The Canadian Writer's World
Essays   SECOND EDITION

- Definition

- Classification

- Arguement

LYNNE GAETZ
Lionel Groulx College

SUNEETI PHADKE
St. Jerome College

RHONDA SANDBERG
George Brown College

The Canadian Writer's World
Essays   SECOND EDITION

Pearson Canada
Toronto

Library and Archives Canada Cataloguing in Publication

Gaetz, Lynne, 1960–

The Canadian writer's world : essays / Lynne Gaetz, Suneeti Phadke, Rhonda Sandberg.
—2nd ed.

Includes index.

ISBN 978-0-13-506666-9

1. English language—Rhetoric—Textbooks. 2. Editing—Textbooks. 3. Report writing—Textbooks.
I. Phadke, Suneeti, 1961– II. Sandberg, Rhonda, 1962– III. Title.

PE1408.G24 2011   808'.042   C2011-901694-X

ISBN 978-0-13-506666-9

Vice-President, Editorial Director: Gary Bennett
Acting Editor-in-Chief: Michelle Sartor
Acquisitions Editor: David S. Le Gallais
Marketing Manager: Loula March
Supervising Developmental Editor: Suzanne Schaan
Developmental Editor: Toni Chahley
Project Manager: Richard di Santo
Production Editor: Susan Adlam
Copy Editor: Tara Tovell
Proofreader: Susan Adlam
Compositor: MPS Limited, a Macmillan Company
Permissions and Photo Researcher: Joanne Tang
Art Director: Julia Hall
Cover Designer: Anthony Leung
Cover image: Getty Images

4 5   15 14

Printed and bound in Canada.

Brief Contents

Editing Handbook 284

Reading Strategies and Selections 480

Appendices

Contents

 PART I — The Writing Process   2

PART II — Essay Patterns   80

PART IV — Editing Handbook   284

Reading Strategies and Selections 480

From Reading to Writing 481

Appendices

Preface

About the Second Edition of *The Canadian Writer's World: Essays*

The Canadian Writer's World can help students produce writing that is technically correct and rich in content. The book's unique features will appeal to both native and non-native students with varying skill levels. Additionally, visual learners will find much to provoke thought in the eye-catching image program.

A Research-Based Approach

From the onset of the development process, we have comprehensively researched the needs and desires of current developmental writing instructors. We personally met with scores of instructors from around the country, asking for their opinions and insights regarding (1) the challenges posed by the course, (2) the needs of today's ever-changing student population, and (3) the ideas and features we were proposing in order to provide a more effective teaching and learning tool. Pearson Education Canada also commissioned several detailed manuscript reviews from instructors, asking them to analyze and evaluate each draft of the manuscript. (They are individually acknowledged at the end of this preface.) These reviewers identified numerous ways in which we could refine and enhance our key features. Their invaluable feedback was incorporated throughout *The Canadian Writer's World*.

How We Organized *The Canadian Writer's World*

The *Canadian Writer's World* presents essay development in five parts.

Part I: The Writing Process teaches students (1) how to formulate ideas (Exploring); (2) how to expand, organize, and present those ideas in a piece of writing (Developing); and (3) how to polish writing so that students convey their message as clearly as possible (Revising and Editing). Students will find the step-by-step approach clear and easy to follow.

Part II: Essay Patterns gives students a solid overview of the patterns of development. Using the same easy-to-understand process (Exploring, Developing, and Revising and Editing), each chapter explains how to convey ideas using specific writing patterns.

Part III: More College and Workplace Writing covers topics ranging from paraphrasing and summarizing to the research essay.

Part IV: The Editing Handbook is a thematic grammar handbook. In each chapter, the exercises correspond to a section theme, such as The Forces of Nature or Human Development. As students work through the chapters, they hone their grammar and editing skills while gaining knowledge about a variety of topics. In addition to helping retain interest in the grammar practices, the thematic material provides a spark that ignites new ideas that students can apply to their writing.

Part V: Reading Strategies and Selections offers tips, readings, and follow-up questions. Students learn how to write by observing and dissecting what they read. The readings contain themes that also are found in Part IV: The Editing Handbook, thereby providing more fodder for generating writing ideas.

How *The Canadian Writer's World* Meets Students' Diverse Needs

You will find many unique elements in *The Canadian Writer's World* including our visual program, our coverage of non-native speaker material, and strategies for addressing students' varying skill levels.

To meet your students' diverse needs, we asked reviewers to critique features that would enhance the learning process of their students. The result has been the integration of the following items.

The Visual Program

A stimulating, full-colour book, *The Canadian Writer's World* recognizes that we live in a visually-oriented world, and it encourages students to become better communicators by responding to images. In Parts I, II, and III, **chapter opening images use similes, analogies, and metaphors** to help students to think about each chapter's key concept in a new way. For example, in the Chapter 10 opener, a photograph of a shoe store sets the stage for classification. Shoes are grouped according to style, which helps students understand the premise of classification.

Providing variety and acting as visual cues and writing prompts, Part IV's **chapter opening photos** reflect the themes in the grammar handbook. Coloured tabs at the sides of the pages are designed to guide students through the six separate sections of Part IV.

The Canadian Writer's World completes its visual program by offering students and instructors full access to MyCanadianCompLab—is a state-of-the-art interactive and instructive website designed to help students meet the challenges of their writing courses; including basic skill development exercises, writing activities, and research tools. Housed within MyCanadianCompLab is also a gradebook for instructors and students.

MyCanadianCompLab provides access to the Pearson eText. Users can create notes, highlight text, create bookmarks, etc.

Seamless Coverage for Non-native Speakers

Instructors in our focus groups noted the growing number of non-native/ESL speakers enrolling in the developmental writing courses. To meet the challenge of this rapidly changing dynamic, we have carefully implemented and integrated content throughout to assist both native and non-native speakers.

The Canadian Writer's World does not have separate ESL boxes, ESL chapters, or tacked-on ESL appendices. Instead, information that traditionally poses a challenge to non-native speakers is woven seamlessly throughout the book. In our extensive experience teaching writing to both native and non-native speakers of English, we have learned that both groups learn best when they are not distracted by ESL labels. With the seamless approach, non-native speakers do not feel self-conscious and segregated, and native speakers do not tune out detailed explanations that may also benefit them. Many of these traditional problem areas receive more coverage than you would find in other developmental writing textbooks, arming the instructor with the material to effectively meet the needs of non-native speakers. Moreover, the online Annotated Instructor's Edition provides ESL Teaching Tips designed specifically to help instructors better meet the needs of their non-native speaking students.

Issue-Focused Thematic Grammar

In our survey of the marketplace, many of you indicated that one of your primary challenges is finding materials that are engaging to students in a contemporary context. This is especially true in grammar instruction. **Students come to the course with varying skill levels**, and many students are simply not interested in grammar. To address this challenge, we have introduced **issue-focused thematic grammar** into *The Canadian Writer's World*.

Each section in Part IV revolves around a common theme. These themes include **Conflict, Urban Development, International Trade, Forces of Nature, Flora and Fauna,** and **Human Development**. Each chapter within a section addresses issues related to the theme. The thematic approach enables students to broaden their awareness of important subjects, allowing them to infuse their writing with reflection and insight. Also, we believe (and our students concur) that the themes make grammar more engaging. And the more engaging grammar is, the more likely students will retain key concepts.

To emphasize the importance of teaching grammar in the context of the writing process, we open each grammar chapter with a **Grammar Snapshot** activity. To further highlight that grammar is not isolated from the writing process, in each of the six grammar sections we offer writing prompts and links to the readings in Part V that relate to the chapter theme.

Key Learning Aids in *The Canadian Writer's World*

Overwhelmingly, reviewers asked that both a larger number and a greater diversity of exercises and activities be incorporated into the book. In response to this feedback, we have developed and tested the following learning aids in *The Canadian Writer's World*. These tools form the pedagogical backbone of the book, and we are confident they will help your students become better writers.

Hints In each chapter, **Hint** boxes highlight important writing and grammar points. Hints are useful for all students, but many will be particularly helpful for non-native speakers. For example, in Chapter 7: Description, there is a hint about how to create a dominant impression, and in Chapter 18: Run-Ons, there is a hint about how to recognize transitional expressions.

The Writer's Desk Parts I, II, and III include **The Writer's Desk** exercises to help students practice all stages and steps of the writing process. Students begin with prewriting and then progress to developing, organizing (using paragraph and essay plans), drafting, and, finally, revising and editing to create a final draft.

Essay Patterns "at Work" To help students appreciate the relevance of their writing tasks, Chapters 6–13 begin with an authentic writing sample. Titled **Cause and Effect at Work, Narration at Work,** and so on, this feature offers a glimpse of the writing patterns people use in different types of workplace writing.

Vocabulary Boost In Chapters 6–13, the vocabulary boost is a collaborative activity that helps students to broaden their vocabulary. For example, in Chapter 13, the Vocabulary Boost helps students understand *connotation*.

Checklist Major points in each chapter are reviewed in the checklist box, which appears at the end of the chapter.

Writers' Exchanges Students who learn best by collaborating and sharing ideas will appreciate the discussion and group work activities that open each chapter in **Part II: Essay Patterns**. Each Writers' Exchange activity introduces the students to the writing pattern in a fun and nonintimidating way.

The Writer's Room These writing activities correspond to general, academic, and workplace topics. Some prompts are brief to allow students to form ideas freely while others are expanded to give students more direction. Students who respond well to visual cues will appreciate the photo writing exercises in **The Writer's Room**. In Part II: Essay Patterns, students can respond to thought-provoking quotations. To help students see that grammar is not isolated from the writing process, there are also **The Writer's Room** activities in each chapter in Part IV: The Editing Handbook.

New to the Second Canadian Edition

Vibrant and Engaging 4-Colour Interior Design

One of the key changes to this edition is the move to a vibrant and engaging 4-colour interior design.

Streamlined Table of Contents

Part IV: The Editing Handbook has been streamlined from 20 to 15 chapters, to reflect the top fifteen common errors in student writing. A sixteenth chapter provides additional editing practice.

Enhanced eText on MyCanadianCompLab

The eText on MyCanadianCompLab includes three chapters that have been moved from the textbook:

- The Resume and Letter of Application
- Responding to Film and Literature
- Becoming a Successful Student

In response to reviewer feedback, the eText contains a brand new chapter, "Research, Plagiarism, and Academic Integrity."

The MyCanadianCompLab also includes "The Writer's Room" activities for film and photo writing that correspond to the themes found in Part V of the text.

New Canadian Reading Selections

We have revamped the readings in the book to include more relevant, Canadian selections that place a greater emphasis on current affairs. Among the new readings in this edition are:

- *A Modest Proposal*, by Heather Mallick
- *Yonge St., a Seedy Mystery in Plain View*, by Sheila Heti
- *Make a Difference*, by David Suzuki and David R. Boyd
- *Canada Misses Its Chance to Join Major Pacific Free Trade Deal*, by John Ibbitson

Student Supplements

mycanadiancomplab

MyCanadianCompLab is a state-of-the-art interactive and instructive solution designed to help you meet the challenges of your writing courses and to assist in all your future writing. MyCanadianCompLab provides access to a wealth of resources all geared to meet your learning needs. See the opening pages of this text for details.

Pearson eText gives you access to the text whenever and wherever you have access to the Internet. eText pages look exactly like the printed text, offering powerful new functionality for students and instructors. Users can create notes, highlight text in different colours, create bookmarks, zoom, click hyperlinked words and phrases to view definitions, and view in single-page or two-page view. Pearson eText allows for quick navigation to key parts of the eText using a table of contents and provides full-text search.

A student access card for MyCanadian-CompLab is packaged with every new copy of the text. Access codes can also be purchased through campus bookstores or through the website.

CourseSmart for Students CourseSmart goes beyond traditional expectations—providing instant, online access to the textbooks and course materials you need at an average savings of 60%. With instant access from any computer and the ability to search your text, you'll find the content you need quickly, no matter where you are. And with online tools like highlighting and note-taking, you can save time and study efficiently. See all the benefits at www.coursesmart.com/students.

Instructor Supplements

Annotated Instructor's Edition (978-0-13-265472-2) The Annotated Instructor's Edition contains the answers to all of the exercises in the text and over 150 teaching tips in the margins, derived from the authors' first-hand experience or suggested by users of this text and experts in the field of English language training. The Annotated Instructor's Edition is available in electronic format, for instructors only, through CourseSmart, at www.coursesmart.com/instructors.

Technology Specialists Pearson's Technology Specialists work with faculty and campus course designers to ensure that Pearson technology products, assessment tools, and online course materials are tailored to meet your specific needs. This highly qualified team is dedicated to helping schools take full advantage of a wide range of educational resources, by assisting in the integration of a variety of instructional materials and media formats. Your local Pearson Education sales representative can provide you with more details on this service program.

Acknowledgments

Many people have helped me produce *The Canadian Writer's World*. First and foremost, I would like to thank Lynne Gaetz and Suneeti Phadke for their superb text on which to build and my students for their constant inspiration and honest feedback. Their words and ideas are included throughout the book.

I also benefited greatly from the insights and contributions of my academic colleagues from across the country, all of whom are listed below. Their ideas and suggestions provided me with a broader perspective on what the text could become. Thanks to my exceptional colleagues and administration at George Brown College for their continuous support.

Gordon Beveridge, University of Winnipeg
John Lehr, George Brown College
Aurelea Mahood, Capilano University
Peter C. Miller, Seneca College
Tatiana Mitchell, Instructor, General Arts and Sciences Program, Humber College of Applied Arts & Technology
Cynthia Rowland, Algonquin College
Michelle Semeniuk, Northern Alberta Institute of Technology

I am indebted to the team of dedicated professionals at Pearson Education Canada who have helped make this project a reality. They have boosted my spirits and have believed in me every step of the way. Special thanks to Freelance Editor, Toni Chahley, for her fabulous job in polishing this book and to Acquisitions Editor, David Le Gallais, for trusting my instincts and enthusiastically propelling me forward. Thanks as well to Project Manager, Richard di Santo, Production Editor, Susan Adlam, and Copy Editor, Tara Tovell. Their attention to detail in the production process kept me motivated and on task and made *The Canadian Writer's World* a much better resource for both instructors and students.

Finally, I would like to dedicate *The Canadian Writer's World: Essays* to my children, Skyelar and Dylan, who supported and encouraged me. They are my inspiration.

A Note to Students

Your knowledge, ideas, and opinions are important. The ability to communicate those ideas clearly is invaluable in your personal, academic, and professional life. When your writing is error-free, readers will focus on your message, and you will be able to persuade, inform, entertain, or inspire them. *The Canadian Writer's World* includes strategies that will help you improve your written communication. Quite simply, when you become a better writer, you become a better communicator. It is our greatest wish for *The Canadian Writer's World* to make you excited about writing, communicating, and learning.

Enjoy!

Lynne Gaetz, Suneeti Phadke, and
Rhonda Sandberg

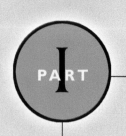

PART I

The Writing Process

The writing process is a series of steps that most writers follow to advance from thinking about a topic to preparing the final draft. Generally, you follow the process step by step. However, sometimes you may find that your steps overlap. For example, you might do some editing before you revise, or you might think about your main idea while you are prewriting. Ensure that you have completed all the steps of the process before preparing your final draft.

Before you begin the next chapters, review the steps in the writing process.

Exploring

Chapter 1

Step 1 Think about your topic.

Step 2 Think about your audience.

Step 3 Think about your purpose.

Step 4 Try exploring strategies.

Developing

Chapters 2, 3, 4

Step 1 Express your main idea.

Step 2 Develop your supporting ideas.

Step 3 Make a plan or an outline.

Step 4 Write your first draft.

Revising and Editing

Chapter 5

Step 1 Revise for unity.

Step 2 Revise for adequate support.

Step 3 Revise for coherence.

Step 4 Revise for style.

Step 5 Edit for technical errors.

Exploring

Before planting seeds or shrubs, a gardener might look for ideas in magazines, on the internet, or in nurseries. Similarly, a writer uses various prewriting strategies to explore topics for writing.

Visualizing the Paragraph and the Essay

A **paragraph** is a series of sentences that are about one central idea. Paragraphs can stand alone, or they can be part of a longer work such as an essay, a letter, or a report. A paragraph contains a **topic sentence** that expresses the main idea and **body sentences** that develop that idea. Most paragraphs end with a **concluding sentence** that brings the paragraph to a satisfactory close.

Sample Paragraph

People learn negotiation skills through sports. Children playing informally at recess must decide what game to play and what rules to follow. They must negotiate with the other children about game boundaries. Every day, my daughter comes home from school telling me that she and her friends have invented a new game. The children make up the rules of the new game by bargaining with each other. In team sports, athletes must make choices about who will play a certain position or which player will play for how much time. Such decisions require negotiation skills, which help people in other areas of their lives.

An **essay** contains several paragraphs that revolve around one central idea. The **introductory paragraph** includes a **thesis statement** expressing the main idea of the essay. **Body paragraphs** support the thesis statement. Finally, the essay closes with a **concluding paragraph** that wraps up the main ideas the writer has presented throughout the paper.

Sample Essay

Sports: A Vital Necessity

Humans have been playing sports since the beginning of civilization. Cave art in France and Africa depicts people playing archery, wrestling, and horse racing. Indigenous North Americans engaged in team sports such as lacrosse or running. The ancient Greeks, Romans, Chinese, and Egyptians also enjoyed many physical activities. Similarly, most people enjoy sports today. Young girls and boys play in soccer leagues, or they may play a baseball game during recess. Adults, too, play or watch sports. Athletic activities are very necessary to people's well-being. In fact, sports help people to develop good character because they learn many skills.

First, when people play games, they learn how to make friends. In Canada, according to Statistics Canada, "Youth aged 15 to 19 years generally have better aerobic fitness and body composition indicators than 20- to 39-year-olds." Whether it is exercising informally or playing a team sport, people interact with strangers. Going to the gym, participating in a hiking club, and playing in a team sport bring different people into close personal contact with each other. These strangers all have something in common. They like to engage in the same activity, so most people end up developing friendships.

People learn negotiation skills through sports. Children playing informally at recess must decide what game to play and what rules to follow. They must negotiate with the other children about game boundaries. Every day, my daughter comes home from school telling me that she and her friends have invented a new game. The children make up the rules of the new game by bargaining with each other. In team sports, athletes must make choices about who will play a certain position or which player will play for how much time. Such decisions require negotiation skills, which help people in other areas of their lives.

> Each **body** paragraph contains details that support the topic sentence.

Players learn how to deal with disappointments and pressure. Disappointment about the level of play or an important loss is common for most people involved in sports. For example, many Olympic athletes are very discouraged when they lose, but most continue training to become even better. Players on high school and college teams also learn to win and lose. For example, my neighbour's son plays on the volleyball team. His team had a winning streak, but the team lost in the semi-finals. All the players on the team were extremely disappointed but vowed to play better in the next season. Sports teach people how to win and lose gracefully. Such a lesson is invaluable in life.

People build character through sports. In fact, they learn many valuable life lessons, including social skills. They learn practical skills such as how to negotiate. As Jeff Kemp, in his article "A Lesson in Humility," says, "In fact, sports teach important moral lessons that athletes can apply on and off the playing field." So don't just sit around at home; go participate in a sport.

> The **concluding** paragraph brings the essay to a satisfactory close.

Essay-length prose is the backbone of written communication in and out of college. Throughout your life, you will use principles of essay writing in various formats, including research papers, emails, reports, formal letters, newsletters, and webpages. Essays help you explore ideas and share those thoughts with others. By reading through this text and completing the many helpful writing practices in it, you will significantly improve your chances of getting more out of your courses and jobs. Enjoy the journey!

Key Steps in Exploring

Perhaps you have been given a writing assignment and then stared at the blank page, thinking, "I don't know what to write." Well, it is not necessary to write a good essay immediately. There are certain things that you can do to help you focus on your topic.

Understand Your Assignment

As soon as you are given an assignment, make sure that you understand your task. Answer the following questions about the assignment.

- How many words or pages does the assignment require?
- What is the due date for the assignment?
- Are there any special qualities my writing should include? For example, should my writing be double-spaced? Should I include a list of works cited?

After you have considered your assignment, consider the following four key steps in the exploring stage of the writing process.

EXPLORING

STEP 1	➤	**Think about your topic.** Determine what you will write about.
STEP 2	➤	**Think about your audience.** Consider your intended readers and what interests them.
STEP 3	➤	**Think about your purpose.** Ask yourself why you want to write.
STEP 4	➤	**Try exploring strategies.** Experiment with different ways to generate ideas.

Topic

Sometimes your topic has been assigned and is already very specific. At other times, it may be very general. For example, if your assigned topic is "food," narrow it down so that you can focus on something specific about food. You might write about the dangers of diets or how to cook a certain type of cuisine. You might describe the symbolism of food in a literary work or try to explain the chemical makeup of a specific food. When you are given a general topic, find an angle that interests you and make it more specific.

To find a focus for your topic, ask yourself the following questions.

- What about the topic interests me? Will it interest other readers?
- Do I have special knowledge about the topic?
- Does anything about the topic arouse my emotions?

Audience

Your **audience** is your intended reader. In your personal, academic, and professional life, you will often write for a specific audience; therefore, you can keep your readers interested by adapting your tone and vocabulary to suit them.

Tone is your general attitude or feeling toward a topic. You might write in a tone that is humorous, sarcastic, serious, friendly, or casual. For example, imagine you are preparing an invitation to an event. To determine the design, phrasing, and format, you need to know some important information about your recipients. What are their ages and lifestyles? Are they mostly males or females?

Would they prefer printed invitations or email invitations? Questions like these can help you connect with your audience.

Knowing your readers is especially important when preparing academic or workplace documents. When you consider your audience, ask yourself the following questions:

- Who will read my assignment—an instructor, other students, or people outside the college?
- Do the readers have a lot of knowledge about my topic?
- How will I need to adjust my vocabulary, writing style, or tone to appeal to my readers?

In academic writing, your audience is generally your instructor or other students, unless your instructor specifically asks you to write for another audience such as the general public, your employer, or a family member.

 **Instructor as the Audience**

Your instructor represents a general audience. Such an audience of educated readers will expect you to reveal what you have learned or what you have understood about the topic. Your ideas should be presented in a clear and organized manner. Do not leave out information because you assume that your instructor is an expert in the field. Also, you should write in standard English. In other words, try to use correct grammar, sentence structure, and vocabulary.

PRACTICE I   As you read the following messages, consider the differences in both the tone and the vocabulary the writer uses. Then answer the questions that follow.

A

yo, :)

im in ur english class on 2sday. how ru? can u help with my essay? >:o b4 i write, i need 2 know what the topic is? what is # of words? plz check my plan cuz i don't no if i'm on the rite track... :'(is it ok? btw, will c u in class.

gtg Andrea :)

B

Dear Professor Gonzales,

I am in your Tuesday morning English class. I have started working on my essay and have prepared an essay plan, but I am not sure if my thesis statement is appropriate and focused enough. Could you please look at my plan and let me know if I am on the right track? Also, could you please remind me of the length of the assignment? Thank you,

Reginald Harper

1. Why is the language inappropriate in the first instant message?

   _____

   _____

2. What judgments might the instructor make about the two students based on the messages?

   _____

   _____

   _____

   _____

Purpose

Your **purpose** is your reason for writing. Keeping your purpose in mind will help you focus your writing.

When you consider your purpose, ask yourself the following questions.

- Is my goal to **entertain**? Do I want to tell a story?
- Is my goal to **persuade**? Do I want to convince readers that my point of view is the correct one?
- Is my goal to **inform**? Do I want to explain something or give information about a topic?

It is possible to write for a combination of reasons. In fact, most essays have more than one purpose. For example, an essay describing a personal experience with fraud could also inform readers about protecting themselves from identity theft, or an essay describing how the heart pumps blood could simultaneously persuade readers to reconsider smoking.

 **General and Specific Purpose**

Your **general purpose** is to entertain, to inform, or to persuade. Your **specific purpose** is your more precise reason for writing. For example, imagine that you have to write about an election. You can have the following general and specific purposes.

General purpose: to inform
Specific purpose: to compare platforms of two different candidates

PRACTICE 2   The following selections are all about food; however, each excerpt has a different purpose, has been written for a different audience, and has been taken from a different source. Read each selection carefully. Then underline any language clues (words or phrases) that help you identify its source, audience, and purpose. Finally, answer the questions that follow each selection.

EXAMPLE:

I just made my very first dessert. It looks awesome. I hope it tastes ◄ slang
alright. I almost <u>freaked out</u> when I realized I forgot to turn the oven ◄ slang
on. My instructor is <u>super</u>, and he's <u>got a great sense of humour</u> with ◄ slang, informal tone
me and the other students. Next, I am going to try to make a more
complicated dessert.

What is the most likely source of this paragraph?
a. website article   (b. personal letter) c. textbook   d. memoir

What is its primary purpose?___*to inform*_____

Who is the audience?___*friend or family member*_____

---

1. I went out with my old friends Nuzhat Ahmad and Ayla, as the three of us often did, in a comradeship of girlhood. We went driving to Bagh-e-Jinnah, formerly known as Lawrence Gardens, located opposite the Governor's House along the Mall in Lahore. We were trying to locate the best *gol guppa* vendor in town and stopped by to test the new stand in Lawrence Gardens. Gol guppas are a strange food: I have never located an equivalent to them or their culinary situation. They are an outdoor food, a passing whim, and no one would dream of recreating their frivolity inside his or her own kitchen. A gol guppa is a small hollow oval of the lightest pastry that is dipped into a fiery liquid sauce made of tamarind and cayenne and lemon and cold water. It is evidently a food invented as a joke, in a moment of good humour.

What is the most likely source of this paragraph?
a. website article   b. personal letter   c. textbook   d. memoir

What is its primary purpose?_____

Who is the audience?_____

---

2. Eat regularly. Eating is one of life's great pleasures, and it is important to take time to stop, relax, and enjoy mealtimes and snacks. Scheduling eating times also ensures that meals are not missed, resulting in missed nutrients that are often not

compensated for by subsequent meals. This is especially important for school-age children, adolescents, and elderly people.

What is the most likely source of this paragraph?
a. website article   b. personal letter   c. textbook   d. memoir

What is its primary purpose?_____

Who is the audience?_____

_____

3. About 5000 years ago, another revolution in technology was taking place in the Middle East, one that would end up changing the entire world. This was the discovery of agriculture, large-scale cultivation using plows harnessed to animals or more powerful energy sources. So important was the invention of the animal-drawn plow, along with other breakthroughs of the period—including irrigation, the wheel, writing, numbers, and the use of various metals—that this moment in history is often called "the dawn of civilization."

What is the most likely source of this paragraph?
a. website article   b. personal letter   c. textbook   d. memoir

What is its purpose?_____

Who is the audience?_____

_____

Exploring Strategies

After you determine your topic, audience, and purpose, try some **exploring strategies**—also known as **prewriting strategies**—to help get your ideas flowing. Four common strategies are *freewriting*, *brainstorming*, *questioning*, and *clustering*. It is not necessary to do all of the strategies explained in this chapter. Find the strategy that works best for you.

You can do both general and focused prewriting. If you have writer's block, and do not know what to write about, use **general prewriting** to come up with possible writing topics. Then, after you have chosen a topic, use **focused prewriting** to find an angle of the topic that is interesting and that could be developed in your essay.

 **When to Use Exploring Strategies**

You can use the exploring strategies at any stage of the writing process:

- To find a topic
- To narrow a broad topic
- To generate ideas about your topic
- To generate supporting details

Narrow Your Topic

An essay has one main idea. If your topic is too broad, you might find it difficult to write a focused essay about it. For example, imagine that you are given the topic "mistakes." If the topic is not narrowed, it will lead to a meandering and unfocused essay. To narrow the topic, think about types of errors, examples of errors, or people who make errors. A more focused topic could be "mistakes newlyweds make" or "mistakes first-year college students make." Find one angle of the topic that you know a lot about and that you personally find interesting. If you have a lot to say, and you think the topic is compelling, chances are that your reader will also like your topic.

Review the following examples of general and narrowed topics.

Topic	Narrowed Topic
jobs	preparing for a job interview
music	protest songs from the past and present

To help narrow and develop your topic, you can use the following exploring strategies.

Step 1: Freewriting

Freewriting gives writers the freedom to write without stopping for a set period of time. The goal of this exercise is to record the first thoughts that come to mind. If you run out of ideas, don't stop writing. Simply fill in the pause with phrases like "blah blah blah" or "What else can I write?" As you write, do not be concerned with word choice, grammar, or spelling. If you use a computer, let your ideas flow and do not worry about typing mistakes. You could try typing without looking at the screen.

Alicia's Freewriting

College student Alicia Parera thought about mistakes college students make. During her freewriting, she wrote down everything that came to mind.

> Mistakes students make? Not doing the homework. Not asking for help when they need it? I sometimes feel shy to speak up when I don't understand something. What else? Some college students leave college early. Why do they leave? Tim. He only stayed for one semester. I don't think he was ready for college life. He treated college like high school and always came late. Goofed off. Cut class. What else? What about Amanda who had that family crisis? She had to leave when her mother was sick. Of course, finances. It's tough. Sometimes I go crazy trying to keep up with my job, friends, schoolwork . . . it's really hard.

Step 2: Brainstorming

Brainstorming is like freewriting, except that you create a list of ideas, and you can take the time to stop and think when you create your list. As you think about the topic, write down words or phrases that come to mind. Do not worry about grammar or spelling; the point is to generate ideas.

Alicia's Brainstorming

Topic: Mistakes that college students make

- party too much
- not doing homework
- feeling too shy to speak with instructors when they have problems
- getting too stressed
- choosing the wrong career path
- don't know what they want to do
- feeling intimidated in class

Step 3: Questioning

Another way to generate ideas about a topic is to ask yourself a series of questions and write responses to them. The questions can help you define and narrow your topic. One common way to do this is to ask yourself *who, what, when, where, why,* and *how* questions.

Alicia's Questioning

Who makes the most mistakes?	— first-year students because they aren't always prepared for college life
Why do some students miss classes?	— feel like there are no consequences, don't feel interested in their program
When do most students drop out?	— administrators say that November is the most common month that students drop out
How should colleges encourage students who are at risk of dropping out?	— give more financial aid — offer career counseling
Where can students get help?	— guidance counsellors, instructors, friends, family, professionals doing student's dream job
Why is it an important topic?	— new students can learn about pitfalls to avoid, administrators can develop strategies for helping students

Step 4: Clustering

Clustering is like drawing a word map; ideas are arranged in a visual image. To begin, write your topic in the middle of the page and draw a box or a circle around it. That idea will lead to another, so write the second idea and draw a line connecting it to your topic. Keep writing, circling, and connecting ideas until you have groups or "clusters" of them on your page.

Alicia's Clustering

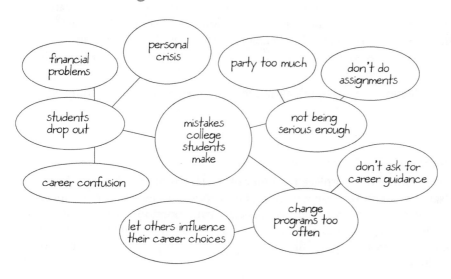

> ## Writer's Desk **Exploring**
>
> Explore the next three topics. Use a different exploring strategy for each topic. You can choose to do freewriting, brainstorming, questioning, or clustering.
>
> stereotypes   mistakes   volunteer work

Journal and Portfolio Writing

Keeping a Journal

You may write for work or school, but you can also practise writing for pleasure. One way to practise your writing is to keep a journal. A **journal** can be a book, computer file, or even a blog where you record your thoughts, opinions, ideas, and impressions. Journal writing gives you a chance to practise your writing without worrying about the audience and what they might think about it. It also gives you a source of material when you want to write about a topic of your choice.

In your journal, you can write about any topic that appeals to you. Here are some possible topics for journal writing.

- Anything related to your personal life, such as your feelings about your career goals, personal problems and solutions, opinions about your college courses, reflections about past and future decisions, or feelings about your job
- Your reactions to controversies in your family, neighbourhood, college, city, country, or world
- Your reflections on the opinions and philosophies of others, including your friends or people whom you read about in your courses

Keeping a Portfolio

A **writing portfolio** is a place (a binder or an electronic file folder) where you keep samples of all of your writing. The purpose of keeping a portfolio is to have a record of your writing progress. In your portfolio, keep all drafts of your writing assignments. When you work on new assignments, review your previous work in your portfolio. Identify your main problems and try not to repeat the same errors.

The Writer's Room **Topics to Explore**

Writing Activity 1

Choose one of the following topics, or choose your own topic. Then generate ideas about the topic. You may want to try the suggested exploring strategy.

General Topics

1. Try freewriting about people who have helped you succeed.
2. Brainstorm a list of thoughts about different types of fear.
3. Create a cluster diagram about a useful invention.
4. Ask and answer questions about voting.

College and Work-Related Topics

5. Try freewriting about an unforgettable day at work or college. Include any emotions or details that come to mind.
6. Brainstorm a list of ideas about career goals.
7. Ask and answer questions about bosses.
8. Create a cluster diagram about the pressures students face.

Writing Activity 2

Use questioning to generate ideas about the following image. Ask and answer *who*, *what*, *when*, *where*, *why*, and *how* questions.

✔ **CHECKLIST: EXPLORING**

When you explore a topic, ask yourself these questions.

☐ What is my **topic**? Consider what you will write about.

☐ Who is my **audience**? Think about your intended reader.

☐ What is my **purpose**? Determine your reason for writing.

☐ Which exploring strategy will I use? You could try one of the following strategies, or a combination of strategies.
Freewriting is writing without stopping for a limited period of time.
Brainstorming is making a list.
Clustering is drawing a word map.
Questioning is asking and answering a series of questions.

How Do I Get a Better Grade?

mycanadiancomplab

Go to www.mycanadiancomplab.ca for additional help with your grammar, writing, and research skills. You will have access to a variety of exercises, instruction, and video that will help you improve your basic skills and help you get a better grade.

Developing the Main Idea

Faced with so many plant and flower varieties, a gardener narrows down which ones are most appropriate for his or her garden. Similarly, a writer considers many ideas before choosing a main idea for an essay.

Key Steps in Developing the Main Idea

In Chapter 1, you learned how to consider your reading audience and your purposes for writing. You also practised using exploring strategies to formulate ideas. In this chapter, you will focus on developing a main idea that can be expanded into a complete essay. There are two key steps in this process.

DEVELOPING THE MAIN IDEA

STEP I ➤ **Write a thesis statement.** Write a statement that expresses the main idea of the piece of writing.

STEP 2 ➤ **Develop the supporting ideas.** Find facts, examples, or anecdotes that best support your main idea.

Writing a Thesis Statement

The **thesis** is your main idea that you want to express. A clear thesis statement presents the topic of the essay, and it includes a **controlling idea** that expresses the writer's opinion, attitude, or feeling about the topic. The controlling idea can appear at the beginning or end of the thesis statement.

topic   controlling idea
Art courses should be compulsory in all high schools.

controlling idea   topic
School districts should stop funding **art courses.**

PRACTICE I   Circle the topic and underline the controlling idea in each thesis statement.

EXAMPLE: Insomnia is caused by several factors.

1. Three strategies can help you become a better public speaker.
2. Moving to a new country was a traumatic experience for me.
3. There should not be racial profiling at borders.
4. School uniforms should be compulsory in public schools.
5. There are several reasons for Australia's compulsory voting system.
6. Phishing is a dangerous internet scam.
7. My office is an obstacle course.
8. There are three types of annoying office workers.

Writing an Effective Thesis Statement

When you develop your thesis statement, ask yourself the following questions to help you avoid thesis statement errors.

1. **Is my thesis a complete statement?**
   Ensure that your thesis does not express an incomplete idea or more than one idea. A thesis statement should reveal one complete thought.

Incomplete:	Allergies: so annoying.
	(This is not a complete statement.)
More than one idea:	There are many types of allergens, and allergies affect people in different ways.
	(This statement contains two distinct ideas. Each idea could become an essay.)
Thesis statement:	Doctors suggest several steps people can take to relieve symptoms related to pet allergies.

2. **Does my thesis statement have a controlling idea?**
   Rather than announcing the topic, your thesis statement should make a point about the topic. It should have a controlling idea that expresses your attitude or feeling about the topic. Avoid phrases such as *My topic is* or *I will write about.*

Announces:	I will write about computers.
	(This sentence says nothing relevant about the topic. The reader does not know what the point of the essay is.)
Thesis statement:	When Microsoft develops a new operating system, there are political, financial, and environmental consequences.

3. **Can I support my thesis statement in an essay?**
   Your thesis statement should express an idea that you can support in an essay. If it is too narrow, you will find yourself with nothing to say. If it is too broad, you will have an endless composition.

Too broad:	There are many childless couples in our world.
	(This topic needs a more specific and narrow focus.)
Too narrow:	The average age of first-time mothers is approximately twenty-six years old.
	(It would be difficult to write an entire essay about this fact.)
Thesis statement:	Many couples are choosing to remain childless for several reasons.

4. **Does my thesis statement make a valid and interesting point?**
   Your thesis statement should make a valid point. It should not be a vaguely worded statement or an obvious and uninteresting comment.

Vague:	Censorship is a big problem.
	(For whom is it a big problem?)
Obvious:	The internet is important.
	(So what? Everyone knows this.)
Invalid:	The internet controls our lives.
	(This statement is difficult to believe or prove.)
Thesis statement:	The internet has become a powerful presence in our personal, social, and working lives.

   ## PRACTICE 2   Examine each statement.

   - Write **TS** if it is an effective thesis statement.
   - Write **I** if it is an incomplete idea.
   - Write **M** if it contains more than one complete idea.
   - Write **A** if it is an announcement.

   EXAMPLE: This essay is about spousal abuse.   _A_

   1. The high price of oil.   _I_

   2. My college has a great sports stadium, but it needs to give more help to female athletes.   _M_

   3. Nursing is extremely demanding.   _A_

   4. In this paper, I will discuss global warming.   _A_

   5. My subject is the torture of war prisoners.   _A_

   6. There are many excellent commercials on television, but some are too violent.   _M_

   7. The loss of a job can actually have positive effects on a person's life.   _TS_

   8. The problem of negative election advertisements.   _I_

   ## PRACTICE 3   Examine each statement.

   - Write **TS** if it is a complete thesis statement.
   - Write **V** if it is too vague.
   - Write **O** if it is too obvious.

   EXAMPLE: Canadians are more nationalistic.   _V_

   1. Toronto has a large population.   _O_

2. We had a major problem.   ✓

3. Some adult children have legitimate reasons for moving back into their parents' homes.   T S

4. The roads are very crowded during holiday periods.   O

5. There are several ways to do this.   ✓

6. Children in our culture are changing.   ✓

PRACTICE 4   Examine each pair of sentences.

- Write **B** if the sentence is too broad.
- Write **TS** if the sentence is an effective thesis statement.

EXAMPLE: *B*   Plants can help people.

     TS   Learning to care for plants gave me unexpected pleasure.

1. B Music is important around the world.

   TS Some simple steps can help you successfully promote your music.

2. TS My neighbourhood is being transformed by youth gangs.

   B Violence is a big problem everywhere.

3. B My life has been filled with mistakes.

   TS My jealousy, insecurity, and anger ruined my first relationship.

4. TS The car accident transformed my life.

   B Everybody's life has dramatic moments.

5. TS Good email manners are important in the business world.

   B Good manners are important.

PRACTICE 5   Examine each pair of sentences.

- Write **N** if the sentence is too narrow.
- Write **TS** if the sentence is an effective thesis statement.

EXAMPLE: *N*   I grow coriander in my garden.

     TS   Learning to care for plants gave me unexpected pleasure.

1. N My poodle's name is Short Stop.

   TS Owning a pet taught me how to be more responsible.

2. N Our roads are very icy.

   TS Driving in the winter requires particular skills.

Fact cannot be TS

? 3. __N__ Carjacking rates have increased by 20 percent in our city.

__TS__ You can avoid being a carjacking victim by taking the next steps.

TS 4. __N__ I hurt myself in various ways during my three days on the beach.

N __TS__ There are many sharp pieces of shell on the local beach.

5. __TS__ Identical twins who are raised together have distinct personalities.

? N __TS__ My twin sisters have similar birthmarks on their necks.

Revising Your Thesis Statement

A thesis statement is like the foundation that holds up a house. If the thesis statement is weak, it is difficult to construct a solid and compelling essay. Most writers must revise their thesis statements to make them strong, interesting, and supportable.

When you plan your thesis, ask yourself if you can support it with at least three ideas. If not, you have to modify your thesis statement. To enliven a dead-end statement, ensure that your thesis can answer the *why, what,* or *how* questions. Sometimes, just by adding a few words, a dead-end statement becomes a supportable thesis.

Poor thesis: Many students drop out of college.

(How could you develop this into an essay? It is a dead-end statement.)

Better thesis: Students drop out of college **for several reasons**.

(You could support this thesis with at least three ideas. This thesis statement answers the question "Why?")

 Hint   **Writing a Guided Thesis Statement**

Give enough details to make your thesis statement interesting. Your instructor may want you to guide the reader through your main points. To do this, mention your main and supporting ideas in your thesis statement. In other words, your thesis statement provides a map for the readers to follow.

Weak: My first job taught me many things.

Better: My first job taught me about the importance of responsibility, organization, and teamwork.

form and function

PRACTICE 6 The next thesis statements are weak. First, identify the problem with the statement (write *vague*, *incomplete*, and so on) and ask yourself questions to determine how you might be able to revise it. Then revise each statement to make it more forceful and focused.

EXAMPLE: Spousal abuse is a big problem.

Comments: *Obvious. Vague. For whom is it a problem? How is it a problem?*

Revision: *Our provincial government should provide better support for victims of spousal abuse.*

1. I will explain how the family is falling apart.
   Comments: _Announces. Too broad_
   Revision: _There are several resons can ~~lead the same~~ families ~~are all~~ apart._
   lead to   _falling_

2. I made a difficult decision.
   Comments: _Incomplete. Announces. Vague_
   Revision: _Everyone has to make difficult decision whether it is ~~suitable~~_
   Join in the army is a difficult decision positive or not me.

3. The media is essential in our lives.
   Comments: _Invalid. The statement is difficult to prove_
   Revision: _The media has become more and more influenced on our life._
   Media is playing a essential role ~~because~~ for several reasons

4. I am an environmentalist.
   Comments: _Obvious._
   Revision: _Unlike what most of people wall chose to do, I am an environmentlist_
   As a environmentalist

5. Fashions are too impractical.
   Comments: _Invalid. Too broad._

   Revision: _Fashions is changing all the time, there always a new form of fashion be found_

   In the fashion world there always be a form and functions

Overview: Writing a Thesis Statement

To create a forceful thesis statement, you should follow these steps.

Step 1

Find your topic. You can use exploring strategies to get ideas.

General topic: Traditions

Brainstorming:
- Commercialization of holidays
- My family traditions
- Important ceremonies
- Why do we celebrate?
- Benefits of traditions
- Initiation ceremonies

Step 2

Narrow your topic. Decide what point you want to make.

Narrowed topic: Initiation ceremonies

Point I want to make: Initiation ceremonies can help people make the transition from childhood to adulthood.

Step 3

Develop a thesis statement that you can support with specific evidence. You may need to revise your statement several times.

Initial thesis statement: Initiation ceremonies serve a valuable function.

Revised thesis statement: Meaningful initiation ceremonies benefit individuals, families, and communities.

Writer's Desk   Write Thesis Statements

Write a thesis statement for each of the next topics. If you explored these topics in Chapter 1, you can use those ideas to help you write your thesis statement. If you have not explored these topics yet, then spend a few minutes exploring them. Brainstorm some ideas for each topic to help you define and narrow them. Then develop a thesis statement that makes a point and is not too broad or too narrow.

stereotypes about beauty   mistakes in relationships   value of volunteer work

EXAMPLE Topic: Mistakes students make   Narrowed topic: _reasons students drop out_

Thesis statement: Students may drop out of college because they are unprepared, have financial problems, or experience an emotional crisis.

1. _____

   _____

2. _____

   _____

3. _____

   _____

Developing the Supporting Ideas

The next step in essay writing is to plan your supporting ideas. Support is not simply a restatement of the thesis. The body paragraphs must develop and prove the validity of the thesis statement.

Each body paragraph has a **topic sentence** that expresses the main idea of the paragraph. Like a thesis statement, a topic sentence must have a controlling idea. Details and examples support the topic sentence. In the following illustration, you can see how the ideas flow in an essay. Topic sentences support the thesis statement, and details bolster the topic sentences. Every idea in the essay is unified and helps to strengthen the essay's thesis.

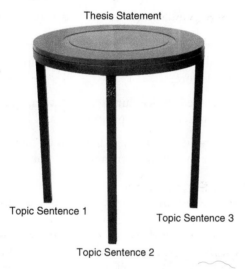

Thesis Statement

Topic Sentence 1

Topic Sentence 3

Topic Sentence 2

PRACTICE 7   Write a thesis statement for each group of supporting ideas. Ensure that your thesis statement is clear, makes a point, and is not too broad or too narrow.

EXAMPLE: Thesis: _When you buy a car, make an informed decision._

   a. Ask family members what type of car they would prefer.

   b. Research on the internet or in car guides to find information about specific models that interest you.

   c. Keeping your budget in mind, compare new and used cars.

1. Thesis: _____ there _____ are _____ several _____ steps _____ in _____ ~~selling~~ ~~presentation~~ sales presentations consists of several steps

   a. First, internalize and believe in your sales pitch.

   b. Speak softly, and do not scare the customer with a commanding voice or aggressive mannerisms.

   c. Finally, involve the customer in your sales presentation.

To make an outstanding

To dramatically improve school success rates, educators should seriously consider dividing students according to gender.

2. Thesis: _People can find some advantages within same-gender classrooms._

    a. When boys are in all-male classrooms, teachers can modify their activities to keep the boys' attention.

    b. All-female classrooms permit the female students to focus on the material and show their intelligence.

    c. Unlike co-education classrooms, same-gender classrooms are easier for teachers to control.

3. Thesis: _The ~~age~~ voters ^preference in an election are largely effected by age._

    a. Most people under twenty-five years of age simply mimic how their parents or friends vote.

    b. To make an informed choice during an election, people need to have life experiences, which include paying rent and bills.

    c. Twenty-five-year-olds are also less likely to be manipulated by a politician because they have a stronger sense of what they want.

The voting age should be raised to twenty-five years.

PRACTICE 8   Read the full essay in this practice and then do the following.

1. Determine the topic of each body paragraph. Then write a topic sentence for each body paragraph. Your topic sentence should have a controlling idea and express the main point of the paragraph.

2. Ask yourself what this essay is about. Then compose a thesis statement that sums up the main point of the essay. You might look in the concluding paragraph to get some ideas.

(Introduction) When I was a child, we had a daily routine. My parents both worked, but they got home at about 5 p.m. They spent about half an hour unwinding over a cup of coffee. Then they worked together to cook the meal, and by 6:30 they called us children to dinner. We ate and talked together. The same thing cannot be said about many families today.

Thesis Statement: _The families in the modern age can not to be as close as the families in the past due to the technology._

(Body 1) Topic Sentence: _When I was a child, we had a daily routine._

Conducive to

Overtime was not so common in the past, but today many employers expect their workers to spend an extra hour or two in the workplace, so employees don't get home until 7 or 8 p.m. Also, children's lives are filled with more activities than they were in past decades. For example, my daughter takes dance class at 7 p.m., and my son gets together with friends for band practice every evening. They dash through the door at different times, throw a frozen pizza in the microwave, and eat alone.

(Body 2) Topic Sentence: _Overtime was not so common in the past._

The little box certainly is entertaining, but people won't talk about their daily experiences when the television is on. According to a researcher at *The Gazette*, "I get asked by parents all the time how am I supposed to make dinner if I can't sit my child in front of the TV." "It keeps the sofas and carpets much cleaner if everybody just watches TV in the kitchen," says Sylvie Labelle, a mother of four. Thirteen-year-old Jeremy Labelle mentions, outside his mother's hearing, that he doesn't really talk to anybody in the family. Daily communication, which is an important staple for healthy family life, is disappearing and being replaced by a television set.

(Body 3) Topic Sentence: _People won't talk about their daily experiences when the television is on_

Even a seven-year-old child can heat up his own dinner. Most parents don't want to cook from scratch after a long workday. Our grocery stores and specialty markets understand this need and provide families with a wide variety of frozen meals. Brigitte Lofgren says that the microwave oven is the most useful appliance in her house: "We all heat up our own meals. Nobody has to cook." When family members heat up their own meals, one after another, it is less likely that they will bother to eat together.

(Conclusion) Most families recognize that they are losing communication time. They watch in frustration as the family dinner disappears. They assure themselves that because of hectic lifestyles, they have no choice but to stagger eating times. Televisions on the kitchen counter provide something to focus on during meals. And the quality of prepackaged and frozen meals is improving, so who really needs to cook? Yet it is tragic that the family meal, a simple and effective way to keep family members linked together, is no longer a priority in many people's lives.

Generating Supporting Ideas

When you develop supporting ideas, ensure that they all focus on the central point that you are making in the thesis statement. To generate ideas for body paragraphs, you could use the exploring strategies (brainstorming, freewriting, clustering, or questioning) that you learned in Chapter 1.

Review the process that student Alicia Parera went through. First, she created a list to support her thesis statement. Then she reread her supporting ideas and removed ideas that she did not want to develop in her essay. She also grouped together related ideas.

Initial Ideas

Draft thesis statement: Students drop out of college for many reasons.

Supporting ideas:
- can't adapt to college life
- feel confused about career goals
- don't have study skills
- can't afford tuition
- part-time job takes time away from schoolwork
- financial problems
- lose a family member
- undergo an emotional crisis such as a breakup
- ~~want to start their own businesses~~

After critically examining her supporting ideas, Alicia chose three that could become body paragraphs. She evaluated each set of linked ideas and summarized the connection between them. These sentence summaries then became her topic sentences. Alicia also reworked her thesis statement.

Revised Thesis and Supporting Points

Thesis Statement: Students may drop out of college because they are unprepared, have financial problems, or experience an emotional crisis.

Topic Sentence: Many students are unable to adapt to college life.

Topic Sentence: Some students face overwhelming financial burdens.

Topic Sentence: Furthermore, they may undergo an emotional crisis.

 **Look Critically at Your Supporting Ideas**

After you have made a list of supporting ideas, look at it carefully and ask yourself the next questions.

- **Which ideas could I develop into complete paragraphs?** Look for connections between supporting ideas. Group together ideas that have a common thread. Then create a topic sentence for each group of related ideas. In Alicia's example, three of her ideas became topic sentences.

- **Does each idea support my thesis?** Choose ideas that directly support the thesis statement and drop any ideas that might go off topic. In Alicia's example, the last idea, "Want to start their own businesses" didn't support her thesis, so she crossed it out.

PRACTICE 9   Brainstorm three supporting ideas for the next thesis statements. Find ideas that do not overlap, and ensure that your ideas support the thesis. (You can brainstorm a list of ideas on a separate sheet of paper, and then add the three best ideas here.)

EXAMPLE: Driving in the city is very stressful.

- *pedestrians and cyclists are careless*

- *poor street planning has led to larger traffic jams*

- *other drivers act in dangerous and erratic ways*

1. Losing a job can have some positive consequences. ~~New opportunity~~
   _____ Expand knowledge. _____ learning mistakes ___
   Improving their skills, is possible.
   _____ with further _____

2. There are several concrete steps that you can take to help preserve the environment.
   _____ Recycling. _____
   ~~Sto~~ _____ Reducing consumption of energy. Managing energy. _
   _____ Stop deforestation into reforestation. _____

3. When young people move away from home, they quickly learn the next lessons.
   __ They have to deal with trouble themselves. Self-Independent
   _____ financial management. _____
   _____ Time management. _____
   House-hold skills.

Writer's Desk Generate Supporting Ideas

Brainstorm supporting ideas for two or three of your thesis statements from the previous Writer's Desk. Look critically at your lists of supporting ideas. Ask yourself which supporting ideas you could expand into body paragraphs, and then drop any unrelated ideas.

 The Writer's Room **Topics to Develop**

Writing Activity 1

Choose one of the Writer's Room topics from Chapter 1 and write a thesis statement. Using an exploring strategy, develop supporting ideas for your thesis.

Writing Activity 2

Narrow one of the following topics. Then develop a thesis statement and some supporting ideas.

General Topics	College and Work-Related Topics
1. good hygiene	6. pressures students face
2. annoying rules	7. credit cards
3. delaying childbirth	8. creative teaching
4. traditions	9. improving services
5. allergies	10. benefits of extracurricular activities

✓ CHECKLIST: THESIS STATEMENT AND TOPIC SENTENCES

When you write a thesis statement, ask yourself these questions.

☐ Is my thesis a complete sentence?

☐ Does it contain a narrowed topic and a controlling idea?

☐ Is my main point clear and interesting?

☐ Can the thesis be supported with several body paragraphs? (Ensure that the topic is not too narrow, or you will hit a dead end with it. Also ensure that the topic is not too broad. Your essay requires a clear focus.)

☐ Can I think of details, examples, and other ideas to support the thesis?

☐ Is my thesis forceful and direct, and not too vague or obvious?

☐ Does my thesis make a valid point?

☐ Do I have good supporting ideas?

☐ Does each topic sentence have a controlling idea and support the thesis statement?

How Do I Get a Better Grade?

mycanadiancomplab

Go to www.mycanadiancomplab.ca for additional help with your grammar, writing, and research skills. You will have access to a variety of exercises, instruction, and video that will help you improve your basic skills and help you get a better grade.

Developing the Essay Plan

Like gardens, essays require careful planning. Some ideas thrive among each other while others do not. Writers develop essay plans to help them decide which ideas support the main idea most effectively and where to place those ideas so that readers can understand them.

Key Steps in Developing the Essay Plan

In the previous chapters, you learned how to use exploring strategies to formulate ideas and narrow topics. You also learned to develop main ideas for essays. In this chapter, you will focus on the third stage of the essay writing process: developing the essay plan. There are two key steps in this process.

DEVELOPING THE ESSAY PLAN

> ❝ *Good plans shape good decisions.* ❞
>
> LESTER R.
> BIDDLE,
> *Management Consultant*

STEP 1 ➤ **Organize your supporting ideas.** Choose an appropriate method of organization.

STEP 2 ➤ **Write an essay plan.** Place your main and supporting ideas in an essay plan.

Organizing Supporting Ideas

Once you have a list of main ideas that will make up the body paragraphs in an essay, you will need to organize those ideas in a logical manner using time, space, or emphatic order.

Time Order

To organize an essay using **time order (chronological order),** arrange the details according to the sequence in which they have occurred. Time order can be effective for narrating a story, explaining how to do something, or describing an event.

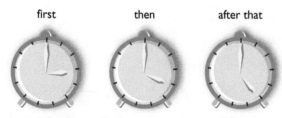

first   then   after that

When you write essays using time order, you can use the following transitional expressions to help your readers understand when certain events happened. (There is a more extensive list of transitions on page 68 in Chapter 5.)

after that	first	last	next
eventually	in the beginning	meanwhile	suddenly
finally	later	months after	then

PRACTICE 1   The supporting ideas for the following thesis statement are organized using time order.

THESIS STATEMENT: My one and only ferry ride was a disaster.

1. To begin with, the only available seat was in a horrible location near the back of the boat.

2. Next, the rain began, and the passengers on deck rushed inside.

3. After that, the ferry began to rock, and some passengers became ill.

One paragraph from the essay also uses time order. Underline any words or phrases that help show time order.

Next, the rain began, and the passengers on deck rushed inside. Suddenly, a sprinkle became a downpour. I was in the middle of the crowd, and water was running in rivulets down my face and down the back of my collar. Then, those behind me got impatient and began to shove. The doorway was narrow, and many people were jostling for position. I was pushed to the right and left. Meanwhile, I was soaked, tired, and cranky. The crowd squeezed me more and more. Finally, I was pushed through the door; I stumbled and tried not to fall. The inner seating room was so crowded that I had to stand in the aisle holding on to the back of one of the seats.

Emphatic Order

To organize the supporting details of an essay using **emphatic order**, arrange them in a logical sequence. For example, you can arrange details from least to most important, from general to specific, from least appealing to most appealing, and so on.

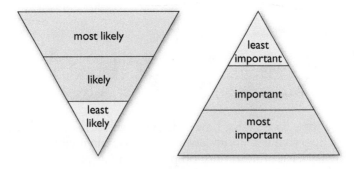

Here are some transitional expressions that help readers understand which ideas you want to emphasize the most or the least in the body paragraphs of an essay.

above all	first	moreover	principally
clearly	in particular	most importantly	the least important
especially	last	of course	the most important

PRACTICE 2   The supporting ideas for the following thesis statement are organized using emphatic order.

THESIS STATEMENT: In our city, some types of public transportation are more dependable and pleasant than others.

1. First, subways can be uncomfortable and even frightening.

2. Bus trips can have certain drawbacks.

3. The most pleasant and reliable way to travel seems to be the streetcar.

One paragraph from the essay also uses emphatic order. Underline any words or phrases that help show emphatic order.

> First, subways can be uncomfortable and even frightening. Above all, subway riders must deal with crowds. In front of the tracks, there is very little seating room, so people line the walls. Of course, the lighting is usually terrible, so ordinary people look sad and even sinister under the fluorescent tubes. Feeling uncomfortable and unattractive, they avoid eye contact. Moreover, for those who feel claustrophobic, being in a subway can feel like being in a grave. There is no sunlight, no sky, and no outdoors for the entire duration of the journey. Passengers can only stare at the sullen faces of the other travellers. Clearly, the entire subway experience can be unpleasant and disturbing.

 **Using Emphatic Order**

When you organize details using emphatic order, use your own values and opinions to determine what is most or least important, upsetting, remarkable, and so on. Another writer may organize the same ideas in a different way.

Space Order

Organizing ideas using **space order** helps the reader to visualize what you are describing in a specific space. For example, you can describe someone or something from top to bottom or bottom to top, from left to right or right to left, or from far to near or near to far.

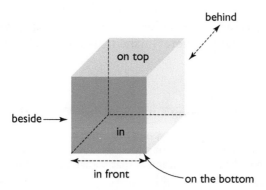

Help readers find their way through your essay by using the following transitional expressions.

above	beneath	nearby	on top
behind	closer in	on the bottom	toward
below	farther out	on the left	under

PRACTICE 3   The supporting ideas for the following thesis statement are organized using space order.

THESIS STATEMENT: With very little money, local students helped turn a tiny old house into a vibrant youth centre.

1. Working outdoors, two students cleared the yard.

2. Focusing on the exterior surfaces of the building, a second team of students painted and made minor repairs.

3. Inside the house, some students turned the living room into a recreation and meeting place.

One paragraph from the essay also uses space order. Underline any words or phrases that indicate space order.

> Inside the house, some students turned the living room into a recreation and meeting place. First, they washed and then painted the walls. At the far end of the room, next to the fireplace, there was an old bar with an orange counter and frayed yellow bar stools. The students stripped and varnished the counter of the bar and cleaned the sink. They turned the space into an art corner. Local teenagers who like to paint and sculpt now have a nice workspace. In the centre of the room, there was an area rope rug that had seen better days. They removed the rug and replaced it with woven straw matting. Beside the rug was a stained and smelly pink and green sofa. The students discarded the sofa. Rather than purchase a new one, which would have cost hundreds of dollars, they used the centre's funds to buy large blue cushions at a discount department store. When the renovations were finished, the room looked like a new and fresh space.

 **Hint**   **Combining Time, Space, or Emphatic Order**

You will likely use more than one type of organizational method in an essay. For example, in a time order essay about a journey, one paragraph might be devoted to a particular place that you visited, and in that paragraph, you might use space order to describe the scene.

PRACTICE 4   Read each list of supporting ideas, and number the items in a logical order. Then write time, space, or emphatic to indicate the organization method.

EXAMPLE: Thesis Statement: Painting a basic picture can be a rewarding experience.

___1___ Choose a location that you find particularly peaceful.

___3___ Add colours to your sketch that best represent the mood you are feeling.

___2___ Settle in and make a preliminary sketch of the place.

Order: ___time___

1. Thesis Statement: Overexposure to the sun can have terrible consequences.

   ___1___ The skin cells lose elasticity and wrinkles set in earlier.

   ___3___ Some people develop cancers that can lead to premature death.

   ___2___ Brown spots can develop on parts of the face.

   Order: ___time___

2. Thesis Statement: We encountered many problems during our trip from Mexico City to Guadalajara.

   ___3___ We arrived late at night and had a lot of trouble finding our friend's house.

   ___1___ We didn't have enough money for the first tollbooth, so we took the side roads.

   ___2___ On a small road halfway there, an accident completely blocked our route.

   Order: ___Space time___

3. Thesis Statement: For an important interview, dress conservatively.

   ___3___ Employers may notice every detail, so pay attention to your footwear.

   _____ If possible, invest in a good haircut a few days before the interview.

   ___1___ Wear a suit jacket and matching pants or a skirt.

   Order: ~~Emphatic~~ Space

4. Thesis Statement: Harold Roos should win the citizen's award for three reasons.

   ___1___ Every Sunday, Mr. Roos does volunteer work at the hospital.

   ___3___ Last September, Mr. Roos saved Eduardo Borsellino's life when he pulled the young man out of a submerged car.

   ___2___ Mr. Roos employs many local citizens in his downtown clothing store.

   Order: ___Emphatic___

Developing an Essay Plan

A contractor would never build a house without making a drawing or plan of it first. In the same way, an **essay plan** or an **outline** can help you to organize your thesis statement and supporting ideas before writing your first draft. Planning your essay actually saves you time because you have already figured out your supporting ideas and how to organize them so your readers can easily follow them. To create an essay plan, follow these steps:

- Looking at the list of ideas that you created while prewriting, identify the ones that most effectively support your thesis statement.
- Next, write topic sentences that express the main supporting ideas.
- Finally, add details under each topic sentence.

A formal essay plan uses Roman numerals and letters to identify main and supporting ideas. A formal plan also contains complete sentences. The basic structure looks like this:

Thesis statement: _____

    I. _____

        A. _____

        B. _____

   II. _____

        A. _____

        B. _____

Concluding Idea: _____

In the planning stage, you do not have to develop your introduction and conclusion. It is sufficient to simply write your thesis statement and an idea for your conclusion. Later, when you write your essay, you can develop the introduction and conclusion.

Alicia's Essay Plan

Alicia Parera wrote topic sentences and supporting examples and organized her ideas into a plan. Notice that she begins with her thesis statement, and she indents her supporting ideas.

> **THESIS STATEMENT:** Students may drop out of college because they have financial problems, experience an emotional crisis, or are unprepared for college life.
>
>   **I.** Some students face overwhelming financial burdens.
>
>   **A.** They may have a part-time job to pay for such things as tuition and rent.

      B. Moreover, a part-time job leaves no time for studying and homework.

      C. Also, transportation may be expensive and beyond a student's means.

  II. Furthermore, some students are faced with life-changing events and must leave college to cope.

      A. A pregnancy and childbirth consume energy and attention.

      B. Also, a serious illness or death in the family can cause a student to miss classes, and it becomes too difficult to catch up.

      C. Of course, a broken relationship can cause a student to feel emotionally fragile and unable to concentrate.

  III. They may be unprepared for college life.

      A. They might have poor study skills.

      B. Furthermore, some students cannot respect schedules.

      C. The increased freedom in college causes some students to skip too many classes.

      D. Additionally, many students feel confused about career goals and decide to leave college.

PRACTICE 5   Read the thesis statement and the list of supporting ideas and details. First, highlight three supporting ideas (topic sentences) and number them 1, 2, and 3. Then, using numbers such as *1a, 1b, 1c, 2a, 2b, 2c,* etc., organize the details that could follow each topic sentence. On a separate piece of paper, place the ideas in an essay plan.

THESIS STATEMENT: *Men have disadvantages at home and in the workplace.*

- High-tower construction work, which is mainly done by males, is very risky. b2
- In family court, men do not get custody of children as often as women do. A3
- According to journalist Ian McArthur, most boys are told to "take it like a man" so they learn to rein in their emotions. c1
- More men do work that puts their lives at risk than women do. A2
- Sheila Siskel, a lawyer, acknowledges that many judges still consider the woman as the child's primary caregiver. a1
- Men are more likely to repair roofs, scale electrical poles, and operate heavy machinery. A1
- Greg Chu says, "It is unsatisfying and heartbreaking when I am reduced to visiting my own children twice a month!" a2
- Over thirty percent of workplace deaths happen to men, according to the Centre for the Study of Living Standards website. b3
- Some men are ridiculed when they show emotion. A

- Manuel Figuera, a graphic designer, says, "Some believe a crying man is an emotional weakling or a wimp." *C2*
- Men's groups, including Divorced Dads, protest the attitudes of the courts toward fathers in their fight for parental rights. *A3*
- Movies such as *Saving Private Ryan* reinforce the stereotype that men must be stoic and control their emotions.

C3

PRACTICE 6   On a separate sheet of paper, create an essay plan for the next thesis statement.

THESIS STATEMENT: Women have disadvantages at home and in the workplace.

PRACTICE 7   Read the following essay plan. Brainstorm and develop three supporting ideas for each topic sentence.

THESIS STATEMENT: Common fairy tales follow a certain model.

Topic Sentence: Fairy tales never mention a real date or place.

Supporting ideas:

The fairy tales are very typical world different from the real place.

_____

_____

_____

Topic Sentence: The main character must overcome great obstacles to achieve his or her goal.

Supporting ideas:

Many famous fairy tales are describing the story about prin ce and princess, and the ones are supposed to beat the monster

enemy

relative or parents died
step mother, step mother.

Topic Sentence: The main character accomplishes his or her goals with the help of magic or some other unnatural phenomena.

Supporting ideas:

Big effects.

legend, magic etc.

1. Harry Potters

2. Green

3. princess with prices

Speaking animals.

PRACTICE 8 Read the following essay plan. Brainstorm and develop three supporting ideas for each topic sentence.

THESIS STATEMENT: I learned valuable lessons during my years in elementary school and high school.

Topic Sentence: First, I learned how to get along with others.

sharing.

1. Volunteering.

Supporting ideas:

1. From the first day of the school life, I had to learn how to talk with teachers and express my ideas.

2. I spent most of my times with classmates, which means I have to learn

3. I learned how to cooperate with others from the group project. negotiation.

flexibility

Topic Sentence: I learned to organize my time.

Supporting ideas: Schedule — prioritize

1. First There is no other people can help students organize their time.

2. Second The percentage between playing and study has to be well distributed.

3. If students not organize timetable properly, sometimes students are not going to going to get good grades.

Time table - plan

punctuality = on time.

procrastination = Defer action

Topic Sentence: Most importantly, I learned about respect, compassion, and gratitude.

Supporting ideas:

PE Course,

Competition.

Listening to others.

Compassion – opportunities to understand and help less fortunate students.

Writer's Desk Write an Essay Plan

Brainstorm ideas for an essay on a separate piece of paper. You can choose ideas that you developed in Chapter 2. Then do the following.

1. Highlight at least three ideas from your list that you think are most compelling and most clearly illustrate the point you are making in your thesis statement. These three ideas will make up your body paragraphs.

2. Group together any related ideas with the three supporting ideas.

3. Organize your ideas for the body paragraphs using time, space, or emphatic order.

4. Create a complete essay plan.

Correp

The Writer's Room   Topics to Develop

Writing Activity 1

Choose one of the Writer's Room topics from Chapter 2, and create an essay plan. Using an exploring strategy, develop supporting ideas for your thesis.

Writing Activity 2

Create a list of supporting ideas for one of the next thesis statements. Then develop an essay plan.

General Topics

1. Single people should (or should not) have the right to adopt children.

2. The three talents I would most like to have are . . .

3. Noise pollution is increasing in our homes and neighbourhoods.

4. There are good reasons to postpone marriage.

College and Work-Related Topics

5. New employees make three types of common mistakes.

6. An elected official should have the following characteristics.

7. I do (or do not) vote for the following reasons.

8. (Choose a story, novel, or film) has important lessons for all of us.

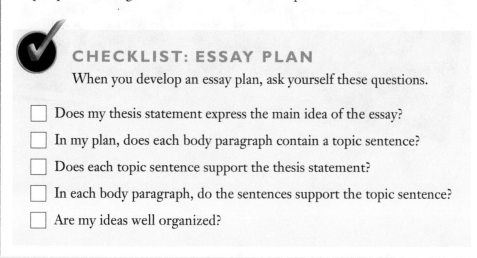

✔ CHECKLIST: ESSAY PLAN

When you develop an essay plan, ask yourself these questions.

☐ Does my thesis statement express the main idea of the essay?

☐ In my plan, does each body paragraph contain a topic sentence?

☐ Does each topic sentence support the thesis statement?

☐ In each body paragraph, do the sentences support the topic sentence?

☐ Are my ideas well organized?

How Do I Get a Better Grade?

mycanadiancomplab

Go to www.mycanadiancomplab.ca for additional help with your grammar, writing, and research skills. You will have access to a variety of exercises, instruction, and video that will help you improve your basic skills and help you get a better grade.

CHAPTER 4

Developing the First Draft

By preparing the soil and planting seeds and shrubs, a gardener creates a landscape's basic foundation. In the same way, a writer plans the main idea, develops the plan, and then prepares the first draft of a writing assignment.

Key Steps in Developing the First Draft

In previous chapters, you learned how to develop a thesis statement, support it with ideas, and create an essay plan. To develop a first draft, follow these five steps.

DEVELOPING THE FIRST DRAFT

STEP 1	➤	**Write an introduction.** Try to attract the reader's attention in the first paragraph of your essay. *[handwritten: Narrow the Topic]*
STEP 2	➤	**Write complete body paragraphs.** Expand each supporting idea with specific details.
STEP 3	➤	**Write a conclusion.** Bring your essay to a satisfactory close.
STEP 4	➤	**Title your essay.** Sum up your essay topic in a few words.
STEP 5	➤	**Write the first draft.** Tie the introduction, body paragraphs, and conclusion into a cohesive essay.

> 66 *Detail makes the difference between boring and perfect writing. It's the difference between a pencil sketch and a lush oil painting. As a writer, words are your paint. Use all the colors.* 99
>
> RHYS ALEXANDER,
> *Author*

Writing an Introduction

The **introductory paragraph** introduces the subject of your essay and contains the thesis statement. A strong introduction will capture the reader's attention and make him or her want to read on. Introductions may have a lead-in, and they can be developed in several different ways.

The Lead-In

The point of writing an essay is to have people read it and to entertain, inform, or persuade them. So, try to grab your readers' attention in the first sentence. There are three common lead-ins that you can try:

- a quotation
- a surprising or provocative statement
- a question   *[handwritten: (usually 1)]*

Introduction Styles

You can develop the introduction in several ways. Experiment with any of the following introduction styles.

- **Give general or historical background information** that gradually leads to your thesis. For example, in an essay about movie violence, you might begin by discussing some classic films.
- **Tell an interesting anecdote** or a story that leads to your thesis statement. For example, you might begin your essay about film violence by describing how aggressive your younger brother and his friends became after they watched the movie *Fight Club*.
- **Describe something in vivid detail,** and then state your thesis. For example, you might begin your essay about movie violence by describing a particularly gory film scene.
- **Define a term,** and then state your thesis. For example, in an essay about ways to avoid marital conflicts, you can begin by defining a happy marriage.

[handwritten: Personal Idea, in which way.]

- **Present a contrasting position,** which is an idea that is the opposite of the one you will later develop, and then offer your thesis. Your readers will not expect you to present one side and then to argue for the other side. For example, in an essay about abortion, you might begin by presenting the arguments of those who would not agree with your particular point of view on the debate.

- **Pose several questions,** and end with a thesis statement. The purpose may be to engage your readers by inviting them to think about the topic. You might also ask questions that you will answer in your essay. For instance, in an essay about lotteries, you might ask: *Have you ever bought a lottery ticket? Why do so many people play lotteries?*

The following example presents the structure of a typical introduction.

Lead-in ➤

Historical background information ➤

Thesis statement ➤

Have good manners disappeared? In past centuries, a gentleman would spread his cloak over a muddy road so that his lady wouldn't dirty her feet. Twenty years ago, an elderly man or woman would never have to stand in a bus because other passengers would offer up their seats. Times have certainly changed. Today, many people lack consideration for others. **Parents and schools should teach children basic good manners.**

PRACTICE I   Read the following introductions. Underline each thesis statement and determine what introduction style the writer used.

1. I got out of bed as usual. I shaved, showered and put on a clean shirt. Trotting out to the kitchen where my wife, Nadine, was standing, I looked at her and asked, "Now what?" The day before, I had accepted a generous buyout offer at Verizon Corp., effectively ending my thirty-year career there as a midlevel manager. I was fifty-one. With the papers in front of me, I listened patiently as my financial adviser cautioned me that some people in my position are not mentally prepared to retire, but I never dreamed that his advice would apply to me. I was wrong. Retirement left a void in my life that I filled in some odd ways.

   Peter Borghesi, "I Was Out of a Job and an Identity," *Newsweek*

   a. Underline the thesis statement.

   b. What is the introduction style? Indicate the best answer.

   _____ general background   _____ anecdote

   _____ definition   _____ questions

2. Adolescent males are dangerous. They join gangs, and they are responsible for most of the crime in our society. They drive too fast, causing accidents on our highways. They all experiment with drugs, and they annoy others with their loud music. But is such a portrayal of our nation's young men really fair? In fact, most stereotypes about adolescent males are incorrect and misleading.

    Abeer Hamad, student

    a. Underline the thesis statement.

    b. What type of lead-in did the writer use?

    _____ quotation   _____ question   __✓__ surprising
                                                       statement

    c. What is the introduction style? Indicate the best answer.

    _____ historical background   _____ anecdote

    _____ definition   __✓__ contrasting position

3. Where did you buy that blouse? I heard the question every time I wore it. It was a truly lovely designer model that had been marked down to $40. It was pale blue with swirling tiny flower buds running down each front panel. The little buttons were topped with imitation pearls. Unfortunately, the middle button kept coming undone. People at a certain angle to my left could peek in and view the lace eyelets on my brassiere. When I wore the blouse, my head kept bobbing down, looking to see if I was exposing myself. Over the years, I have had several humorous and embarrassing wardrobe and makeup malfunctions.

    Catalina Ortega, student

    a. Underline the thesis statement.

    b. What type of lead-in was used?

    __✓__ quotation   _____ question   _____ surprising
                                                       statement

    c. What is the introduction style? Indicate the best answer.

    _____ general background   __✓__ anecdote

    _____ definition   _____ description

4. Nationalism is the sometimes angry belief in the independence of one's people. It often includes resentment or even hatred of alien rulers or threatening foreigners: "No foreigners will push us

around!" It is the strongest and most emotional of the world's ideologies. Most of the world's people—including Americans—are nationalistic.

Michael G. Roskin and Nicholas O. Berry, *The New World of International Relations*

a. Underline the thesis statement.

b. What is the introduction style? Indicate the best answer.

_____ historical background   _____ anecdote

__✓__ definition   _____ contrasting position

5. Reflecting on his trips down a Lancashire coal mine, George Orwell wrote that aside from the lack of fire, "most of the things one imagines in hell are there—heat, noise, confusion, darkness, foul air, and above all, unbearably cramped space." If Orwell had found a few days in a coal mine just this side of hell, imagine what it must be like for the 33 Chilean miners who have been trapped 700 m underground since the main shaft of the San Jose gold and silver mine collapsed on Aug. 5. When the miners were finally discovered on Aug. 22, rescuers quickly realized that it could take as many as four months to bore a hole wide enough to pull the men out. As a result, a great deal of attention has been paid to the urgent need to secure not only the miners' physical well-being, but also their mental health.

Source: Potter, Andrew. "That Far Down, Who Decides What's Law?" *Maclean's*. September 13, 2010, p. 14.

a. Underline the thesis statement.

b. What type of lead-in was used?

__✓__ quotation   _____ question   _____ surprising statement

c. What is the introduction style? Indicate the best answer.

__✓__ historical background   _____ anecdote

_____ definition   _____ questions

6. Why do some hip-hop artists embed jewels and gold in their teeth? Are the grills meant to impress others, or do the grills fit some deep need on the part of the artists to show that they matter? Is the hip-hop artist who shows off his "bling" any different than the accountant who buys a BMW to show that she has succeeded, or the corporate executive who marries a beautiful trophy wife?

Showing off one's wealth is not new. In fact, throughout history, people have found extravagant ways to flaunt their wealth.

Jamal Evans, student

a. Underline the thesis statement.

b. What is the introduction style? Indicate the best answer.

_____ general background   _____ anecdote

_____ definition   _____ questions

PRACTICE 2   Write interesting lead-ins (opening sentences) for the following topics. Use the type of lead-in that is indicated in parentheses.

EXAMPLE: Bicycle helmet laws   (question)

How many cyclists have needlessly died this year from head injuries?

1. dangerous dogs   (a surprising or controversial statement)

_____

_____

2. ridiculous fashions   (a question)

_____

_____

3. the junk food nation   (a surprising fact or idea)

_____

_____

PRACTICE 3   Choose *one* of the next thesis statements. Then write three introductions using three different introduction styles. Use the same thesis statement in each introduction.

It's important to know more than one language.

Famous musicians generally make poor (or good) role models.

Computers have made our lives more complicated.

You can choose any three of the following introduction styles:

- Anecdote
- Description
- Definition

- Contrasting position
- Series of questions
- General or historical background

Writer's Desk **Write Two Introductions**

In Chapter 3, you prepared an essay plan. Now, on a separate piece of paper, write two different styles of introductions for your essay. Use the same thesis statement in both introductions. Later, you can choose the best introduction for your essay.

Writing Complete Body Paragraphs

In your essay plan, you developed supporting ideas for your topic. When you prepare the first draft, you must flesh out those ideas. As you write each body paragraph, ensure that it is complete. Do not offer vague generalizations, and do not simply repeat your ideas. Provide evidence for each topic sentence by inserting specific details. You might include examples, facts, statistics, anecdotes, or quotations.

Examples are people, places, things, or events that illustrate your point. To support the view that some local buildings are eyesores, the writer could give the following examples.

The car dealership on Labelle Boulevard is run-down. *looking bad*

The gray block apartment buildings that line Main Street are monotonous.

The Allen Drive mini-mall has tacky signs and cracked store windows.

Facts are objective details that can be verified by others. **Statistics** are facts *cheap looking* that are expressed in percentages. (Make sure that your statistics are from reliable sources.) To support the view that transportation costs are too high for students, the following facts and statistics could be given as evidence.

A one-way bus ticket now costs $3.50 for students.

The monthly subway pass just increased to $260 for students.

In a college survey of four hundred students, 70 percent expressed concern about the recent rate increases in public transportation.

Anecdotes are true experiences that you or someone else went through. An anecdote expresses what happened. **Quotations** are somebody's exact words, and they are set off in quotation marks. To support the view that lack of sleep can have dangerous consequences, the following anecdote and quotation could be included as evidence.

When Allen Turner finished his nightshift, he got into his car and headed home. On Forest Drive, he started to nod off. Luckily, a truck driver in another lane noticed that Turner's car was weaving and honked.

Turner said, "My eyes snapped open and I saw a wall growing larger in front of me. I slammed on my brakes just before smashing into it."

Essay with Sample Body Paragraphs

Read the following body paragraphs. Notice how they are fleshed out with specific evidence.

Thesis Statement:

> For personal and financial reasons, a growing number of adult children are choosing to live with their parents.

Body Paragraphs

The cost of education and housing is very high, so it is more economical to live at home. First, rents have increased dramatically since the 1990s. In the North Bay Nugget, Anna Reinhold states that   ⋖ fact
rents tripled in the past ten years. During the same period, student wages have not risen as much as the rents. In fact, the minimum wage is still $10.25 an hour. Also, college fees are increasing each   ⋖ fact
year. Canadian full-time students in undergraduate programs paid   ⋖ statistic
4 percent more on average in tuition fees for the 2010–2011 academic year than they did a year earlier, according to the © Living In Canada website.

Many young people want to build a nest egg before moving out of the family home. When they remain at home, they can save income from part-time jobs. "I've saved $14 000 by staying in my   ⋖ quotation
parents' place," says Kyle Nehme, a twenty-four-year-old student at the University of Toronto. Such students do not need to worry about student loans. According to financial analyst Raul Gomez, "Students   ⋖ quotation
who stay in the family home reap significant financial benefits."

Students who remain in their parents' home have a much more relaxed and comfortable lifestyle. Often, the parents do the shopping and housework. For example, Liz Allen, a twenty-six-   ⋖ anecdote
year-old marketing student, moved back in with her parents last May. She discovered how much more convenient it was when someone else did the vacuuming, laundry, and cooking. Moreover, such students feel more secure and safe in the cocoon of home. In a North Bay Nugget survey of ninety adults who live at home, 64   ⋖ statistic
percent cited "comfort" as their major reason.

Hint   **Using Research to Support Your Point**

Your instructor might ask you to back up your ideas with research. You can look in several resources, including books, magazines, and the internet, for relevant quotations, statistics, and factual evidence. For more information about doing research, see Chapter 15, The Research Essay.

Make essay strange

PRACTICE 4   Make the body paragraphs below more complete by adding specific examples. You can include the following:

- examples
- anecdotes from your own life or from the lives of others
- quotations (for this exercise, you can make up punchy quotations)
- facts, statistics, or descriptions of events that you have read about or seen

Do not add general statements. Ensure that the details you add are very specific.

THESIS STATEMENT: Prospective pet owners should become informed before buying an animal.

Body Paragraph 1 First, when families choose a dog, they should consider the inconvenience and possible dangers. Some breeds of dogs can become extremely aggressive. Like _____

_____

_____

_____

_____ Moreover, dog owners must accept that dogs require a lot of time and attention. _____

_____

_____

_____ Furthermore, it is very expensive to own a dog. _____

_____

Body Paragraph 2 Some new pet owners decide to buy exotic pets. However, such pets come with very specific problems and require particular environments.

_____

_____

_____

_____ Also, some exotic pets seem interesting when they are young, but they

can become distinctly annoying or dangerous when they reach maturity.

_____

_____

_____

Hint   Making Detailed Essay Plans

You can shorten the time you spend developing the first draft if you make a very detailed essay plan. In addition to writing main ideas, your plan can include details for each supporting idea. Notice the detailed evidence in the following excerpt from an essay plan.

Thesis Statement: For personal and financial reasons, a growing number of adult children are choosing to live with their parents.

I. **Topic Sentence:** The cost of education and housing is very high.
   A. Rents have increased dramatically in the past ten years.
       Evidence: The <u>North Bay Nugget</u> states that rents tripled in the past ten years.   ◄ fact
   B. Student wages have not risen as much as the rents.
       Evidence: The minimum wage is still $10.25 an hour.   ◄ fact
   C. Tuition fees are very high.
       Evidence: Tuition and fees at four-year colleges rose 4 percent this year, according to the © Living In Canada website.   ◄ statistic

Writer's Desk   Make Complete Body Paragraphs

In Chapter 3, you prepared an essay plan. Now write complete body paragraphs for your essay. Ensure that each body paragraph contains specific details.

Writing a Conclusion

The **concluding paragraph** gives you one last chance to impress the reader and to make your point clear. A good conclusion makes the essay seem complete. One common and effective way to conclude a composition is to summarize the main ideas. The essay then comes full circle, and you remind the reader of your strongest points.

To make your conclusion more interesting and original, you could also close with a prediction, a suggestion, a quotation, or a call to action.

 Hint   **Linking the Conclusion to the Introduction**

One effective way to conclude an essay is to continue an idea that was introduced in the introduction.

- If you began an anecdote in the introduction, you can finish it in the conclusion.
- If you posed some questions in the introduction, you can answer them in the conclusion.
- If you highlighted a problem in the introduction, you might suggest a solution in the conclusion.

Look at the concluding paragraph to an essay about etiquette in our technological age.

> Do not hide behind technology as your excuse for displaying rude or annoying behaviour. You can turn off your cellphone when you are with someone you care about. If someone is writing an email, do not read over his or her shoulder. Also, never send or accept chain emails that promise wealth, happiness, or cures for cancer.

The last sentence in the essay could be one of the following.

Prediction:	If you follow the basic rules of etiquette, you will ensure that your friends and colleagues maintain their respect for you.
Suggestion:	The next time someone forwards you a nasty chain letter asking you to send it to at least ten people or else, return it to the sender ten times.
Quotation:	As the French author Colette once said, "It is wise to apply the oils of refined politeness to the mechanism of friendship."
Call to Action:	To help the next generation learn good manners, offer to teach a class to local high school students about etiquette in the technological age.

PRACTICE 5   Read the following conclusions and answer the questions.

A. Laws designed to spook such scammers may be on the way, in the same way legislators tried to wipe out spam a few years ago. California Governor Arnold Schwarzenegger has approved legislation specifically outlawing such scams, giving prosecutors another tool to pursue the fraudulent. But it's still too early to measure whether such laws will be effective at curbing phishing attacks. Until then, consumers should continue to click carefully and be cautious about how and where they hand over personal information.

Mike Musgrove, "Phishing," The Washington Post

1. What method does the author use to end the conclusion? _Suggestion_

B. Just as a peacock spreads its tail feathers to attract the opposite sex, human beings flaunt their wealth to impress their mates and to establish their power over others. The grills on the teeth of hip-hop artists are simply modern versions of the Taj Mahal, the pyramids, or the elaborate castles of kings and queens. As Mel Brooks said in *The Producers*, "When you've got it, baby, flaunt it."   _etiquette_

Jamal Evans, student

2. What method does the author use to end the conclusion? _Quotation_

C. In this new millennium, let's put the concept of IQ to rest, once and for all. Stop giving IQ tests. Stop all the studies on IQ and birth order, IQ and nutrition, or IQ and Mozart. Let's find newer, more fluid, and more fair ways to debate and enable human potential. Let's use our heads for a change.

Dorothy Nixon, "Let's Stop Being Stupid About IQ"

3. What method does the author use to end the conclusion? _Call to Action_

 Hint   **Avoiding Conclusion Problems**

In your conclusion, do not contradict your main point, and do not introduce new or irrelevant information. Also, avoid ending your essay with a rhetorical question, which is a question that cannot be answered, such as "When will humans stop having wars?"

Writer's Desk   Write a Conclusion

Write a conclusion for the essay you've been preparing in the previous Writer's Desk exercises.

Choosing an Essay Title

Think of a title *after* you have written your essay because you will have a more complete impression of your essay's main point. The most effective titles are brief, depict the topic and purpose of the essay, and attract the reader's attention.

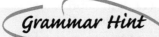 **Capitalizing Titles**

Place your title at the top centre of your page. Capitalize the first word of your title, and capitalize the main words except for prepositions (*in, at, for, to,* etc.) and articles (*a, an, the*). Leave about an inch of space between the title and the introductory paragraph.

Descriptive Titles

Descriptive titles are the most common titles in academic essays. They depict the topic of the essay clearly and concisely. Sometimes, the writer takes key words from the thesis statement and uses them in the title. Here are two examples of descriptive titles.

> Etiquette in the Technological Age
>
> Avoiding Mistakes in the First Year of College

Titles Related to the Writing Pattern

You can also relate your title directly to the writing pattern of your essay. Here are examples of titles for different writing patterns.

Illustration:	Problems with Internet Dating
Narration:	My Worst Nightmare
Description:	The Anniversary Party
Process:	How to Handle a Workplace Bully
Definition:	The Meaning of Tolerance
Classification:	Three Types of Fathers
Comparison and Contrast:	Fads Versus Timeless Fashions
Cause and Effect:	The Reasons People Pollute
Argument:	Why Writing Matters

 **Avoiding Title Pitfalls**

When you write your title, watch out for problems.

- Do not view your title as a substitute for a thesis statement.
- Do not write a really long title because it can confuse readers.
- Do not put quotation marks around the title of your essay.

PRACTICE 6   Read the next introductions and underline the thesis statements. Then write titles for each essay.

1. Some people fear mistakes more than others fear snakes. Perfectionism refers to self-defeating thoughts and behaviours aimed at reaching excessively high, unrealistic goals. Unfortunately, nobody is perfect. In fact, there are many problems associated with the desire to be perfect.

    Title: _____

2. Gang life, once associated with large urban centres in Canada, has become a common part of adolescent experience in towns and rural areas. Many of the gang members have no strong role models at home, and their gang affiliation makes them feel like part of a powerful group. To combat the problems associated with youth gangs, adolescents need to be given more responsibilities in our society.

    Title: _____

3. "A person who is not initiated is still a child," says Malidoma Somé. Somé is from the Dagara Tribe in West Africa, and he underwent a six-week initiation ceremony. Left alone in the bush with no food or clothing, he developed a profound appreciation of nature and of magic. When he returned to his village, everyone welcomed him and other initiates with food and dancing. Somé had passed from childhood into adulthood and was expected to assume adult responsibilities. The ceremony helped Somé and the other initiates feel like valued participants in village life. Our culture should have formal initiation ceremonies for adolescents.

    Title: _____

PRACTICE 7   Read the following body paragraphs of a short essay. First, highlight the topic sentence in each body paragraph. Then, on a separate sheet of paper, develop a title, a compelling introduction, and a conclusion.

Add a title

Add an introduction

Body 1   First, family communication suffers when a television is present. The TV is turned on from morning to night. Families install televisions in the kitchen, living room, and bedrooms. Thus, in locations where families traditionally congregated to talk, they now sit mutely—sometimes next to each other—staring at the screen. Instead of reading a bedtime story together, families deposit children in front of the television to watch a bedtime video. Fourteen-year-old Annie Wong says, "When I get home from school, I head straight for my bedroom. I watch my shows in my room, and my brother watches the TV in the living room. I never have to talk to him."

Body 2   Too often, when people do communicate, their discussions revolve around television shows. It is common to hear people quoting Dr. Phil or Oprah, and water cooler conversations often revolve around the latest hot series. Thirty-year-old William and his friend Jay love nothing more than to reminisce about their favourite programs. When *Lost* was at its peak, they discussed each episode in detail. They also love theme songs. "I know the songs for about fifteen television shows," William says, as he proceeds to do the *Fresh Prince of Bel-Air* rap. Jay admits that his conversations with William rarely stray beyond the lightness of the television world.

Body 3   Most importantly, the health of children has changed since the introduction of television. Before televisions existed, children played outdoors and spent most of their free time doing physical activities. Today, most children pass hours sitting or lying down as they stare at the television screen. According to Anna Franklin, a researcher at the Mayo Clinic, such inactivity is contributing to the obesity epidemic in our nation. Ben Tyler, a 10-year-old from Regina, admits that he watches between six and eight hours of television each day. "I can watch whatever I want," he says proudly. But Ben is also overweight and suffers from asthma.

Add a conclusion

Writing the First Draft

After creating an introduction and conclusion, and after arranging the supporting ideas in a logical order, you are ready to write your first draft. The first draft includes your introduction, several body paragraphs, and your concluding paragraph.

Writer's Desk **Write the First Draft**

In the previous Writer's Desk exercises, you wrote an introduction, a conclusion, and an essay plan. Now write the first draft of your essay.

 The Writer's Room **Topics to Develop**

Writing Activity 1

Choose an essay plan that you developed for Chapter 3, and write the first draft of your essay.

Writing Activity 2

Write the first draft of an essay about one of the following topics.

General Topics

1. In divorce cases, grandparents should receive visitation rights.
2. Movies and television shows glorify crime and criminals.
3. Lying is appropriate in certain situations.
4. I would like to improve three of my traits.

College and Work-Related Topics

5. People go to college for the following reasons.
6. Getting fired can be a liberating experience.
7. Compare learning from experience versus learning from books.
8. I do (or do not) have the skills to be a salesperson.

✓ CHECKLIST: FIRST DRAFT

When you develop the first draft, ask yourself these questions.

☐ Do I have a compelling introduction?

☐ Does my introduction lead into a clear thesis statement?

☐ Do my body paragraphs contain interesting and sufficient details?

☐ Do the body paragraphs support the idea presented in the thesis statement?

☐ Do I have an interesting title that sums up the essay topic?

☐ Does my conclusion bring my essay to a satisfactory close?

How Do I Get a Better Grade?

mycanadiancomplab

Go to www.mycanadiancomplab.ca for additional help with your grammar, writing, and research skills. You will have access to a variety of exercises, instruction, and video that will help you improve your basic skills and help you get a better grade.

Revising and Editing

CONTENTS

The revising and editing stage of the writing process is similar to adding the finishing touches to a garden. Like a gardener, a writer considers what he or she needs to add or trim to make it the best creation possible.

Key Steps in Revising and Editing

Revising and editing is the final step in the writing process. When you **revise**, you modify your writing to make it stronger and more convincing. To revise, read your first draft critically, and look for faulty logic, poor organization, or poor sentence style. Then reorganize and rewrite it, making any necessary changes. When you **edit**, you proofread your final draft for errors in grammar, spelling, punctuation, and mechanics.

> *If you have made mistakes, there is always another chance for you. You may have a fresh start any moment you choose, for this thing we call 'failure' is not falling down, but the staying down.*

MARY PICKFORD, *Canadian-born American actress*

There are five key steps to follow during the revising and editing stage.

REVISING AND EDITING

STEP 1	➤	**Revise for unity.** Ensure that all parts of your work relate to the main idea.
STEP 2	➤	**Revise for adequate support.** Determine that your details effectively support the main idea.
STEP 3	➤	**Revise for coherence.** Verify that your ideas flow smoothly and logically.
STEP 4	➤	**Revise for style.** Ensure that your sentences are varied and interesting.
STEP 5	➤	**Edit for technical errors.** Proofread your work and correct errors in grammar, spelling, mechanics, and punctuation.

Revising for Unity

Unity means that the ideas in an essay clearly support the focus of the essay. All information heads in the same direction, and there are no forks in the road. If an essay lacks unity, then some ideas drift away from the main idea a writer has expressed in the essay. To check for unity in an essay, consider the following:

- Ensure that all topic sentences in the body paragraphs support the thesis statement of the essay.
- Ensure that all sentences within a body paragraph support the topic sentence of that paragraph.

Essay Without Unity

The following essay plan looks at the reasons for deforestation. The third topic sentence veers away from the writer's central focus that deforestation has implications for the quality of life.

Thesis Statement: Deforestation in the Amazon has tremendous implications for people's quality of life.

Topic Sentence 1: First, logging, mining, and agriculture displace indigenous peoples in the Amazon.

Topic Sentence 2: Also, scientists believe that deforestation in the Amazon will lead to a rapid increase in global climate change, which will affect people worldwide.

Topic Sentence 3: Many development experts are trying to find methods to have sustainable development in the Amazon. ◄ This topic sentence strays from the thesis of this essay.

PRACTICE 1   The following thesis statements have three supporting points that can be developed into body paragraphs. Circle the point that does not support the thesis statement.

1. Thesis Statement: North America is developing a culture of victimization.

   a. First, many people blame their personal and professional problems on addiction.

   b. Furthermore, the increase in personal injury lawsuits suggests that more people see themselves as victims.

   c. In addition, lobbyists are petitioning on behalf of special interest groups.

2. Thesis Statement: International adoptions should be banned.

   a. An internationally adopted child will often lose contact with his or her culture.

   b. Too many celebrities have adopted internationally.

   c. By adopting from poor countries, westerners are complicit in the exploitation of poor people forced to give up their babies due to poverty.

Paragraph Without Unity

Not only must your essay have unity, but each body paragraph must have unity. The details in the paragraph must support the paragraph's topic sentence. The next paragraph is part of a larger work. In it, the writer drifted away from his main idea. Some sentences do not relate to the topic sentence. If the highlighted sentences are removed, then the paragraph has unity.

> Canadians should not fear the practice of outsourcing by businesses. First, outsourcing is the same practice as subcontracting. In the past, many companies subcontracted work to companies within the same country. Now, businesses simply subcontract to other nations. Furthermore, outsourcing usually leads to higher profits because the product or service is produced more cost effectively. Therefore, the head company's profit margin increases, allowing it to reinvest in domestic markets. In addition, when a company increases its profit, not only do the stockholders benefit, but so do the employees of the

company. The stockholders receive more value for their stock, and the employees receive more salaries and benefits. My sister worked in computers and her job became obsolete when her company outsourced the work to India. Now my sister is devastated. She has lost her house and car, and she cannot find another job in her field. Thus, with more disposable incomes, people can help the domestic economy by buying more products.

The writer detours here.

PRACTICE 2   Paragraphs A and B contain problems with unity. In each paragraph, underline the topic sentence and cross out any sentences that do not support the controlling idea.

Paragraph A

The gated community is an attempt to create a modern utopia. First, many people are buying property in gated communities because they want to feel more secure. Gated communities are surrounded by fences and guarded entrances. Therefore, tenants feel that crime will stop at the gate. People also buy homes in gated communities because they do not want to spend time maintaining the yard. Most gated communities have lawn mowing or snow clearing services available. In fact, home maintenance services are becoming very popular in all types of neighbourhoods. Such services are not only meant for the elderly, but they are also meant for busy young families. For some people, gated communities give them a lifestyle choice. Since there are rules to follow in a gated community, some homeowners feel that they will be able to live in a community with likeminded neighbors. For example, people with similar religious values may want to live in one community. Thus, gated communities seem to be an attempt at creating utopian living conditions.

Paragraph B

The electric car is not as good for the environment as many people think. First, many people buy electric cars thinking that such vehicles produce no carbon dioxide emissions. Consumers forget how electricity is produced. Most electricity plants generate power by burning coal, oil, or diesel fuel. In fact, burning coal releases many contaminants into the air, which create a great deal of air pollution. Moreover, electric car batteries contain toxic ingredients. If these are not properly recycled, they could contaminate landfill sites. My friend is in the market for a car, and we are going to test-drive a few on the weekend. He is considering both new and used cars. So think carefully about environmental concerns before buying your next car.

Revising for Adequate Support

An arch is built using several well-placed stones. Like an arch, an essay requires **adequate support** to help it stand on its own.

When revising an essay for adequate support, consider the following:

- Ensure that your thesis statement is broad enough to develop several supporting points. It may be necessary to revise the thesis statement to meet the length requirements of the essay.
- When you write the body paragraphs of the essay, insert specific details and try to include vivid descriptions, anecdotes, examples, facts, or quotations.

Avoid Circular Reasoning

Circular reasoning means that a paragraph restates its main point in various ways but does not provide supporting details. Like driving aimlessly around and around a traffic circle, the main idea never seems to progress. Avoid using circular reasoning by directing your paragraph with a clear, concise topic sentence and by supporting the topic sentence with facts, examples, statistics, or anecdotes.

Paragraph with Circular Reasoning

The following paragraph contains circular reasoning. The main point is repeated over and over. The writer does not provide any evidence to support the topic sentence.

> Travelling is a necessary educational tool. Students can learn a lot by visiting other countries. Many schools offer educational trips to other places for their students. Students may benefit from such cultural introductions. Clearly, travelling offers students an important educational opportunity.

≺ This writer leads the reader in circles.

In the second version of this paragraph, the paragraph contains specific examples that help to illustrate the main point.

Revised Paragraph

Travelling is a necessary educational tool. Students can learn a lot by visiting other places. Many schools and colleges offer educational trips. On such trips, students visit museums, art galleries, and historical sites. For example, the art department of our college sponsored a trip to Ottawa, and the students visited the Canadian Museum of Civilization. Other travel programs are work programs. Students may travel to another region or country to be involved in a community project. Students in the local high school, for example, helped build a community centre for children in a small town in Nicaragua. The students who participated in this project all said that they learned some very practical lessons, including organizational and construction skills. Clearly, travelling offers students an important educational opportunity.

Anecdotes and examples provide supporting evidence. ➤

PRACTICE 3   Read the following paragraphs and write OK next to the ones that have adequate support. Underline the specific details in those paragraphs. Then, to the paragraphs that lack adequate support, add details such as descriptions, examples, quotations, or anecdotes. Use arrows to indicate where you should place specific details.

The following example is from an essay. In the first paragraph, the writer was repetitive and vague. After the writer added specific examples and vivid details, the paragraph was much more interesting.

Weak Support

To become a better dresser, follow these steps. First, ask friends or family members what colours suit you. Also, don't be a slave to the latest fashion. Finally, spend money on a few good items rather than filling your closet with cheap outfits. My closet is half-full, but the clothing I have is of good quality.

Better Support with Details

To become a better dresser, follow these steps. First, ask friends or family members what colours suit you. *I love green, for instance, but when I wore an olive green shirt, a close friend said it brought out the green in my skin and made me look ill.* Also, don't be a slave to the latest fashion. *Although tank tops and low-waist jeans were popular for several years, I didn't have the right body type for that fashion because my belly spilled over the tops of my jeans. Instead, I wore longer shirts with my jeans, so I looked stylish but not ridiculous.* Finally, spend money on a few good items rather than filling your closet with cheap outfits. My closet is half-full, but the clothing I have is of good quality.

1. **Many cyclists are inconsiderate.** Some think that they don't have to obey traffic rules and that traffic signs are just for car drivers. Also, some cyclists are pretty crazy and do dangerous things and risk their lives or the lives of others. People have ended up in the hospital after a run-in with these two-wheeled rebels. Cyclists should take safety courses before they ride on public roads.

   Write OK or add details

2. **During my first job interview, I managed to overcome my fright.** I sat in a small, brightly lit room in front of four interviewers. A stern woman stared at me intently and curtly asked me why I wanted the job. Perspiration dripped into my eyes as I stammered that I had seen an advertisement. She smirked and asked me to be more specific. Feeling that I didn't have a chance anyway, I relaxed and stopped worrying about the faces gazing at me. I spoke about my first experience in a hospital, and I described the nurses who took care of me and the respectful way the orderlies treated me. I expressed my heartfelt desire to work as an orderly, and I got the job.

   Write OK or add details

3. **Hollywood producers should stop making movies based on old television shows.** Many of the original series were on television in the 1960s or 1970s, and younger audiences cannot relate to movies based on those television shows. Even when those programs were first on the air, they were mediocre. The remakes are boring for young people even when studios hire stellar actors and spend fortunes on special effects. Then the studio bosses are surprised when the remakes are not successful. Hollywood studios should realize that the public doesn't want any more remakes of old television shows.

   Write OK or add details

Revising for Coherence

Make your writing as smooth as possible by using expressions that logically guide the reader from one idea to the next. When revising an essay for **coherence**, consider the following:

- Ensure that sentences within each body paragraph flow smoothly by using transitional expressions.
- Ensure that the supporting ideas of an essay are connected to each other and to the thesis statement by using paragraph links.

Transitional Expressions

Just as stepping stones can help you cross from one side of the water to the other, **transitional expressions** can help readers cross from idea to idea in an essay.

Here are some common transitional expressions.

Function	Transitional Word or Expression
Addition	again, also, besides, finally, first (second, third), for one thing, furthermore, in addition, in fact, last, moreover, next, then
Comparison and contrast	as well, equally, even so, however, in contrast, instead, likewise, nevertheless, on the contrary, on the other hand, similarly
Concession of a point	certainly, even so, indeed, of course, no doubt, to be sure
Effect or result	accordingly, as a result, consequently, hence, otherwise, then, therefore, thus
Emphasis	above all, clearly, first, especially, in fact, in particular, indeed, least of all, most important, most of all, of course, particularly, principally
Example	for example, for instance, in other words, in particular, namely, specifically, to illustrate
Reason or purpose	because, for this purpose, for this reason, the most important reason
Space	above, behind, below, beneath, beside, beyond, closer in, farther out, inside, near, nearby, on one side/the other side, on the bottom, on the left/right, on top, outside, to the north/east/south/west, under
Summary or conclusion	in conclusion, in other words, in short, generally, on the whole, therefore, thus, to conclude, to summarize, ultimately
Time	after that, at that time, at the moment, currently, earlier, eventually, first (second, etc.), gradually, immediately, in the beginning, in the future, in the past, later, meanwhile, months after, now, one day, presently, so far, subsequently, suddenly, then, these days

 **Use Transitional Expressions with Complete Sentences**

When you add a transitional expression to a sentence, ensure that your sentence is complete. Your sentence must have a subject and a verb, and it must express a complete thought.

Incomplete: For example, violence on television.

Complete: For example, <u>violence on television is very graphic</u>.

Adding Transitional Words Within a Paragraph

The following paragraph shows transitional words linking sentences within a paragraph.

> Learning a new language provides invaluable benefits to a person's life. **First**, researchers have found that learning a foreign language is a kind of exercise for the brain. It improves the area in the brain that processes information. Such people display better problem-solving abilities. **Furthermore**, people who know a second language can communicate with more people. **Therefore**, they can use this skill to acquire greater understanding of different cultures. **For example**, knowing a foreign language may give them more personal satisfaction when they are travelling because it allows them more opportunities to communicate with other people. **In addition**, bilingual people are more competitive in the job market. Because they know another language, they may be more mobile in their careers. They may **also** be able to take advantage of more job opportunities. In their spare time, people should learn a second language. They won't regret it.

PRACTICE 4   Add appropriate transitional expressions to the following paragraph. Choose from the following list, and use each transitional word once. There may be more than one correct answer.

in addition	therefore	in fact	for instance
first	then	for example	moreover

Counterculture is a pattern of beliefs and actions that oppose the cultural norms of a society. ___for example___ hippies are the best-known counterculture group in the recent past, and they are known for rebelling against authority. ___first___ they rejected the consumer-based capitalist society of their parents in favour of communal living arrangements.

_____[then]_____ the hippie generation valued peace and created a massive antiwar movement. _____[Moreover furthermore]_____ there were mass protests against the Vietnam War. _____[In fact]_____ small religious groups belong to the countercultural current. These groups live with other like-minded people and turn away from widely accepted ideas on lifestyle. _____[For example]_____ the Amish are pacifists, and they reject modern technology. _____[Therefore]_____ militant groups and anarchist groups reject conventional laws. Some of these groups want to eliminate legal, political, and social institutions. Countercultural social patterns will always remain part of the mainstream society.

PRACTICE 5   The next paragraph lacks transitional expressions. Add appropriate transitional expressions wherever you think they are necessary.

People in our culture tend to idolize notorious gangsters. [For example] Al Capone operated during Prohibition, selling alcohol and building a criminal empire. He became infamous and his name is instantly recognizable. [In fact] The Gotti family's patriarch was the head of a large and vicious crime family in New Jersey. The family members are celebrities and one of the daughters, Victoria Gotti, had her own reality television show. Filmmakers contribute to the idealization of criminals. Movies such as *The Godfather* and *Live Free or Die Trying* celebrate gangsters and criminals. [Therefore] Gangsters appear to have exciting and glamorous lives. It is unfortunate that our culture elevates criminals to heroic status.

Making Links in Essays

To achieve coherence in an essay, try the following methods to transition from one idea to the next.

1. **Repeat words or phrases from the thesis statement in the topic sentence of each body paragraph.**   In this example, *giftedness* and *ambiguity* are repeated words.

Thesis Statement:	Although many schools offer a program for <u>gifted</u> children, there continues to be <u>ambiguity</u> concerning the definition of <u>gifted</u>.
Body Paragraph 1:	One <u>ambiguity</u> is choosing the criteria for <u>assessing the gifted</u>.
Body Paragraph 2:	Another <u>ambiguity</u> pertains to defining the fields or areas <u>in which a person is gifted</u>.

2. **Refer to the main idea in the previous paragraph, and link it to your current topic sentence.** In the topic sentence for the second body paragraph, the writer reminds the reader of the first point (*insomnia*) and then introduces the next point.

Thesis Statement:	Sleeping disorders cause severe disruption to many people's lives.
Body Paragraph 1:	Insomnia, a common <u>sleep disorder</u>, severely limits the <u>sufferer's quality of life</u>.
Body Paragraph 2:	The <u>opposite condition of insomnia</u>, narcolepsy also causes <u>mayhem as the sufferer struggles to stay awake</u>.

3. **Use a transitional word or phrase to lead the reader to your next idea.**

Body Paragraph 3:	<u>Moreover</u>, when sufferers go untreated for their sleep disorders, they pose risks to the people around them.

Revising for Style

When you revise for sentence **style**, you ensure that your essay has concise and appropriate language and sentence variety. You can also ask yourself whether your sentences are parallel in structure. (To practise revising for parallel structure, see Chapter 19.)

Alicia's Revision

In Chapter 3, you read Alicia's essay plan about college dropouts. After writing her first draft, she revised her essay. Look at her revisions for unity, support, coherence, and style.

Add title. ➤

Dropping Out of College

I live in a small coastal town on the Atlantic. The town attracts tourists from all over the country. Because of its beautiful beach. My college roommate, Farrad, works as a cook at the local pizza stand. Last year, Farrad started working a few hours per week, but then because of his efficiency, his boss increased Farrad's hours. My roommate then joined a growing group of people. He became a college dropout. **Students may drop out of college**

Thesis statement ➤ **because they lack financial support, experience an emotional crisis, or are unprepared.**

Add transition. ➤ *First*
~~S~~some students drop out because they face overwhelming financial burdens. Like Farrad, they may have a part-time job to help pay for tuition and rent. If the job requires students to work for many hours, they might not have time to study or to do homework.

Add detail. ➤ *A recent Statistics Canada study showed that student borrowers between the ages of 20 and 45 were less likely to have savings or investments compared to non-borrowers.* **Nadia, for exemple, works in the computer lab four nights a week.**

Add detail. ➤ *The number of hours is overwhelming and she may drop out of college.*
Clarify pronoun. ➤ *Some students*
~~They~~ also drop out because they live far from campus, and transportation may be too expensive or inconvenient.

events, and they
Furthermore, some students undergo life-changing events. ~~They~~

Combine sentences. ➤ *In a recent report by the Ottawa Citizen, "Money, or lack of it, doesn't appear to play a major role in the decision [to stay in post-secondary education]. While students who get scholarships or grants are less likely to leave than those who get loans, of all those who start post-secondary education, only 1.8 per cent of those in college and 2.3 per cent of those in university depart for lack of funds."*

Revise for unity. ➤ must leave college. ^A college student may get married or a female student may become pregnant and taking care of a baby may consume all of her time and energy. ~~There are public~~

Add transition. ➤ ~~and private daycare centers. But parents must choose very carefully.~~
In addition, an
~~An~~ illness in the family may cause a student to miss too many

classes. A student may feel emotionaly fragile because of a broken relationship. The student may not be able to cope with their feelings and wanted to leave college.

Moreover, some students may be unable to ~~get into~~ *adapt to* college life. Some have poor study skills and fall behind in homework assignments. Students may not be able to organize there time. Or a student might be unused to freedom in college and skip too many classes. For instance, my lab partner has missed about six classes this semester. *In addition, not* ~~Not~~ every student has clear career goals. *According to the National Academic Advising Association (NACADA) website, 75 percent of first-year students do not have clear career goals.* Those who are unsure about their academic futur may drop out rather than continue to study in a field they do not enjoy. *For instance, my cousin realized she did not want to be an engineer, so she left school until she could figure out what she really wanted to do.* Even though students drop out of college for many good reasons, some decide to return to college life. *For example,* Farrad hopes to finish his studies next year. *He knows he would have to find a better balance between work and school to succeed, but he is motivated to complete his education.*

> ◄ Find better word.
>
> ◄ Add transition.
>
> ◄ Add detail.
>
> ◄ Add detail.
>
> ◄ Add transition.
>
> ◄ Improve conclusion.

 **Hint** **Enhancing Your Essay**

When you revise, look at the strength of your supporting details. Ask yourself the following questions.

- Are my supporting details interesting and will they grab my reader's attention? Should I use more vivid vocabulary?
- Is my concluding sentence appealing? Could I end the paragraph in a more interesting way?

Editing for Errors

When you **edit**, you reread your writing and make sure that it is free of errors. You focus on the language, and you look for mistakes in grammar, punctuation, mechanics, and spelling.

There is an editing guide on the inside back cover of this book. It contains some common error codes that your instructor may use. It also provides you with a list of errors to check for when you proofread your text.

GRAMMAR LINK

To practise your editing skills, try the practices in Chapter 31.

Editing Tips

The following tips will help you to proofread your work more effectively.

- Put your text aside for a day or two before you do the editing. Sometimes, when you have been working closely with a text, you might not see the errors.

- Begin your proofreading at any stage of the writing process. For example, if you are not sure of the spelling of a word while writing the first draft, you could either highlight the word to remind yourself to verify it later, or you could immediately look up the word in the dictionary.

- Use the grammar and spelling checker that comes with your word processor. However, be vigilant when accepting the suggestions. Do not always choose the first suggestion for a correction. For example, a grammar checker cannot distinguish between when to use *which* and *that*. Make sure that suggestions are valid before you accept them.

- Keep a list of your common errors in a separate grammar log. When you finish a writing assignment, consult your error list and make sure that you have not repeated any of those errors. After you have received each corrected assignment from your instructor, you can add new errors to your list. For more information about a grammar and spelling log, see Appendix 5.

Alicia's Edited Essay

Alicia edited her essay about college dropouts. She corrected errors in spelling, punctuation, and grammar.

Dropping Out of College

I live in a small coastal town on the Atlantic. The town attracts tourists from all over the country. ~~Because~~ *country because* of its beautiful beach. My college roommate, Farrad, works as a cook at the local pizza stand. Last year, Farrad started working a few hours per week, but then because of his efficiency, his boss increased Farrad's hours. My roommate then joined a growing group of people, and he became a college dropout. Students may drop out of college because they lack financial support, experience an emotional crisis, or are unprepared.

First, some students drop out because they face overwhelming financial burdens. Like Farrad, they may have a part-time job to help pay for tuition and rent. According to *The Ottawa Citizen*, "Investments in post-secondary education must be part of the federal government's economic recovery plan, and it must help relieve massive student debt, which hit $13 billion." If the job requires students to work for many hours, they might not have time to study or to do homework. Nadia, for ~~exemple~~ *example*, works in the computer lab four nights a week. The number of hours is overwhelming, and she may drop out of college. Some students also drop out because they live far from campus, and transportation may be too expensive or inconvenient.

Furthermore, some students undergo life-changing events, and they must leave college. In an interview with CNN, Dr. William Pepicello, President of the University of Phoenix, stated that one reason that students drop out is "life gets in the way." A college student may get married or a female student may become pregnant *, [add comma]* and taking care of a baby may consume all of her time and energy. In addition, an illness in the family may cause a student to miss too many classes. A student may also feel ~~emotionaly~~ *emotionally* fragile because of a broken relationship. The student may not be able to cope with ~~their~~ *his or her* feelings and ~~wanted~~ *want* to leave college.

Moreover, some students may be unable to adapt to college life. Some have poor study skills and fall behind in homework assignments. Also, students may not be able to organize ~~there~~ *their* time. Or a student might not be used to freedom in college and skip too many classes. For instance, my lab partner has missed about six classes this semester. In addition, not every student has clear career goals. According to the National Academic Advising Association (NACADA) website, 75 percent of first-year students do not have clear career goals. Those who are unsure about their academic ~~futur~~ *future* may drop out rather than continue to study in a field they do not enjoy. For instance, my cousin realized she did not want to be an engineer, so she left school until she could figure out what she really wanted to do.

Even though students drop out of college for many good reasons, some decide to return to college life. Farrad, for example, hopes to finish his studies next year. He knows he ~~would~~ *will* have to find a better balance between work and school to succeed, but he is motivated to complete his education.

Writer's Desk Revise and Edit Your Paragraph

Choose an essay that you have written for Chapter 4, or choose one that you have written for another assignment. Carefully revise and edit the essay. You can refer to the Revising and Editing checklists on the inside covers.

Peer Feedback

After you write an essay, it is useful to get peer feedback. Ask a friend, family member, or fellow student to read your work and give you comments and suggestions on its strengths and weaknesses.

> ## Hint   **Offer Constructive Criticism**
>
> When you peer edit someone else's writing, try to make your comments useful. Phrase your comments in a positive way. Look at the examples.
>
> | **Instead of saying . . .** | **You could say . . .** |
> |---|---|
> | You repeat the same words. | Maybe you could find synonyms for some words. |
> | Your paragraphs are too short. | You could add more details here. |

You can use this peer feedback form to evaluate written work.

Peer Feedback Form

Written by _____ Feedback by _____

Date: _____

1. What is the main point of the written work?_____

    _____

    _____

2. Which details effectively support the thesis statement?_____

    _____

    _____

3. What, if anything, is unclear or unnecessary? _____

    _____

    _____

4. Give some suggestions about how the work could be improved. _____

    _____

    _____

5. What is the most interesting or unique feature of this written work?_____

    _____

    _____

Writing the Final Draft

When you have finished making revisions on the first draft of your essay, write the final draft. Include all the changes that you have made during the revising and editing phases. Before you submit your final draft, proofread it one last time to ensure that you have caught any errors.

Writer's Desk **Write Your Final Draft**

You have developed, revised, and edited your essay. Now write the final draft.

 **Spelling, Grammar, and Vocabulary Logs**

- **Keep a Spelling and Grammar Log.** You probably repeat, over and over, the same types of grammar and spelling errors. You will find it very useful to record your repeated grammar mistakes in a Spelling and Grammar Log. You can refer to your list of spelling and grammar mistakes when you revise and edit your writing.

- **Keep a Vocabulary Log.** Expanding your vocabulary will be of enormous benefit to you as a writer. In a Vocabulary Log, you can make a list of unfamiliar words and their definitions.

See Appendix 5 for more information about spelling, grammar, and vocabulary logs.

 The Writer's Room **Essay Topics**

Writing Activity 1

Choose an essay that you have written for this course or for another course. Revise and edit that essay, and then write a final draft.

Writing Activity 2

Choose any of the following topics, or choose your own topic, and then write an essay. Remember to follow the writing process.

General Topics	College and Work-Related Topics
1. online shopping	6. something you learned in college
2. heroes in sports	7. bad work habits
3. a problem in politics	8. reasons to accept a job
4. unfair gender roles	9. unpleasant jobs
5. making the world better	10. a funny co-worker

CHECKLIST: REVISING AND EDITING

When you revise and edit your essay, ask yourself the following questions.

☐ Does my essay have **unity**? Ensure that every paragraph relates to the main idea.

☐ Does my essay have **adequate support**? Verify that there are enough details and examples to support your main point.

☐ Is my essay **coherent**? Try to use transitional expressions to link ideas.

☐ Does my essay have good **style**? Check for varied sentence patterns and exact language.

☐ Does my essay have any errors? **Edit** for errors in grammar, punctuation, spelling, and mechanics.

☐ Is my **final draft** error-free?

How Do I Get a Better Grade?

mycanadiancomplab

Go to www.mycanadiancomplab.ca for additional help with your grammar, writing, and research skills. You will have access to a variety of exercises, instruction, and video that will help you improve your basic skills and help you get a better grade.

Essay Patterns

What Is an Essay Pattern?

A pattern or mode is a method used to express one of the three purposes: to inform, to persuade, or to entertain. Once you know your purpose, you will be able to choose which writing pattern to use.

Patterns may overlap. You can combine writing patterns. You may use one predominant pattern, but you can also introduce other patterns as supporting material.

Narration

to narrate or tell a story about a sequence of events that happened

Process

to inform the reader about how to do something, how something works, or how something happened

Description

to describe using vivid details and images that appeal to the reader's senses

Definition

to explain what a term or concept means by providing relevant examples

Classification

to classify or sort a topic to help readers understand different qualities about that topic

Comparison and Contrast

to present information about similarities (compare) or differences (contrast)

Cause and Effect

to explain why an event happened (the cause) or what the consequences of the event were (the effects)

Argument*

to argue or to take a position on an issue and offer reasons for your position

*Argument is included as one of the eight patterns, but it is also a purpose in writing.

Narration

CONTENTS

When investigating a story, a reporter must try to find answers to the questions who, what, when, where, why, and how. You answer the same questions when you write a narrative essay.

Writers' Exchange

Try some nonstop talking. First, sit with a partner and come up with a television show or movie that you have both seen. Then, starting at the beginning, describe what happened in that episode or film. Remember that you must speak without stopping. If one of you stops talking, the other must jump in and continue describing the story.

EXPLORING

What Is Narration?

Narrating is telling a story about what happened. You generally explain events in the order in which they occurred, and you include information about when they happened and who was involved in the incidents.

The following examples show how you might use narration in everyday situations.

Audience: Neighbour

The car accident was really my fault.

- When I left the house, I was late for work, so I was driving too fast.
- My favourite CD, which I'd been playing, had finished.
- As I reached into my glove compartment to find another CD, I crashed into the stop sign.
- Luckily, I wasn't hurt, but my car needs major repairs.

Audience: Instructor

My homework isn't ready because of events beyond my control.

- My binder containing the instructions was in my basement when it flooded.
- I called a classmate to give me the instructions, but he gave me the incorrect information.
- I then tried to contact you, but you were not available during your office hours.

Audience: Clients

Our marketing campaign will work like a puzzle to pique the consumers' interest.

- The first billboard will not have any words—just a stunning photograph of the product with a question mark.
- Two weeks later, we will include variations of the brand name with the letters mixed up and a giant question mark.
- In four weeks, consumers will view the completed image with the brand name.

Narration at Work

After real-estate agent Francine Martin has shown a home, she records the client's reactions. Here is an excerpt from one of her client records.

Clients: The Nguyens

Needs: The Nguyens have twin sons, and Mrs. Nguyen works at home. They would like a three-bedroom home and prefer two bathrooms or a full bath and powder room. A garage is unnecessary. They will accept townhouses, but cannot spend more than $150 000, which limits their possibilities in this region. They are not willing to view other municipalities.

March 14: We visited 114 Philippe Street. Their first impressions were not favourable. The master bedroom was too small. Cracks in the wall near the ceiling worried them. (Discuss repair of cracks with owner.) However, they appreciated the view. They liked the main floor and especially appreciated the kitchen, which may sell the house. The price is in their range. Suggest a second visit.

The Narrative Essay

When you write a narrative essay, consider your point of view.

Use **first-person narration** to describe a personal experience. To show that you are directly involved in the story, use *I* (first-person singular) or *we* (first-person plural). This is an example of first-person narration: "When I got on the tiny plane, I tried to calm myself. I strapped myself in beside the pilot. As the plane lurched down the runway, I screamed."

Use **third-person narration** to describe what happened to somebody else. Show that you are simply an observer or storyteller by using *he*, *she*, *it* (third-person singular), or *they* (third-person plural). This is an example of third-person narration: "Every morning, Joe cut out pieces of cardboard and placed them in his shoes. Then Joe buttoned up his only good shirt, and smoothed down his hair. He was going to look for a job, and he had to look his best."

 **Combining Essay Patterns**

Narration is not only useful on its own; it also enhances other types of writing. For example, student writer Omar Hakim had to write an essay about the effects of gambling. His essay was more compelling than it might otherwise have been because he included an anecdote about his uncle's gambling addiction.

A Student Essay

Read the essay and answer the questions that follow.

My Journey Down the Grand Canyon
by Andrew Wells

1   Twenty years old, on a break from studies, I decided to set out backpacking to see where it would take me. Having found myself in a youth hostel in Flagstaff, Arizona, I spontaneously decided to see the Grand Canyon. My plan was to hike right from the top of the canyon, down to the Colorado River, and then back up. What I didn't realize was that this sort of hiking is not a simple test of aerobic fitness or personal desire. No, it's a type of brutal self-destruction. The next two days hiking in the canyon left me dazed and depleted.

2   On the first day, I walked and hitchhiked the 115 kilometres from Flagstaff and descended 8 kilometres before nightfall. I set out the next morning toward the river, and my physical condition rapidly deteriorated. First, the soles of my boots gave out, partially tearing from the seams and flapping against the pads of my feet with every step I took. My blisters ached continuously. The straps from my backpack tore into my shoulder blades and pain ran down my spine. But the dull pounding of my boots against the rocky terrain drowned out my thoughts. My focus remained on the path in front of me. I knew that if I lost concentration, at any point I could trip and fall over the edge. At least the awe-inspiring surroundings made it easier to forget the pain.

3   In the canyon, my surroundings were ever changing. At one moment, I was following a winding dirt path under light tree cover, with deer roaming, birds chirping, and small mammals scurrying about. Then suddenly I was on a sandy ledge following a stream that cut between towering walls of red rock. I could see nothing but the three feet in front of me where the wall curved with the stream. Then when I turned a corner, the walls opened up into a majestic gorge 1.5 kilometres across; it was green,

lush, and lightly snow-covered. A little farther, as I looked down below me, I could trace the trail winding down the gorge and gradually disappearing.

4   Eventually I reached Phantom Ranch at the bottom of the canyon. It serves as a rest stop for die-hard hikers and is so popular that people have to reserve years ahead of time. At the ranch I encountered two types of people. There are retired couples who are passionate hikers and who wait a year and a half for reservations. Some that I met had scaled Mount Everest. And then there are those who work at the ranch. Most of them don't leave the canyon for months on end because the only way out is a gruelling 24-kilometre trek or a rather expensive ride on the back of a mule. To further their isolation, the media is virtually nonexistent. The ranger has a radio, and there's one emergency telephone.

5   I spoke with the man working the canteen desk. He was a calm slow talker in his early thirties, tall and thin, with ear-length tangled hair and a dull, emotionless expression. While poking at a block of wood with a steel pick, he droned on and on about all the people he knew about who had died in the canyon. "Once, some parents let their three-year-old girl walk alone, and she just walked right off the edge. Another time a couple tried to hike in from the far west, ran out of water, and expired." He kept tapping the wood with his pick. "Then there was the guy who was knocked off the edge by one of the sheep." In my head, I begged for him to stop.

6   If a hiker is tired at the bottom of the canyon, he's in serious trouble. Trouble was what I came face-to-face with. Climbing back up, I encountered a big-horned sheep on a narrow ledge. It wanted to go where I was, and I wanted to go where it was, but there was no room to pass. For minutes on end the sheep and I engaged in a stare-down. Then all of a sudden, it got bored with me and climbed up an 85-degree sheer rock face! I was dumbfounded. It was so smart, and as soon as I passed, it climbed back down, turned, looked at me, and walked on. It understood perfectly what was going on.

7   After several hours of nonstop hiking, I had absolutely no drive left. The rock face kept getting steeper and the air significantly thinner. Each layer of the canyon above me was hidden behind the nearest sheet of towering sandstone. So when I thought I had gotten to the top, to my great dismay, a whole new area opened up above me. Then a woman in at least her late seventies plowed past me on her way uphill out of the canyon. She was no more than five feet tall, with short gray hair and a hunched back. I was honestly in pretty good hiking shape from all the heavy walking I had done. I passed just about everyone else, but this woman was unbelievable. (I was carrying a twenty-pound pack, though, so I call it a no-contest and want a rematch.)

8   At certain points, I felt like saying, "That's it. I'm living the rest of my life on this ledge. I'm not moving." And then I started making deals with myself, planning what I was going to do with my life once I got out, just to motivate myself to keep going. When I reached the top, I looked down into the bowels of the canyon and felt relieved that I had done it. It's something that does not need to be done more than once. I can retain the knowledge of what I have accomplished. I have come out believing that there's nothing that can stop me, and there's no greater feeling.

PRACTICE I

1. Highlight the thesis statement.

2. Highlight the topic sentence in paragraphs 2 and 3. Remember, the topic sentence is not necessarily the first sentence in the paragraph.

3. Using your own words, sum up what happened in each body paragraph. Begin with paragraph 4.

    Paragraph 4: _____

    _____

    Paragraph 5: _____

    _____

    Paragraph 6: _____

    _____

    Paragraph 7: _____

    _____

4. In paragraph 5, Wells describes a man he met. Which images help you visualize the man?

    _____

    _____

5. Why did the writer write about his experience? You will need to make a guess based on the information in the essay.

    _____

Explore Topics

In the Writer's Desk Warm Up, you will try an exploring strategy to generate ideas about different topics.

Writer's Desk **Warm Up**

Read the following questions, and write the first ideas that come to your mind. Think of two to three ideas for each topic.

EXAMPLE: What difficult realizations have you made?

My choice to stay in college was hard. Leaving home was difficult. When I broke up with my girlfriend. What else? My friend told me that I interrupt others too much. When I let my brother take the blame for something I did, I realized that I have a dark side.

1. What are some disagreements or misunderstandings that you have had with someone you love?

_____

_____

_____

2. What were some significant moments in your childhood?

_____

_____

_____

3. Think about some stressful situations that brought out the best or worst in you. List some ideas.

_____

_____

_____

DEVELOPING

The Thesis Statement

When you write a narrative essay, choose a topic that you personally find very interesting, and then share it with your readers. For example, very few people would be interested if you simply list what you did during your recent vacation. However, if you write about a particularly moving experience during your vacation, you could create an entertaining narrative essay.

Ensure that your narrative essay expresses a main point. Your thesis statement should have a controlling idea.

topic   controlling idea

The day I decided to get a new job, <u>my life took a dramatic turn.</u>

controlling idea   topic

<u>Sadie's problems began</u> **as soon as she drove her new car home.**

 How to Make a Point

In a narrative essay, the thesis statement should make a point. To help you find the controlling idea, you can ask yourself the following questions:

- What did I learn?
- How did I change?
- How did it make me feel?
- What is important about it?

For example:

  Topic: *ran away from home*

  Possible controlling idea: *learned the importance of family*

          topic   controlling idea

  When I ran away from home at the age of fifteen, <u>I discovered the</u> <u>importance of my family.</u>

PRACTICE 2 Practise writing thesis statements. Complete the following sentences by adding a controlling idea.

1. During my sister's wedding, she realized _____

   _____

2. Because my family is large, I know _____

   _____

3. When I graduated, I discovered _____

   _____

Writer's Desk **Write Thesis Statements**

Write a thesis statement for each of the following topics. You can look for ideas in the Warm Up on page 87. Each thesis statement should mention the topic and express a controlling idea.

EXAMPLE: Topic: A difficult realization

Thesis statement: <u>When I betrayed my brother, I made an unpleasant discovery about myself.</u>

1. Topic: A disagreement with a loved one

   Thesis statement: _____

   _____

2. Topic: A significant moment in childhood

   Thesis statement: _____

   _____

3. Topic: A stressful situation

   Thesis statement: _____

   _____

The Supporting Ideas

A narrative essay should contain specific details so that the reader understands what happened. To come up with the details, ask yourself a series of questions and then answer them as you plan your essay.

- **Who** is the essay about?
- **What** happened?
- **When** did it happen?
- **Where** did it happen?
- **Why** did it happen?
- **How** did it happen?

When you orally recount a story to a friend, you may go back and add details, saying, "Oh, I forgot to mention something." However, you do not have this luxury when writing narrative essays. When you write, organize the sequence of events clearly so that your reader can follow your story easily.

 **Narrative Essay Tips**

Here are some tips to remember as you develop a narrative essay.

- Do not simply recount what happened. Try to indicate why the events are important.
- Organize the events in chronological order (the order in which they occurred). You could also reverse the order of events by beginning your essay with the outcome of the events, and then explaining what happened that led to the outcome.
- Use some descriptive language. For example, you could use images that appeal to the senses. For more information on using descriptive imagery, see page 104 in Chapter 7.

Writer's Desk **Develop Supporting Ideas**

Choose one of your thesis statements from the Writer's Desk on page 89. Then generate supporting ideas. List what happened.

EXAMPLE: A difficult realization   Topic: _____

—about four years old   _____

—broke sister's glass ornaments   _____

—blamed brother   _____

—Mark was scolded   _____

—didn't admit the truth, kept denying it   _____

—felt extremely guilty   _____

The Essay Plan

Before you write a narrative essay, make a detailed essay plan. Write down main events in the order in which they occurred. To make your narration more complete, include details about each event.

THESIS STATEMENT: When I betrayed my brother, I made an unpleasant discovery about myself.

    I. I wanted to touch my sister's glass ornaments.
        A. I snuck into her room.
        B. I climbed her dresser.
        C. My brother watched me climb.

II. The dresser fell forward.
  A. I jumped off.
  B. A glass deer crashed to the floor and broke.
III. Our mother asked who did it, and I blamed my brother.
  A. My brother was scolded.
  B. He was confined to his bedroom.
  C. I heard him crying.
IV. I never admitted that I had done it.
  A. My brother was sad more than angry.
  B. I felt really guilty, but I still couldn't confess.
  C. I realized that my actions made me a liar and a coward.

Writer's Desk **Write an Essay Plan**

Refer to the information you generated in previous Writer's Desks, and prepare a detailed essay plan. Include details for each supporting idea.

The First Draft

After you outline your ideas in a plan, you are ready to write the first draft. Remember to write complete sentences and to use transitions to help readers understand the order in which events occur or occurred. Here are some transitions that are useful in narrative essays.

To show a sequence of events

afterward	finally	in the end	meanwhile
after that	first	last	next
eventually	in the beginning	later	then

Enhancing Your Essay

One effective way to enhance your narrative essay is to use dialogue. A **direct quotation** contains the exact words of an author, and the quotation is set off with quotation marks. When you include the exact words of more than one person in a text, you must make a new paragraph each time the speaker changes.

"Who did this?" my mom shrieked, as my brother and I stood frozen with fear.

"Mark did it," I assured her shamelessly, as my finger pointed at my quivering brother.

An **indirect quotation** keeps the author's meaning but is not set off by quotation marks.

As Mark and I stood frozen with fear, our shrieking mother asked who did it. I assured her shamelessly that Mark did it, as my finger pointed at my quivering brother.

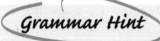 **Using Quotations**

When you insert a direct quotation into your writing, capitalize the first word of the quotation, and put the final punctuation inside the closing quotation marks.

- Place a comma after an introductory phrase.

  The boy said, "Everyone was terrified."

- Place a colon after an introductory sentence.

  The boy described the atmosphere: "Everyone was terrified."

See Chapter 30 for more information about using quotations.

Writer's Desk **Write the First Draft**

In the previous Writer's Desk, you developed an essay plan. Carefully review your essay plan, make any necessary changes to the details or chronology, and then write the first draft of your narrative essay.

REVISING AND EDITING

Revise and Edit a Narrative Essay

When you finish writing a narrative essay, carefully review your work and revise it to make the events as clear as possible to your readers. Check that you have organized events chronologically, and remove any irrelevant details. Before you revise and edit your own essay, practise revising and editing a student essay.

A Student Essay

Read the essay, and then answer the questions that follow. As you read, correct any errors that you find, and make comments in the margins.

Crashing Glass Deer
by Adele Berridge

1   My brother and I grew up in a suburban bungalow near a freeway. Built in the 1950s, my house boasted a living room with a picture window, three bedrooms, and a bathroom. My older sister and I shared the middle bedroom, and my younger brother Mark, as the only boy, was given his own room next to ours. He was my fraternal twin and my best friend. On the day that I betrayed Mark, I made an unpleasant discovery about myself.

2   Sherry, my sister, had just turned eight, and my brother and I were both four. We had celebrated my sister's birthday a few days before, and some of her prized possessions were on display in our shared bedroom. Most impressive of all was a set of glass deer. My sister placed the three fragile deer on top of her dresser, well out of reach of my grubby little hands. Those deer fascinated me, and I thought they represented Bambi's family. I longed to hold them, but I can't reach them.

3   That morning, my sister had gone to school, and my mother was doing laundry at the opposite end of the house. I brought my brother into my room and told him that we would play with Sherry's deer. We would be carefull, I assured him. He didn't want to proceed, but he watched me as I pulled out each drawer on my sister's dresser, starting with the bottom drawer, then the middle, and then the top, until I made a series of steps.

4   I had my slippers on, and I climbed up, carefully stepping on the edge of each drawer. I reached the second drawer from the top, and was just reaching for the deer when the dresser started to tip toward me. I leapt off the drawer to safety just as the large piece of furniture crashed to the ground. The glass ornaments smashed on the hardwood floor. My brother and I stared in stunned silence as hard footsteps clomped down the hall.

5   "Who did this?" my mom shrieked, as my brother and I stood frozen with fear. "He did it," I assured her shamelessly, as my finger pointed at my quivering brother. My brother denied it, of course.

6   Peering closely at us both, my mother's eyes rested on her son. The next minutes were a torrent of shouting and loud wailing as my brother was punished for the act. I remained perfectly still, numb. Noises and colours swirled around me, the occasional image registering like a snapshot. Then, as I backed out of the room and slunk down the hall to the living room, I heard the distant sound of my brother's muffled sobs. At the time, I knew that I was being *really, really bad*, but there was no turning back.

7   That incident haunted me for years to come. As a child, I thought that the human soul was a round white pie plate and that sins were like black specks of dirt on it. In my mind's eye, my soul was stained with the mud of sin. I knew what I was: a liar and a coward. My brother's tear-streaked face burned into my brain, I saw his disappointed eyes staring at me not with anger but with bewilderment. I was his sister and best friend, and I had betrayed him in order to save myself. The guilt wouldn't go away, nor would my sense that I was inherently bad. Occasionaly my brother would remind me of the incident, and I pretended that I couldn't remember that time, yet I couldn't forget it. Denying it only intensified the guilt, of course.

8   I wish I could say I changed overnight, but I'm a slow learner. I lied again and again. However, that incident planted a seed in me that budded and grew with time. I would have to overcome my own inherent cowardice and learn to take responsibility for my actions. It had to feel better than lying and living with horrible guilt.

9   Today, I get it. On that day all those years ago, if I had simply told the truth and taken the punishment, most likely I would'nt even remember the incident today. Because I lied, I've never forgotten it.

PRACTICE 3

Revising

1. Write down the two parts of the thesis statement.

   topic   +   controlling idea

   _____

2. What type of order do the specific details follow? Circle your response.

   a. space   b. time   c. emphatic

3. What type of narration is this?

   a. first person   b. third person

4. Paragraph 4 lacks a topic sentence. An appropriate topic sentence for paragraph 4 could be

   a. The glass deer was on top of the dresser.

   b. I concentrated on my goal of getting my hands on those glass deer.

   c. My brother didn't move.

   d. The glass deer were fragile.

5. Underline a dialogue problem in paragraph 5, and then write a rule regarding quotations and dialogue.

   _____

Editing

6. Underline a tense consistency error in paragraph 2. The tense shifts for no apparent reason. Write the correction on the line below.

   Correction: _____

7. This essay contains misspelled words in paragraphs 3 and 7. Underline and correct them.

   Corrections: _____   _____

8. Paragraph 7 contains a run-on sentence. Underline the error, and show three ways to correct the sentence

   Corrections: _____

   _____

   _____

9. Underline an apostrophe error in paragraph 9. Write the correct word on the line below.

   Correction: _____

GRAMMAR LINK

See the following chapters for more information about these grammar topics:
Run-Ons, Chapter 18
Verb Consistency, Chapter 23
Spelling, Chapter 27
Apostrophes, Chapter 29

---

vo•cab•u•lar•y BOOST

Writers commonly overuse words. To make your writing more vivid and interesting, identify five common and overused verbs in your essay. Replace each verb with a more vivid and specific verb.

First draft: We walked to the edge of the cliff and looked at the sea.

Revision: We strolled to the edge of the cliff and gazed at the sea.

Writer's Desk Revise and Edit Your Essay

Revise and edit the essay that you wrote for the previous Writer's Desk. You can refer to the revising and editing checklists at the end of this chapter and on this book's inside covers.

A Professional Essay

In his memoir, *Cockeyed*, Ryan Knighton, an author and teacher, describes his slow descent into blindness. In the following excerpt from an article, he narrates what happened.

Out of Sight
by Ryan Knighton

1   On my 18th birthday, my first retina specialist, a man who delivered his bedside manner like napalm, informed me that I would be blind within a few years. "No cure," he said. "Sorry." The specialist told me the name of the condition, retinitis pigmentosa. He described how it would soon **eradicate** my remaining night vision, limit me to tunnel vision, and eventually blinker me altogether. The whole scene took less than ten minutes.

eradicate:
remove completely

2   For four years, I had exhibited clumsy behaviour nobody could account for. As a warehouse worker during summer vacations, I drove a forklift and ran over nearly everything possible, including one of my co-workers. True, I hated him and his insistence that we play nothing but Iron Maiden on the shipping area stereo, but it wasn't in my character to crush him.

3   But the real giveaway came when I drove my father's Pontiac into a ditch. Lots of friends crashed their parents' cars, but my accident stood out. I did my teenaged duty at roughly five miles per hour. How do you miss a turn at that speed unless your eyes are closed? After sundown, mine might as well have been.

4   When I reported to my mother that, as a new driver, I was having trouble on rainy nights, she said they gave everybody trouble and told me not to worry. I was on my way out the door, about to drive to work. "But do you use the cat's eyes sometimes?" I asked.

5   "Sure," she said. "That's what they're for, reflecting light when it's hard to see the yellow line."

6   "No, I mean do you use them? Do you drive on them?"

7   When I couldn't see the yellow line, I had taken to steering onto the cat's eyes. This, I found, helped position me on the road. I was a little close to the middle, maybe, but better than anything I could determine on my own. The clunk clunk clunk of the reflectors under my tires let me know where I was. I suppose I drove Braille.

8   "You drive on the cat's eyes?" my mother asked.

9   "Well, only at night." I would wager my mother called for my first ophthalmological appointment by the time I had shut the front door behind me.

10   Retinitis pigmentosa is the loss of photoreceptors associated with pigmentary changes in the retina. Another way to put it is that my retina is scarring itself to death. I've enjoyed the slow loss of all peripheral and night vision. By my own estimate, I have a year to go until that tiny pinhole of clarity in which I live will consume itself, and the lights will go out. To know what's filling up my little tunnel, I rely mostly on context.

11   Once I asked a red-headed waitress for directions to the washroom. I didn't know she was a waitress by the colour of her hair, of course—the bit of it I saw—but by the smell of coffee, which was quickly overwhelmed by a perfumy fog.

12   "Would you like more coffee?"

13   "I'd love coffee," I said, "but I'd love to be in the men's room even more."

14   "Um, okay, the men's room is over that way."

15   I stared vacantly ahead while she, I imagine, continued to point "that way." Then I heard the pleasant sound of coffee being poured.

16   "I'm sorry," I said, "but I don't know what *that way* means." I plucked my white cane from the bag beside me. "I guess it wasn't obvious, and I forgot to—"

17   "Oh my God, I'm sorry, I didn't know you're blind! You didn't look—you don't look—not at all—I mean really."

18   I smiled with that warm sensation you get when you are sixteen and someone says you look like you're in your twenties. "Thanks. That is very kind. Where did you say the washroom is?"

19   "At the back."

20   "Which way is back?"

21   "It's over there," she said, and walked away.

22   All I wanted were specific directions. Instead, my waitress gave me a demonstration of the fact that, along with vision, parts of language disappear into blindness. The capacity of language to guide me has atrophied. Not even Braille can substitute for some words. *This way. Right here, in front of you. No, there. Right there, under your nose.* Such directional cues have lost their meaning. Who would have guessed that a disease can alter language as it alters the body, disabling parts of speech—that language is, in this way, an extension of the body and subject to the same pathologies.

23   "EXCUSE ME."

24   My waitress was back, not a second too soon. I really did need to use the facilities.

25   "I don't mean to intrude," she said, "but didn't you go to Langley Secondary School?"

26   "Yes, I did."

27   "It's Ryan, right? I'm Danielle! We were in drama class together. God, I didn't recognize you at all. You look so different now," she said.

28   I braced myself. "I'm not sure what it is. Maybe it's—" *The fierce squint? The white cane? The expression of perpetual disorientation?*

29   "It's—well. I know!" She put a hand on my head with daring compassion. "You shaved your hair off. When did you do that?"

30   Now I was free to burn with embarrassment at my self-centeredness. Just because it's a sighted world doesn't mean blindness is the first thing people notice about me, nor the first thing that comes to mind. Along with mutant celebrity and meaningless words, I suppose paranoia is another side effect. "A couple of years ago, I guess," I replied.

31   "Looks cool."

32   "Thanks."

33   "I remember in high school your hair used to be long," she said. "Really long. It was down to here, right?"

PRACTICE 4

1. What type of narration is this text?

   a. first person   b. third person

2. The thesis of this essay is not stated directly, but it is implied. Using your own words, write the thesis of this essay.

   _____

3. Describe how Knighton introduces his topic. What introduction style does he use? Circle the letter of the best answer.

   a. definition   b. general   c. anecdote   d. historical

4. Knighton divides his essay into two time periods. What are they?

   _____   _____

5. How does Knighton realize that he is losing his sight? In two or three sentences, explain what happens.

   _____

   _____

   _____

6. In which paragraph is there a definition of a term? _____

7. Describe what happens during Knighton's encounter with the waitress. Use your own words.

_____

_____

_____

_____

8. Write down one example of an indirect quotation from the essay.

_____

9. Write down one example of a direct quotation from the essay.

_____

10. Narrative writers do more than simply list a series of events. Knighton explains why the events were meaningful. What did he learn?

_____

_____

_____

 The Writer's Room **Topics for Narrative Essays**

Writing Activity 1

Choose any of the following topics, or choose your own topic, and write a narrative essay.

General Topics

1. a breakup
2. a risky adventure
3. a personal ritual
4. a thrilling or frightening moment
5. a news event that affected you

College and Work-Related Topics

6. an interesting encounter
7. a sudden realization at school or work
8. an uncomfortable incident at work
9. a positive or negative job interview
10. a difficult lesson at work or school

Writing Activity 2

Choose a quotation you agree or disagree with, and then write a narrative essay based on it.

Canada is hockey.

—Mike Weir, Canadian golfer

Always do what you are afraid to do.

—Ralph Waldo Emerson, essayist

There's always one who loves and one who lets himself be loved.

—W. Somerset Maugham, author

Blind belief is dangerous.

—Kenyan proverb

READING LINK

More Narrative Readings

"Yonge St., a Seedy Mystery in Plain View," by Sheila Heti (page 498)

"The Rules of Survival," by Laurence Gonzales (page 515)

"The Other Side of the Mountain," by Geoff Powter (page 520)

"Monsoon Time," by Rahul Goswami (page 522)

Writing Activity 3

Write about a physical or spiritual journey that you have been on. Describe what happened.

WRITING LINK

More Narrative Writing Topics

See the following grammar sections for more narrative writing topics.

Chapter 26, Writer's Room topic 1 (page 418)

Chapter 28, Writer's Room topic 2 (page 446)

✓ CHECKLIST: NARRATION ESSAY

After you write your narration essay, review the checklist on the inside front cover of this book. Also ask yourself these questions.

☐ Does my thesis statement clearly express the topic of the narration?

☐ Does my thesis statement contain a controlling idea that is meaningful and interesting?

☐ Does my essay answer most of the following questions: who, what, when, where, why, how?

☐ Do I use transitional expressions that help clarify the order of events?

☐ Do I include details to make my narration more vivid?

How Do I Get a Better Grade?

mycanadiancomplab

Go to www.mycanadiancomplab.ca for additional help with your grammar, writing, and research skills. You will have access to a variety of exercises, instruction, and video that will help you improve your basic skills and help you get a better grade.

Description

CONTENTS

Sculptors chisel features and other details in their work to express their artistic vision. Similarly, writers use the tools of descriptive writing to create images that readers can visualize in their mind's eye.

Writers' Exchange

Choose one of the objects from the following list. Then, brainstorm a list of descriptive words about the object. Think about the shape, texture, smell, taste, colour, and so on. List the first words that come to your mind.

For example: cake   *gooey, sweet, chocolate, smooth, pink icing, layered*

panther   old car   sweater   baby   apple

What Is Description?

Description creates vivid images in the reader's mind by portraying people, places, or moments in detail. Here are some everyday situations that might call for description.

Audience: Roommate

The apartment we will rent is close to the campus.

- The north side of the campus has student housing.
- Our apartment is in the middle of Grove Street, which is still a dusty, unpaved road.
- The building is next to the wooded lot.

Audience: Classmate

The experiment in chemistry class went well.

- We dissolved Epsom salts on construction paper.
- Crystals of many different shapes formed as the paper dried.
- The crystals were mainly bright coral and sunny yellow.

Audience: Intern

Our company has renovated the front lobby.

- The walls are painted in warm browns and beiges.
- There are two overstuffed chairs and a soft leather couch.
- There are oil paintings on the walls and dried flowers in ceramic vases on the tables.

> 66 *Be careful that you do not write or paint anything that is not your own, that you don't know in your own soul.* 99
>
> EMILY CARR,
> *Canadian artist and writer*

Description at Work

To help hikers plan camping trips effectively, the website www.americansouthwest.net describes hiking trails in Zion National Park.

The trail descends quite steeply, close to the course of the South Fork of Taylor Creek, and soon reaches the main stream. Here, the canyon is deep but wide and V-shaped, with red rocks and sandy soils, quite densely covered by trees, bushes, and cacti. The path follows the valley upstream, at first on the south side but later on either side as it crosses the creek several times. The water is fast flowing but shallow and easily forded.

The Descriptive Essay

When you write a descriptive essay, focus on three main points.

1. **Create a dominant impression.** The dominant impression is the overall atmosphere that you wish to convey. It can be a strong feeling, mood, or image. For example, if you are describing a casual Sunday afternoon party, you can emphasize the relaxed ambience in the room.

2. **Express your attitude toward the subject.** Do you feel positive or negative toward the subject? For instance, if you feel pleased about your last vacation, then the details of your essay might convey the good feelings you have about it. If you feel tense during a business meeting, then your details might express how uncomfortable the situation makes you feel.

3. **Include concrete details.** Details will enable a reader to visualize the person, place, or situation that you are describing. You can use active verbs and adjectives so that the reader imagines the scene more clearly. You can also use **imagery,** which is description using the five senses. Review the following examples of imagery.

Sight:	A Western Tiger Swallowtail dipped by my face. About three inches across, its lemon yellow wings were striped improbably and fluted in black. They filliped into a long forked tail with spots of red and blue. (Sherman Apt Russell, "Beauty on the Wing")
Sound:	The tree outside is full of crows and white cranes who gurgle and screech. (Michael Ondaatje, *Running in the Family*)
Smell:	I think it was the smell that so intoxicated us after those dreary months of nostril-scorching heat, the smell of dust hissing at the touch of rain and then settling down, damply placid on the ground. (Sara Suleri, *Meatless Days*)
Touch:	The straps from my backpack tore into my shoulder blades and pain ran down my spine. (Andrew Wells, "My Journey Down the Grand Canyon")
Taste:	Entirely and blessedly absent are the cloying sweetness, chalky texture, and oily, gummy aftertaste that afflict many mass-manufactured ice creams. (R.W. Apple, Jr., "Making Texas Cows Proud," *The New York Times*)

A Student Essay

Read the following student essay and answer the questions that follow.

The Wake-Up Call
by Jennifer Alvira

1   My hands were covered in flavoured syrup, and my hair sat in a messy bun on the top of my head. I cringed at the sight of last-minute customers. I had had enough of people for one day and was ready to close the shop for the night.

2   I picked up the dingy mop from an old pail and started mopping the chocolate encrusted tiles. Our milkshake machine had splattered the chequerboard walls in a vanilla mess while the eight glass jars of candies had spilled out over the marble countertop. After five long minutes of hard scrubbing, the black and white of the wall started to shine through. I swept up the broken candies from the floor. When the stressful day finally came to an end, I grabbed my purse and headed for the door. Little did I know that in the next hour, I was about to destroy my car and my self-confidence as a driver.

3   The air grew heavy with storm clouds, and a thin layer of car oil residue coated the road. If driving in the dark was not terrifying enough, it was pouring rain. I climbed into my silver '92 Dodge Spirit, the car given to me on my sixteenth birthday. The interior was a deep burgundy red and emanated a distinct aroma of wet tennis shoes and old carpet. The exterior had its own collection of dents and scratches but remained beautiful to me. It was my personal dream car despite what anyone else said; it always started and never gave me any real problems.

4   Night blanketed the roads, and my nerves started to twist in knots. I hated driving at night. I arrived about a half a mile from the intersection at Eber and Dairy Road. An abandoned white chapel sat peacefully to the right, and a humble section of mysterious houses thrived in a community called Little Oak Creek further up the road. It appeared to me that I was the only car on the road at this hour. As I neared the intersection, I pressed on the gas pedal to make sure I would fly through before the light turned yellow.

5   I had just made it past the light when the glare of a pair of headlights caught the corner of my left eye. I slammed on the brakes only to feel my tires lose traction and slide across pavement. The abrupt impact barely gave me enough time to close my eyes. I gripped the steering wheel so tightly that my palms stung when I finally let go. The two-ton weight of my car shoved the other car completely off the road into a patch of trees in front of Little Oak Creek.

6   My air bag deployed with a loud bang and burst with white powder. I pushed open the door and stumbled out. The smell of burnt tires and exhaust smoke permeated the night. The accident seemed like a nightmare.

7   By then, I couldn't hold back fear anymore. Tears smeared my stunned face, while cars passed by with none stopping to assist me. I hyperventilated, and my entire body shook. Everything happened so quickly; I didn't have a chance to feel the throbbing in my wrist from the sprain or the enormous bruise from where my knee had slammed into the dashboard.

8   Finally, a young woman and her son appeared in the warm rays of the streetlamp. The woman clutched a small blue jacket, with her son closely behind.

9   "Darling, are you okay?"

10   She draped a light jacket over my frail shoulders and proceeded to cup my trembling hands within hers. I noticed a metallic taste in my mouth, and I could barely form a coherent sentence. "I'm alive and can feel all my limbs. I'm okay."

11   The young lady rubbed my shoulders, and made sure to stand next to me in case my body gave way to the shock. "What's your mom's phone number so that I can tell her you're fine?" Her sweet voice eased my terror, and I could finally take a deep breath. I looked over at her son, who stood quietly beside his mother. His eyes widened as he stared at my now nonexistent source of transportation.

12   The police showed up after two hours of waiting for their arrival. I found out that the sixteen-year-old girl driving the other vehicle jumped out of her car in a bout of panic. Her knees bled from the rough impact of asphalt. Her boyfriend and mother were at the scene and stayed close to her side. The police ticketed the girl with failure to yield to passing cars while making a left turn. The accident was not my fault, and I welcomed the flood of relief.

PRACTICE 1

1. Look in the opening paragraphs and highlight the thesis statement.

2. The writer describes in detail the events of the fateful night. Find examples of imagery from the essay.

   a. Sight _Covered in Flavored syrup_

   _____

   b. Sound _sweet voice_

   _____

   c. Taste _metallic taste_

   _____

   d. Touch _The young lady ... shoulders._

   _____

e. Smell _The smell of burnt tires ... the night._

_____

3. What dominant impression does the writer create in this essay? Underline examples in the essay to support your answer.

The air grew heavy with storm clouds, ... coated the road.

Explore Topics

In the Writer's Desk Warm Up, you will try an exploring strategy to generate ideas about different topics.

Writer's Desk **Warm Up**

Read the following questions, and write the first ideas that come to your mind. Think of two or three ideas for each topic.

EXAMPLE: List some memorable trips you have taken.

—*my trip to Africa*

—*the time I stayed with my grandmother in Montreal*

—*a field trip to the Royal Ontario Museum*

1. Who are your best friends?

_____

_____

_____

2. What are some unattractive fashion trends?

_____

_____

_____

3. List some memorable trips that you have taken.

_____

_____

_____

DEVELOPING

When you write a descriptive essay, choose a subject that lends itself to description. You should be able to describe images or objects using some of the five senses. To get in the frame of mind, try thinking about the sounds, sights, tastes, smells, and feelings you would experience in certain places, such as a busy restaurant, a hospital room, a subway car, a zoo, and so on.

The Thesis Statement

In the thesis statement of a descriptive essay, you should convey a dominant impression about the subject. The dominant impression is the overall impression or feeling that the topic inspires.

       topic   controlling idea

The photograph of me as a ten-year-old has an embarrassing story behind it.

    controlling idea   topic

Feeling self-satisfied, **Odysseus Ramsey started his first day in public office.**

 **How to Create a Dominant Impression**

To create a dominant impression, ask yourself how or why the topic is important.

Poor: Land developers have built homes on parkland.

              (Why should readers care about this statement?)

                               topic   controlling idea

Better: **The once pristine municipal park** has been converted into giant estate homes that average families cannot afford.

Writer's Desk   Thesis Statements

Write a thesis statement for each of the following topics. You can look for ideas in the Warm Up on page 107. Each thesis statement should state what you are describing and contain a controlling idea.

EXAMPLE: Topic: a memorable trip

Thesis Statement: *My first day in Ghana left me enthralled but exhausted.*

1. Topic: a close friend

   Thesis Statement: _____

   _____

2. Topic: unattractive fashion trends

   Thesis Statement: _____

   _____

3. Topic: a memorable trip

   Thesis Statement: _____

   _____

The Supporting Ideas

After you have developed an effective thesis statement, generate supporting details.

- Use prewriting strategies such as freewriting and brainstorming to generate ideas.
- Choose the best ideas. Most descriptive essays use imagery that describes the person or scene.
- Organize your ideas. Choose the best organizational method for this essay pattern.

Show, Don't Tell

Your audience will find it more interesting to read your written work if you show a quality or an action of a place or person rather than just state it.

Example of Telling: Mr. Leon was a very kind man.

Example of Showing: Our neighbour, Mr. Leon, a grim-faced, retired seventy-year-old grandfather, always snapped at the neighbourhood children, telling us not to play street hockey, not to make so much noise, and not to throw the ball near his roses. When it came to important matters, however, he was always supportive of us. Mr. Leon taught all the local youths to ride bikes. He used to walk along beside us holding on to the cycle as we wobbled down the sidewalk. One day, we learned that Mr. Leon had been donating fifty bicycles to the local children's charity annually for many years.

PRACTICE 2   Choose one of the following sentences, and write a short description that shows—not tells—the quality of the person or place.

1. Today was a perfect day.
2. I was frightened as I walked down the street.
3. The weather did not co-operate with our plans.

Use Different Figurative Devices

When writing a descriptive essay, you can use other figurative devices (besides **imagery**) to add vivid details to your writing.

- A **simile** is a comparison using *like* or *as*.

  My thoughts ran as fast as a cheetah.

  Let us go then you and I,
  When the evening is spread out against the sky
  Like a patient etherised upon a table;
  (from "The Love Song of J. Alfred Prufrock" by T.S. Eliot).

- A **metaphor** is a comparison that does not use *like* or *as*.

  Life is sweet-and-sour soup.

  You need a blue sky holiday
  (from "Bad Day" by Daniel Powter)

- **Personification** is the act of attributing human qualities to an inanimate object or animal.

  The chocolate cake winked invitingly at us.

  Life has a funny way of helping you out.
  (from "Ironic" by Alanis Morrissette).

PRACTICE 3   Practise using figurative language. Use one of the following to describe each item: simile, metaphor, or personification. If you are comparing two things, try to use an unusual comparison.

EXAMPLE: toddler: *The toddler climbed like a monkey out of his crib.*
(simile)

1. mountain: The mountain's shape is like a standing giant.
2. hair: The girl's hair is wavy to the others in the breeze
3. ocean: Ocean would offers every thing to the the gentle generally people live in the shoreline.

etherise

---

vo•cab•u•lar•y BOOST

Use Vivid Language

When you write a descriptive essay, try to use **vivid language**. Use specific action verbs and adjectives to create a clear picture of what you are describing.

livid
My boss was ~~angry~~.   Use a more vivid, specific adjective.

whimpered
The child ~~cried~~.   Use a more vivid, specific verb or image.

Think about other words or expressions that more effectively describe these words: *laugh, talk, nice, walk.*

Writer's Desk   **List Sensory Details**

Choose one of your thesis statements from the previous Writer's Desk and make a list of sensory details. Think about images, impressions, and feelings that the topic inspires in you.

EXAMPLE: Topic: a memorable trip

—*colourful clothes*

—*bright, warm sand*

—*appetizing smell of food*

—*putrid odour of sewers*

—*a cool breeze*

—*powerful drumbeat of music*

—*bodies moving to a beat*

Your topic: _____

Your list of sensory details: _____

_____

_____

_____

_____

The Essay Plan

An essay plan helps you organize your thesis statement, topic sentences, and supporting details before writing a first draft. When you make an essay plan, remember to include concrete details and to organize your ideas in a logical order. If you want to emphasize some descriptive details more than others, arrange them from least affecting to most affecting. If you want your readers to envision a space (a room, a park, and so on), arrange details using spatial order.

THESIS STATEMENT: <u>My first day in Ghana left me enthralled but exhausted.</u>

    I. I was overwhelmed by my surroundings.
        A. People wore traditional African clothing.
        B. Some walked balancing objects on their heads.
        C. Mothers carried babies tied to their backs.
        D. I could smell different types of food.
   II. The beach was unlike any other beach I'd seen.
        A. I felt a cool breeze and saw orange sand.
        B. I sat in the shade and had a cold beverage.
        C. People were swimming and dancing.
  III. The scenery of the countryside was breathtaking.
        A. There were mud huts with straw roofs.
        B. People were cooking on open fires.
        C. Many animals roamed, including dogs and goats.
        D. I saw immense anthills.

Writer's Desk **Write an Essay Plan**

Choose one of the ideas that you have developed in previous Writer's Desks and prepare an essay plan. Remember to use vivid details and figurative language to help create a dominant overall impression.

The First Draft

After you outline your ideas in a plan, you are ready to write the first draft. Remember to write complete sentences. Also, as you write, think about which transitions can effectively help you lead your readers from one idea to the next. Descriptive writing often uses space order. Here is a list of transitions that are useful for describing the details of a person, place, or thing.

To show place or position

above	beyond	in the distance	outside
behind	closer in	nearby	over there
below	farther out	on the left/right	under
beside	in front	on top	underneath

Writer's Desk Write the First Draft

In the previous Writer's Desk on page 112, you developed an essay plan. Now write the first draft of your descriptive essay. Before you write, carefully review your essay plan and make any necessary changes.

REVISING AND EDITING

Revise and Edit a Descriptive Essay

When you finish writing a descriptive essay, review your work and revise it to make the description as vivid as possible to your readers. Check that you have organized your ideas, and remove any irrelevant details. Before you work on your own essay, practise revising and editing a student essay.

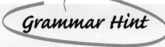 **Grammar Hint**   **Using Adjectives and Adverbs**

When you revise your descriptive essay, check that you have used adjectives and adverbs correctly. For example, many people use *real* when the adjective is actually *really*.

Incorrect use of an adjective: My brother, Magnus, is real tall and powerful.

Correct use of an adjective: My brother, Magnus, is really tall and powerful.

See Chapter 25 for more information about adjectives and adverbs.

A Student Essay

Read the essay, and then answer the questions that follow. As you read, correct any errors that you find, and make comments in the margins.

African Adventure
by Natalia MacDonald

1   My trip to Africa began with a twenty-hour journey filled with boring flights and long layovers. When I finaly arrived in Ghana, it was 9:00 P.M. local time, and I was exhausted. I went straight to my hotel to get some rest for the long day I had ahead of me. My first day in Ghana left me enthralled but exhausted.

2   On waking, Kwame, the coordinator of my volunteer program, picked me up to accompany me for the day. As I left the hotel, I was overwhelmed by the heat and the surroundings. Although many people dressed in Western-style clothing, the majority wore traditional African dress. The colours were incredibly vibrant: bright blues, purples, and yellows. Men, women, and children alike walked by carrying incredible amounts of goods balanced on their heads with such amazing grace and poise. Mothers also carried their babies in a way you had never seen before, tied to their backs with colourful scarves in almost a piggy-back position with their little feet sticking out at either side. As we hurried through the centre, I noticed the strong smells of food being cooked by street vendors, fruit being sold in baskets, and of course the not-so-pleasant smell of the open sewers lining the roads. After getting to the bank and cashing my traveller's checks, it was off to the beach.

3   Everything from the sand to the activities people were doing was unique. The first thing I felt was the much-needed cool breeze from the ocean brush against my face as I approached. After being in the hustle and bustle of the capital, feeling the rich, dark orange sand between my toes felt very relaxing. I then took a seat in the shade to enjoy a cold beverage and observe my surroundings. Some people were swimming and sunbathing, and others were dancing. There was a particular group of young boys dressed in colourful loincloths dancing to traditional music. The powerful drumbeat of the music was moving. The boys moved their bodies with such a natural fluidity along with the music that I was completely captivated. I was thoroughly enjoying myself, but it was time to catch my bus.

4   The bus was a large white van that left from a station not too far from the beach. As we drove out of the city and on to the dirt road, the scenery was breathtaking. We drove past many different types of villages along the way. Some of the villages were large and had schools, stores, and houses while others were much smaller and more basic and consisted of a

circle of around twenty little mud huts with straw roofs with people cooking over an open fire in the middle. Along the road there were many animals walking around such as dogs and mules, but mostly there were small goats. A month later I went to visit a national park to see wild animals. The road itself was the same rich, dark orange colour that the sand had been at the beach. One of the most incredible sights were the numerous huge anthills that were formed from the dark orange dirt. They stood about four feet high! After driving through some rain, we finally arrived in Manya Krobo, my new home.

5   My first full day in Ghana was one filled with new discoveries and adventure. In a mere matter of hours, I saw things that I had only read about in books and seen in movies. In one day, I had gone from the snowy minus 18-degree weather of Montreal to the humid 90 degrees of Ghana. My long planned and awaited adventure in Africa was finally a reality.

PRACTICE 4

Revising

1. Highlight the thesis statement.

2. Highlight the topic sentences in paragraphs 2 and 4.

3. Paragraph 3 lacks a topic sentence. One possible topic sentence could be:
    a. I went to the beach that evening.
    b. La Pleasure beach was unlike any other beach I had ever seen.
    c. There were many people at La Pleasure beach.
    d. Everyone goes to La Pleasure beach in Ghana.

4. What overall dominant impression does the writer convey in the essay? Underline examples in the essay to support your answer.

     _____ # ____ Surprise. amazement. ____

5. In paragraph 4, cross out the sentence that does not support the topic sentence.

Editing

6. Paragraph 1 contains a spelling mistake. Underline and correct the mistake.
    Correction: ___finally___

7. Paragraph 2 contains a pronoun shift. Underline and correct the error.
    Correction: ___babies.___

    _____

GRAMMAR LINK

See the following chapters for more information about these grammar topics:
Subject–Verb Agreement, Chapter 21
Spelling, Chapter 27
Commas, Chapter 28

8. Underline and correct a comma error in paragraph 2. _____

    _____

9. Underline and correct one subject–verb agreement error in paragraph 4.
    Correction: _____

    _____

Writer's Desk Revise and Edit Your Essay

Revise and edit the essay that you wrote for the previous Writer's Desk.
You can refer to the revising and editing checklists at the end of this
chapter and on this book's inside covers.

A Professional Essay

Lucie L. Snodgrass, a regular contributor to *Vegetarian Times*, is a passionate gardener
and a college teacher. She is also the author of *Green Roof Plants: A Resource and
Planting Guide*. In the following essay, she reflects on the importance of bees.

Living Among the Bees
by Lucie L. Snodgrass

1   Scattered along a gently sloping hill on our farm is a series of white
wooden boxes that resemble fallen tiles from a game of giant dominos.
The boxes arrived one spring six years ago in an old pickup truck driven
by Ed Yoder, a longtime neighbor and beekeeper who sells his honey at
local supermarkets. Always searching for open land in this county of
dwindling farms, Ed approached my husband and me, asking whether we
would mind having some hives on our property. Since we didn't, twenty of
them—home to about a million bees—came to share our 135 acres. At least
that's how we described it initially. In reality, we've come to understand, it
is the bees who have consented to share their workspace with us, and we,
clumsy and often inadvertently destructive humans, are the better for it.

2   Our coexistence did not get off to an auspicious start. Shortly after the
bees moved in, I began, as I always do in spring, spending most of my free
time in the vegetable garden—tilling the raised beds, pulling early weeds,
and carrying out flats of plants started in the greenhouse some fifty feet
away. The bees, I quickly learned, disapproved of my activity. They had

claimed this formerly quiet area as their own. They had chosen well, packed as the garden was with nectar-dripping flowers and fruit trees in brilliant bloom, a veritable juice bar that they frequented from early to late.

3   Each of my trips into the garden brought an angry protest as dozens of them dive-bombed my head, just as barn swallows do to cats when their territory is encroached upon. I had always found that funny, but being the victim myself was eminently less amusing. I tried varying the hours that I gardened; I tried apologizing to the bees each time I walked in; I even tried singing to them—all to no avail. Whether I was early or late, contrite or in song, the bees were piqued to see me, a fact made clear by the number of welts on various parts of my body. After six stings, I'd had enough.

4   "Ed," I complained on the beekeeper's next visit, "every time I go into the vegetable garden, your bees sting me. Something's got to give." He returned my gaze, his sympathy evident. "Of course they sting you," he said after a long silence. "You're walking right into their flight path."

5   And so my real experience began of living with the bees and their fiercely protective keeper. I quickly learned that Ed's devotion was complete, his concern solely for them. Implicit in his reply was the suggestion that I, and not the bees, was at fault for getting stung. Only after I pointed out that the garden had been there longer than the hives and that it wasn't feasible to move the orchard did he agree to move the hives that were closest to the garden—a concession I'm sure he secretly regrets even today.

6   That was the only disagreement we've ever had, and perhaps if I had avoided the garden for a while, as Ed bluntly suggested, the problem would have resolved itself. In retrospect, perhaps the bees, like people moving into a new neighborhood, needed some time to settle in without the threat of interference. In any event, they have long since accepted my presence, whether I am picking raspberries, walking on the road back to our nursery—a trip that takes me within ten feet of some of the hives—or simply sitting beside a hive for long stretches, watching the bees come and go. I've never again been stung, not when I've scooped some into my hand to rescue them from drowning in the birdbath or when I've picked them up, so covered with pollen they couldn't fly, to avoid someone trampling them. Ed says that the bees have come to trust me, and I believe that I, in turn, have given them my trust.

7   As wonderful as watching the bees is watching Ed, who is an old-fashioned suitor. He visits the bees almost every day, wooing them with presents, fixing things, delighting in the offerings they give back to him. When he has to disturb the bees, he calms them first, moving among them with his smoker like a priest with incense burners. **Loquacious** by nature, Ed can spend the day talking about his charges: waxing on about their

loquacious:
talkative

cleanliness, their loyalty to their queen, and their industriousness. Ed's love is infectious. We felt no small amount of pride when he told us after the first year's harvest that their honey production increased dramatically after the bees moved to our farm, certain that our unsprayed fields and flower gardens were responsible. We mourned with him when he lost many of his colonies to mites several years ago and others to a harsh winter. And we have done things that we would never have contemplated, like plowing up a few acres to plant clover because Ed told us that the bees would love it.

8   As with any good teachers, the bees have made me see things in a new light. About a half a mile from the hives is a small, perpetually muddy bog with a boardwalk of old heart pine running through it. In early spring, when the skunk cabbage blooms, I find bees there by the thousands, humming happily and drinking greedily. It is, I now know, their first source of nectar in spring. I am glad, and wiser, to know that the skunk cabbages, which always make my nose wrinkle, are to bees what poached strawberries are to me: both a delectable perfume and a welcome harbinger of spring.

9   The bees' contributions to the farm are everywhere. Berry bushes that bore modestly before the bees' arrival now hang heavy with fruit; my vegetable plants produce an embarrassing abundance of heirloom squash, cucumbers, and runner beans. Even seemingly barren fruit trees, far from the house and orchard in what were once cow pastures, have suddenly begun producing again. And, of course, there is the honey itself, velvety brown and perfectly sweet, dissolving in my tea and rippling across my bread. None of this is my work; it is all the bees' doing, and in their labor I have found wonder, gratitude, and a welcome sense of my own very modest place in the world.

PRACTICE 5

1. What is the writer's attitude toward the subject? Circle the best answer.

   a. positive   b. negative   c. neutral

2. Highlight the thesis statement.

3. How has the relationship between the writer and the bees changed? Explain, using your own words. First, they try to gaint Ea, hother, after a while, they love in peale.

4. The writer describes her life with the bees. Highlight some of the most effective examples of imagery.

5. A simile is a comparison using *like* or *as*. Highlight one simile in paragraph 6 and another in paragraph 7.

6. Circle some examples where the writer personifies or attributes human qualities to the bees.

7. Throughout the essay, the writer shows how the bees have had a positive influence on her life. In your own words, give some examples of how the bees have helped the writer.

Bees made a big contribution to the writer's
farm, they showed some precious human
qualities to writer as well. And, the bees
have made writer see things in a new light.

 The Writer's Room **Topics for Descriptive Essays**

READING LINK

Another Descriptive Reading

"Monsoon Time" by Rahul Goswami, page 522

Writing Activity 1

Write a descriptive essay about one of the following topics, or choose your own topic.

General Topics

1. a music concert
2. the day _____ went to the _____
3. a family meal
4. a night out
5. an exciting sports event

College and Work-Related Topics

6. a beautiful building or area on campus
7. a frustrating day
8. an eccentric professor
9. a new person I have met
10. an exciting event

WRITING LINK

More Descriptive Writing Topics

Chapter 17, Writer's Room topic 1 (page 303)
Chapter 21, Writer's Room topic 1 (page 346)
Chapter 22, Writer's Room topic 1 (page 365)
Chapter 23, Writer's Room topic 1 (page 380)
Chapter 26, Writer's Room topic 1 (page 418)

Writing Activity 2

Choose a quotation that you agree or disagree with, and then write a descriptive essay based on it.

> Everything has its wonders, even darkness and silence, and I learn whatever state I am in to be content.
>
> —Helen Keller, blind and deaf educator

> Art is the concrete representation of our most subtle feelings.
>
> —Agnes Martin, Canadian/American artist

> A few days ago I walked along the edge of the lake and was treated to the crunch and rustle of leaves with each step I made. The acoustics of this season are different, and all sounds, no matter how hushed, are as crisp as autumn air.
>
> —Eric Sloane, artist

> Train up a fig tree in the way it should go, and when you are old sit under the shade of it.
>
> —Charles Dickens, novelist

Writing Activity 3

Have you or someone you know ever seen an unusual event or been in an unusual situation? Describe the scene or event. Include vivid details.

✓ **CHECKLIST: DESCRIPTIVE ESSAY**

After you write your descriptive essay, review the essay checklist on the inside front cover. Also ask yourself these questions.

☐ Does my thesis statement clearly show what I will describe in the essay?

☐ Does my thesis statement have a controlling idea that makes a point about the topic?

☐ Does my essay have a dominant impression?

☐ Does each body paragraph contain supporting details that appeal to the reader's senses?

☐ Do I use vivid language?

How Do I Get a Better Grade?

PEARSON
mycanadiancomplab

Go to www.mycanadiancomplab.ca for additional help with your grammar, writing, and research skills. You will have access to a variety of exercises, instruction, and video that will help you improve your basic skills and help you get a better grade.

8 CHAPTER

Process

- What Is Process?
- The Process Essay
- Explore Topics

Developing
- The Thesis Statement
- The Supporting Ideas
- The Essay Plan
- The First Draft

Revising and Editing
- Revise and Edit a Process Essay
- A Professional Essay: "Are You Breathing the Right Way?" by Meredith Dault

Every industry uses processes. For example, builders need to study architectural designs, take measurments of their materials, construct structures with tools, and so on. Along similar lines, writers not only have to follow the writing process, but sometimes they need to be able to explain processes to their readers as well.

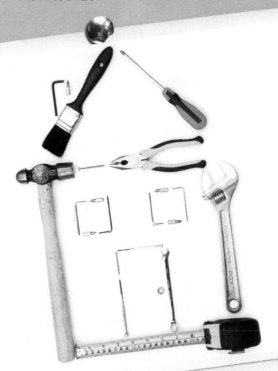

Writers' Exchange

Choose one of the following topics and have a group or class discussion. Describe the steps you would take to do that process.

- How to become an annoying neighbour
- How to write an essay
- How to get rich quickly
- How to parallel park

EXPLORING

What Is Process?

A **process** is a series of steps usually done in chronological order. In process writing, you explain how to do something, how an incident took place, or how something works. Take a look at the following examples of processes that people discuss in everyday life.

> *I am always doing that which I cannot do, in order that I may learn how to do it.*
>
> PABLO PICASSO, *Cubist painter*

Audience: Family member

Cook pasta in the following way.

- Boil a pot of water.
- Add a pinch of salt.
- Put pasta into boiling water.
- Cook for 8 minutes.
- Drain water.
- Serve pasta hot.

Audience: Classmate

Follow these steps to become a tutor.

- Decide what subject you want to tutor.
- See the person responsible for hiring a tutor.
- Find out the number of hours you need to tutor.

Audience: Intern

Take the customer's order by following these procedures.

- First, check to ensure that the order form is filled out correctly.
- Next, call our warehouse to verify stock.
- Then, send the order form to the warehouse manager.

Process at Work

Frank Morelli is a mechanic who specializes in repairing Toyotas and Volvos. In this pamphlet excerpt, he advises customers on how to buy a car.

First, decide if you want a new or used car. There are some advantages and disadvantages for both. A new car will be more expensive, but you can buy an extended warranty, and a new car will likely not incur expensive repairs. A used car is, of course, more economical. However, if the previous owner has not properly maintained the car, you may have to pay for costly repairs, and the car may not last for very long.

Next, research the safety record of the car that you want to buy. Some types of cars offer extensive safety features such as dual airbags and a reinforced frame. To find information about the safety statistics of the car you want to buy, consult the car insurance websites or read some consumer magazines that deal with cars.

The Process Essay

Before planning a process essay, you need to determine your purpose. Do you want to tell readers how to complete a process or how to understand a process?

1. **Complete a process.** This type of essay contains directions for completing a particular task. For example, a writer might explain how to change a flat tire, how to decorate a room, or how to use a particular computer program.

2. **Understand a process.** This type of essay explains how something works or how something happens. For example, a writer might explain how the admissions process at a college works or how food goes from the farm to the table.

A Student Essay

Read the essay and answer the questions that follow.

Learning Good Finances
by Tony Ruiz

1   Every year, when you apply for more student aid, it takes a toll on your fiscal confidence. If you are anything like I am, no matter how well you think you have curbed your spending, you always find yourself staring at your T-4 tax return form in disbelief. Your humble living standards do not reflect the overwhelming discrepancy between your alleged total earnings and your most recent bank statement. Students can begin making smart financial decisions today and help reduce the financial burden they are likely to experience after graduation.

2   Students should avoid spending money on unnecessary gadgets. For example, the iPod is a terrible investment for students who are trying to save money. Besides paying at least $199 for the iPod nano or $269 for the iPod Video, consumers end up buying crucial trendy accessories. An FM transmitter that will let listeners wire their iPod through a car's sound system costs $29.95. For those who want to listen to FM radio while walking to class, the FM Radio Remote costs another $49.95. And before long, the iPod's dead battery will have to be replaced for $59 (plus shipping and handling). Some students might even be tempted to buy a newer model of iPod. Meanwhile, an impressive iTunes library costs $0.99 for every song and $1.99 for every episode of *The Hour* that could be watched weeknights at no cost.

3   Another common mistake students make is adopting expensive daily regimens. They should reduce "treat" spending by half. For the sluggish, a $4.50 personalized Starbucks coffee is the only way to function. Booster Juice is the formidable, health-conscious counterpart. Replacing the

designer drink every day with generic coffee or fruit juice would amount to substantial savings. Skipping the Chai Latte or the Mocha Cappuccino Delight three days out of five is painless but effective.

4   Students can earn more money by investing carefully. Setting aside even as little as $500 every year toward student debt means that after a four-year period, they will have $2000 less to worry about paying off. The elimination of interest charges will generate pocket change in the long term as well. Furthermore, student loans also offer a unique advantage since the cost to students will not be felt until graduation, so they should make that money work for them. Those who are absolutely sure that they will not need a certain amount of money until graduation can lock up the money with a certificate of deposit and let it earn interest yields typically higher than those of savings and money market accounts.

5   Nobody expects students to invest all of their time and money in scholarly endeavours. Everybody needs to have some leisure activities. But they should be reasonable. New gadgets and expensive habits are unnecessary indulgences.

PRACTICE I

1. Highlight the thesis statement.

2. Highlight the topic sentence in each body paragraph.

3. Who is the audience for this essay? _____

4. For each of the body paragraphs, list some supporting details the writer gives.

    Paragraph 2: _____

    _____

    Paragraph 3: _____

    _____

    Paragraph 4: _____

    _____

Explore Topics

In the Writer's Desk Warm Up, you will try an exploring strategy to generate ideas about different topics.

Writer's Desk **Warm Up**

Read the following questions, and write the first ideas that come to your mind. Think of two or three ideas for each topic.

EXAMPLE: Imagine that you are choosing a college to begin your higher education. What are some steps that you should follow to choose an appropriate college?

—find out the programs the college offers

—find out the cost

—think about the size of the college

1. How can you become a better friend?

_____

_____

_____

2. What can you do to fall out of love?

_____

_____

_____

3. How can someone become competent in another language?

_____

_____

_____

DEVELOPING

When you write a process essay, choose a process that you know something about. For example, you might be able to explain how to become more environmentally conscious; however, you might not know how to reduce nuclear waste.

The Thesis Statement

In a process essay, the thesis statement states what process you will be explaining and what readers will be able to do after they have read the essay.

topic   controlling idea

Remaining attractive to your spouse can help keep your relationship exciting.

controlling idea   topic

Consistency, patience, and time are essential **to becoming a good parent**.

Writer's Desk Thesis Statements

Write a thesis statement for each of the following topics. You can look for ideas in the Warm Up on page 126. Each thesis statement should state the process and contain a controlling idea.

EXAMPLE: Topic: how to choose an appropriate college

  Thesis Statement: *The following steps are important when choosing an appropriate college.*

_____

1. Topic: how to become a better friend

   Thesis Statement: _____

   _____

2. Topic: how to fall out of love

   Thesis Statement: _____

   _____

3. Topic: how to learn another language

   Thesis Statement: _____

   _____

The Supporting Ideas

A process essay contains a series of steps. When you develop supporting ideas for a process essay, think about the main steps that are necessary to complete the process.

- Use prewriting strategies such as freewriting and brainstorming to generate ideas.
- Choose the best ideas. Clearly explain the steps of the process.
- Organize your ideas. Choose the best organizational method for this essay pattern. Process essays generally use chronological or time order.

 **Give Steps, Not Examples**

When you explain how to complete a process, describe each step. Do not simply list examples of the process.

Topic: How to Plan an Interesting Vacation

List of Examples	Steps in the Process
• go to a tropical island	• decide what your goal is
• ride a hot air balloon	• research possible locations
• swim with the sharks	• find out the cost
• tour an exotic city	• plan the itinerary according to budget

Writer's Desk   List the Main Steps

Choose one thesis statement from the previous Writer's Desk. List the main steps to complete the process.

EXAMPLE:

Thesis Statement: _The following steps are important when choosing an appropriate college._

1. Ask about programs.

2. Find out the cost.

3. Consider the size of the college.

4. Ask about student housing.

Thesis Statement: _____

_____

Steps to complete the process:

_____

_____

_____

_____

_____

The Essay Plan

An essay plan helps you organize your thesis statement, topic sentences, and supporting details before writing a first draft. Decide which steps and which details your reader will really need to complete the process or understand it.

THESIS STATEMENT: The following steps are important for choosing an appropriate college.

I.   Find out which programs the college offers.
   A. Look for different options like majors and minors.
   B. Make note of the number of years to complete the program.
   C. Figure out the prerequisites necessary to get accepted.
II. Determine what you can afford to spend on your education.
   A. Ask the administration for details on tuition and other expenses.
   B. Research the available student loans and grants.
   C. Find out about other sources of financial aid, including scholarships.
III. Consider the size of the college.
   A. A smaller college may have smaller class sizes and more individualized attention.
   B. It may be easier to make friends in smaller classes.
   C. A bigger college may have more programs, a more heterogeneous student population, and more student services.

Writer's Desk **Write an Essay Plan**

Refer to the information you generated in previous Writer's Desks, and prepare a detailed essay plan. Add details and examples that will help to explain each step.

The First Draft

As you write your first draft, explain the process in a way that would be clear for your audience. Address the reader directly. For example, instead of writing, "You should scan the newspaper for used cars," simply write, "Scan the newspaper for used cars." Also, remember to use complete sentences and transitions to smoothly string together the ideas from your essay plan. Here are some time-order transitions that are useful for explaining processes.

To begin a process	To continue a process		To end a process
(at) first	after that	later	eventually
initially	afterward	meanwhile	finally
the first step	also	second	in the end
	furthermore	then	ultimately
	in addition	third	

Grammar Hint   **Avoid Sentence Fragments**

Ensure that you do not use sentence fragments to list the steps of the process. A sentence must have a subject and a verb to express a complete idea.

check

Consider your airline's carry-on luggage requirements. First, the weight of

your suitcase.

See Chapter 17 for more information about sentence fragments.

Writer's Desk **Write the First Draft**

In the previous Writer's Desk, you developed an essay plan. Now, carefully review your essay plan, make any necessary changes, and write the first draft of your process essay.

REVISING AND EDITING

Revise and Edit a Process Essay

When you finish writing a process essay, carefully review your work and revise it to make the process as clear as possible to your readers. Check to make sure that you have organized your steps, and remove any details that are not relevant to being able to complete or understand the process. Before you revise and edit your own essay, practise revising and editing a student essay.

A Student Essay

Read the essay, and then answer the questions that follow. As you read, correct any errors that you find, and make comments in the margins.

The Right College
by Jose Luis Fonseca

1   When I first thought about a college to attend, I really did not know what to do. It was very lucky that Dave Hunt, my good friend, was more organized than me and could help me make such an important decision. One Sunday afternoon, very close to the deadline, we sat in a café, and he proceeded to explain exactly what I should think about when choosing a college. The following steps are crucial for finding an appropriate college.

2   Learn about the programs different colleges offer. Some important factors to consider are the number of years to complete the program that interests you. You need to know about different program options like major and minor subjects. It is necessary to know the prerequisite courses or experience necessary to get accepted into a program. If you want to pursue social work, perhaps you need some experience working with people. If you are interested in bookkeeping, maybe you need a particular high school math course to get accepted into the program. For instance, when I applied to our college's nursing program, I needed my Grade 12 science credit.

3   Also, the cost. Education is very expensive. When determining which college to go to, find one where you can afford to spend several years studying. For example, a college in a large city with a great reputation might cost a lot for tuition, housing, and transportation. I live far from the campus. The traffic is incredibly heavy, and it takes me a long time to get there. The local college might not be as well known or respected, but perhaps you will be able to afford the tuition, or you may be able to live at home, and your transportation costs might be much lower. For example, Trang Hoang, a mechanical engineering student, saved money by going to our local college. "My decision to study locally has never hurt my career prospects," she says.

4   You may not know what you want to study. In such a case, it is advisable to take a variety of courses to see where your interests lie. When Dave Hunt was eighteen, he started out majoring in art, but after one term, he worried about earning a good living, and he switched to administration. He realized that he loves working with numbers, so he is very happy about his decision. Keep your mind open to different subjects.

5   A smaller college will have smaller class sizes and more individualized attention. It is easier to make friends in smaller classes. But a larger college may have more programs. It may also have a more heterogeneous student

population, which would enable you to meet students with different backgrounds. A larger college may also provide more student services, clubs, and other activities, you may find such experiences enriching.

6   So think very carefully when choosing a college. The right college will provide you with innumerable advantages such as a good education, the right career opportunity, and long-lasting friendships. Take advantage of different sources and become informed. You will never regret it.

PRACTICE 2

Revising

1. Highlight the thesis statement.

2. Highlight the topic sentences for paragraphs 2 and 3.

3. Which of the following would make an effective topic sentence for paragraph 5? Circle the best answer.
    a. It is easy to make friends at college.
    b. Participate in different activities at a bigger college.
    c. Small colleges are not as interesting as big colleges.
    d. Keep the size of the college in mind when making your decision.

4. Which paragraph is unnecessary for the development of ideas? __ Explain why. _____

    _____

5. In paragraph 3, cross out the sentence that does not support the topic sentence.

6. Paragraph 5 lacks adequate support. Think of a detailed example that would help flesh out the paragraph.

    _____

    _____

7. Paragraph 2 lacks transitions. Add at least three transitions to link the sentences.

    _____   _____   _____

Editing

8. Underline a pronoun problem in the introductory paragraph. Write the correction in the following space.

    Correction: _____

    _____

GRAMMAR LINK

See the following chapters for more information about these grammar topics:
Run-Ons, Chapter 18
Pronouns, Chapter 26
Fragments, Chapter 17

9. Underline the sentence fragment in paragraph 3. Then correct it here.

Correction: _____

_____

10. Underline the run-on sentence in paragraph 5. Then correct it here.

Correction: _____

_____

---

vo•cab•u•lar•y BOOST

Look at the first draft of your process essay. Underline the verb that you use to describe each step of the process. Then, when possible, come up with a more evocative verb. Use your thesaurus for this activity.

Writer's Desk **Revise and Edit Your Process Essay**

Revise and edit the essay that you wrote for the previous Writer's Desk. You can refer to the revising and editing checklists at the end of this chapter and on this book's inside covers.

A Professional Essay

Meredith Dault, a print and broadcast journalist, has published articles on a variety of topics (visual arts, dance, business, health) in the *Globe and Mail*, the *Chronicle Herald*, and *Canadian Art*, among other print and online journals. She can also be heard on CBC Radio. In the following essay, Dault reflects on the importance of proper breathing.

"Are You Breathing the Right Way?"
by Meredith Dault

1   Good breathing is a major component of good health, yet many of us spend our lives taking too-shallow breaths that can increase our stress levels. Find out how to breathe the right way and get some breathing techniques to try.

2   For most of us, breathing is nothing more than an automatic function that keeps us alive, a steady flow that brings in vital oxygen and expels carbon dioxide. But unlike heartbeat or digestion, breath is a bodily

function we can consciously control. If you've ever taken a deep breath to keep a panic attack at bay, then you already know the wonders breathing can have on your well-being. Not only will paying regular attention to your breath give you a good reading on your mental and emotional state, you'll also tap into an easy and effective way to manage stress and anxiety.

3   Though we usually take it for granted, we use the breath in lots of different ways every day: gasping when we cry, hyperventilating when we're panicked and breathing deeply when we laugh. But most of us still live day-to-day taking shallow, unconscious breaths—and that's not good for us. "A lot of people don't realize they aren't breathing properly," says Adam Prinsen, a naturopathic doctor based in Peterborough, Ont. "They are breathing in a way that reflects stress—and by breathing that way, they're actually sending a message to their nervous system that they *are* stressed. It's a vicious circle."

How to breathe properly

4   For an example of proper breathing, Prinsen suggests watching an animal or newborn baby while they're sleeping —they breathe steadily and effortlessly from their bellies. But by the time we're four or five years old, we've already learned improper breathing habits, and they soon become ingrained. "Eventually you're 40 and you've been breathing in an unhealthy way for years," says Prinsen. "If you want to change your breathing, you have to put effort into changing your habits."

5   The first step toward using your breath more effectively is to pay attention to it. "Notice what your breath is doing when you're stressed, when you're happy, during sex, and while doing exercise," says Seth Daley, a Halifax-based yoga teacher, explaining that once you understand the way you breathe, you can start to modify it. Daley says breathing is integral to most forms of yoga—and is ultimately a more important part of the practice than the physical postures. As he explains, the Sanskrit word for breath, *prana*, also means energy, and it's a vital indicator of our overall well-being. That's why practices that incorporate the breath—like yoga, tai chi and Pilates—are good places to start in learning how to use yours more effectively.

Learning good breathing techniques

6   The key to good technique is learning how to breathe with your diaphragm. That's the muscle beneath your rib cage, the same one you use for singing or laughing. "If you're breathing properly, you can feel your diaphragm pushing down into your belly," says Prinsen, who points out that though it isn't crucial for the abdomen to go in and out while you're breathing, it can be a good technique. If you're guilty of holding in your

stomach so that it looks flatter—and many women are—then you definitely aren't using your diaphragm properly. And utilizing the diaphragm is the key to letting go of stress. "It sends a message to the nervous system that you're relaxed," says Prinsen.

7   Daley says learning to control the breath is as simple as taking long, deliberate inhales at designated times throughout the day. He recommends counting to three as you breathe in, and then again as you exhale, making each inhale and exhale the same length, without pausing. "Not only does it make you aware of your breathing patterns, but it forces you to calm down and it draws your focus inward, like meditation does," says Daley. He also suggests lying down with a pillow under your upper back as an even easier method to practise calm breathing. Once you get good at it, you can practise calm breathing while you're walking, doing dishes or sitting in your car at a stoplight.

Finding a daily breathing routine

8   Though Prinsen recommends deep breathing for 10 to 20 minutes a day, he says even practising for a minute every hour will have noticeable benefits. "It will completely change your mental and emotional state," he says. As an added bonus, he adds that good breathing has physical benefits for the whole body, as it helps reduce acidity and makes the body more alkaline. "If you have chronic acidity in your body tissue," he explains, "you'll have a greater tendency to develop chronic disease." Isn't that worth taking a deep breath for?

PRACTICE 3

1. What is the writer's specific purpose? _____

2. Highlight the thesis statement. It may not be in the first paragraph.

3. Read the topic sentence of each body paragraph. Circle the verbs in each topic sentence.

4. In each topic sentence, the subject is implied but not stated. What is the subject?

   _____

5. In the last paragraph, list the examples the writer gives to support the topic sentence.

   _____

   _____

7. Underline the names of two experts whom the writer quotes.

8. The writer uses transitional words or phrases to link the steps of the process. What are they?

_____

 The Writer's Room **Topics for Process Essays**

Writing Activity 1

Write a process essay about one of the following topics or choose your own topic.

General Topics

How to . . .

1. buy a used car

2. become a good driver

3. communicate more effectively with family members

4. win a _____

5. live on a budget

College and Work-Related Topics

How to . . .

6. look for a new job

7. assemble a _____

8. become a better manager or supervisor

9. change a law

10. make a good impression at an interview

Writing Activity 2

Choose a quotation that you agree or disagree with, and then write a process essay based on it.

In my last years of high school, I finally decided to use my brain.
—Naomi Klein, political activist and writer

We now accept the fact that learning is a lifelong process of keeping abreast of change. And the most pressing task is to teach people how to learn.

—Peter Drucker, writer

There was a definite process by which one made people into friends, and it involved talking to them and listening to them for hours at a time.

—Rebecca West, journalist

Civilization is a slow process of adopting the ideas of minorities.

—Anonymous

Writing Activity 3

What are some steps people can take to have an enduring personal relationship?

READING LINK

More Process Readings

"The Rich Resonance of Small Talk" by Roxanne Roberts (page 509)

"The Rules of Survival" by Laurence Gonzales (page 515)

"Medicating Ourselves," by Robyn Sarah (page 534)

WRITING LINK

More Process Writing Topics

Chapter 19, on page 323, see Writer's Room Topic 2.

Chapter 20, on page 332, see Writer's Room Topic 1.

Chapter 24, on page 390, see Writer's Room Topic 1.

✔ **CHECKLIST: PROCESS ESSAY**

As you write your process essay, review the checklist on the inside front cover. Also ask yourself these questions.

☐ Does my thesis statement make a point about the process?

☐ Do I include all of the steps in the process?

☐ Do I clearly explain each step so my reader can accomplish the process?

☐ Do I mention all of the supplies that my reader needs to complete the process?

☐ Do I use transitions to connect all of the steps in the process?

How Do I Get a Better Grade?

mycanadiancomplab

Go to www.mycanadiancomplab.ca for additional help with your grammar, writing, and research skills. You will have access to a variety of exercises, instruction, and video that will help you improve your basic skills and help you get a better grade.

Definition

CONTENTS

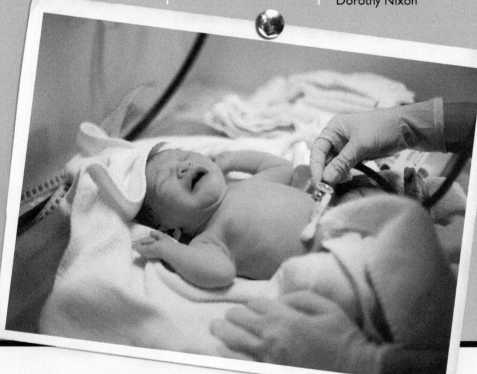

To help patients understand a diagnosis, doctors may define the illness itself or explain related medical terms. Similarly, you may write an entire essay in which you define a term. Or, you may need to define only a few terms within an essay to ensure that your readers understand specific concepts.

Writers' Exchange

Brainstorm some common slang expressions. Think about words you use to express pleasure or disgust. You can also consider words describing a specific type of person. Choose one expression and define it without using a dictionary. Make your definition clear so that a non-native speaker will understand the word.

EXPLORING

What Is Definition?

When you define, you explain the meaning of a word. Some terms have concrete meanings, and you can define them in a few words. For example, a *town* is "a small city." Other words, such as *values*, *faith*, or *human rights*, are more abstract and require more detailed definitions. It is possible to write a paragraph, an essay, or even an entire book about such concepts. Here are some examples of terms people regularly define in different situations.

Audience: Children

I expect you to be *reliable*.

- Phone if you are going to be late.
- Do your chores to help out.
- Do your homework every night.

Audience: Classmate

In my sociology class we are discussing the term *poverty*.

- Poverty means different things to different cultures.
- In this country, the government always talks about low-income families.
- Some countries, like China, define poverty by the minimum caloric intake of an individual.

Audience: Colleague

My supervisor said my presentation "needs improvement."

- I spoke too quickly.
- I relied too heavily on my PowerPoint slides.
- My presentation was too long.

The Definition Essay

When you write a definition essay, try to explain what a term means to you. For example, if someone asks you to define *overachiever*, you might give examples of over-achievers and what you think those people do that goes beyond the limits. You may also explain what an overachiever is not. Also, remember the following two points.

1. **Choose a term that you know something about.** You need to understand a term to say something relevant and interesting about it.
2. **Give a clear definition.** Write a definition that your reader will easily understand, and support your definition with examples.

Definition at Work

*In the following excerpt,
Michigan's 2004 Teacher of the Year, Heidi Capraro,
defines what makes a great teacher.*

We have a passion for teaching. We care about our students, parents, and the communities in which we work and teach. We celebrate the positive accomplishments in the field of teaching and look for brighter possibilities for the future.

I think teachers have to be sensitive to each student's tolerance for frustration and recognize that each one handles this kind of stress differently. We want to engage and motivate students, not force them to shut down and quit. This applies to students at every age. I think people assume that as children grow up, they don't need the same support and understanding. In reality, they have more difficulties to face as they reach their teenage years. Kindness, empathy, opportunities for success, modifications, and adults with a personal interest in them—these are what every child needs.

 Consider Your Audience

Consider your audience when you write a definition essay. You may have to adjust your tone and vocabulary, depending on who will be reading the essay. For example, if you write a definition essay about cloning for your political science class, you may have to explain concepts using basic, non-technical terms. If you write the same essay for your biology class, you may be able to use more technical terms.

A Student Essay

Read the student essay and answer the questions that follow.

Journalists Are History's Record Keepers
by Lindsey Davis

1   When you want to find research for that paper on World War II for class, you hit the books in the library, looking for the historian who summed up the events or the political scientist who offered critical insight as to why it happened. But when you want to find out what is happening in the world right now, you pick up the *National Post* or log on to your computer and browse the **plethora** of news sites. Journalists play multiple roles in society. From **The Canadian Press** as the check on government and business to the responsibility of creating a forum for debate and free speech, the job of journalists is crucial to society's progress. But beyond this role, journalists are historians. They are the note takers and storytellers who document today's activities and events to safeguard their accuracy and preserve the record of history.

2   First, different types of media are crucial for preserving historical records. Newspapers, news websites, and television news programs are the only place you can turn to find the latest breaking developments of what is happening in Ottawa, what reforms Prime Minister Harper is planning, the status of the war in Iraq, and the crucial stats of the last CFL playoff game. Before it goes in the history books, it goes in the newspaper. Before you can find it in the library, you can find it in the news.

3   Moreover, journalists are the record keepers for the community. They will give you the plain and simple facts. They will find out how much those tickets were selling for at the Vanier Cup. They will tell you who won the basketball games and what the upcoming baseball season looks like. But beyond simple facts, they will record the emotions of a Vanier Cup defeat. How about those new movies and CDs that are coming out next week? They will give you the scoop on what's good and what's bad. They will tell you what you can't miss in Toronto. You can find the thoughts and analyses of a vast array of differing voices.

4   Furthermore, journalists are also crucial to preserving the spirit of the times. It is within the media that you'll find the record of the year's events. But this history won't be complete unless it includes your voice, your opinion, and your perspective on events. Tell the journalists what's going on and what you would like to see covered. Send them an email. Talk to reporters and tell them what you think. The media will never be able to create an accurate record of history unless you help gather all the facts by saying what you know or what you saw. Do you think something was wrongly covered? Let the media know. Do you disagree with a column you

plethora:
a large amount

The Canadian Press:
the entire press, including newspapers, television news programs, magazines, etc.

have read? Send a letter to the editor and make sure your viewpoint is printed and recorded as well.

5   Journalists are committed to ensuring that whatever happens is recorded forever. Some people say that journalists write the rough draft of history. But they strive to report accurately enough that it will be the final draft. Their dedication ensures that you get the news and ensures that history is recorded. All they ask is that you read to keep the history alive.

PRACTICE 1

1. What is the specific purpose of this essay? _To give the definition of journalists. / To inform us what is journalist._

2. Highlight the thesis statement.

3. Highlight the topic sentence of each body paragraph.

4. What introductory style is used? Circle the best answer.
   a. anecdote
   b. historical
   c. contrasting position
   d. general background

5. In your own words, list some of the specific examples in each body paragraph.
   1. Find what happened in the past on
   newspapers / news websites / TV news programs
   2. Learn about the latest events around the us / sports.. tickets...
   3. Our efforts are needed

6. Circle the transitional links in this essay.

Explore Topics

In the Writer's Desk Warm Up, you will try an exploring strategy to generate ideas about different topics.

Writer's Desk **Warm Up**

Read the following questions, and write the first ideas that come to your mind. Think of two or three ideas for each topic.

EXAMPLE: What is a volunteer? Think of some characteristics of a volunteer.

—*is involved in charitable causes*

—*wants to help people*

—*has love for humankind*

1. What is a home?

   Is the protection.

   A place can go back.

   motivates people to work.

2. What is the Canadian dream?

   The more you pay, the more you gain.

   ~~Canada~~ Wants to achieve equality.

   Party

3. What is a religion?

   A belief.

   respects secret

   backs people up

DEVELOPING

The Thesis Statement

A clear thesis statement for a definition essay introduces the term and provides a definition. There are three basic ways to define a term.

Definition by Synonym

Providing a definition by synonym is useful if the original term is difficult to understand, and the synonym is a more familiar word.

term   +   synonym

He is a neophyte,   which means he is a beginner or novice.

Definition by Category

When you define by category, you determine the larger group to which the term belongs. Then you determine what unique characteristics set the term apart from others in that category.

term   +   category   +   detail

A forest ranger   is a worker   who is trained to protect
                                                   wildlife in national parks.

Definition by Negation

When you define by negation, you explain what a term does not mean. You can then include a sentence explaining what it does mean.

term   +   what it is not   +   what it is

Obsession   is not an eccentricity;   it is a mental illness.

Grammar Hint   **Using Semicolons**

You can join two related and complete ideas with a semicolon, as the writer has done in this example of a definition.

EXAMPLE: Marriage is not the end of your freedom; it is the beginning of a shared journey.

See Chapter 18 for more information about using semicolons.

Making a Point

Defining terms by synonym, category, and negation are only guidelines for writing thesis statements for a definition essay. Keep in mind that your essay will be more interesting if you express your attitude or point of view in your thesis statement.

No point: Avarice means greed.

Point: Human avarice, or greed, invariably leads to tragedy.

PRACTICE 2   Write thesis statements by defining the following terms using your own words. Try to make definitions by synonym, category, and negation. Remember to indicate your controlling idea in the thesis statements.

EXAMPLE: Road rage *is not a momentary lapse of judgment; it is serious*

criminal behaviour.

1. A misfit _____

_____

2. A jock _is not a positive word to describe athlete_
it is way for people who abuse their popularity

3. B-list actors _are not a group of unprofessional actors._
they are actors with less reputation.

4. Rush-hour traffic _is a situation that large number_
of people stuck in a way to go back home caused by
traffic congestion

5. A mentor _is_

_____

Hint   **Be Precise!**

When you write a definition essay, it is important to use precise words to define the term. Moreover, when you define a term by category, make sure that the category for your term is correct.

Anorexia nervosa is the <u>inability</u> to eat.
(Anorexia nervosa is not an ability or an inability.)

Anorexia nervosa is <u>when</u> you want to be thin.
(*When* refers to a time, but anorexia nervosa is not a time.)

Anorexia nervosa is <u>where</u> it is hard to eat properly.
(*Where* refers to a place, but anorexia nervosa is not a place.)

Now look at a better definition of this illness.

Anorexia nervosa is a tragic **eating disorder** characterized by the desire to become very thin.

PRACTICE 3   Revise each sentence using precise language.

EXAMPLE: Multitasking is when you do many activities at once.

Multitasking is doing many activities at once.

1. A blacklist is when a list of people comes under suspicion.

   A blacklist is ~~list~~ of people under suspicion.
   A record

2. A poor loser is the inability to accept defeat graciously. walk

   A poor loser is a person who cannot accept defeat graciously.

3. A <u>twixter</u> is overdependence on parents by adult children.

   A twixter is young people who overdependent on parents.

4. Feedback is when you get <u>constructive criticism</u>. To make people better.

   Feedback is a process that you get constructive criticism.

5. Networking is where you keep in contact with people to help your career.

   Networking is a system in which you keep in contact with people to help your career.

---

vo•cab•u•lar•y BOOST

Some words have neutral, positive, or negative associations. Look at each set of words and categorize each as neutral, positive, or negative. Do this with a partner.

1. thin, cadaverous, lean, emaciated, wiry, skinny, slender
2. home, shack, cottage, slum, stomping ground, dump, sanctuary
3. dainty, delicate, finicky, fussy, prissy, fragile, elegant, frail
4. honest, coarse, crude, open, gross, straightforward
5. brat, child, sweetheart, cutie, munchkin, delinquent, heir, mama's boy

Writer's Desk **Write Thesis Statements**

Write a thesis statement in which you define each of the following topics. You can look for ideas in the previous Writer's Desk. Remember to make a point in your thesis statement.

EXAMPLE: Topic: a volunteer

Thesis Statement: *A volunteer is a necessary and generous person who is emotionally*

invested in the betterment of humankind.

1. Topic: home

Thesis statement: _____

_____

2. Topic: the Canadian dream

Thesis statement: _____

_____

3. Topic: a religion

Thesis statement: _____

_____

The Supporting Ideas

After you have developed an effective thesis statement, generate supporting ideas. In a definition essay, you can give examples that clarify your definition. To develop supporting ideas, follow these three steps:

- Use prewriting strategies to generate ideas. Think about facts, anecdotes, and examples that will help define your term.
- Choose the best ideas. Use examples that clearly reveal the definition of the term.
- Organize your ideas. Choose the best organizational method for this essay pattern.

Writer's Desk Generate Supporting Ideas

Choose one of your thesis statements from the previous Writer's Desk. List three or four ideas that most effectively illustrate the definition.

EXAMPLE: Thesis statement: *A volunteer is a necessary and generous person who is*

emotionally invested in the betterment of humankind.

—*offers to help others*

—*brings attention to charitable causes*

—*is selfless*

—*is important for society*

Thesis statement: _____

_____

Supports: _____

_____

_____

_____

The Essay Plan

An essay plan helps you organize your thesis statement and supporting details before writing the first draft. A definition essay includes a complete definition of the term and provides adequate examples to support the central definition. When creating a definition essay plan, ensure that your examples provide varied evidence and do not just repeat the definition. Organize your ideas in a logical sequence.

THESIS STATEMENT: A volunteer is a necessary and generous person who is emotionally invested in the betterment of humankind.

   I. Volunteers do not earn money; they gain a sense of personal satisfaction.

      A. Donne wrote Meditation XVII: No man is an island.

      B. He believed that people are not isolated, but interconnected.

      C. Donne's philosophy influenced people such as Martin Luther King, Jr.

II. Many people of all types are volunteers.
  A. Extremely rich people contribute to charity.
  B. Ordinary people donate their time.
III. By giving their time and money, volunteers are crucial for charities to function.
  A. Non-profit organizations help develop public awareness of different issues and problems.
  B. International organizations rely on volunteers.
  C. Volunteers also work at local community churches and schools.

Writer's Desk **Write an Essay Plan**

Refer to the information you generated in previous Writer's Desks and prepare a detailed essay plan.

The First Draft

Your essay plan is the backbone around which you can craft your first draft. Use it to write your first draft. As you write, remember to vary your sentence structure and to write complete sentences. Also include transitional words or expressions to help your ideas flow smoothly. Here are some transitional expressions that can help you show different levels of importance in a definition essay.

To show the level of importance

clearly	next
first	one quality . . . another quality
most important	second
most of all	undoubtedly

Writer's Desk **Write the First Draft**

Carefully review the essay plan you prepared in the previous Writer's Desk. Make any necessary changes to the definition or its supporting details, and then write your first draft.

REVISING AND EDITING

Revise and Edit a Definition Essay

When you finish writing a definition essay, carefully review your work and revise it to make the definition as clear as possible to your readers. You might have to adjust your definition and supporting ideas to suit their knowledge. Also keep in mind the tone of your essay. Certain words have either negative or positive connotations. Finally, check that you have organized your ideas logically and remove any irrelevant details. Before you revise and edit your own essay, practise revising and editing a student essay.

A Student Essay

Read the essay, and then answer the questions that follow. As you read, correct any errors that you find, and make comments in the margins.

Volunteers
by Michael Newberg

1   "What do we live for, if it is not to make life less difficult for each other"? wrote the English writer George Eliot. This question has been discussed throughout history during times of prosperity and poverty. Human beings need to be kind and giving to each other. Volunteers are the backbone of a kind world, and we desperately need their acts of charity. A volunteer is a necessary and generous person who is emotionally invested in the betterment of humankind.

2   Volunteers do not work to earn money; they work to gain a sense of personal satisfaction. One of the English poets, John Donne (1572–1631), believed that humanity has a collective responsibility. In a powerful poem, *Meditation XVII*, Donne wrote, "No man is an island, entire of itself . . . any man's death diminishes me, because I am involved in mankind." According to Donne, people must care for each other. His philosophy has influenced many people such as Martin Luther King, Jr. Volunteers want to help people because they want to make the world a more just society.

3   Some very wealthy people donate tremendous amounts of time and money to help others. Oprah, for example, She spends a lot of time and money with her girls' school in South Africa. Many middle-class and poor people also volunteer and help those in need. Soup kitchens, for instance, could not function without the service of many unpaid workers. Bae Kim is a cook in our college cafeteria, but he also volunteers once a week for the Meals on Wheels program in our district.

Margin annotations:
prosperity:
poverty :
diminishes:
tremendous:

epidemic :

tragedy :

4   By giving their time and money, volunteers are crucial for charities to function. Non-profit organizations, such as Doctors Without Borders or the Red cross, help raise public awareness about different issues, including the AIDS epidemic, war, political injustices, and so on. Most of these organizations rely on large numbers of volunteers from all walks of life. ~~Doctors Without Borders won the Nobel Peace Prize several years ago.~~ Volunteers not only work in large international organizations, but they also donate their own time and money to local churches, schools, and youth centres. Our community refugee help centre could not function without the local high school students who regularly volunteer there.

5   Volunteers are increasingly necessary to create a kinder world. With powerfull communication technology, we see tragedy every day in our living rooms. Those volunteers from all walks of life who give their time and skills help to alleviate the suffering of others. As Martin Luther King, Jr., said, "Life's most persistent and urgent question is, what are you doing for others?"

PRACTICE 4

Revising

1. Highlight the thesis statement.

2. What type of definition does the thesis statement have? Circle the best answer.
    a. synonym   b. category   c. negation

3. Highlight the topic sentences in paragraphs 2 and 4.

4. What type of definition is in the topic sentence for paragraph 2? Circle your answer.
    a. synonym   b. category   c. negation

5. Paragraph 3 does not have a topic sentence. Which sentence would be an effective topic sentence for that paragraph? Circle the best answer.
    a. Oprah Winfrey is one of the most generous people in America.
    b. Many people reflect on the act of giving.
    c. Many poor people donate their time to charitable organizations.
    d. Volunteers are found in all social classes.

6. Cross out the sentence in paragraph 4 that does not support the topic sentence.

Editing

7. The quotation in the introductory paragraph is incorrectly punctuated. Underline and correct the error.

    ?"

    _____

    _____

8. Paragraph 3 has a fragment. Underline and correct the error.

   Correction: ___*Oprah, for example, spends*___

9. There is one spelling mistake in paragraph 5. Underline and correct the mistake.

   Correction: ___*powerful*___

GRAMMAR LINK

See the following chapters for more information about these grammar topics:
Fragments, Chapter 17
Spelling, Chapter 27
Quotations, Chapter 30

Writer's Desk Revise and Edit Your Essay

Revise and edit the essay that you wrote for the previous Writer's Desk. You can refer to the revising and editing checklists at the end of this chapter and on this book's inside covers.

A Professional Essay

Dorothy Nixon, a freelance writer, has written for *Salon.com*, *Chatelaine*, and *Today's Parent* magazine. In the following article, Nixon ponders the meaning of genius.

On Genius
by Dorothy Nixon

1   When Albert Einstein was chosen as *Time* magazine's Man of the Century, I was not surprised. Our society is simply obsessed with the idea of genius, and no man embodies that concept in this scientific age better than Albert Einstein, with his godlike grasp of mathematics and his messy mad-scientist hair.

2   Around the same time, a group of Canadian researchers were grabbing headlines. The researchers, while analyzing Einstein's brain, had discovered some extra connections in the famous physicist's grey matter. They theorized that Einstein's brain held the secret to the man's genius. "I held Einstein's brain, and I was in awe," said a researcher, revealing the fact that the research was not entirely objective on his part. After all, *awe* is usually a feeling reserved for religious experiences.

3   Rationally speaking, holding Einstein's brain cannot feel too differently from holding a chimp's brain or a Vegas chorus girl's brain.

Still, everyone understood what he meant: he was moved by the idea of Einstein's genius, which seems almost mystical in nature and therefore something to be "in awe of." The question remains, why were the scientists trying to quantify Einstein's genius by locating it somewhere in his brain in the first place? Genius is not quantifiable. Genius cannot be captured in a butterfly net or put in a bottle. Genius is not even that mysterious, really: it exists all around us, almost always in unrecognized form.

4   Societies tend to value some forms of genius over others. In the Renaissance, artists, sculptors, and architects were esteemed above all; in sixteenth century Vienna, musicians were revered; today, mathematicians and scientists are lauded. Da Vinci, Mozart, and Einstein arose from these environments.

nurtured:
encouraged

5   Genius has to be given a chance; it has to be **nurtured**. It has to be rigorously trained, too. (Remember, genius is one percent inspiration and ninety-nine percent perspiration, according to Thomas Edison.) Genius has to have good timing, or it is liable to be labeled lunacy. Above all, it has to be recognized for what it is.

6   A while back, I was sitting on the Montreal–Toronto train. To my dismay, the grandmotherly woman beside me wanted to talk. I don't normally like talking on trains, but within minutes I was truly mesmerized by the old woman's story. In broken English, the old woman told me about her life; how she had grown up in a poor country and spent only a few years in school; how she had eloped to Canada with a hardworking young man from her village; how she had helped out her husband with his landscaping business "doing the money part" until they had enough cash scraped together to buy a small apartment building. She told me how her husband had died soon thereafter and left her with three young boys, and how, with good business "luck" (for she had never remarried), she made enough money to put all her boys through graduate school. Indeed, she was on her way this minute to visit her youngest son and his wife, both law school professors.

7   She felt sorry for young people these days, she said. They were all so busy juggling careers and kids that they found it so hard to cope. That is why she often visited her sons' homes to help out. While there, she cooked all the meals, mostly Italian specialties (as she described them my mouth watered uncontrollably), and even whipped up some outfits for the kids.

8   By modern definitions, this woman was not a genius: she did not discover a new element or the reason the stars stay up in heaven. She had not even been to high school. But as I got off the train, I felt that I had been in the presence of someone very special; someone with extraordinary gifts who had lived and was continuing to live a full and balanced life.

9   If that is not pure genius, what is?

PRACTICE 5

1. Highlight the thesis statement of the essay.

2. According to the writer, what four things does genius need to flourish?

    Renaissance, artists, sculptors, and
    architects / Nurture, trained, good timing,
    and lunacy.

3. According to the writer, how has the definition of genius changed over time?

    Genelous in the past are Arts related,
    Genlus nowadays are Siends related

4. Highlight the topic sentence of paragraph 6. Remember that it may not always be the first sentence of the paragraph.

5. The old woman tells the writer her life story. What can you infer (conclude) about the old woman's personality from this tale?

    She is really courgeous, hardworky, and
    emotionally strong person.

6. The writer acknowledges that society recognizes Einstein as a genius. But why does the writer think that the old woman is also a good example of genius?

    She had lived and was continuing
    to live a full and balanced Life. / Taking
    care her children, and battled through diversity.

7. In paragraph 6, why does the author place quotation marks around "doing the money part" and "luck"?   _Understand?_

    It doesn't really because of Luck.
    She said is luck, the author does not.

The Writer's Room   **Topics for Definition Essays**

Writing Activity 1

Write a definition essay about any of the following topics, or choose your own topic.

General Topics

1. a soul mate
2. meltdown
3. a saint
4. family
5. a good sport

College and Work-Related Topics

6. teamwork
7. poor workplace communication
8. equal opportunity
9. good education
10. healthy competition

Writing Activity 2

Choose a quotation that you agree or disagree with, and then write a definition essay based on it.

> The deepest definition of youth is life as yet untouched by tragedy.
>
> —Alfred North Whitehead, mathematician

> The absence of flaw in beauty is itself a flaw.
>
> —Havelock Ellis, sexual psychologist

> The fearless are merely fearless. People who act in spite of their fear are truly brave.
>
> —James A. LaFond-Lewis, restaurateur

> A good hockey player plays where the puck is. A great hockey player plays where the puck is going to be.
>
> —Wayne Gretzky, former Canadian hockey player

Writing Activity 3

The Irish writer Oscar Wilde once said that all art is useless. Is art only paintings and sculptures, or does it also include folk art, advertising, music, writing, theatre, dance, and so on? Does art have to be original, or can it include something that is copied? Does the definition of art depend on a person's background, such as his or her ethnicity? Write an essay in which you define what art means to you.

READING LINK

Another Definition Reading
"Twixters" by Betsy Hart (p. 529)

WRITING LINK

More Definition Writing Topics
Chapter 23, Writer's Room topic 2 (page 380)
Chapter 29, Writer's Room topic 2 (page 455)

✓ **CHECKLIST: DEFINITION ESSAY**

As you write your definition essay, review the checklist on the inside front cover. Also ask yourself the following set of questions.

☐ Does my thesis statement contain a definition by synonym, category, or negation?

☐ Do I use concise language in my definition?

☐ Do I make a point in my thesis statement?

☐ Do all of my supporting paragraphs relate to the thesis statement?

☐ Do the body paragraphs contain enough supporting details that help define the term?

How Do I Get a Better Grade?

mycanadiancomplab

Go to www.mycanadiancomplab.ca for additional help with your grammar, writing, and research skills. You will have access to a variety of exercises, instruction, and video that will help you improve your basic skills and help you get a better grade.

Classification

CHAPTER 10

CONTENTS

Exploring
- What Is Classification?
- The Classification Essay
- Explore Topics

Developing
- The Thesis Statement
- The Supporting Ideas
- The Essay Plan
- The First Draft

Revising and Editing
- Revise and Edit a Classification Essay
- A Professional Essay: "Types of Correctional Officers" by Frank Schmalleger

To make it easier for shoppers, many shoe stores display footwear according to different styles and purposes, such as sandals, sneakers, and boots. Similarly, when writing a classification essay, you divide a topic into categories to help your readers understand your ideas.

Writers' Exchange

Work with a partner or group. Divide the following words into three or four different categories. What are the categories? Why did you choose those categories?

art	studio	medicine
construction	stethoscope	workshop
doctor	paintbrush	hospital
hammer	welder	sculptor

EXPLORING

What Is Classification?

When you classify, you sort a subject into more understandable categories. For instance, if a bookstore simply put books randomly on shelves, you would have a hard time finding the book that you need. Instead, the bookstore classifies according to subject area.

In classification writing, each of the categories must be part of a larger group, yet they must also be distinct. For example, you might write an essay about the most common types of hobbies and sort those into board games, sports, and crafts. Take a look at some ways people use classification in common situations.

Audience: Family member	**Audience: Classmate**	**Audience: Customer**
Your dirty laundry should be sorted in the following way.	Different labs on our campus are high-tech, quaint, and outdated.	Our beds come in three categories.
▪ Put the coloured clothing in the red basket.	▪ Our science lab has the latest technology.	▪ Innerspring mattresses have a variety of coil gauges and numbers of springs.
▪ Put your whites in the beige basket.	▪ The music lab is old, but quite beautiful and quaint.	▪ Air mattresses can be pumped for a softer or firmer feel.
▪ Put all bath towels in the green bin by the door.	▪ The language lab is outdated, and the audio needs to be upgraded to digital.	▪ Foam beds may be made from polyurethane foam, memory foam, or latex.

The Classification Essay

To find a topic for a classification essay, think of something that you can sort or divide into different groups. Also, determine a reason for classifying the items. When you are planning your ideas for a classification essay, remember the following points.

1. **Use a common classification principle.**
   A **classification principle** is the overall method that you use to sort the subject into categories. To find the classification principle, think about one common characteristic that unites the different categories. For example, if your subject is "jobs," your classification principle might be any of the following:

   ▪ jobs in which people work with their hands
   ▪ dangerous jobs
   ▪ outsourced jobs

2. **Sort the subject into distinct categories.**
A classification essay should have two or more categories.

Topic: jobs

Classification principle: dangerous jobs

Category 1
public security jobs

Category 2
construction jobs

Category 3
hazardous materials jobs

 **Categories Should Not Overlap**

When sorting a topic into categories, make sure that the categories do not overlap. For example, you would not classify *roommates* into aloof, friendly, and messy because a messy roommate could also be aloof or friendly. Although the categories share something in common, each category should be distinct.

Classification at Work

Ahmad Bishr is a web design consultant. In the following excerpt from an email to a client, he makes suggestions about classifying a website.

The second thing you need to do is decide how to divide your site. The opening page should contain only the most pertinent information about the cottage you are trying to rent. For instance, include the number of rooms, the location, the most spectacular traits of the cottage, and so on. Each subcategory will become a link. Because you are trying to rent your cottage, I suggest that one link contain photos of the interior, with details about each room. You will also need a link that includes a rental calendar and rates. A fourth section might contain information about local attractions. Remember that too many categories will confuse the viewer. You'll want a simple, uncluttered site. Keep the divisions down to four or five pages at the most.

A Student Essay

Read the student essay and answer the questions that follow.

Heroes
by Diego Pelaez

1   The word "hero" comes from the Greek word *heros*, which means a person of superhuman ability. *Webster's Dictionary* defines a hero as a person "admired for courage, fortitude, prowess, nobility, etc." Certainly, heroes come in many forms throughout a person's life. Somewhere out there, there is always a model, real or fictional, that drives people to better themselves and gives them the dream of being heroic. The three general ideas of a hero that most people embrace are the fictional superhero, the sports or media hero and, finally, the practical hero.

2   The dominant heroes of childhood are fictional superheroes. Action figures represent these titans and are the absolute blueprint for the average young person. Be they on television, in comic books, or in children's movies, characters such as Batman, Superman, and Spiderman usually dominate the imaginations of youngsters. It is common to see children blazing down the street wearing the capes of their idols. Thankfully, the female crowd has gotten away from Barbie; female action heroes such as Buffy the Vampire Slayer and Sydney Bristow from *Alias* are models of strength for young girls. These heroes defy the laws of physics and are capable of superhuman feats that any child dreams of.

3   However, as time wears on, children outgrow the superhero phase and idolize another form of superior humans: celebrities. With the information age, celebrities are **ubiquitous**. The internet, television, newspapers, and magazines feature images of athletes, singers, and movie stars, providing them with more exposure than they could have ever possibly wanted. Thus, the superhero stage is followed by the "I want to be famous" stage, where adolescents start trying to shoot like Steve Nash, act like Paul Gross, or sing like Sarah McLachlan. A good example is the unbelievable amount of worldwide acclaim for soccer player David Beckham; some nations have even erected statues in his image. These people are superheroes who make the game-winning shot on a basketball court, kill the bad guy on film, or perform on stage in front of thousands of screaming fans.

4   Alas, for the vast majority of people, there will come a day when fantasies of fame must give way to more realistic goals. Along with these goals come more practical, real-life heroes. Teachers, although they sometimes get a bad reputation, are heroes to far more people than they realize. Many teachers become mentors to their pupils, providing guidance

ubiquitous:
everywhere

and inspiration. Young adults also look to inspirational figures in their field; thus, an aspiring journalist might idolize a writer from the local paper. Of course, most people, as they grow older, realize that the most potent figures in their lives are those family members—parents, grandparents, siblings, aunts, or uncles—who have guided them and been compelling role models.

5   Heroes fill people with a sense of their own possibilities. Children think they are indestructible, and this attitude is reflected in larger-than-life heroes who always seem to achieve the impossible. However, with the passage of time, goals become more realistic and so do definitions of heroes. Heroes drive children to dream of the impossible, and heroes encourage young adults to strive toward an ideal.

PRACTICE 1

1. Highlight the thesis statement.

2. Highlight the topic sentence in each body paragraph.

3. State the three categories that the writer discusses and list some details about each category.

   a. _____ Common ____ heros _____

   Details: _____ actro ____ action figure ___ en ___

   _____

   b. _____ Celebrus . superior people in society ___

   Details: _____ are ubiquitous . movie stars. ___

   _____

   c. _____ (categor) real-life heros. ___

   Details: _____ real-life heros is teachers ___

   _____

4. Which introductory style does this essay use? Circle your answer.

   a. anecdote   c. historical

   b. definition   d. opposing position

Explore Topics

In the Writer's Desk Warm Up, you will try an exploring strategy to generate ideas about different topics.

Writer's Desk **Warm Up**

Read the following questions, and write the first ideas that come to your mind. Think of two to three ideas for each topic.

EXAMPLE: What are some types of lawbreakers?

—petty thieves (pickpockets, scam artists)

—people who break traffic laws

—violent criminals like carjackers and terrorists

1. What are some different categories of families?

— Traditional families. (Nuclear)

— Single-Parent families

— Pink families

2. What are some different types of shoppers?

Bargain shoppers (hereditary stuff)

Impulse shoppers

Smart Shoppers

3. When an election comes around, people act in different ways. What are some categories of political responses?

Positive response

Negative response

Unconcerned response

Uninterested

Making a Classification Chart

A **classification chart** is a visual representation of a main topic and its categories. Making a classification chart can help you to identify the categories more clearly so that you will be able to write more exact thesis statements.

When you classify items, remember to use a single method of classification and a common classification principle to sort the items. For example, you could classify friends according to the length of time you have known them. You could also classify friends according to the activities you do with them or the places where you met them.

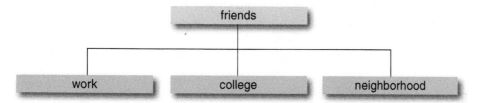

Classification Principle: places to make friends

You can also use a pie chart to help you classify items.

Places to Meet Friends

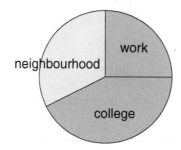

Hint   **Categories Versus Examples**

When you are trying to find a topic for a classification essay, don't simply list examples. Each category of items should have subcategories. The following lists are for an essay about the physical and psychological benefits of playing certain sports. In the list of examples, the sports are all active team sports, so the advantages in each sport would be similar. In the second list of categories, each type of sport has particular benefits.

Topic: sports
Classification principle: physical and psychological benefits

List of examples	**Categories**
football	solo sports
baseball	pair sports
hockey	team sports

PRACTICE 2   In the following classification charts, a subject has been broken down into distinct categories. The items in the group should have the same classification principle. Cross out one item in each group that does not belong. Then write down the classification principle that unites the group.

EXAMPLE:

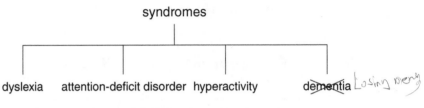

syndromes

dyslexia   attention-deficit disorder   hyperactivity   ~~dementia~~ Losing memory

Classification principle: _childhood learning disorders_

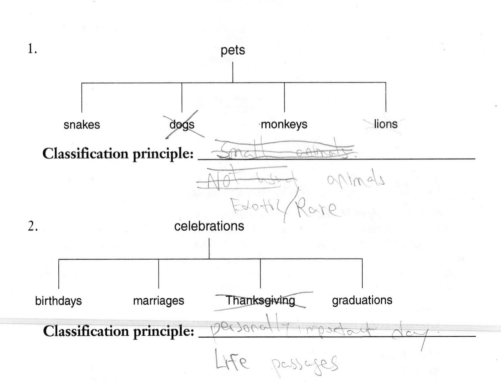

1.

pets

snakes   ~~dogs~~   monkeys   lions

Classification principle: ~~Small animals~~

~~Not used~~ animals
Exotic/Rare

2.

celebrations

birthdays   marriages   ~~Thanksgiving~~   graduations

Classification principle: ~~personally important day~~
Life passages

3.

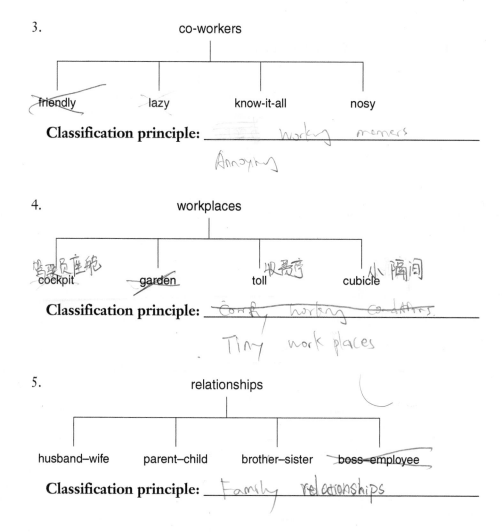

co-workers

~~friendly~~ · lazy · know-it-all · nosy

Classification principle: _____ Working manners _____

Annoying

4.

workplaces

苗驾及准驰 cockpit · ~~garden~~ · 收费亭 toll · cubicle 小隔间

Classification principle: ~~Comf. working conditions.~~

Tiny work places

5.

relationships

husband–wife · parent–child · brother–sister · ~~boss–employee~~

Classification principle: Family relationships

Hint **Make a Point**

To write interesting classification essays, try to express an attitude, opinion, or feeling about the topic. For example, in an essay about discipline, your classification principle might be types of discipline methods; however, the essay needs to inform readers of something specific about those methods. You could write about discipline methods that are most effective, least effective, ethical, unethical, violent, non-violent, and so on.

Writer's Desk **Find Distinct Categories**

Break down the following topics into three distinct categories. Remember to find categories that do not overlap. You can look for ideas in the Writer's Desk Warm Up on page 164.

EXAMPLE:

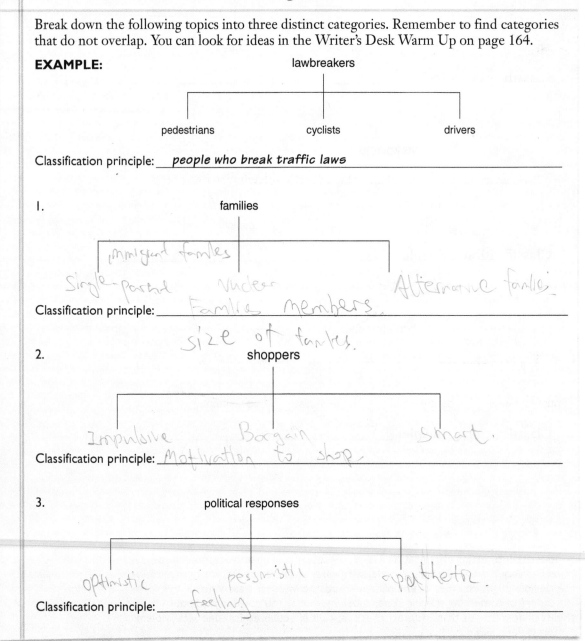

lawbreakers

pedestrians   cyclists   drivers

Classification principle: *people who break traffic laws*

1.   families

immigrant families

Single-parent   Nuclear   Alternative families

Classification principle: _Families members_

size of familes.

2.   shoppers

Impulsive   Bargain   Smart.

Classification principle: _Motivation to shop_

3.   political responses

Optimistic   pessimistic   apathetic.

feeling

Classification principle: _____

DEVELOPING

The Thesis Statement

The thesis statement in a classification essay clearly indicates what you will classify. It also includes the controlling idea, which is the classification principle that you will use.

> Several types of co-workers can completely destroy a workplace environment.

You can also mention the types of categories in your thesis statement.

> Nosy, lazy, and know-it-all coworkers can completely destroy a workplace environment.

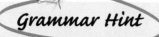 **Grammar Hint** **Parallel Structure**

Use parallel structure when words or phrases are joined in a series.

Some annoying sales methods include <u>calling customers on the phone</u>, <u>putting</u>

~~leaving~~
<u>popup ads on the internet</u>, and <s>when people leave</s> leaving <u>flyers on car windows</u>.

See Chapter 19 for more information about parallel structure.

Criminals.

Corrupt leaders

Online criminals

Terrorists

Writer's Desk   Write Thesis Statements

Write clear thesis statements. You can refer to your ideas in previous Writer's Desks. Remember that your thesis statement can include the different categories you will be discussing.

EXAMPLE: Topic: lawbreakers

Thesis Statement: *Pedestrians, cyclists, and drivers regularly break the rules of the road.*

1. Topic: family

   Thesis statement: _Immigrant, nuclear, and alternative families are the main ingredients of families._

2. Topic: shoppers

   Thesis statement: _Shoppers can be divided into three types of families, impulsive, bargain, and smart shoppers._

3. Topic: political responses

   Thesis statement: _Optimistic, pessimistic, and apathetic feelings are three main responses to politics._

The Supporting Ideas

After you have developed an effective thesis statement, generate supporting ideas. In a classification essay, you can list details about each of your categories.

- Use prewriting strategies to generate examples for each category.
- Choose the best ideas.
- Organize your ideas. Choose the best organizational method for this essay pattern.

One way to visualize your categories and your supporting ideas is to make a detailed classification chart. Break down the main topic into several categories, and then list supporting ideas for each category.

Most davastcty crimirels.

political.

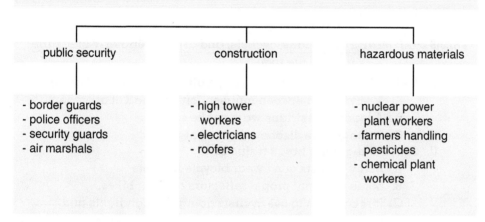

The public should be grateful to those who perform dangerous jobs in three particular areas.

public security	construction	hazardous materials
- border guards - police officers - security guards - air marshals	- high tower workers - electricians - roofers	- nuclear power plant workers - farmers handling pesticides - chemical plant workers

Writer's Desk **Develop Supporting Ideas**

Choose one of the thesis statements from the Writer's Desk on page 170, and list supporting ideas.

Thesis statement: _____

The Essay Plan

Before you write a classification essay, make a detailed essay plan. Add supporting details for each category.

THESIS STATEMENT: <u>Pedestrians, cyclists, and drivers regularly break the rules of the road.</u>

   I. Pedestrians are supposed to obey traffic rules, but most do not.
      A. Many cross between intersections instead of at corners.
      B. A lot of pedestrians walk on the road.
      C. Some people disobey walking signals.
  II. Cyclists regularly break traffic laws.
      A. Many cyclists don't wear bicycle helmets.
      B. Some don't put proper reflectors on their bikes.
      C. It is common to see cyclists going through lights and stop signs.
 III. Drivers are the most dangerous lawbreakers.
      A. Speeding is common on roads and highways.
      B. Some people drive on the shoulders of roads.
      C. Many drivers disobey traffic signs.
      D. There are even drivers who go the wrong way on one-way streets.

Writer's Desk   **Make an Essay Plan**

Refer to the information you generated in previous Writer's Desks, and prepare a detailed essay plan. Arrange the supporting details in a logical order.

The First Draft

After you outline your ideas in a plan, you are ready to write the first draft. Weave together the ideas you have in your essay plan. Remember to write complete sentences and to include transitional words or expressions to help your ideas flow smoothly. Here are some transitions that can help you express which category is most important and to signal a movement from one category to the next.

To show importance
above all
clearly
most of all
the most important
particularly

To show types of categories
one kind . . . another kind
the first/second kind
the first/second type
the last category

Writer's Desk **Write the First Draft**

Carefully review the classification essay plan you prepared in the previous Writer's Desk and make any necessary changes. Then, write the first draft of your classification essay.

REVISING AND EDITING

Revise and Edit a Classification Essay

When you finish writing a classification essay, carefully review your work and revise it to make sure that the categories do not overlap. Check to make sure that you have organized your essay logically, and remove any irrelevant details. Before you work on your own essay, practise revising and editing a student essay.

A Student Essay

Read the essay, and then answer the questions that follow. As you read, correct any errors that you find, and make comments in the margins.

Breaking Traffic Laws
by Lonzell Courtney

1   Ask most people, and they will insist they are law-abiding. Dig a little deeper, though, and the hidden criminal emerges. Stand on any street corner for a few hours, and you probably will observe all types of people breaking traffic laws. Pedestrians, cyclists, and drivers regularly break the rules of the road.

2   There are many traffic laws that pedestrians ignore. For example, jaywalking. When people arrive at a crossing with traffic lights, they are supposed to wait for the walk signal. They should also cross the street at corners and proper crossings, and they should not walk on the road. Yet most people be breaking these rules. Armando Guzman, an exterminator

break

from Vancouver, is an unapologetic jaywalker. When ~~him~~ *he* and I go for a walk, he crosses between intersections rather than make the long walk to the corner. Kate Shapiro, a hairdresser, admits that she always crosses when the "Don't Walk" signal is blinking if there is no traffic. "It is ridiculous to wait when I know I can cross safely," she argues. ~~Some pedestrians are also very rude. They push through crowds, knock people over, and are basically very unpleasant.~~

3   Cyclists also disrespect traffic laws. For example, many municipalities have bicycle helmet laws, but citizens regularly flout the law and drive with bare heads. In all provinces, bicycles must be equipped with reflectors, but many cyclists do not bother getting them. Other rules of the road apply to cyclists, yet they regularly plow past stop signs or zoom through red lights. Most unpleasant are the cyclists who speed along busy sidewalks even though that is illegal. Thus, most cyclists are lawbreakers, too.

4   Drivers, of course, are the ~~worse~~ *worst* offenders. They can harm or even kill others, yet virtually every driver has occasionally broken a traffic law. Who hasn't gone over the speed limit, for example? Many people believe that the maximum speed limit sign generally means, "I can go ten or fifteen miles per hour over that limit." Drivers also change lanes without signalling, they drive on the shoulder to pass slow traffic, and they allow children to ride without seatbelts. In 2006, Britney Spears famously placed her infant on her lap while driving. Of course, if she ~~would have~~ *had* known about the subsequent scandal, she might have acted differently.

5   Most lawbreakers are unrepentant, and some of them have original excuses for ignoring traffic rules. They claim that everyone else does it. Some people condemn seatbelt and helmet laws as infringements on their rights.

PRACTICE 3

Revising

1. Highlight the thesis statement.

2. In paragraph 2, one of the examples is not a valid support. Cross it out. Explain why it is not valid. _It is not related to law breaking._

3. This essay does not have a concluding sentence. Write a concluding sentence here. _Three types of traffic law breakers are pedestrians, cyclists, and drivers. feel they know more than others, the law of traffic will continue be broken._

Editing

4. A fragment lacks a subject or a verb and is an incomplete sentence. Underline one fragment in paragraph 2. Then write a correct sentence here.

   Correction: _For example, jaywalking is a_ _____

5. Paragraph 2 contains a verb-tense error. Underline the error and correct it.

   Correction: _____ People are breaking these rules. ____

6. The writer uses a pronoun incorrectly in paragraph 2. Underline and correct the error.

   Correction: _____ ~~people~~ He _____

7. In paragraph 4, there is an error with the superlative form of an adjective. Underline the error and correct it.

   Correction: _____ Worst _____

8. In paragraph 4, there is an error with conditional forms (*if . . . would*). Underline the error and correct it.

   Correction: _____ ~~she would act differently~~ _____
   If she had known.

GRAMMAR LINK

See the following chapters for more information about these grammar topics:
Fragments, Chapter 17
Verb Tenses, Chapter 22
Conditionals, Chapter 23
Adjectives, Chapter 25
Pronouns, Chapter 26

---

vo•cab•u•lar•y BOOST

Writers commonly overuse the same vocabulary. To make your writing more vivid and interesting, look at your first draft and underline at least ten repeated nouns and verbs. (Remember that a noun is a person, place, or thing.) Then add details or specific descriptions to five of the nouns and write more vivid verbs. Here is a brief example of how you might avoid repetition of nouns and verbs.

Dull, repetitive:	Patrice likes cycling. Patrice often cycles to work at his bookstore. Often Patrice is reckless and cycles without a helmet.
Detailed, uses synonyms:	**Patrice** likes **cycling** and **commutes** to work on his **bike**. Although **the thirty-year-old bookstore owner** knows better, **he** often **recklessly rides** without a helmet.

Writer's Desk Revise and Edit Your Essay

Revise and edit the essay that you wrote for the previous Writer's Desk. You can refer to the revising and editing checklists at the end of this chapter and on this book's inside covers.

A Professional Essay

Frank Schmalleger is director of the Justice Research Association, a private consulting firm that focuses on issues relating to crime and justice. The following excerpt is from his book *Criminal Justice Today*.

Types of Correctional Officers
by Frank Schmalleger

1   Prison staff culture, in combination with naturally occurring personality types, gives rise to a diversity of officer types. Correction staff can be classified according to certain distinguishing characteristics. Among the most prevalent types are the dictator, the friend, the merchant, the turnkey, the climber, and the reformer.

The Dictator

2   Some officers go by the book; others go beyond it, using prison rules to reinforce their own brand of discipline. The guard who demands signs of inmate subservience, from constant use of the word *sir* or *ma'am* to frequent free shoeshines, is one type of dictator. Another goes beyond legality, beating or "macing" inmates even for minor infractions or perceived insults. Dictator guards are bullies.

3   Dictator guards may have sadistic personalities and gain ego satisfaction through feelings of near omnipotence, which come from the total control of others. Some may be fundamentally insecure and employ a false bravado to hide their fear of inmates. Officers who fit the dictator category are the most likely to be targeted for vengeance should control of the institution temporarily fall into the hands of the inmates.

The Friend

4   Friendly officers try to fraternize with inmates. They approach the issue of control by trying to be "one of the guys." They seem to believe that they can win inmate cooperation by being nice. Unfortunately, such guards do not recognize that fraternization quickly leads to unending requests for special favors—from delivering mail to bending "minor" prison rules. Once a few rules have been bent, the officer may find that inmates have the upper hand through the potential for blackmail.

5   Many officers have amiable relationships with inmates. In most cases, however, affability is only a convenience that both sides recognize can quickly evaporate. "Friendly officers," as the term is being used here, are *overly* friendly. They may be young and inexperienced. On the other

hand, they may simply be possessed of kind and idealistic personalities built on successful friendships in free society.

The Merchant

6   Contraband could not exist in any correctional facility without the merchant officer. The merchant participates in the inmate economy, supplying drugs, pornography, alcohol, and sometimes even weapons to inmates who can afford to pay for them.

7   Probably only a very few officers consistently perform the role of merchant, although a far larger proportion may occasionally turn a few dollars by smuggling some item through the gate. Low salaries create the potential for mercantile corruption among many otherwise "straight-arrow" officers. Until salaries rise substantially, the merchant will remain an institutionalized feature of most prisons.

The Turnkey

8   The turnkey officer cares little for what goes on in the prison setting. Officers who fit this category may be close to retirement, or they may be alienated from their jobs for various reasons. Low pay, the view that inmates are basically "worthless" and incapable of changing, and the monotonous ethic of "doing time" all combine to numb the professional consciousness of even young officers.

9   The term *turnkey* comes from prison argot where it means a guard who is there just to open and shut doors and who cares about nothing other than getting through his or her shift. Inmates do not see the turnkey as a threat, nor is such an officer likely to challenge the status quo in institutions where merchant guards operate.

The Climber

10   The climber is apt to be a young officer with an eye for promotion. Nothing seems impossible to the climber, who probably hopes eventually to be warden or program director or to hold some high-status position within the institutional hierarchy. Climbers are likely to be involved in schooling, correspondence courses, and professional organizations. They may lead a movement toward unionization for correctional personnel and tend to see the guard's role as a profession that should receive greater social recognition.

11   Climbers have many ideas. They may be heavily involved in reading about the latest confinement or administrative technology. If so, they will

suggest many ways to improve prison routine, often to the consternation of complacent staff members. Like the turnkey, climbers turn a blind eye toward inmates and their problems. They are more concerned with improving institutional procedures and with their own careers than they are with the treatment or day-to-day control of inmates.

The Reformer

12   The reformer is the "do-gooder" among officers, the person who believes that prison should offer opportunities for personal change. The reformer tends to lend a sympathetic ear to the personal needs of inmates and is apt to offer armchair counseling and suggestions. Many reformers are motivated by personal ideals, and some of them are highly religious. Inmates tend to see the reformer guard as naive but harmless. Because the reformer actually tries to help, even when help is unsolicited, he or she is the most likely of all the guard types to be accepted by prisoners.

13   Correctional officers have generally been accorded low occupational status. Historically, the role of prison guard required minimal formal education and held few opportunities for professional growth and career advancement. Such jobs were typically low paying, frustrating, and often boring. Growing problems in our nation's prisons, including emerging issues of legal liability, however, increasingly require a well-trained and adequately equipped force of professionals. As correctional personnel have become better trained and more proficient, the old concept of guard has been supplanted by that of correctional officer. Thus, many states and a growing number of large-city correctional systems make efforts to eliminate individuals with potentially harmful personality characteristics from correctional officer applicant pools.

PRACTICE 4

1. What is the topic of this essay? _Correctional officers._

2. What are the main characteristics of the following types of guards?
   a. the dictator _Bullies, Despires_

   _____

   b. the friend _Nice, inexperiecned, successful friend._

   c. the merchant _~~Town Shop~~ Making Money_

   _____

  d. the turnkey _Close to retirement_

    _____

  e. the climber _Young teenagers with an eye for promotion_
  Want to improve institutional procedures

  f. the reformer _High religion_

    _____

3. What is the writer's purpose? Circle your answer. _C_
  a. to entertain   b. to persuade   c. to inform

4. Consider the order in which the guards are listed. Think of another effective way to organize the guards, and list them in order here.

  Organizational method: _Close to prisoners or not._

  a. _The Dictator_ c. _The climber_ e. _The Merchant_

  b. _The Friend_ d. _The Turkey_ f. _The Reformer_

The Writer's Room   Topics for Classification Essays

READING LINK

Another Classification Reading

"Living Environments," by Avi Friedman (page 503)

Writing Activity 1

Choose any of the following topics, or choose your own topic, and write a classification essay. Determine your classification principle and ensure that your categories do not overlap.

General Topics

Types of . . .

1. computer games
2. politicians
3. living arrangements
4. siblings
5. punishment

College and Work-Related Topics

Types of . . .

6. electronic modes of communication
7. procrastination techniques
8. success
9. risks
10. work spaces

WRITING LINK

More Classification Writing Topics

Chapter 20, Writer's Room topic 2 (page 332)
Chapter 24, Writer's Room topic 2 (page 390)
Chapter 30, Writer's Room topic 2 (page 469)

Writing Activity 2

Choose a quotation that you agree or disagree with, or one that inspires you, and then write a classification essay based on it.

Canada is the homeland of equality, justice and tolerance.
—Kim Campbell, Canada's nineteenth prime minister

There are really only three types of people: those who make things happen, those who watch things happen, and those who say, "What happened?"
—Ann Landers, advice columnist

The wit makes fun of other persons; the satirist makes fun of the world; the humorist makes fun of himself.
—James Thurber, author

I'll keep it short and sweet—family, religion, and friendship. These are the three demons you must slay if you wish to succeed in business.
—Matt Groening, creator of *The Simpsons*

Writing Activity 3

Examine this photo of the man doing tai chi, and think about some classification topics. For example, you might write about types of athletes, attitudes toward exercise, fitness programs, places to work out, or healthy activities. Determine a classification principle and then follow the writing process to write a classification essay.

CHECKLIST: CLASSIFICATION ESSAY

After you write your classification essay, review the checklist on the inside front cover. Also, ask yourself these questions.

☐ Does my thesis statement explain the categories that I will discuss?

☐ Do I use a common classification principle to unite the various items?

☐ Do I offer sufficient details to explain each category?

☐ Do I arrange the categories in a logical manner?

☐ Does all of the supporting information relate to the categories that I am discussing?

☐ Do I include categories that do not overlap?

How Do I Get a Better Grade?

mycanadiancomplab

Go to www.mycanadiancomplab.ca for additional help with your grammar, writing, and research skills. You will have access to a variety of exercises, instruction, and video that will help you improve your basic skills and help you get a better grade.

11
CHAPTER

Comparison and Contrast

When you plan to move to a new place, you compare the features of different houses or apartments to help you make a decision. When you write a comparison and contrast essay, you examine two or more items or issues to help yourself and your readers make conclusions about them.

Writers' Exchange

What were your goals as a child? What are your goals as an adult? Think about work, money, and family. Compare your answers with a partner, and discuss how childhood goals are different from adult goals.

What Is Comparison and Contrast?

When you want to decide between options, you compare and contrast. You **compare** to find similarities and **contrast** to find differences. The exercise of comparing and contrasting can help you make judgments about things. It can also help you to better understand familiar things. The following examples show comparisons and contrasts people might use in everyday situations.

" I know not anything more pleasant, or more instructive, than to compare experience with expectation, or to register from time to time the difference between idea and reality. It is by this kind of observation that we grow daily. "

Samuel Johnson, *writer*

Audience: Family member	Audience: Another student	Audience: Customer
A laptop is more sensible than a desktop computer.	The summer course is easier than the fall course.	Our product is better than the competitor's product.

Audience: Family member

A laptop is more sensible than a desktop computer.

- The desk is small and a laptop takes less space than a desktop computer.
- Modern laptops have screens that are just as large and clear as many desktop monitors.
- Unlike a clunky desktop computer, we can easily transport a laptop to other rooms or to school or work.

Audience: Another student

The summer course is easier than the fall course.

- The summer course lasts for three weeks and the material is condensed, so there is less homework.
- The fall course has more reading and writing homework.
- The summer course has fewer students, so you can get more help if you need it.
- The fall course has large groups, so if you don't understand something, it is difficult to get help.

Audience: Customer

Our product is better than the competitor's product.

- Our product is less expensive than the competitor's.
- Our product is smaller and easier to use.
- The competition does not offer a rebate.
- The competition does not offer a variety of colours and sizes.

The Comparison and Contrast Essay

In a comparison and contrast essay, you can compare and contrast two different subjects, or you can compare and contrast different aspects of a single subject. When you write using this essay pattern, remember to think about your specific purpose.

- Your purpose could be to make judgments about two things. For example, you might compare and contrast two cars to convince your readers that one is preferable.
- Your purpose could be to describe or understand two familiar things. For example, you might compare two movies to help your readers understand their thematic similarities.

Comparison and Contrast at Work

Eric Hollymead works in public relations. In the following memo, he compares two job candidates. To respect each person's privacy, he has numbered the candidates.

Although both candidates have the required education, I suggest that we go with Candidate 1. Her experience is more relevant to this industry. I also believe she will be a better fit for the sales department because her energy level is high, and she seems like a real team player. Candidate 2, although highly competent, is less experienced in sales. He was quite nervous in the interview, and I sense he may be less at ease with clients. On the other hand, his questions were thoughtful, and he seemed interested in the business. I also appreciated his sense of humour. Perhaps we should keep his resumé on file should we have future positions that are more suitable to his skills.

Comparison and Contrast Patterns

Comparison and contrast essays follow two common patterns.

Point by Point   Present one point about Topic A and then one point about Topic B. Keep following this pattern until you have a few points for each topic. Go back and forth from one side to the other like tennis players hitting a ball back and forth across a net.

Topic by Topic   Present all of your points about one topic, and then present all of your points about the second topic. Offer one side and then the other side, just as opposing lawyers would do in the closing arguments of a court case.

Marina's Example

Marina is trying to decide whether she would prefer a part-time job in a clothing store or in a restaurant. Marina can organize her information using a topic-by-topic pattern or a point-by-point method.

Thesis Statement: <u>The clothing store is a better place to work than the restaurant.</u>

Point-by-Point Comparison	Topic-by-Topic Comparison

Point-by-Point Comparison

Topic sentence: Salaries
    Job A
    Job B

Topic sentence: Working hours
    Job A
    Job B

Topic sentence: Working environments
    Job A
    Job B

Topic-by-Topic Comparison

Topic sentence: Job A
- salary
- hours
- working environment

Topic sentence: Job B
- salary
- hours
- working environment

A Student Essay

Read the student essay and answer the questions that follow.

Working Life
by Alfonso Castillo Zavas

1   My uncle Cayetano spent the first thirty years of his life in Mexico City. When he moved to Canada, he rented a room in our house, and he tried to get used to life in Toronto. Many evenings, my uncle told stories about his workplace, and he reminisced about his younger days when he was an office worker in Mexico City. We realized that the workplace culture is more relaxed in Canada than it is in Mexico.

2   One noticeable difference between the two nations is the attitude about arrivals and departures of employees. In the 1980s, my uncle Cayetano worked as an accountant for a company in Mexico City. He was supposed to arrive at 8:00 a.m. each morning, but he was often late. He ran from the subway station to the door of the office building, hoping to arrive before 8:30 a.m., which was the time that the doors were locked for the day. Guards at the door ensured that employees arrived and left at the proper time. Local street vendors encouraged my uncle, yelling "Correle" when they saw him sprinting past. Every three months, his pay was docked because three late days counted for an absence. When my uncle came to Toronto in 1992, he found a job with a computer company. The first thing he noticed was that there were no guards at the doors of his workplace. Attendance at work depended on an honour system. Employees were only accountable to their immediate superiors. My uncle learned to be punctual

not because of a guard locking a door, but because he wanted to complete his work in the amount of time allotted to him.

3   Another major difference in work cultures is mealtimes. In Mexico, there is no concept of lunch. Instead, most people eat the main meal, the "comida," at around 2:00 p.m. When my uncle worked for a Mexican company, he took a two-hour break for his main meal. In the cafeteria, he often had a plate filled with meat, rice, beans, avocados, and chili peppers, and a side dish filled with warm tortillas. After his meal, he returned to work from 4:00 to 6:00 p.m. Later, when he arrived at home, he ate a small snack. In his Toronto job, he became acquainted with the lunch hour, which was earlier than he was used to. He learned that lunch is not the time to have a large meal; instead, most employees just have a bland sandwich or soup. He also learned that Canadians finish work by 4:00 or 5:00 p.m. and then eat their main meal between 6:00 and 8:00 p.m. So Canadians have a longer and more relaxed evening. In Mexico, my uncle had to work much later in the day and was quite tired when he finally got home from the office.

4   The most visible distinction between Mexican and Canadian workplaces is the level of formal dress in the workplace. Although Mexican dress codes are becoming slightly more relaxed, men in most offices and banks wear suits and ties, and women wear suit jackets, skirts, pantyhose, and heels. My aunt Lucia, who lives in Mexico City, never goes to work without manicured nails, makeup, and a very nice outfit. When my uncle Cayetano received his job in Toronto, he starched his shirt collar, put on a tie, and ensured that his shoes were shiny. He was surprised to see that some of his co-workers wore baggy casual trousers and even sneakers. Very few co-workers wore dress shirts, with most wearing polo shirts. He quickly learned that people dress nicely at his office in Canada, but much less formally than workers at his Mexican workplace.

5   When immigrants come to a new country, they must get used to food, eating times, dress codes, and workplace rules that may be very different from those they encountered in their native countries. While they adjust to the differences, they are sometimes judged. My uncle said that co-workers didn't understand why he always shined his shoes, and for a while his nickname was "shiny." When a new immigrant arrives in your workplace, show tolerance and respect for cultural differences.

PRACTICE I

1. Highlight the thesis statement.

2. Highlight the topic sentence in each body paragraph.

3. What pattern of comparison does the writer follow in the entire essay?
   a. point by point   b. topic by topic

4. What pattern of comparison does the writer follow in body paragraphs 2, 3, and 4?

   a. point by point   b. topic by topic

5. Using your own words, sum up the main subjects in this essay.

   Paragraph 2: _____

   Paragraph 3: _____

   Paragraph 4: _____

6. What does this essay mainly focus on? Circle the correct answer.

   a. similarities   b. differences

7. Underline transitional words or phrases that link ideas between body paragraphs.

8. How does the writer organize his arguments?

   a. time order   b. space order   c. emphatic order

---

vo•cab•u•lar•y BOOST

In the student essay "Working Life," the writer uses the terms *accountable* and *accountant* in paragraph 2. The root word—or base word for those terms is *count*. Prefixes and suffixes alter a word's meaning and are added to the root word. Prefixes appear at the beginning of a root word; suffixes appear at the end. Here are some examples.

Prefixes	Examples	Suffixes	Examples
anti = against	antiwar	*able* = ability	understandable
bi = two	bilingual	*al* = pertaining to	physical
hyper = excessive	hypersensitive	*dom* = a quality or state	freedom
il = not	illegal	*ful* = filled with	respectful
inter = between	interfaith	*ism* = belief	communism
mis = wrong	misspell	*ist* = practitioner	scientist
multi = many	multifunctional	*ive* = tends toward	regressive
pre = before	prenatal	*less* = without	helpless
re = again	rebirth	*ment* = condition	argument
un = not	unfaithful	*ness* = state of being	happiness

   Brainstorm at least three variations of the following root words by using various prefixes and suffixes. Keep in mind that the previous list is not complete. There may be other prefixes or suffixes that you can think of.

1. use

2. act

3. social

Explore Topics

In the Writer's Desk Warm Up, you will try an exploring strategy to generate ideas about different topics.

Writer's Desk **Warm Up**

Read the following questions, and write the first ideas that come to your mind. Think of two to three ideas for each topic.

EXAMPLE: What are some key differences between girls' and boys' toys?

girls' toys	boys' toys
—pastel colours	—noisy
—stuffed animals	—toy cars, trucks, fire engines
—dolls with clothes	—action figures

1. What were your fears when you were a child? What are your current fears?

childhood fears	current fears

2. What are the key features of your generation and your parents' generation?

your generation	your parents' generation

3. How are your actions and appearance different in your public and private life?

public life	private life

DEVELOPING

The Thesis Statement

In a comparison and contrast essay, the thesis statement indicates what you are comparing and contrasting, and it expresses a controlling idea. For example, the following thesis statement indicates that the essay will compare the myths and reality of mould to prove that it does not seriously threaten human health.

Common household mould is not as dangerous as many people believe.

PRACTICE 2   Read each thesis statement, and then answer the
questions that follow. State whether the essay would focus on similarities or
differences.

1. The weather in our region is more extreme than it was in the past.
    a. What is being compared?   _____
    b. What is the controlling idea?   _____
    c. What will the essay focus on?   _____ similarities   _____ differences

2. Students need technical courses as well as academic courses for a well-
    rounded education.
    a. What is being compared?   _____
    b. What is the controlling idea?   _____
    c. What will the essay focus on?   _____ similarities   _____ differences

3. Before marriage, people expect to feel eternally lustful toward their "soul
    mate," but the reality of married life is quite different.
    a. What is being compared?   _____
    b. What is the controlling idea?   _____

                                         _____
    c. What will the essay focus on?   _____ similarities   _____ differences

 **Grammar Hint**   **Comparing Adjectives and Adverbs**

When comparing or contrasting two items, ensure that you have correctly
written your comparative forms. For instance, never put *more* with an adjective
ending in *-er*.

    City life is ~~more~~ better than country life.

If you are comparing two actions, remember to use an adverb instead of an adjective.

                        more easily
    Children learn lessons ~~easier~~ when they are treated with respect.

See Chapter 25 for more information about making comparisons with adjectives
and adverbs.

Writer's Desk **Write Thesis Statements**

For each topic, write a thesis statement that includes what you are comparing and contrasting and a controlling idea.

EXAMPLE: Topic: girls' and boys' toys

Thesis statement: *Both girls' and boys' toys reinforce gender stereotypes.*

1. Topic: childhood fears and adult fears

   Thesis statement: _____

   _____

2. Topic: two generations

   Thesis statement: _____

   _____

3. Topic: public versus private life

   Thesis statement: _____

   _____

The Supporting Ideas

After you have developed an effective thesis statement, generate supporting ideas. In a comparison and contrast essay, think of examples that help to clarify the similarities or differences, and then incorporate some ideas in your final essay plan.

To generate supporting ideas, you might try using a Venn diagram. In this example, you can see how the writer draws two circles to compare traditional boys' and girls' toys and how some ideas fall into both categories.

Boys
Bold red and black
Fighting figures
Uniforms, weapons
Hard plastic
Animals
Toy guns

Both
Human figure toys
Active toys such as balls, hacky sacks, skateboards
Video games
Blocks

Girls
Pastel colours
Baby-like dolls
Doll fashions
Stuffed animals
Bake ovens

Writer's Desk **Develop Supporting Ideas**

Choose one of your thesis statements from the previous Writer's Desk. List some similarities and differences.

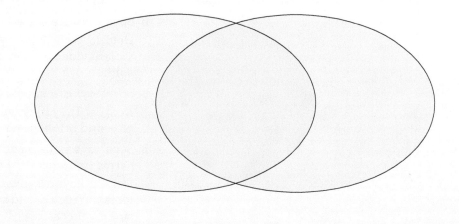

The Essay Plan

Before you write a comparison and contrast essay, make a detailed essay plan. Decide which pattern you will follow: point by point or topic by topic. Then add supporting details. Make sure that each detail supports the thesis statement. Also think about the best way to organize your ideas.

THESIS STATEMENT: Both girls' and boys' toys reinforce gender stereotypes.

Point by Point

A/B Girls' toys focus on activities in the home, whereas boys' toys focus on outside activities.

Details: Girls have dollhouses and baking ovens whereas boys have carpenter sets and race cars.

A/B Colours are different in girls' and boys' toys.

Details: Girls' toys are pastel colours and boys' toys are bold colours.

Topic by Topic

A Girls' toys reinforce the importance of looks, body image, and fashion.

Details: They receive fashion dolls with clothing, shoes, and other accessories.

A Girls' toys are in soft pastel colours.

Details: They play with pink ponies and hug pale blue stuffed animals.

Point by Point (cont.)

A/B Girls' toys focus on nurturing, and boys' toys focus on heroic fighters.

Details: Girls have baby dolls and boys have GI Joes and guns.

Topic by Topic (cont.)

A Girls' toys encourage nurturing by focusing on home and the family.

Details: They have dolls with baby bottles, baking ovens, toy vacuums, and shopping carts.

B Boys' toys are more violent.

Details: Boys have toy guns, violent video games, and soldier toys.

B Boys' toys are in bold colours.

Details: They play with red toy cars and bright green soldiers.

B Boys' toys focus on activities and heroic fighters.

Details: Boys are given carpenter's tools, car racing, and service station play sets.

Writer's Desk **Write an Essay Plan**

Refer to the information you generated in previous Writer's Desks and prepare a detailed essay plan using a point-by-point or topic-by-topic pattern. You can use the letters A and B to indicate which side you are discussing in your plan. Include details about each supporting idea.

The First Draft

After you outline your ideas in an essay plan, you are ready to write the first draft. Remember to follow the topic-by-topic or the point-by-point pattern you used in your plan. Write complete sentences and use transitions to help your ideas flow smoothly. The following transitions can be helpful for guiding readers through a comparison and contrast essay.

To show similarities		To show differences	
additionally	in addition	conversely	nevertheless
at the same time	in the same way	however	on the contrary
equally	similarly	in contrast	then again

Writer's Desk **Write the First Draft**

Write the first draft of your comparison and contrast essay. Before you write, carefully review your essay plan to see if you have enough support for your points and topics. Flesh out each body paragraph with specific details.

REVISING AND EDITING

Revise and Edit a Comparison and Contrast Essay

When you finish writing a comparison and contrast essay, carefully review your work and revise it to make sure that the comparison or contrast is as clear as possible to your readers. Check that you have organized your essay logically, and remove any irrelevant details. Before you work on your own essay, practise revising and editing a student essay.

A Student Essay

Read the essay, and then answer the questions that follow. As you read, correct any errors that you find, and make comments in the margins.

Gender and Toys
by Ashley Lincoln

1   As a young mother, I am trying to avoid the pitfalls that parents so easily fall into. I try not to call my daughter cute and my son strong, thus reinforcing any cultural notions about their self-worth. I encourage my five-year-old daughter to play sports, and I bought my son a baby doll when he asked for one. My friends been saying they have the same concerns about gender roles. But insulating children against male or female role expectations is almost impossible. Most parents, in spite of their best efforts, reinforce gender stereotypes every time they shop for toys.

2   Girls' toys reinforce the importance of looks, body image, and fashion. Parents can buy their daughters makeup sets that include child-friendly lipstick, blush, and eye shadow. Fashion dolls of all shapes and sizes abound. Barbies, Bratz, and other teenage dolls stare at the buyer. Hanging next to the dolls are rows of clothing, shoes, hats, and tiny doll necklaces and bracelets. Girls can also play with a large doll head,

changing and curling the hair and adding makeup. Of course, none of the dolls are pudgy, pimply, large-boned, or just plain unattractive. When girls play with these toys, they quickly learn that beauty and the right clothes and makeup are very important.

3   If a little girl does not like fashion toys, they will surely enjoy baby dolls with their fake bottles of milk, soft little blankets, and strollers. Girls' toys encourage nurturing by focusing on the home and the family. At a very young age, girls learn to be competent mothers when they change the little diapers of their dolls. Girls can learn to cook with their Easy-Bake ovens, and they learn to shop with tiny shopping carts and cash registers. My daughter and her friends love playing "house" with one child acting as the mother. They shop, pull the "cry" strings on their dolls, and feed their "babies."

4   Boys' toys, on the other hand, stress jobs and activities outside the home. My son begged for, and received, a miniature workshop complete with a plastic saw, drill, screwdriver, and wrench. Lego sets prepare boys for creative occupations such as architecture and auto design. Computer and video games prepare boys for jobs in the high-tech industries. Finally, there is a lot of toy cars, trucks, and racetracks to remind boys that cars are very important to their identities.

5   Toys aimed at young males also permit boys to be the heroes in their fantasy games. In the boys' aisle of the toy store, there are rows of action figures. The GI Joes fight soldiers from other armies. Batman, Superman, and the X-Men fight fantasy villains. Curiously, the X-Men figures include female characters such as Storm, but the toys are not call "X-People." Aimed predominantly at boys, fighting action figures bolster ideas boys have about rescuing others. In their fantasy lives, boys learn early on that they are the heroes and the saviours.

6   Some suggest that it is useless to fight against the male and female roles. They point out that girls in previous centuries made their own dolls out of straw and rags, and boys made cars out of tin cans and wood. While that is true, toy stores take the stereotyping to extremes. One solution is to try to buy gender-neutral toys such as modelling clay, painting supplies, or balls and other sporting equipment.

PRACTICE 3

Revising

1. Highlight the thesis statement.

2. Highlight the topic sentence in each body paragraph.

3. Circle a transitional word or phrase in the topic sentence of paragraph 4. Then add transitional words or phrases to the other topic sentences.

4. What pattern does the writer use to organize this essay? Circle your response.
   a. point by point   b. topic by topic

5. The student writer uses the word "reinforce" at the end of the introduction and in the first sentence of the second paragraph. To avoid repeating the same word, what synonym could the student use?

   _____

Editing

GRAMMAR LINK

See the following chapters for more information about these grammar topics:
Subject–Verb Agreement, Chapter 21
Passive Voice, Chapter 22
Verbs, Chapter 23
Pronouns, Chapter 26

6. Underline the verb error in the introduction. Write the correction on the line.

   Correction: _____

7. Underline and correct the pronoun shift in paragraph 3.

   Correction: _____

8. Underline and correct the subject–verb agreement error in paragraph 4.

   Correction: _____

9. Underline and correct the passive verb that has been incorrectly formed in paragraph 5.

   Correction: _____

Writer's Desk Revise and Edit Your Essay

Revise and edit the essay that you wrote for the previous Writer's Desk. You can refer to the revising and editing checklists at the end of this chapter and on this book's inside covers.

A Professional Essay

Writer and translator Naomi Louder has published poetry in *The Fiddlehead Review* and *The New Quarterly*, among other journals. In the following essay, she uses the comparison and contrast pattern. Read the essay and answer the questions that follow.

The Dating World
by Naomi Louder

1   Dating has changed a lot over the years. Many people, post millennium, can't help associating the word "date" with a more innocent time and scenarios involving ice-cream sodas, varsity jackets, and drive-in movies. In smaller and more traditional communities, vestiges of this remain, and high school sweethearts who paired up early on wind up getting married straight out of school. Compared to previous generations, today's singles have a new dating ethic that involves flying straight into a whirlwind affair.

2   The most obvious difference between the past and the present is in dating methods. In the 1950s and 1960s, potential sweethearts met at school dances, the lunch-line at the school cafeteria, or at school sports events. There were certain formal rules of etiquette to be followed, down to the "base" system, dictating when, where, and how the relationship was to progress to its logical conclusion. People were concerned, after a date, with whether "first base"—a kiss—was attained. Nowadays, it is more common to obsess over the other party's sexual history, his or her expectations, and whether a relationship might be a possibility. The "base" system has been supplanted, in junior high or even elementary school, by the "gummy" trend, where cheap rubber bracelets, coded by color, announce the sexual experience or willingness of the wearer.

3   In a traditional dating context, couples worried primarily about pregnancy, and—mainly in the case of the girls—about losing their reputations. An ill-timed boast on the part of a boy could jeopardize a girl's dating career, while a pregnancy could result in the ultimate shame to the girl and her family or a rushed and gossiped-over wedding. In a contemporary urban center, these worries seem naïve. Early sexual relationships are more the norm than before, and the concerns are sexually transmitted infections, date rape, and abortion or adoption versus single parenthood. Certainly, some young people have reacted to these threats by rejecting the ethic of sexual freedom popularized in the 1960s. The revival of traditional religious values has influenced many young Americans, and chastity rings and church events make even the dating system of a more innocent era seem fraught. However, the majority of teens and young adults are more determined than ever to fulfill their sexual and emotional needs, sometimes before they are clearly aware of the consequences.

4   Both the traditional and the new dating methods have downsides. The new generation, with all its scorn of traditional and prudish dating

etiquette, finds itself lost and lonelier than ever. The old-fashioned courtship ritual has been condensed to a witty remark, a compliment or two, and an animal assault on a balcony, on a street corner, or in a taxi. Once the deed is done, people often find that they have no idea who they're dating. On the other hand, some would argue that when a mutual attraction is felt, holding back from intimacy is counter-productive. For instance, using the traditional method, people may try to represent themselves dishonestly, behaving with courtesy, unselfishness, or generosity that they would never bother with if they weren't trying to impress. The person's true personality—perhaps that of a slob or a diva—may only be unveiled when a commitment has been made. Advocates of casual encounters argue that when the formalities are dispensed with, people show themselves as they truly are.

5   There are pitfalls to both of these ways of dating, but the fact is, most people are looking for a partner in life, and the only way to find one is to trust somebody. A high school sweetheart or the best-looking person at a party is not necessarily the ideal partner. For the most part, relationships succeed because there is a sounder basis to them than passion or romance. If a true friendship is possible between two people, when passion and excitement fade, there will still be a reason to stay together.

PRACTICE 4

1. Highlight the thesis statement.

2. Highlight the topic sentence in paragraphs 2 and 4.

3. Paragraph 3 does not have a topic sentence. Which sentence best expresses the implied point?

    a. In the past, women worried about losing their reputations.

    b. Courtship rituals have changed.

    c. Dating concerns have also transformed since the 1950s.

    d. Today, there is a revival of religious values among young people.

4. In this essay, what pattern of comparison does the writer follow? Circle the correct answer.

    a. point by point   b. topic by topic

5. Using your own words, sum up the main subjects in this essay.

    Paragraph 2: _____

    Paragraph 3: _____

    Paragraph 4: _____

6. Does this essay focus mainly on similarities or differences? Circle the correct answer.

   a. similarities   b. differences

7. What is the writer's purpose?

   a. to make a judgment   b. to understand two things

 The Writer's Room   **Topics for Comparison and Contrast Essays**

Writing Activity 1

Choose any of the following topics, or choose your own topic, and write a comparison and contrast essay.

General Topics

Compare or contrast . . .

1. team sports versus solo sports
2. an early bird and a night owl
3. a true friend and an acquaintance
4. a watcher versus a doer
5. living near family versus living away from family

College and Work-Related Topics

Compare or contrast . . .

6. courage versus recklessness
7. living on campus versus living off campus
8. being self-employed versus working for others
9. work and drudgery
10. expectations about a job versus the reality of the job

Writing Activity 2

Choose a quotation that you agree or disagree with, or one that inspires you, and then write a comparison and contrast essay based on it.

> A wise man can see more from the bottom of a well than a fool can from a mountaintop.
>
> —Unknown

It seemed the world was divided into good and bad people. The good ones slept better while the bad ones seemed to enjoy the waking hours much more.

—Woody Allen, filmmaker

Imagination is more important than knowledge.

—Albert Einstein, physicist

People who work sitting down get paid more than people who work standing up.

—Ogden Nash, poet

Writing Activity 3

Examine the photo, and think about things that you could compare and contrast. You can focus on something in the photo, or use it to spark ideas about related topics. Some ideas might be two homes that you lived in, two buildings that you have worked in, two architectural styles, two neighbourhoods, the city versus the countryside, or your dream home versus your actual home. Then write a comparison and contrast essay.

READING LINK

More Comparison and Contrast Readings

"Seeing Red Over Myths," by Drew Hayden Taylor (page 495)

"Religious Faith versus Spirituality," by Neil Bissoondath (page 531)

WRITING LINK

More Comparison and Contrast Writing Topics

Chapter 16, Writer's Room topic 2 (page 292)

Chapter 17, Writer's Room topic 2 (page 303)

Chapter 21, Writer's Room topic 1 (page 346)

Chapter 25, Writer's Room topic 1 (page 402)

✔ CHECKLIST: COMPARISON AND CONTRAST

After you write your comparison and contrast essay, review the checklist on the inside front cover. Also, ask yourself the following set of questions.

☐ Does my thesis statement explain what I am comparing and contrasting?

☐ Does my thesis statement make a point about the comparison?

☐ Does my essay have a point-by-point or topic-by-topic pattern?

☐ Does my essay focus on similarities or on differences?

☐ Do all of my supporting examples clearly relate to the topics that I am comparing or contrasting?

How Do I Get a Better Grade?

mycanadiancomplab

Go to www.mycanadiancomplab.ca for additional help with your grammar, writing, and research skills. You will have access to a variety of exercises, instruction, and video that will help you improve your basic skills and help you get a better grade.

Cause and Effect

CONTENTS

When a flood occurs, people ask themselves, "How did this happen?" and "What is the extent of the damage?" Writers use the cause and effect pattern to explain the answers to these types of questions.

Writers' Exchange

Work with a group of students. Each group has two minutes to brainstorm as many reasons as possible to explain why people eat fast food. Then, each team will have two minutes to explain the effects of eating fast food. The team with the most causes and effects wins.

EXPLORING

What Is Cause and Effect?

Cause and effect writing explains why an event happened or what the consequences of such an event were. A cause and effect essay can focus on causes, effects, or both.

You often analyze the causes or effects of something. The following examples show you causes and effects of decisions in your home, college, and work.

Audience: Family member

My car accident happened for a few reasons.

- The fog had reduced visibility.
- The driver behind me was following too closely.
- There was a sudden traffic jam, and I had to stop quickly.

Audience: College administrator

Several events have caused a lack of student housing.

- There has been an increase in enrollment in our college.
- One student residence burned down during the summer.
- Another student residence was converted into condominiums.

Audience: Colleague

My company is downsizing for the following reasons.

- There is too much competition.
- We rely more on machines than on labour.
- The owners want to retire soon.

The Cause and Effect Essay

When you write a cause and effect essay, focus on two main tasks.

1. **Indicate whether you are focusing on causes, effects, or both.**
   If you do decide to focus on both causes and effects, make sure that your thesis statement indicates your purpose to the reader.
2. **Ensure that your causes and effects are valid.**
   You should determine real causes and effects and not simply list things that happened before or after the event. Also, verify that your assumptions are logical.

Illogical: Our furnace stopped working because the weather was too cold.
(This is illogical; cold weather cannot stop a furnace from working.)

Better: Our furnace stopped working because the filters needed replacing and the gas burners needed adjusting.

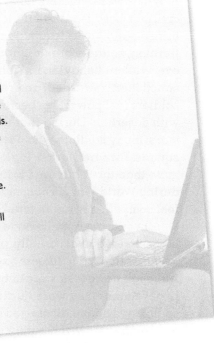

Cause and Effect at Work

In this community newsletter about safety, the writer explains about the causes and effects of computer-related injuries.

Musculoskeletal disorders (MSDs) are a family of painful disorders affecting tendons, muscles, nerves, and joints in the neck, upper and lower back, chest, shoulders, arms, and hands. They include repetitive strain injuries (RSIs), which may take years to develop. Recovery can be difficult and may even require surgery in extreme cases.

MSDs are the scourge of the computerized workplace. Workers can develop chronic pain if their workstations are set up without proper attention to ergonomics. A small change, such as repositioning the screen or keyboard or using an adjustable chair, can often eliminate the problem.

A Student Essay

Read the student essay and answer the questions that follow.

The Causes of Aggressiveness in Ordinary People
by Catherine Belisle Prevost

1   During World War II, many German citizens behaved in an inhuman manner toward the people who were put in concentration camps. In 1961, in an effort to understand how people could behave so callously, Stanley Milgram conducted a series of experiments. He wondered how ordinary people could be led to commit aggressive and horrible acts. A few years later, another researcher named Philip Zimbardo conducted his own tests to determine how social roles influence behaviour. The experiments led to some astounding conclusions. Ordinary people can be persuaded to commit cruel acts when they are in submissive or dominant positions.

2   Many idealistic young men and women join the military. These ordinary soldiers and marines, who are in a submissive relationship with superior officers, sometimes have no choice but to act violently. During

previous wars, soldiers have shot others, set fire to villages, and terrorized civilians because they had to do what their commanders asked. Thomas Brinson and Vince Treanor, in an article for *Veteran*, wrote, "In military training, soldiers are taught to react when threatened with aggressive, even violent behavior. In Vietnam there were no rules. Violence was sanctioned, rewarded, and reinforced as crucial to survival." Furthermore, soldiers feel powerless because those who refuse orders can be charged with desertion. During the American Civil War and during previous world wars, many soldiers who deserted were imprisoned or sent before firing squads. Richard Norton Taylor, in an article for *The Guardian*, says that more than three hundred British soldiers were executed for desertion during World War I. Thus, many ordinary people who join the military may feel compelled to act in cruel and inhuman ways.

3   Even when people have the option of disobeying orders, they can still be persuaded to act cruelly. In Stanley Milgram's experiment, a professor asked ordinary volunteers to give electric shocks to another human. Although no shocks were actually given, the subjects in the experiment believed that they were hurting someone. In that case, the participants could easily have disobeyed and left the room with no consequences. Yet, as Joseph Dimow, the author of "Resisting Authority," says, "Of forty participants in Milgram's first experiment, fifteen refused to continue at some point, while twenty-five went all the way to 450-volt shocks." In a more recent case, managers of fast-food restaurant chains were telephoned by someone pretending to be a police officer. The "officer" said that a female employee was guilty of theft, and he convinced several restaurant managers in different locations across the nation to strip-search young employees. Donna Jean Summers, an assistant manager at McDonald's, received one of those calls on April 9, 2004. She obeyed the caller and strip-searched eighteen-year-old employee Louise Ogborn. Summers could easily have disobeyed the person on the phone, yet she did as she was told. Therefore, dominated people can commit cruel acts even when they simply think they are obeying orders.

4   People in submissive positions are not the only ones who can be persuaded to act aggressively. A lot of people in dominant positions also act in horrible ways. The news is filled with stories of prison guards, police officers, and others in authoritarian roles who abuse their power. When some people are in powerful positions, they can become filled with a sense of superiority and strength, and they may end up seeing those under their authority as objects. In Philip Zimbardo's Stanford Prison Experiment, students were randomly selected to be guards or prisoners. According to Kathleen O'Toole, in her article "The Stanford Prison

Experiment," guards "increased their coercive aggression tactics, humiliation, and dehumanization of the prisoners. For example, the student guards forced prisoners to clean out toilet bowls with their bare hands." Christina Maslach, the woman credited with stopping the experiment, describes the change in one of the participants. When she first spoke with the student who was nicknamed "John Wayne," she thought that he was charming. Later, she saw him in the experiment; she was shocked by his transformation into a sadistic and cruel guard: "He was talking in a different accent, a Southern accent, which I hadn't recalled at all. He moved differently. [. . .] It was like Jekyll and Hyde," said Maslach. The experiment demonstrated that some ordinary people in authoritarian positions can become cruel and aggressive toward those under their command.

5   Ordinary people in controlling or submissive positions have the capacity to become tyrants. Perhaps those in positions of power should get leadership training, and those who are dominated should be taught that there are logical and legal limits they must not cross. As George Eliot, the English novelist, once wrote, "Cruelty, like every other vice, requires no motive outside of itself; it only requires opportunity."

PRACTICE 1

1. Highlight the thesis statement.

2. Does the thesis statement express causes, effects, or both? _____

3. What introductory style does the writer use?
    a. anecdote   b. contrasting position   c. historical background

4. Highlight the topic sentences in paragraphs 2, 3, and 4.

5. Using your own words, sum up the causes that contribute to tyrannical behaviour.

    _____

    _____

    _____

    _____

    _____

6. The writer concludes her essay with which of the following?
    a. a suggestion b. a call to action c. a prediction   d. a quotation

Explore Topics

In the Writer's Desk Warm Up, you will try an exploring strategy to generate ideas about different topics.

Writer's Desk **Warm Up**

Read the following questions, and write the first ideas that come to your mind. Think of two or three ideas for each topic.

EXAMPLE: Why are reality television shows so popular?

—*voyeurism*

—*people are bored with sitcoms and other regular television programs*

—*a large variety for every taste*

1. Why do people get into debt?

2. What are some causes and effects of addictions? Specify the type of addiction.

3. Why do people want to be famous? What are the effects of fame?

DEVELOPING

The Thesis Statement

When writing a thesis statement for a cause and effect essay, clearly demonstrate whether the focus is on causes, effects, or both. Also, make sure that you state a controlling idea that expresses your point of view or attitude.

controlling idea (causes)   topic
There are many reasons for **global warming.**

topic   controlling idea (effects)
Global warming may have a profound influence on our lifestyles.

topic   controlling idea (causes and effects)
Global warming, which has developed for many reasons, may have a profound influence on our lifestyles.

PRACTICE 2   Look carefully at the following thesis statements. Decide if each sentence focuses on the causes, effects, or both. Look at the key words that give you the clues and circle the best answer.

1. Poverty persists in developing countries because of lack of education, scarcity of jobs, and political corruption.
   a. causes   b. effects   c. both

2. In our college, the high student dropout rate, which is triggered by the tourist industry, results in long-term problems for the community.
   a. causes   b. effects   c. both

3. The Asian tsunami has created many problems for the environment, as well as in people's mental and physical health.
   a. causes   b. effects   c. both

Grammar Hint   **Affect and Effect**

Use *affect* as a verb and *effect* as a noun. *Affect* means "to influence or change" and *effect* means "the result."

verb
How does the ban on fast food in public schools <u>affect</u> children's health?

noun
What <u>effects</u> will the ban on fast food in public schools have on children's health?

You can also use *effect* as a verb that means "to cause or to bring about a change or implement a plan."

verb
Health care professionals lobbied to <u>effect</u> changes in public school lunch menus.

See Chapter 27 for more information about commonly confused words.

Writer's Desk **Write Thesis Statements**

Write a thesis statement for each of the following topics. You can look for ideas in the previous Writer's Desk. Determine if you will focus on the causes, effects, or both in your essay.

EXAMPLE: Topic: popularity of reality shows

Thesis Statement: *Reality television shows have become increasingly popular for several reasons.*

1. Topic: getting into personal debt

   Thesis Statement: _____

   _____

2. Topic: having an addiction

   Thesis Statement: _____

   _____

3. Topic: having fame

   Thesis Statement: _____

   _____

The Supporting Ideas

After you have developed an effective thesis statement, generate supporting ideas. In a cause and effect essay, think of examples that clearly show the causes or effects. To develop supporting ideas follow these three steps:

- Use prewriting strategies such as freewriting and brainstorming to generate ideas.
- Choose the best ideas. Use examples that clearly reveal the causes and effects.
- Organize your ideas. Choose the best organizational method for this essay pattern.

Hint **Do Not Oversimplify**

Avoid attributing a simple or general cause to a very complex issue. When you use expressions such as *it appears that* or *a possible cause is,* it shows that you are aware of the complex factors involved in the situation.

Oversimplification: Global warming is caused by cars.

Better: One possible cause of global warming is the CO_2 emissions from cars.

Identifying Causes and Effects

Imagine that you had to write a cause and effect essay on gambling. You could brainstorm and think of as many causes and effects as possible.

Causes
- need money quickly
- advertisements entice people to buy lottery tickets
- think winning is possible
- availability of gambling establishments

Gambling

Effects
- bankruptcy
- may cause problems in marriage or at work
- depression
- criminal behaviour such as forging cheques

Writer's Desk **Identify Causes and Effects**

Choose the topic of one of the thesis statements from the previous Writer's Desk. Then write some possible causes and effects.

EXAMPLE: Topic: *Popularity of reality television programs*

Causes	Effects
new television concept	*become TV junkie*
empathize with the contestants	*contestants become famous*
each episode has a hook ending	*take pleasure in others' humiliation*
feel superior to contestants	*live vicariously through others*

Focus on: *causes*

Topic: _____

Causes	Effects
_____	_____
_____	_____
_____	_____
_____	_____

Focus on: _____

The Essay Plan

In many courses, instructors ask students to write about the causes or effects of a particular subject. Take the time to plan your essay before you write your first draft. Also, think about how you would logically arrange the order of ideas. As you make your plan, ensure that you focus on causes, effects, or both.

THESIS STATEMENT: Reality television shows have become increasingly popular for several reasons.

I. Many situation comedies and movies of the week are no longer innovative, so people turn to reality shows.
    A. Some television comedies retell old jokes.
    B. Characters are often stereotypical.
    C. Many shows have predictable endings.

II. Reality television programs cater to a variety of tastes.
    A. Some shows focus on family dynamics.
    B. Some shows focus on romance.
    C. Other shows focus on extreme situations.
III. Home audiences live vicariously through contestants.
    A. Audiences may feel superior to contestants.
    B. An audience member can empathize with a contestant.
    C. Audience members think they can become famous like the contestants.

Writer's Desk **Write an Essay Plan**

Choose one of the ideas that you have developed in previous Writer's Desks and prepare an essay plan. If you think of new details that will explain your point more effectively, include them in your plan.

The First Draft

After you have developed and organized your ideas in your essay plan, write the first draft. Remember to write complete sentences and to use transitional words or expressions to help your ideas flow smoothly. Most writers arrange cause and effect essays using emphatic order, which means that they place examples from the most to the least important or from the least to the most important. The following transitional expressions are useful for showing causes and effects.

To show causes	To show effects
for this reason	accordingly
the first cause	as a result
the most important cause	consequently

Writer's Desk **Write the First Draft**

Carefully review and, if necessary, revise your essay plan from the previous Writer's Desk, and then write the first draft of your cause and effect essay.

vo•cab•u•lar•y **BOOST**

If you use inappropriate vocabulary in a particular context, it can affect the way people respond to you. For example, you would not use street language in a business meeting. Replace the following words with terms that can be used in academic or professional writing.

buddy   guy   kid   chill   stuff   crook

REVISING AND EDITING

Revise and Edit a Cause and Effect Essay

When you finish writing a cause and effect essay, review your work and revise it to make the examples as clear as possible to your readers. Check that you have organized your ideas logically and remove any irrelevant details. Before you work on your own essay, practise revising and editing a student essay.

A Student Essay

Read the essay, and then answer the questions that follow. As you read, correct any errors that you find, and make comments in the margins.

Reality Television Is Here to Stay
by Ivan Pogrebkov

1   Matt is a twenty-one-year-old college student. Each Thursday evening, he and his friends get together to watch television. They are hooked on reality shows, which have changed the television landscape since they first arrived on the screen a few years ago. These television shows have become increasingly popular for several reasons.

2   First, the traditional situation comedies have become repetitive; therefore, bored viewers are looking for more innovative programming that will hold their attention. For example, many weekly comedy programs have the same mind-numbing plot in which the parents have to deal with their children getting into superficial trouble. The jokes are the same and the endings are predictable. The parents help the children solve the problem, and everybody learn a valuable life lesson. Most viewers are tired of this format where family problems can be solved in thirty minutes. Some comedies in the past were very good, though. *Seinfeld* was a great situation comedy that was very popular and ran for a decade. Reality

television is more interesting than run-of-the mill television shows because ordinary people can react in unexpected ways.

3   There are reality shows that focus on family dynamics, shows concentrating on romance, and on extreme situations. Although reality shows are scripted to some degree, they do provide viewers with a degree of suspense and unpredictability. One never knows who is going to loose the competition. This factor attracts audiences to keep watching to find out the outcome for each participant.

4   Finally, reality shows are all the rage because audiences can relate to the situations and participants on some level. Most of the people appearing on reality shows are ordinary citizens as opposed to glamorous stars with expensive hairdos and clothes. Spectators' emotions may range from empathy for the participants to feeling superior to them. Because they are just like the participants, viewers enjoy envisioning themselves doing the same things and achieving fifteen minutes of fame. And, if the reality show is a contest, the winner usually wins money, prizes, and some amount of recognition.

5   People are loyal to reality shows because they offer variety, humour, and suspense. In fact, these programs are today's new soap operas. Although many critics find reality shows uninspiring, those programs are probably going to continue to be popular for a long time.

PRACTICE 3

Revising

1. Does the essay focus on causes, effects, or both? _____

2. Each body paragraph lacks adequate details. List some examples that could support the main idea of each body paragraph.

   Paragraph 2 _____

   _____

   Paragraph 3 _____

   _____

   Paragraph 4 _____

   _____

3. Highlight the topic sentence in paragraph 2, and then cross out any sentences that do not support the topic sentence.

4. An appropriate topic sentence for paragraph 3 is
    a. Reality programs, unlike most sitcoms, soap operas, and made-for-TV movies, cater to a variety of tastes.
    b. Contestants of reality shows must follow a script, so they are not "real."
    c. Reality shows are unpredictable.
    d. Not everyone likes reality shows because their premises are often tedious.

5. What is the introductory style of this essay? _____

6. How does the writer conclude the essay?
    a. with an observation   b. with a prediction   c. with a suggestion

Editing

7. In paragraph 2, there is a subject–verb agreement error. Underline and correct the error.

    Correction: _____

8. In paragraph 3, a sentence has faulty parallel structure. Underline and rewrite the sentence.

    Correction: _____

    _____

9. Underline and correct the misspelled word in paragraph 3.

    Correction: _____

GRAMMAR LINK

See the following chapters for more information about these grammar topics:
Parallel Structure, Chapter 19
Subject–Verb Agreement, Chapter 21
Spelling, Chapter 27

Writer's Desk **Revise and Edit Your Essay**

Revise and edit the essay that you wrote for the previous Writer's Desk. You can refer to the revising and editing checklists at the end of this chapter and on this book's inside covers.

A Professional Essay

Ellen Goodman is a Pulitzer Prize–winning columnist for the *Boston Globe*, and her articles appear in over 370 newspapers. She has also written several books, including *Value Judgments* and *Keeping in Touch*. In the next essay, she examines why North Americans are becoming more isolated socially.

Friendless in North America
by Ellen Goodman

1   Lynn Smith-Lovin was listening in the back seat of a taxi when a woman called the radio talk-show hosts to confess her affairs with a new boyfriend and a not-yet-former husband. The hosts, in their best therapeutic voices, offered their on-air opinion, "Give me an S, give me an L, give me a U," You can spell the rest. It was the sort of exchange that would leave most of us wondering why anyone would share her intimate life story with a radio host. Didn't she have anyone else to talk with? Smith-Lovin might have been the only one in the audience with an answer to the question: Maybe not.

2   The Duke University sociologist is co-author of one of those blockbuster studies that makes us look at ourselves. This one is labeled "Friendless in America." A face-to-face study of 1467 adults turned up some disheartening news. One-fourth reported that they have nobody to talk to about "important matters." Another quarter reported they are just one person away from nobody. But this was the most startling fact. The study is a replica of one done twenty years ago. In only two decades, from 1985 to 2004, the number of people who have no one to talk to has doubled. And the number of confidants of the average person has gone down from three to two.

3   The people to whom we are closest form our own informal safety net. They're the ones who see us through a life crisis, lend us their spare bedroom, or pick up our kids at school in a pinch. Social isolation is as big a risk factor for premature death as smoking. Robert Putnam has already chronicled the erosion of the ties that bind in *Bowling Alone*. But we've paid less attention to "coping alone" or "suffering alone." Imagine if some other piece of the social safety net had frayed that furiously. Imagine if income had gone down by a third or divorce doubled or the medical system halved. We would be setting up commissions and organizing rallies.

4   Not everything in the study was gloomy. Deep in the data is the suggestion that families—husbands and wives, parents and adult children—might be closer. Spouses who call each other "my best friend" might be right. We might have fewer intimates but we're more intimate with them. On average, we see them more than once a week and have

known them seven years. Nevertheless, the big news is that circles have tightened, shrunk, and gone nuclear. As Smith-Lovin says, "Literally nothing takes the place of family." The greatest loss has been in neighbors and friends who will provide help, support, advice, and connections to a wider world.

5   There is no shortage of speculation about why our circle of friends is eroding. The usual suspect is the time crunch. It's knocked friendship off the balancing beam of life as we attend to work and family. It's left less time for the groups and associations that bind us. But in the past twenty years, technology has changed the way we use our "relationship time." Walk along any city street and people talking on cell phones are more common than pigeons. Go into Starbucks and a third of the customers are having coffee dates with their laptops. "It could be that talking to people close to us on cell phones has caused our social circle to shrink," says Smith-Lovin. It could be that we are both increasingly in-touch and isolated. It's become easier to keep extensive relationships over time and distance but harder to build the deep ones in our backyard. In the virtual neighborhood, how many have substituted email for intimacy, contacts for confidants, and Facebook for face to face?

6   A few years ago, when my friend Patricia O'Brien and I wrote a book on the power of friendship in women's lives, we noted that there was no official status for friends, no pro-friendship movement, no cultural or political support system for friends. Yet this voluntary relationship can be the most sustaining one of life.

7   Now we are living in smaller, tighter circles. We are ten degrees of separation from each other and one or two people away from loneliness. And many now outsource intimacy from friends to professional therapists and *gawd* help us, talk shows. Who can we talk to about important matters? Who can we count on? As we search for tools to repair this frayed safety net, we can take poor, paradoxical comfort from the fact that if we are feeling isolated, we are not alone.

PRACTICE 4

1. Who is the audience for this essay? _____

2. The thesis of this essay is not stated directly, but it is implied. Using your own words, write the thesis of this essay.

   _____

   _____

3. Circle the type of introduction Goodman uses.
   a. historical background   b. anecdote   c. general background

4. In your own words, how have the socialization habits of North Americans changed in the past twenty years?

   _____

   _____

5. What specific reasons does Goodman give for this social change?

   _____

   _____

6. Goodman writes, "It could be that we are both increasingly in-touch and isolated." What does she mean?

   _____

   _____

   _____

 The Writer's Room **Topics for Cause and Effect Essays**

Writing Activity 1

Write a cause and effect essay about one of the following topics, or choose your own topic.

General Topics

Causes and/or effects of

1. a good/bad sports parent
2. getting married
3. a fear of _____
4. road rage
5. a natural phenomenon

College and Work-Related Topics

Causes and/or effects of

6. a public policy
7. becoming successful
8. giving somebody a second chance
9. learning a skill
10. a hostile workplace

READING LINK

More Cause and Effect Readings

"The Hijab," by Naheed Mustafa (page 488)

"Canada Misses its Chance to Join Major Pacific Free-Trade Deal," by John Ibbitson (page 506)

"Make a Difference," by David Suzuki and David R. Boyd (page 525)

WRITING LINK

More Cause and Effect Writing Topics

Chapter 16, Writer's Room topic 1 (page 292)

Chapter 22, Writer's Room topic 2 (page 365)

Writing Activity 2

Choose a quotation that you agree or disagree with, and then write a cause and effect essay based on it.

> Usually when people are sad, they don't do anything. They just cry over their condition. But when they get angry, they bring about a change.
>
> —Malcolm X, political activist

> Human beings, by changing the inner attitudes of their minds, can change the outer aspects of their lives.
>
> —William James, psychologist

> Those who can make you believe absurdities can make you commit atrocities.
>
> —Voltaire, satirist

> Fire and swords are slow engines of destruction, compared to the tongue of a gossip.
>
> —Richard Steele, essayist

Writing Activity 3

Why do nations go to war? What are some causes and effects of war? Write about war.

CHECKLIST: CAUSE AND EFFECT ESSAY

As you write your cause and effect essay, review the checklist on the inside front cover. Also, ask yourself the following questions.

☐ Does my thesis statement indicate clearly that my essay focuses on causes, effects, or both?

☐ Do I have adequate supporting examples of causes and/or effects?

☐ Do I make logical and valid points?

☐ Do I use the terms *effect* and/or *affect* correctly?

How Do I Get a Better Grade?

mycanadiancomplab

Go to www.mycanadiancomplab.ca for additional help with your grammar, writing, and research skills. You will have access to a variety of exercises, instruction, and video that will help you improve your basic skills and help you get a better grade.

Argument

CONTENTS

Medical practitioners often use argument to convince colleagues about the best treatment for a patient. In the same way, you use argument writing to convince readers to see things from your point of view.

Writers' Exchange

For this activity, you and a partner will take turns debating an issue. To start, choose which one of you will begin speaking. The first speaker chooses one side of any issue listed below, and then argues about that issue, without stopping, for a set amount of time. Your instructor will signal when to switch sides. After the signal, the second speaker talks non-stop about the other side of the debate. If you run out of ideas, you can switch topics when it is your turn to speak. Possible topics:

too general ←

(Technology) has improved our lives.	Technology has hurt our lives.
It is better to be an only child.	It is better to have brothers and sisters.
Adolescence is the best time of life.	Adolescence is the worst time of life.
Our college needs improvements.	Our college does not need improvements.

EXPLORING

What Is Argument?

When you use **argument**, you take a position on an issue, and you try to prove or defend your position. Using effective argument strategies can help you convince somebody that your point of view is a valid one.

Argument is both a writing pattern and a purpose for writing. In fact, it is one of the most common aims, or purposes, in most college and work-related writing. For example, in Chapter 9, there is an essay called "On Genius," in which the author uses definition as the predominant pattern. At the same time, the author uses argument to convince the reader that true genius exists all around us. Therefore, in most of your college and work-related writing, your purpose is to persuade the reader that your ideas are compelling and legitimate.

The following examples show arguments people might make every day.

Audience: Mate

We need to move to a larger home.

- My home office space in the corner of our bedroom is not adequate.
- Our son and daughter are approaching ages where they will need separate bedrooms.
- We can have a larger apartment or duplex for the same cost if we are just willing to relocate slightly north of the city.

Audience: College dean

The Graphic Arts Department needs new computers.

- The department has grown, and there are not enough computers.
- The existing computers do not support new graphics programs.
- To make our education relevant, students must understand current high-tech tools.

Audience: Customer

Our company has the best cellphone package.

- We have the lowest rates.
- We give more free daytime minutes than the competitors.
- We include call display and voice messaging in all of our packages.

The Argument Essay

When you write an argument essay, remember four key points.

1. **Consider your readers.** What do your readers already know about the topic? Will they likely agree or disagree with you? Do they have specific concerns? Consider what kind of evidence would be most effective with your audience.

2. **Know your purpose.** In argument writing, your main purpose is to persuade the reader to agree with you. Your specific purpose is more focused. You may want the reader to take action, you may want to support a viewpoint, you may want to counter somebody else's argument, or you may want to offer a solution to a problem. Ask yourself, What is my specific purpose?

3. **Take a strong position and provide persuasive evidence.** The first thing to do in the body of your essay is to prove that there is, indeed, a problem. Then back up your point of view with a combination of facts, statistics, examples, and informed opinions.

4. **Show that you are trustworthy.** Respect your readers by making a serious argument. If you are condescending, or if you try to joke about the topic, your readers may be less inclined to accept your argument. You can also help your readers have more respect for your ideas when you choose a topic that you know something about. For example, if you have been in the military or know people in the military, you might be able to make a very convincing argument about the lack of proper equipment for soldiers.

Argument at Work

Network administrator Octavio Pelaez uses argument writing in this excerpt from a memo to his director.

We need to invest in a new email server. First, the slow speed and unreliability of the present equipment is becoming a serious inconvenience. While the cost of replacing the server and the accompanying software will be very high, the cost of not doing it is going to be much higher in lost time and productivity. It would not be an exaggeration to say that for the last three months, we have lost over a thousand billable hours due to the poor condition of our equipment. The average hourly rate per user is $30, thus those lost hours of productivity have cost the company over $30 000. Also, consider the impact on our company's reputation when the clients have problems communicating with us. We cannot afford to wait any longer to invest in new equipment and technology. In fact, over the long term, replacing the email server would actually increase productivity and profitability.

A Student Essay

Read the student essay and answer the questions that follow.

Changing Face of Cosmetic Surgery
by Kate Howell

1   Many people who undergo cosmetic surgery are regarded as vapid, shallow, and lacking in self-esteem. The phrases "Be happy with who you are" and "God made you perfect as is" are thrown around to provide assurance. For instance, a woman who attempts to change her appearance is told that such an act signals a level of dishonesty toward herself, her family and, possibly, her creator. The stigma associated with plastic surgery clearly exists—note the negative connotation of the word "plastic." However, such attitudes ignore reality. Anyone who uses cosmetic surgery to enhance his or her appearance should be applauded, not condemned.   *thesis statement*

2   "It is better to look good than to feel good." This line was made famous in the 1980s by Billy Crystal's "Fernando" character on *Saturday Night Live*, but few would have imagined that it was more than a catchphrase. It was actually an indication of a cultural phenomenon that exploded shortly thereafter. Cosmetic surgery has become popular on TV, in the office, and all around campus. TV shows such as *Extreme Makeover* have become hits. Prices for all kinds of procedures, from eyelifts to liposuction, have gone down, so more and more people can afford them. The age of plastic surgery recipients has also gone down, with college-aged girls opting for breast implants and nose jobs.

3   It is not just women who are body-obsessed. According to *HealthDay News*, men are the newest arrivals to the cosmetic surgery party. In 2000, there was a 16 percent increase in body-altering procedures performed on males. Competition in the business world is fierce, and men are looking for any advantage they can find. Bags under the eyes and a weak chin just won't cut it when there is an army of young bucks with MBAs gunning for every job. The idea that men are not supposed to care or show interest in their personal appearance is outdated and unfortunate. We do not live in a society of cattle ranchers and frontier explorers anymore. The beaten-up faces and callused hands of yore are no longer necessary tools of the trade; in today's society, they have been replaced by cheek lifts and palm scrubs, and that is not necessarily a bad thing.

4   There remains a degree of disapproval of plastic surgery, yet the importance of personal appearance is everywhere. Consumers spend billions of dollars each year on makeup, haircuts, tanning salons, manicures, and pedicures. Studies show that good-looking people tend to get hired for jobs. In the movies, some distinct qualities belong to the majority of the stars: trim bodies, immaculate grooming, and gleaming teeth. Yet nobody likes to acknowledge the fact that looks matter. Science

tells us we are attracted to certain features, and it is ridiculous to deny that fact. Appearance certainly isn't everything, but to downplay its importance is self-righteous hypocrisy.

5   If, as is widely believed, it is what is on the inside that matters, then people should not get in such a huff about altering one's outside. If a person feels unattractive, he or she should not be held back from making a change because friends or family cling to some half-hearted notion of "playing the cards one has been dealt." If people desire to remake their body as they see fit, then more power to them. In this time of laziness and apathy, at least these people are taking steps to try to improve their lot in life. As humans, we adapt to our society, and ours is now one of aesthetics. To borrow an oft-used phrase from hip-hop: Don't hate the player, hate the game.

PRACTICE 1

1. Highlight the thesis statement.

2. What introduction style does the author use?
   a. an anecdote
   b. a definition
   c. a contrasting position
   d. a description

3. Highlight the topic sentence in paragraphs 2 and 4. Be careful because the topic sentence may not be the first sentence.

4. The topic sentence in paragraph 3 is implied but is not stated directly. Choose the most effective topic sentence for this paragraph.
   a. Men are obsessed about their bodies.
   b. In 2000, the percentage of males getting cosmetic surgery increased.
   c. Men no longer want to have wrinkled, beaten-up faces and callused hands.
   d. To gain an advantage in the competitive workplace, men are increasingly opting to have cosmetic surgery.

5. What is the author's specific purpose? _To argue it is important to do cosmetic surgery_

6. The writer supports her point of view with specific evidence. Underline a quotation and a statistic.

7. In your own words, sum up the writer's main point about cosmetic surgery.

   Adapting social demand.

Explore Topics

In the Writer's Desk Warm Up, you will try an exploring strategy to generate ideas about different topics.

Writer's Desk **Warm Up**

Read the following questions, and write the first ideas that come to your mind. Think of two to three ideas for each topic.

EXAMPLE: Should alcohol advertising be banned?

Yes, I think so. It doesn't make sense that cigarette advertising is banned, when alcohol is much more dangerous. The ads make drinking seem glamorous.

1. Are some laws invalid, irrational, or unfair? To find ideas, you might think about laws related to drinking, driving, cycling, smoking, and voting.

_____

_____

_____

2. Should the custom of tipping for service be abolished? Why or why not?

_____ No _____ It depends on customers.

_____

_____

3. What are some of the major controversial issues in your neighbourhood, workplace, college, province, or country? List some issues.

_____ Gullang

_____

_____

DEVELOPING

The Thesis Statement

In the thesis statement of an argument essay, state your position on the issue.

topic   controlling idea (the writer's position)

Many corporate executives <u>are overpaid for very substandard work.</u>

A thesis statement should be debatable, not a fact or a statement of opinion.

Fact: Some car companies have produced electric cars.
(This is a fact. It cannot be debated.)

Opinion: I think that people should buy electric cars.
(This is a statement of opinion. Nobody can deny that you feel this way. Therefore, do not use phrases such as *In my opinion, I think*, or *I believe* in your thesis statement.)

Argument: To address global warming and energy shortages, the automobile industry should focus on the production of electric cars.
(This is a debatable statement.)

 **Be Direct**

Many students feel reluctant to take a stand on an issue. They may feel that it is too personal or impolite to do so. However, in academic writing, it is perfectly acceptable, and even desirable, to state an argument in a direct manner and then support it.

PRACTICE 2   Evaluate the following statements. Write F for a fact, O for an opinion, or A for an argument.

1. Canada should impose a standard three-week vacation for all workers.

2. Many colleges permit soft-drink companies to sell their products on campus.

3. I disagree with advertising on college campuses.

4. The city's major art gallery spent millions of dollars on an abstract painting.

5. In my point of view, abstract art is ridiculous.

6. Japanese animé should be recognized as an influential art form.

7. I think that no one should use racial profiling at borders.

8. Racial profiling at borders is a legitimate way to defend the nation.

9. In our province, art is not taught in most high schools.

10. Art education should be compulsory in our high schools.

 **Making a Guided Thesis Statement**

Your instructor may want you to guide the reader through your main points. To do this, mention your main and supporting ideas in your thesis statement. In other words, your thesis statement provides a map for the readers to follow.

Art education should be compulsory in high schools because it encourages creativity, it teaches culture, and it develops students' analytical skills.

Writer's Desk **Write Thesis Statements**

Write a thesis statement for the following topics. You can look for ideas in the Warm Up on page 225. Make sure that each thesis statement clearly expresses your position on the issue.

EXAMPLE: Topic: alcohol advertising

Thesis statement: _*Advertisements for alcoholic beverages should be prohibited on*_ _*television or in any form of mass media.*_

1. Topic: unfair laws

   Thesis statement: The Law bans teenager driking should be
   abolished.

2. Topic: tipping customs

   Thesis statement: Tipping custom should be saved by
   United Nation and

3. Topic: a controversial issue

   Thesis statement:

The Supporting Ideas

To make a logical and reasoned argument, support your main point with facts, examples, and statistics. (For details about adding facts, examples, and statistics, see page 50 in Chapter 4.)

You can also include the following types of support.

- **Quote informed sources.** Sometimes experts in a field express an informed opinion about an issue. An expert's thoughts and ideas can add weight to your argument. For example, if you want to argue that people are becoming complacent about AIDS, you might quote an article published by a respected national health organization.
- **Consider logical consequences.** When you plan an argument, think about long-term consequences of a proposed solution to a problem. Perhaps you want to argue that alternative energy sources should be used to fuel automobiles. You could point out that the country will be less reliant on oil imports. As a result, consumers will not be subject to rising gas prices caused by conflicts in other areas of the world.
- **Acknowledge opposing viewpoints.** Anticipating and responding to opposing views can strengthen your position. For instance, if you argue that school uniforms should be mandatory, you might address those who feel that students need freedom to express themselves. Try to refute some of the strongest arguments of the opposition.

Making an Emotional Appeal

reffle
refutation.

Generally, an effective argument appeals to the reader's reason, but it can also appeal to his or her emotion. For example, you could use certain words or descriptions to encourage a reader's sense of justice, humanity, or pride. However, use emotional appeals sparingly. If you use **emotionally charged words** such as *wimp* or *thug*, or if you appeal to base instincts such as fear or cowardice, then you may seriously undermine your argument. Review the following examples of emotional appeals.

Overemotional:	A ferocious, bloodthirsty pit bull broke free of its leash and attacked a defenseless, fragile boy named Jason. The child, who will suffer from lifelong psychological trauma, is disfigured with irreparable facial scars.
Reasonable and more neutral:	Pit bulls can be unpredictable. The pit bull attack on nine-year-old Jason caused significant facial scarring and psychological trauma.

 **Avoid Common Errors**

When you write your argument essay, avoid the following pitfalls.

Do not make generalizations. If you begin a statement with *Everyone knows* or *It is common knowledge*, then the reader may mistrust what you say. You cannot possibly know what everyone else knows or does not know. It is better to refer to specific sources.

> **Generalization:** Everyone knows that our nation is too dependent on oil.
>
> **Better:** Prominent senators have stated that our nation's dependence on oil is a serious problem.

Do not make exaggerated claims. Make sure that your arguments are plausible.

> **Exaggerated:** If marijuana is legalized, drug use will soar in schools across the nation.
>
> **Better:** If marijuana is legalized, drug use may increase in schools across the nation.

PRACTICE 3 You have learned about different methods to support a topic. Read each of the following thesis statements and think of a supporting idea for each item. Use the type of support suggested in parentheses.

1. Volunteer work should be mandatory in all high schools.

   (Logical consequence) _____

   _____

2. Online dating is a great way to meet a potential mate.

   (Acknowledge an opposing view) _____

   _____

3. Children should not be spanked.

   (Emotional appeal) _____

   _____

4. The college dropout rate is too high in our province.

   (Logical consequence) _____

   _____

5. Pointy-toed stilettos are unattractive, uncomfortable, and potentially harmful. (Acknowledge an opposing viewpoint) _____

_____

---

vo•cab•u•lar•y BOOST

Some words can influence readers because they have positive or negative connotations, which are implied or associated meanings. The meaning often carries a cultural value judgment with it. For example, *macho* may have negative connotations in one country and positive connotations in another country. For the word *thin*, synonyms like *skinny* or *skeletal* have negative connotations, while *slender* and *svelte* have positive ones.

Using a thesaurus, try to come up with related terms or descriptions that have either positive or negative connotations for the words in bold.

Gloria is **large.**

Calvin is **not assertive.**

Mr. Wayne **expresses his opinion.**

Franklin is a **liberal.**

Identify terms you chose that might be too emotionally loaded for an argument essay.

Consider Both Sides of the Issue

Once you have decided what issue you want to write about, try to think about both sides of the issue. Then you can predict arguments that your opponents might make, and you can plan your answer to the opposition. Here are examples.

Arguments for Banning Alcohol Advertisements	**Arguments Against Banning Alcohol Advertisements**
▪ Ads encourage drinking among adolescents.	▪ Print advertisers will lose significant income from magazine ads.
▪ Ads are aimed at young males who can become aggressive.	▪ Sporting events rely on advertising dollars.
▪ Alcohol kills more people than cigarettes.	▪ Advertisers should have freedom of speech.

Writer's Desk Consider Both Sides of the Issue

Choose one of the topics from the previous Writer's Desk, and write arguments showing both sides of the issue.

Topic: _____

For	Against
_____	_____
_____	_____
_____	_____
_____	_____
_____	_____

 **Strengthening an Essay with Research**

In some courses, your instructors may ask you to include supporting ideas from informed sources to strengthen your essays. You can find information in a variety of resources, including textbooks, journals, newspapers, magazines, or on the internet. When researching, make sure that your sources are from legitimate organizations. For example, for information about the spread of AIDS, you might find statistics on the World Health Organization website. You would not go to someone's personal rant or conspiracy theory site.

For more information about evaluating and documenting sources, refer to Chapter 15, The Research Essay.

The Essay Plan

Before you write your argument essay, outline your ideas in a plan. Include details that can help illustrate each argument. Ensure that every example is valid and relates to the thesis statement. Also think about your organization. Many argument essays use emphatic order and list ideas from the least to the most important or compelling.

THESIS STATEMENT: <u>Advertisements for alcoholic beverages should be</u> <u>prohibited on television or in any form of mass media.</u>

I. Banning alcohol ads would reduce excessive drinking and alcohol-related assaults and injuries among youths.
   A. Drinking is like a rite of passage, and ads encourage that belief.
   B. Many binge drinkers die from alcohol poisoning.
   C. Many rapes and assaults are blamed on excessive drinking.

II. Alcohol advertising targets young impressionable males who are the most dangerous drivers.
   A. Beer ads reinforce he-man attitudes.
   B. Young males are more likely to drink and drive than any others.
   C. Drunk driving rates are very high among young men.

III. It is hypocritical to ban cigarette advertising but not alcohol advertising.
   A. Cigarette packages carry warnings, but alcohol bottles don't.
   B. Alcohol is addictive.
   C. Alcohol causes many diseases such as cirrhosis of the liver.

Writer's Desk **Write an Essay Plan**

Choose one of the ideas that you have developed in the previous Writer's Desk, and write a detailed essay plan.

The First Draft

Now that you have a refined thesis statement, solid supporting details, and a roadmap of your arguments and the order in which you will present them, you are ready to write the first draft. Remember to write complete sentences and to include transitional words or expressions to lead readers from one idea to the next. Here are some transitions that introduce an answer to the opposition or the supporting ideas for an argument.

To answer the opposition

admittedly
however
nevertheless
of course
on one hand/on the other hand
undoubtedly

To support your argument

certainly
consequently
furthermore
in fact
obviously
of course

 **Keeping Pronouns Consistent**

In argument writing, ensure that your pronouns do not switch between *they*, *we*, and *you*. If you are writing about specific groups of people, use *they* to refer to those people. Only change pronouns when the switch is logical.

> Many hunters argue that they need large collections and varieties of guns. Yet
> *they*
> why would ~~you~~ need a semi-automatic to go hunting?

See Chapter 26 for more information about pronoun usage.

Writer's Desk **Write the First Draft**

Write the first draft of your argument essay. Include an interesting introduction. Also, add specific details to flesh out each body paragraph.

REVISING AND EDITING

Revise and Edit an Argument Essay

When you finish writing an argument essay, carefully review your work and revise it to make the supporting examples as clear as possible to your readers. Check that the order of ideas is logical, and remove any irrelevant details. Before you revise and edit your own essay, practise revising and editing a student essay.

A Student Essay

Read the essay, and then answer the questions that follow. As you read, correct any errors that you find, and make comments in the margins.

Alcohol Advertising
by Kayin Jacobs

1   Magazines feature glossy vodka advertisements. During television sporting events, viewers see one beer ad after another. Alcohol, while society's most accepted drug, is considerably more dangerous than some other substances that cannot be advertised. The current massive promotion of alcoholic beverages has several negative side effects that are ignored because of the cultural significance of alcohol. Advertisements for alcoholic beverages should be prohibited on television or in any form of mass media.

2   Binge drinking is a common pass-time for students entering their first week of college. Eliminating alcohol ads would reduce excessive drinking and alcohol-related assaults and injuries among youths. While some may see drinking as a rite of passage for young people entering adulthood, the reality is that the practice doesn't have no positive benefits. According to Anne Mullens' "The Perils of Binge Drinking, "[W]hat alarms public-health officials is the fact that while illicit drug use has generally been declining, the prevalence of binge drinking has been holding steady and even increasing, particularly among youth age 15 to 25. Moreover, new studies show that some kids start drinking at 13 or younger, and youth are particularly at risk from its effects." The author refers to a "2000 Canadian Campus Survey[, which] found . . . 63 percent of students reporting consuming five or more drinks in a single sitting in the previous year. The Canadian study concluded that campuses are a 'risky milieu for hazardous drinking.'" Mullens further states that "Whatever the age, binge drinking puts a person at much higher risk of death or injuries from motor vehicle crashes, falls, drowning and other hazards of poor judgement and reduced coordination. Violence, vandalism, sexual assault, unprotected sexual encounters with the risk of unplanned pregnancy or infection from sexually transmitted diseases all increase." Alcohol is the only recreational drug that is still actively advertised on television, and this is a large part of the reason why so many young people binge on the drug. Elimination of the advertising could result in a lower number of young people who drink, just as removing cigarette advertising from television has helped reduce the number of young smokers.

3   Alcohol advertising targets young impressionable males who are the most dangerous drivers. Beer ads, for example. These advertisements usually allude to a connection between drinking a certain beer and getting attractive females. In the article "Sobering Drunk Driving Statistics,"

"Mothers Against Drunk Driving Canada estimates that in 2005, there were 3226 traffic fatalities in Canada. Of these, they estimate that at least 1210—37.5%, or more than three deaths per day—involved impaired driving, but that the figure 'is a conservative estimate, due to the underreporting that results from the inability to test surviving impaired drivers and reliance on police reports.' Moreover, they estimate that in 2005, 380 668 individuals were injured in traffic accidents, and approximately 71 413 of these—or 196 per day—were injured in impaired driving crashes. It stands to reason that the elimination of alcohol advertising would result in fewer drunk driving fatalities, as young men are both the primary target of these advertisements and the primary cause of most drunk driving deaths.

4   Cigarette packages contain warnings about negative health effects. Alcohol cans and bottles should also have warning labels explaining the addictive qualities of the product and the long-term effects of excessive drinking. Certainly, both cigarettes and alcohol are highly addictive. A lifetime drinker has health problems that could be compared to a lifetime smoker. Some of the potential health problems that could await an alcoholic include brain cell damage, inflammation and ulcers in the stomach, and cirrhosis, hepatitis, or cancer of the liver. According to *Preventing Chronic Disease*, "in Canada in 2002, there were 1631 chronic disease deaths among adults aged 69 years and younger attributed to alcohol consumption, and these deaths were 2.4% of the deaths in Canada for this age group."

5   Now, don't get the wrong message. This is not an argument for the prohibition of alcohol but for a pause in the incessant marketing of this product to young people, young males in particular. Let's face it: young guys can become idiots when they have a bottle in their hands. Advertising promotes our alcohol culture, which results in many preventable deaths every year. Those who want alcohol can buy it, but it should not be actively marketed. A lesson society seems to have learned with cigarettes. Now let's hope the holocaust of people's lives is curbed with the ban of alcohol advertising.

Skirmish

PRACTICE 4

heedless

Revising

1. Highlight the thesis statement.

2. Highlight the topic sentence in each body paragraph.

3. a. How does the topic sentence in paragraph 4 fail to support the thesis statement?

    The Thesis - is about media Warning problem
    4 — is about health
              cigarette.

Because potential consequences are serious compared to cigarettes

b. Create a topic sentence for paragraph 4 that more effectively links the paragraph to the thesis statement.

Alcohol cans and bottles should contain warnings about negative healths.

4. In the concluding paragraph, the writer uses emotionally charged words and exaggerates. Give examples of each of these problems.

Emotionally charged language ___~~idiots~~ *can become idiots.* - - -

Exaggeration - - *which results in many deaths every yr preventable*

5. Does the writer acknowledge the opposing viewpoint? _____ Yes __✓_No

Editing

6. Underline and correct a spelling mistake in paragraph 2.

Correction: ___*part-time.*___

GRAMMAR LINK

See the following chapters for more information about these topics:
Fragments, Chapter 17
Double Negatives, Chapter 23
Spelling, Chapter 27

7. In paragraph 2, there is a double negative. (Two negative words cancel each other out.) Underline the error and write the correct phrase in the space.

Correction: ___*Doesn't have any positive benefits*___

8. Identify fragments in paragraphs 3 and 5, and write correct sentences on the lines below.

Paragraph 3: ___*Beer ads, for example, are*___

Paragraph 5: ___~~Message this~~___
___*It is a lesson* ...___

Writer's Desk   Revise and Edit Your Essay

Revise and edit the essay that you wrote for the previous Writer's Desk. You can refer to the revising and editing checklists at the end of this chapter and on this book's inside covers.

A Professional Essay

Rex Murphy is a Canadian political and social commentator. He is the host of CBC Radio's *Cross Country Checkup*, and he contributes to CBC TV's *The National*. In this essay, he argues for the preservation of the Tim Hortons brand. Read the essay, and answer the questions that follow.

I'm with the Brand

May 17, 2008

1   On this Victoria Day weekend, back home in Newfoundland, there will be thousands of people hustling off to cabin or pond to make a day of trout fishing and having a boil-up. Very likely it'll snow, since a snowfall is an almost infallible curse of the first long weekend of Newfoundland spring. In the old days, if there was to be a boil-up and a few trout to be fried, everyone brought along a block of Good Luck butter and three or four tins of York wieners and beans. Had to be York, had to be Good Luck.

2   Good Luck and York were the brands of choice. Newfoundlanders, for reasons that defy any substantial analysis, bonded with certain brands. Robin Hood flour, a local bread called (excruciatingly) Mammy's, a chocolate bar that was not a bar at all (Cherry Blossom), Klik canned beef—there were a batch of such brand items that simply belonged. I've seen Libby's beans on camping trips, but I knew, and everyone else did, too, that the dolt who brought them was a stranger and an heretic.

3   Certain items moved into a territory of being more than just commodities. They offered a kind of whimsical identity, a grocery shelf of Newfoundlandia. In the really old days, a plug of Target chewing tobacco was as much a part of a fisherman's kit as nets and lines.

4   All were more emblems than products.

5   The same phenomenon can be seen on a much wider plane today with Tim Hortons. I doubt anyone can locate the moment Hortons stopped being a small doughnut shop, serving, at best, indifferent coffee and transmuted into a hallowed piece of Canadiana, but that it arrived no one can doubt. Outside of *Hockey Night in Canada* and—with reverence—Don Cherry, there are few institutions or companies that have blended into the character of the nation so completely as Tim Hortons.

6   I became a hostage to Boston cream doughnuts so long ago the day is lost in gooey memory. And now, in every town and city across the country, despite the advances of the upscale chains, the aggressive yuppie haunts of Starbucks Corp., the gentrified caffeine oases of Timothy's and Second Cup, Tim Hortons remains the venue of choice for all everyday Canadians. You knew the Canadian effort in Afghanistan had registered with the great Canadian public when Tim Hortons opened in Kandahar. Hortons is not the red Maple Leaf, but it has brewed and baked its way into being an essential piece of Canadiana.

7   Up to now, anyway. I think Tim Hortons is drifting from its special
status. This has nothing to do with the fury of recent weeks over the
woman fired for giving away a Timbit to a crying infant—though that
incident may be a signal of how the brand has strayed. Nor has it to do, in
my judgment, with the consideration that Tim Hortons was, until recently,
purely a Canadian company (Wendy's owns it now).

8   No, the change is more subtle and has crept in by a kind of osmosis.

9   Perhaps the invisible moment was the first time a Canadian went to a
Tim's not for itself, but more because it wasn't a Starbucks. A reverse
preference moment. Perhaps it came when Tim Hortons became conscious
that it really wasn't just selling cheap coffee and doughnuts. (That,
incidentally, was more than a while ago. Just one old-fashioned plain is
eighty cents now; years back, you could buy the whole front counter
display case of doughnuts for about five bucks.) Perhaps it was the
moment when they became self-conscious, and started to see themselves
as a symbol.

10   Something has leaked out of the enterprise. Did the coffee change?
Are the doughnuts still as fresh as once they so proudly boasted they
were? I'm not sure what it was or is, but, for me anyway, the zest has gone
out of the transaction between chain and customer. Their "roll up the rim"
is a farcical gimmick. The signature phrases—"double double" being the
most familiar—gall more than they please. Their ridiculous lineups—in
some places it takes longer to get a coffee than to pick up a licence at a
motor vehicle registration office—have lost the kind of self-congratulatory
charm they had some time back. People used to smile at each other for the
silly indulgence of lining up for a not-very-good cup of coffee. They don't
smile as much anymore. They mutter.

11   Most of all, people don't feel the loyalty they once did. It is no longer a
traitorous act to wander into Second Cup—though, it must be noted,
treading into Starbucks is still a barista too far. All in all, I think Timmy's—
another unfortunate coinage—is past its best-before date. The romance
has wilted. The coffee has cooled. It has had its crowning moment as a
badge of this great white north, but unless something in the chemistry
between coffee and customer changes, real soon, the days of Tim Hortons
as an essential Canadian experience are dwindling and few. ⌡ Thesis

PRACTICE 5

1. Highlight the thesis statement.

2. What technique does the writer use to introduce the topic?

   a. historical background   b. anecdote   c. a definition

3. What synonyms does Murphy use for *business* in this essay?

   _____

4. In which paragraph does the writer acknowledge an opposing viewpoint? __8__

5. Which sentence sums up the writer's implied argument in paragraph 3?

   a. Fishing is a way of life in Newfoundland.

   b. Some items turn into brands.

   c. Branded items often become necessities.

   d. Target chewing tobacco is a necessity for Newfoundlanders.

6. Underline the topic sentence in paragraph 11.

7. Which sentence sums up the writer's implied argument in paragraph 10?   A

   a. Customer attitudes are changing.

   b. Tim Hortons represents more than coffee.

   c. Tim Hortons has undergone major changes.

   d. Customers are frustrated with long line-ups at Tim Hortons.

8. Using your own words, sum up Murphy's main supporting arguments.

   Tim hortons
   The change is more subtle and has crept in "osmosis
   more emblems than products

The Writer's Room **Topics for Argument Essays**

Writing Activity 1

Choose any of the following topics, or choose your own topic, and write an argument essay. Remember to narrow your topic and to follow the writing process.

General Topics	**College and Work-Related Topics**
1. graffiti	6. usefulness of college programs
2. gun laws	7. working while going to college
3. labour unions	8. minimum wage
4. home schooling	9. parental leave
5. same-sex marriage	10. working at home

Writing Activity 2

Choose a quotation that you agree or disagree with, and then write an argument essay based on it.

> Many would be cowards if they had courage enough.
> —Thomas Fuller, historian

> Advertising is the modern substitute for argument.
> —George Santayana, philosopher

> My great hope would be that Quebec would realize itself fully as a distinct part of Canada, and stay Canadian, bringing to Canada a part of its richness.
> —Gabrielle Roy, French-Canadian author

> Everything on the earth has a purpose, every disease an herb to cure it, and every person a mission.
> —Mourning Dove Salish, author

READING LINK

Argument

"A Modest Proposal," by Heather Mallick (page 490)

"Google's China Web" by Frida Ghitis (page 512)

"Medicating Ourselves" by Robyn Sarah (page 534)

WRITING LINK

See the next grammar sections for more argument writing topics.

Chapter 18, Writer's Room topic 2 (page 315)

Chapter 20, Writer's Room topic 1 (page 332)

Chapter 25, Writer's Room topic 2 (page 402)

Chapter 26, Writer's Room topic 1 (page 418)

Chapter 27, Writer's Room topic 2 (page 432)

Chapter 28, Writer's Room topic 2 (page 446)

Writing Activity 3

Examine the photo and think about arguments that you might make, such as controversies related to sex selection, international adoptions, foster care, and celebrity adoptions. For instance, you could argue that adopted children should or should not receive information about their biological fathers. Then write an argument essay.

CHECKLIST: ARGUMENT ESSAY

After you write your argument essay, review the checklist on the inside front cover. Also, ask yourself the following set of questions.

☐ Does my thesis statement clearly state my position on the issue?

☐ Do I make strong supporting arguments?

☐ Do I include facts, examples, statistics, and logical consequences?

☐ Do my supporting arguments provide evidence that directly supports the thesis statement?

☐ Do I acknowledge and counter opposing arguments?

☐ Do I use valid arguments? (Do I avoid making broad generalizations? Do I restrain any emotional appeals?)

☐ Do I use a courteous tone?

How Do I Get a Better Grade?

mycanadiancomplab

Go to www.mycanadiancomplab.ca for additional help with your grammar, writing, and research skills. You will have access to a variety of exercises, instruction, and video that will help you improve your basic skills and help you get a better grade.

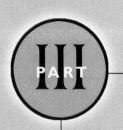

PART III

More College and Workplace Writing

In the following chapters, you will learn about additional writing skills. Chapter 14, Paraphrasing and Summarizing, provides you with details about these important skills. Chapter 15 leads you through the process of writing a research essay.

Source: *Understanding Music* by Jeremy Yudkin, Fifth Edition, 2008, Prentice Hall, Upper Saddle River, New Jersey

Page 411. "Jazz singers also deliberately make use of unusual sounds. A special kind of singing in which the vocalist improvises with nonsense syllables . . . is known as 'scat' singing."

423: bebop uses "nonsense syllables used in scat singing." Different from swing—not as predictable.

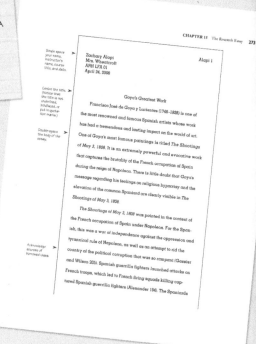

Paraphrasing and Summarizing

CHAPTER 14

CONTENTS

- Integrating Borrowed Information
- Paraphrasing
- Summarizing

When cooking, you combine small amounts of specific ingredients to create an appetizing meal. When writing a research-supported essay, you combine other people's ideas with your own to support your main points.

Integrating Borrowed Information

During your college career, your instructor may ask you to support your essay ideas using quotations, paraphrases, or summaries. These useful strategies strengthen your research paper and make it more forceful and convincing.

A **quotation** permits you to use another person's exact language. A **paraphrase** lets you use your own words to present someone else's essential information or ideas. Finally, a **summary** allows you to use borrowed information by presenting only the main points of one or several works in your own words. A summary is a shortened version of the original work.

All of these strategies are valid ways to incorporate research into your writing, as long as you give credit to the author or speaker.

> 66 *After all, the ultimate goal of all research is not objectivity, but truth.* 99
>
> HELENE DEUTSCH,
> *psychoanalyst*

Avoid Plagiarism

Plagiarism is the act of using—intentionally or unintentionally—someone else's words or images without giving that person credit. Plagiarism is a very serious offence and can result in expulsion from college or termination from work. **Always** acknowledge the source when you borrow material. Here are some ways to avoid plagiarizing someone else's work.

- Do not buy another work and present it as your own.
- Do not use another student's work and present it as your own.
- Do not use someone's exact words or ideas without citing that source.
- Do not make slight modifications to an author's sentences and then present the work as your own.

To avoid plagiarism, keep detailed notes about your sources. Then, when you want to borrow words, phrases, or ideas, you can acknowledge the source.

GRAMMAR LINK

To find out more about using quotations, see Chapter 30.

Paraphrasing

Paraphrasing allows you to support your essay using other people's ideas. By paraphrasing, you can make the ideas of a source clearer in your own paper. In addition, paraphrasing forces you to grasp a text completely, which may be useful for fully understanding the subject of your research paper. Clarifying ideas by paraphrasing may also help when you are studying. When you paraphrase, use only your own words.

How to Paraphrase

- Read the original text carefully and underline any key ideas. You will have to restate the main ideas and supporting details of the text when you paraphrase.
- Use your own words to restate the main and supporting ideas of the original text. To help prevent copying, try not to look at the original source. Use a dictionary and thesaurus to find exact meanings and synonyms of words in the original text.
- Mention the source of the original text. State the author and title.
- Put quotation marks around any words or phrases used from the original source. Words that are specific names or generic words do not have to be put into quotation marks.

- Use approximately the same number of words as the original passage. A paraphrase is a restated version of the original text.
- Do not change the meaning of the original text. Do not include your own opinions.
- Verify that your paraphrase expresses the ideas and intent of the author of the original text.

The following paragraph is from a longer article written by John Stanton and appeared in the October 5, 2010, edition of the *National Post* online edition. Read the selection and paraphrase.

Original Selection

Sport drinks or fluid/electrolyte replacement beverages help to "top up" blood glucose levels. This, in turn, helps to preserve or "spare" your glycogen stores and promote endurance. Sport drinks also replace minerals like potassium and sodium that are lost during exercise. But not all runners can tolerate sport drinks. Recognizing this, it is important to experiment during training to assess their impact on your individual performance. Never try a sport drink on race day if you have not already tested it during training.

Effective Paraphrase

On the *National Post* website, John Stanton states that sport beverages can enhance runners' training performance. The author stresses the importance of exercisers trying the drink prior to training to see if it works for them.

Unacceptable Paraphrase

Sport drinks aid in increasing blood glucose levels, which aids in preserving glycogen stores and promoting endurance. It is crucial for trainers to experiment with sport drinks to see if it impacts their training experience.

This paraphrase is unacceptable because it contains exact words from the text without enclosing them in quotation marks.

PRACTICE I   Read the following selections and answer the questions that follow. The original selection, written by Mike Oliveira, appeared in The *Montreal Gazette* on December 4, 2006, on page D5.

ORIGINAL SELECTION

While Apple has sold 70 million units and has legions of devotees, the iPod has also received unfavourable attention for problems that have been known to kill the pricey gadgets—including screens that break, batteries that fade, damaged headphone jacks that distort sound, and failing hard drives. In rare cases, some iPods were even sold with a virus.

PARAPHRASE A

In the *Montreal Gazette*, Mike Oliveira writes that iPod sales are in the millions. However, some iPods contain many problems that lead to breakage. Such problems are breaking screens, fading batteries, damaged headphone jacks that distort sound, and failing hard drives. Some iPods even contain a virus.

1. How does this paraphrase plagiarize the original piece of writing?

_____

_____

_____

PARAPHRASE B

Apple computers have sold millions of iPods, but some customers are experiencing difficulties with the popular product. Some iPod users complain that screens fracture, batteries weaken, and headphones do not work. Also, iPod hard drives collapse and some have a virus.

No Citation

2. How does this paraphrase plagiarize the original piece of writing?

_____

_____

Summarizing

Summarizing is a vital skill for writing and studying. When you summarize, you condense a text to its key ideas. Reducing a long work to its bare essentials requires that you fully understand the message of the text. It also helps you understand how ideas are organized in a text.

How to Summarize

- Read the original text carefully.
- Underline any key ideas. In a summary, you will present only the main ideas of a text.
- Ask yourself *who, what, when, where, why,* and *how* questions. These questions will help you to synthesize the ideas of the original text.
- Restate the essential ideas in your own words. Refer to a dictionary and thesaurus for the meanings of words and for useful synonyms.
- Maintain the original meaning of the text. Do not include your own opinions.

- Mention the author and title of the original source.
- Reread your summary. Verify that you have explained the key message of the text.

PRACTICE 2

The folowing paragraph is from page 101 of the textbook *Core Concepts in Sociology*, by Linda L. Lindsey, Stephen Beach, and Bruce Ravelli. Compare the paraphrase and summary of the original text. Then answer the questions that follow by underlining the appropriate response.

ORIGINAL SELECTION

In much of the world, health care is provided by traditional or folk healers. The ethnocentric notion long prevalent in the Western world that traditional healing would be replaced by scientific medicine is now questioned. Folk healers are successful because they understand patient concerns from the viewpoint of the patient's culture. China's "barefoot doctors" are recruited from the villages they eventually serve. They understand village culture and combine techniques from both traditional and scientific medicine.

PARAPHRASE

In *Core Concepts in Sociology*, Linda L. Lindsey and others state that indigenous medical practices are used by many societies around the world. Occidental medical experts were wrong when they thought that modern Western medicine would take the place of native health care customs. By being sensitive to culture, health care givers around the world gain the confidence of their patients. Chinese doctors practising in rural areas often are villagers themselves. They are successful because they blend local and Western medicine (101).

SUMMARY

According to Linda L. Lindsey in *Core Concepts in Sociology*, indigenous health care givers around the world are successful in treating patients because they blend local and Western medicine practices (101).

1. Which is about the same length as the original text?
   paraphrase _
   summary   _
   both   _

2. Which contains only the main idea of the original text?
   paraphrase _
   summary   _
   both   _

3. Which maintains the author's intent of the original text?
   paraphrase _
   summary   _
   both   _

4. Which includes all the details of the original text?
   paraphrase _
   summary   _
   both   _

5. Which mentions the source of the original text?
   paraphrase _
   summary   _
   both   _

 **Consider Your Audience**

When you decide whether to paraphrase or summarize, think about your audience.

- Paraphrase if your audience needs detailed information about the subject.
- Summarize if the audience needs to know only general information.

PRACTICE 3   The following article is by Noreen Rasbach and was published in the *Globe and Mail*. Read the article and then write a summary. To make summarizing a longer text a little easier, follow these steps:

Read the complete article.

- Underline the main ideas in the text.
- Write the summary by answering *who, what, when, where, why,* and *how* questions.
- Write a first draft of the summary.
- Remove any unnecessary details.
- Ensure that you have not used the exact words or phrases from the original text.
- Reduce your writing to only a paragraph by revising and condensing your draft.
- Reread your summary to verify that you have stated the essential ideas of the text.

Bridging the Spender–Saver Divide
by Noreen Rasbach

1   A few years back, Valentina Naranjo Velasquez and her husband Gary Verrinder found themselves in a place that is probably very familiar to a vast majority of Canadian couples: They began to fight about money.

2   Their story, as told by Ms. Velasquez, is common: The Kitchener, Ont., couple, who together earn about $130 000 a year, was constantly short of cash. "I felt for me it was always, 'Well, where's the money?' or 'Where did the money go?'"

3   "It was very stressful."

4   Ms. Velasquez, 29, and Mr. Verrinder, 42, also had different attitudes toward money: He was a spender, she was more of a saver.

5   "And when he spends, he spends big," she says.

6   Theirs is the story with which many Canadian couples can identify. A national survey by Credit Canada and Capital One Canada last year found that 86 per cent of couples say they argue about money and 48 per cent say they don't believe their spouses have the same philosophy when it comes to managing money.

7   Opposites attract: So say therapists and personal-finance experts, who see the saver-spender divides in a large number of couples. These couples have opposite approaches to money, and can develop strong frustration and resentment toward their spouses.

8   "I deal with a lot of women across the country, and the perfect emotional financial storm happens when there's misalignment, there's a lack of trust and there are differing financial values," says Patricia Lovett-Reid, senior vice-president with TD Waterhouse Canada Inc.

9   "I have seen many couples who actually don't understand each other's spending or saving personalities until a year or two into the relationship and then—wow—fireworks," says Alison Griffiths, a personal-finance author and host of television show *Maxed Out*.

10   "But I don't believe that finances are like leopards and spots. I do believe that people can alter their financial personalities."

11   That begins by having a conversation about money, experts say, preferably with a third party who can cut through the intense emotions. "When those conversations start, there is a floodgate of emotions that get unleashed," says Karin Mizgala, a financial planner who also is co-founder of the Women's Financial Learning Centre in Vancouver.

12   "Typically when the conversation happens, it's a fight. There are pent-up fears and insecurities on the part of the saver, who sees that his or her

financial well-being may be jeopardized by their partner. On the spender's part, there can be a real sense that they don't want to be told what to do, that they're tired of having every move being watched."

13   Those conversations should also touch on how each spouse was raised and what influenced their attitudes about money, says Ed Santana, a psychotherapist and executive-director for the Ontario Association for Marriage and Family Therapy.

14   "When they understand where the other person is coming from and when they [learn] some of their choices about money, [their fight] becomes less personal," he says.

15   Mr. Santana and financial experts also agree on some of the ways to bring together spenders and savers to find the middle ground.

16   The first step: Figure out exactly how much the household spends and what the money goes toward.

17   The next: Find common goals and let each other know individual goals. Whether it's getting out of debt, or saving for a house, a car or a vacation—setting up a budget and a financial plan to meet those goals can help couples stay on the right path.

18   It's what Devon Beaton and Kristin Campbell of Calgary did. The couple—she's 20 and he's 22—are engaged and had planned to get married this past summer. But first they had to sort out their financial differences— he was a saver and she was a spender.

19   The difference has caused friction at times, she says, but they have learned not to fight and to talk it out.

20   "I think we've both kind of rubbed off on each other," Ms. Campbell says. "We've both grown to accept each other. He tries to not be a penny pincher and I try not to spend as much. It's a compromise."

21   The couple talks regularly about what they can and can't afford. In the "can't" category: the summer wedding. When they realized they would have to go into debt for it, Ms. Campbell says, they decided to postpone it.

22   Ms. Lovett-Reid advises that couples also rotate financial responsibilities, so that each has an intimate knowledge of the household finances.

23   "If there's a dominant person in the family that handles the money, then switch it for six months, and the other will get a far better appreciation and understanding of how much money is coming in and where it is being spent," she says.

24   In the case of Ms. Velasquez, getting involved with the family's finances was a huge breakthrough. The couple may have had different attitudes toward money, but she says that she wasn't really taking any responsibility for the finances.

25 "Things are really good now. I'm more involved. We keep track of everything we spend. We probably talk about [household finances] every week.

26 "We definitely talk about it more without fighting about it."

27 The couple followed a lot of the experts' advice—they went to a third party, the Meridian Credit Union, where financial consultant Amie Daminato worked with the couple to come up with a budget plan, a savings plan and a financial wish list.

28 Ms. Velasquez says having financial goals—such as saving for retirement and their child's education—has made the couple focus on what's really important.

29 And a few months ago, when the couple's car broke down, they realized just how far they have come.

30 "It wasn't, 'Oh my God, how are we going to pay for that.' It was, 'Oh, we have money in savings.' It wasn't stressful at all."

The Writer's Room   **Paraphrasing or Summarizing**

Writing Activity 1

Choose one of the photos in this textbook and briefly summarize what seems to be taking place in it.

Writing Activity 2

Exchange an essay with a classmate and paraphrase or summarize it.

Writing Activity 3

Summarize the information found in the online chapter, Becoming a Successful Student.

Writing Activity 4

Summarize the plot of a novel, movie, or television program.

Writing Activity 5

Read one of the essays in this textbook and paraphrase a section of it.

✓ **CHECKLIST: PARAPHRASING AND SUMMARIZING**

When you paraphrase or summarize, ask yourself these questions.

☐ In a paraphrase, have I kept the original intent of the author?

☐ In a summary, have I kept only the key ideas?

☐ Have I used my own word when paraphrasing or summarizing?

☐ Have I mentioned the source when paraphrasing or summarizing?

How Do I Get a Better Grade?

mycanadiancomplab

Go to www.mycanadiancomplab.ca for additional help with your grammar, writing, and research skills. You will have access to a variety of exercises, instruction, and video that will help you improve your basic skills and help you get a better grade.

The Research Essay

CONTENTS

Before legislators plan new laws, they might examine previous case studies, survey public opinion, and consult with legal experts. In the same way, when you prepare to write a research essay, you look for resources in books, magazines and newspapers, and on the internet.

Planning a Research Essay

Conducting **research** means looking for information that will help you better understand a subject. Knowing how to locate, evaluate, and use information from other sources is valuable in your work and day-to-day activities. It is also crucial in college writing because, in many of your assignments, you are expected to include information from outside sources. In this chapter, you will learn some strategies for writing a research paper.

Determining Your Topic

In some courses, your instructor will ask you to write a research paper about a specific topic. However, if you are not assigned one, then you will need to think about issues related to your field of study or to your personal interests.

The scope of your topic should match the size of the assignment. Longer essays might have a broader topic, but a short research essay (of three or four pages) must have a rather narrow focus. For instance, you would not write about the history of Spanish art in a short research paper, but you could write about a particular artwork or artist. To help find and develop a topic, you can try exploring strategies such as freewriting, questioning, or brainstorming. (See Chapter 1 for more information about prewriting strategies.)

Finding a Guiding Research Question

The point of a research essay is not to simply collect information and summarize it; the idea is to gather information that relates directly to your central question. To help you determine your central question, brainstorm a list of questions that you would like your research to answer. For example, Zachary Alapi must write a research essay for his art history class. He might ask himself the following questions in order to narrow his topic.

What is my favourite artwork?

Why is Goya's "firing squad" painting so powerful?

What compelled Goya to paint?

Zachary's next step is to find the most promising research question that can become the focus of his essay.

Why is Goya's "firing squad" painting so powerful?

Writer's Desk Find a Research Topic

Choose a general topic that you might like to write about.

Topic: _____

Now ask five or six questions to help you narrow the topic.

_____

_____

_____

_____

_____

_____

Decide which question will become your guiding research question, and write it here.

_____

_____

Gathering Information

Once you know what information you seek, you can begin gathering ideas, facts, quotations, anecdotes, and examples about the research topic you have chosen. Before you begin to gather information, consider how to find it and how to sort the valid information from the questionable information.

Consulting Library-Based Sources

Today's technological advances in both print and electronic publishing make it easier than ever to access information. For sources, you can consult encyclopedias, online catalogues in libraries, periodical databases, and the internet. Here are some tips for finding information about your topic through library resources.

- **Ask a reference librarian** to help you locate information using various research tools, such as online catalogues, CD-ROMs, and microfiches. Before meeting with the librarian, write down some questions that you would like the answers to. Possible questions might be _Can I access the library's online databases from my home computer?_ and _Can you recommend a particular online database?_

- **Search the library's online holdings.** You can search by keyword, author, title, or subject. The listing gives the call number, which helps you locate the book on the library shelves. If the catalogue is part of a library network, the online listing will explain which library to visit. Because books are organized by topic, chances are good that you will find other relevant books near the one you have chosen.

- **Use online periodical services in libraries.** Your library may have access to _EBSCOhost®_ or _INFOtrac_. By typing keywords into EBSCO_host®_, you can search through national or international newspapers, magazines, or reference books. When you find an article that you need, print it or cut and paste it into a word processing file and then email the document to yourself. Remember to print or copy the publication data because you will need that information when you cite your source.

Searching the Internet

Search engines such as *Google* and *Yahoo!* can rapidly retrieve thousands of documents from the internet. However, most people do not need as many documents as those engines can generate. Here are some tips to help make your internet searches focused and efficient.

Choose your keywords with care. Imagine you want information about new fuel sources for automobiles. If you type in the words *alternative energy* in Google's keyword search space, you will come up with over ten million entries (also known as "hits"). Think about more precise terms that could help you limit your search. For instance, if you are really interested in fuel sources for automobiles, you might change your search request to *alternative fuel sources*. Other options might be *alternative car fuel*. To limit the search, type only the keywords that are most relevant to your research question. If you do not find information on your topic, think about synonyms or alternative ways to describe it.

Use quotation marks to limit the search. Remember that you are driving the search engine, and you can control how many hits you get. By putting quotation marks around your search query, you limit the number of sites to those that contain all of the words that you requested. For example, when you input the words *alternative car fuel* into Google without quotation marks, you will have over three million hits. When the same words are enclosed with quotation marks, the number of hits is reduced to about one thousand, and the displayed webpages are more relevant.

Use bookmarks. When you find information that might be useful, create a folder where you can store the information in a "bookmark" or "favourites" list. Then you can easily find it later. (The bookmark icon appears on the toolbar of your search engine.)

Use academic search engines. Sites such as *Google Scholar* (scholar.google.com) or *Virtual Learning Resources Centre* (virtuallrc.com) help you look through academic publications such as theses, peer-reviewed papers, books, and articles. To find more academic sites, simply do a search for "academic search engines."

Conducting Interviews or Surveys

Another excellent way to find information about your topic is to conduct **interviews**. You can speak to an expert in the field or people who are directly affected by the issue. If you record the interview, ensure that your subject gives you permission to do so. Remember to plan the interview before you meet the person, and list key questions that you would like answered. Include the person's complete name and qualifications in your research notes.

Another source of information can be a **survey**, which is an assessment of the views of many people. For example, if you are writing about the tuition fee increase, you can survey students to gather their opinions. When you plan your survey, follow some basic guidelines:

- **Determine your goal.** What do you want to discover?
- **Determine the age, gender, and status of the respondents** (people you will survey). For example, in a survey about the legalization of marijuana, you might decide to survey equal-sized groups of males and females or those over and under twenty-five years of age.
- **Decide how many people you will survey.** Try to survey at least twenty people. If you are working with a partner or a team of students, you can increase that number.
- **Determine the type of survey you will do.** Will you survey people by phone, internet, or with written forms? Keep in mind that people are more likely to obscure the truth when asked questions directly, especially if the questions are embarrassing or very personal. For example, if you ask someone whether he agrees or disagrees with legalized abortion, he might present a viewpoint that he thinks you or nearby listeners will accept. The same person might be more honest in an anonymous written survey.
- **Plan your survey questions.** If gender, age, marital status, or job status are important, place questions about those items at the beginning of your survey. When you form your questions, do not ask open-ended, essay-type questions because it will be difficult to compile the results. Instead, ask yes/no questions or provide a choice of answers. Sample questions:

What is your gender?

_____ male
_____ female

How often do you use the public transit system (the bus, subway, or train)?

_____ weekdays
_____ about once a week
_____ about once a month
_____ rarely or never

If you want to determine your respondents' knowledge about a topic, include an "I don't know" response. Otherwise, people will make selections that could skew your survey results.

Has Jackson Monroe done a good job as student union leader?

_____ yes
_____ no
_____ I don't know

Writer's Desk   **Research Your Topic**

Using the guiding research question that you developed in the previous Writer's Desk, list some keywords that you can use to research your topic.

_____

_____

Using the library and the internet, find some sources that you can use for your research essay. You might also conduct interviews or prepare a survey.

Evaluating Sources

When you see sources published in print or online, especially when they are attention-grabbing with colour or graphics, you may forget to question whether those sources are reliable. For instance, a company's website advertising an alternative cancer therapy might be less reliable than an article in a scientific journal by a team of oncologists (doctors who treat cancer).

When you evaluate internet sites, you can often determine which type of sponsor or organization runs the website by looking at the last two or three letters of the web address.

Common Domain Names and Website Sponsors

domain name	sponsor	example
.ca	educational institution	www.ubc.ca
.ca	government	www.cra-arc.gc.ca
.com	company	www.nytimes.com
.org	organization (often not-for-profit)	www.magazines.org
.net	network	www.jobs.net

PRACTICE I   Imagine that you are writing an essay about the dangers of internet dating. Your audience is other college students. To enhance your argument, you want to add some facts, statistics, anecdotes, and quotations to your essay. Answer the questions by referring to the list of web-search hits that follows.

1. Which sites would likely contain useful information? For each site that you choose, explain why it could be useful.

   _____

   _____

   _____

2. Which sites are probably not useful for your essay? For each site you choose, explain why.

   _____

   _____

   _____

   a. **Internet Dating Directory**   Interactive Views of Online Dating Resources. The Most Popular Directory of 2009.

   internetdating.net/

   b. **Stop Internet Dating Petition [powered by iPetitions.com]**
   Petition Stop Internet Dating. This is a petition to stop Internet Dating.

   www.ipetitions.com/petition/endinternetdating/

   c. **globeandmail.com: Technology**   Police issue warning on Internet dating. Canadian Press. Toronto—Police forces around the world spend fortunes trolling for and arresting Internet . . .

   www.theglobeandmail.com/eceRedirect?articleId=743575

   d. **Internet dating: sucks for guys, good for women.** It is deplorable how much it sucks for guys on dating sites for many reasons. There is usually a hugely uneven ratio of men vs women, with men in the great . . .

   forums.plentyoffish.com/datingPosts2568515.aspx

   e. **CNN.com - Transcripts** . . . And also with us is CNN.com technology correspondent Daniel Sieberg. . . . I would say that Internet dating in some fashion or another has been around really . . .

   transcripts.cnn.com/TRANSCRIPTS/0207/28/sm.25.html

   f. **Internet Dating Stories: The good, the bad, and the OH MY GOD . . .** Stories from people about their Internet dating experiences, the good, the bad and the bizarre. Includes online safety advice.

   www.internetdatingstories.com

 **Questions for Evaluating a Source**

Each time you find a source, ask yourself the following questions:

• Will the information support the point that I want to make?

• Is the information current? Check the date of publication of the material you are considering.

• Is the information relevant and directly related to my topic?

• Is the source reliable and highly regarded? For instance, is the source from a respected newspaper, journal, or website?

• Is the author an expert on the subject?

• Does the author present a balanced view, or does he or she clearly favour one viewpoint over another? Ask yourself if the author has a financial or personal interest in the issue.

• On various sites, do different authors supply the same information? Information is more likely to be reliable if multiple sources cite the same facts.

PRACTICE 2   Working on your own or with a partner, complete the following tasks.

1. Use exploring strategies to come up with a narrowed research question about the legalization of marijuana.

2. Searching the internet, find two websites that you do not consider valid sources. Explain how you determined that the two sources are not useful for an academic research paper.

3. Next, find two websites that you consider valid. Explain how you determined that the two sources are reliable for an academic research paper.

Taking Notes

As you research your topic, keep careful notes on loose-leaf paper, on note cards, or in computer files. Do not rely on your memory! You would not want to spend several weeks researching, only to accidentally plagiarize because you had not adequately acknowledged some sources.

Look for sources that support your thesis statement. Each time you find a source that seems relevant, keep a detailed record of its publication information so that you can easily cite the source when you begin to write your research essay. You will find important information about preparing in-text citations and Works Cited (MLA) or References (APA) lists later in this chapter.

For example, Lenny Bukowski searched for information on jazz, and he created the following note card after finding source material in the library.

Source: Understanding Music by Jeremy Yudkin, Third Edition, 2002, Prentice Hall, Upper Saddle River, New Jersey

Page 411: "Jazz singers also deliberately make use of unusual sounds. A special kind of singing in which the vocalist improvises with nonsense syllables . . . is known as 'scat' singing."

423: bebop uses "nonsense syllables used in scat singing." Different from swing—not as predictable.

Finding Complete Source Information

Source information is easy to find in most print publications. It is usually on the copyright page, which is often the second or third page of the book, magazine, or newspaper. On many internet sites, however, finding the same information can take more investigative work. When you research on the internet, look for the home page to find the site's title, publication date, and so on. Record as much information from the site as possible.

Book, Magazine, Newspaper

author's full name
title of article
title of book, magazine, or newspaper
publishing information (name of publisher,
   city, and date of publication)
page numbers used

Website

author's full name
title of article
title of website
date of publication or update
date that you accessed the site
complete website address

 **Avoid Plagiarism**

Do not plagiarize. When you use someone else's work without giving that person credit, it is considered stealing, and it is a very serious offence. To eliminate your chances of inadvertently plagiarizing, ensure that your notes contain detailed and clear source information. Then, when you later quote, paraphrase, or summarize another's work, you can cite the source. For more information about plagiarism, paraphrasing, and summarizing, see online chapter on Research, Plagiarism, and Academic Integrity.

Writer's Desk **Take Notes**

Use your topic from the previous Writer's Desk. Take notes from the sources that you have found. In your notes, include direct quotations, paraphrases, and summaries. Organize your sources and keep a record of your sources.

Organizing the First Draft

For research essays, as for any other type of essay, planning is essential. After you have evaluated the material that you have gathered, decide how you will organize your material. Group your notes under the main points that you would like to develop. Then arrange your ideas in a logical order. You might choose to use spatial, chronological, or emphatic order.

Writing a Thesis Statement

After taking notes, plan your thesis statement. Remember that the thesis statement expresses the main focus of the essay. One way to form the thesis statement is to convert your guiding research question into a statement. For instance, student writer Zachary Alapi decided to use the following as his guiding question: *Why is Goya's "firing squad" painting so powerful?* After researching and gathering material on the topic, he then reworked the question to create a thesis statement.

> Thesis: Goya's message regarding his feelings on religious hypocrisy and the elevation of the common Spaniard are clearly visible in The Shootings of May 3, 1808.

Creating an Informal Outline

A general **outline** or **plan** will help you organize your ideas. List some of the supporting details that you will insert into your essay. Then, ask yourself the following questions as you evaluate your outline.

- Do I have sufficient supporting examples?
- Is my plan organized in a logical manner?
- Do I need to research more sources?

Zachary's Preliminary Outline

Introduction: General info about Goya

Thesis: Goya's message regarding his feelings on religious hypocrisy and the elevation of the common Spaniard are clearly visible in <u>The Shootings of May 3, 1808</u>.

    Context of French occupation under Spain
        Much bloodshed (Alexander, page 194)
        King Ferdinand VIII's position (See Gasier and Wilson, page 205)
    Revolutionary techniques that Goya used
        Views about colour expressed by Myers (see pages 5–12)
        Description of painting
        Political expressions about war (see Schickel, pages 132–36)
    Goya's relationship with Spanish people
        Shows "religion without mercy" (Lassaigne, page 96)
        Role of church

An outline also helps you check whether you have any "holes" in your research. If you need more support for certain ideas, do more research and fill in any holes before starting on your first draft. For reminders about the writing process, see Chapters 1 through 5.

 **Inserting Quotations, Paraphrases, and Summaries**

Using your outline, you can plan your first draft. Smoothly integrate supporting paraphrases, summaries, and quotations. Rather than repeating *Yudkin says* over and over, try to use a variety of verbs when you integrate information from your sources. For instance, you could include the following verbs:

states	suggests	notes	indicates
concurs	reiterates	discusses	mentions

Refer to Chapter 14 for more detailed information about paraphrasing and summarizing, and see Chapter 30 for information about punctuating quotations.

Writer's Desk Make a Preliminary Plan

Organize your topic and make a plan. In your preliminary plan, include source information. Remember that this is not a final plan. You can add or remove information afterward.

Incorporating Visuals

Visuals—such as charts, maps, graphs, photos, or diagrams—can provide useful information as you research a topic. They can also enhance your own research essay if you know how to include them and cite them properly. For example, a graph showing the falling crime rate can be an effective way to support an argument that policing methods have become increasingly successful. Visuals help to clarify, summarize, or emphasize a concept. However, use visuals sparingly and only when they help to illustrate a point.

Most word processing programs offer templates for visuals, such as graphs and charts. For example, the toolbar in MS Word allows you to select *Chart* under *Insert* to create line, bar, pie, and other types of charts. Simply input your own data, and the program will create the chart for you. The following are standard examples of what you can create.

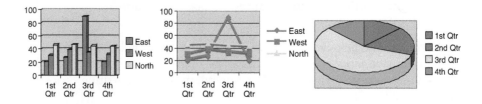

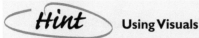

Hint   **Using Visuals**

Here are some recommendations for using visuals in an academic research essay:

- Ask your instructor whether you are permitted to use visuals in your essay. If so, find out if you should use them in the body of your essay near the point that you are supporting, or if you should place them in an appendix.
- Include a label above each visual to clearly identify it. For example, you can number figures and tables sequentially: *Figure 1, Figure 2,* or *Table 1, Table 2,* and so on.
- Place a caption beside or under the visual to help the reader understand it.
- Acknowledge the source of any visual that you borrow.
- Explain how the visual supports a point.

  Example: The crime rate has fallen steadily since the 1990s (see fig. 2).

Citing Sources

Each time you borrow someone's words, ideas, or images, you must **cite** or credit the source. If you fail to properly acknowledge the source of your information, you will be committing a serious academic offence called plagiarism (see page 244 of Chapter 14).

There are two ways you need to cite sources in your research essays. The first is in the body of your essay. When incorporating quotations, paraphrases, or summaries, offset the source information using parentheses. These **in-text citations**, also known as **parenthetical citations**, allow you to acknowledge where you obtained the information. The second place to cite sources is in an alphabetized list at the end of your essay. The title of this source list depends on the documentation style you choose. For example, the Modern Language Association (MLA) refers to the list as Works Cited and the American Psychological Association (APA) refers to it as References.

 **Choose a Documentation Style**

A **documentation style** is a method of presenting the material that you have researched.

The three most common styles for documenting sources are the Modern Language Association (MLA), the American Psychological Association (APA), and the *Chicago Manual of Style* (CMS). Before writing a research essay, check with your instructor about which documentation style you should use and where you can find more information about it.

For more information about where to find the most up-to-date guidelines and samples, check each organization's website: **www.mla.org** or **www.apastyle.org**.

Using MLA Style
MLA: In-Text Citations

In an MLA-style research essay, there are two ways you can show readers that you have borrowed an idea or a quote from a source.

1. **Enclose the author and page number in parentheses.** Include the last name of the author along with the page number where the material appears. If there is more than one author, write both authors' names in parentheses. Do not use a comma between the name(s) and page reference. Place the final period after the final parenthesis.

   > Sometimes a group of rioters will direct their hostility at one person, even if that person has never attacked them or their ideals (Locher 92).

   > The consequences of a nuclear attack would be devastating: "Nuclear winter could produce climatic disaster" (Roskin and Berry 236–237).

   If you are using several works by the same author, then you can place a shortened version of the title—perhaps the first two or three words—within the parentheses.

   > Martin Luther King attended the rally (Kofsky, *Black Nationalism* 48).

 **Quoting from a Secondary Source**

If your source material includes a quotation, and you do not know the original source of the quotation, then use *Qtd. in* (a shortened form of "quoted in").

> David York, co-founder of Toughlove International, said, "Our society's fearful of our kids" (Qtd. in Schmalleger 533).

2. **Introduce the source in the text and write the page reference in parentheses.** You can mention the author's name in the introductory phrase, with only the page number in the parentheses. Place the final period *after* the parentheses.

> "Violent mobs often take out their anger and frustration on any individual," writes David A. Locher (92).

> According to sociologist David A. Locher, mobs display violent behaviour as a way of venting hostility and frustration (92).

 Citing Certain Web Sources

If you are using a web-based source, no page number is necessary. If you cannot find the author's name, then put the title of the site in parentheses.

> Peer support networks are essential: "Many witnesses identified peer support groups as one of the most important services needed on the road to recovery from mental illness" ("Out of the Shadows").

GRAMMAR LINK

To find out more about writing titles, see pages 465–466 in Chapter 30.

MLA: Making a Works Cited List

An MLA-style Works Cited list appears at the end of a research essay. It gives readers details about each source from which you have borrowed material to write your essay. Works Cited is not the same as a running bibliography, which is a list of all of the sources you consulted while you were researching your essay topic. In a Works Cited list, only include works you have quoted, paraphrased, or summarized.

To prepare a Works Cited list, follow these basic guidelines.

1. Write "Works Cited" at the top of the page and centre it. Do not italicize it, underline it, or put quotation marks around it.
2. List each source alphabetically, using the author's last name.
3. Indent the second line and all subsequent lines of each entry five spaces.
4. Double-space all lines.

 **Writing the Name, Title, and Publishing Information Using MLA Style**

Name
On the Works Cited page, write the author's complete last name and first name.

Title
Add quotation marks around the titles of short works. Italicize titles of longer works such as books, newspapers, and magazines.

Place and Year of Publication
Mention the name of the city and the shortened name of the publisher. MLA does not require the name of the province or state. If the work is published outside Canada, add a shortened form of the country name, such as Eng. for England. Also mention the year of publication.

Publisher's Name
Use a shortened form of the publisher's name. Omit *A*, *An*, or *The* from the beginning, and omit words such as *Co.*, *Corp.*, *Books*, *Press*, and *Publishers*. The short form for University Press is UP.

Medium of Publication
Indicate the medium of publication: print, web, CD Rom, etc.

Complete Reference
Here is an example of a basic Works Cited entry.

> Brainard, Shirl. *A Design Manual.* Upper Saddle River: Prentice Hall, 2006. Print.

Sample MLA-Style Works Cited Entries

The following are a few sample entries for various publications. The *MLA Handbook for Writers of Research Papers* has a complete list of sample entries. Before you look at the samples for each type of source, review how the punctuation varies for each.

Books

> Last name, First name. *Title of the Book.* Place of Publication: Publisher, Year. Medium of Publication.

ONE AUTHOR

> Findley, Timothy. *Famous Last Words.* Toronto: Penguin, 1982. Print.

TWO OR THREE AUTHORS   Write the last name and first name of the first author. Follow with *and*, and then write the first and last name of subsequent authors. If the book is a second, third, or subsequent edition, write just the abbreviated form of the edition after the title.

> Bovée, Courtland and John Thill. *Business Communication Essentials.* 2nd ed. Upper Saddle River: Prentice Hall, 2006. Print.

FOUR OR MORE AUTHORS   Add *et al.*, which means "and others," after the first author's name.

Coon, Dennis, et al. *Psychology, a Journey*. Scarborough: Thomson, 2003. Print.

BOOK WITH AN EDITOR INSTEAD OF AN AUTHOR   Write the editor's name followed by *ed.*

Koppleman, Susan, ed. *Old Maids: Short Stories by Nineteenth-Century US Women Writers*. Boston: Pandora, 1984. Print.

TWO OR MORE BOOKS BY THE SAME AUTHOR   Write the author's name in the first entry only. In subsequent entries, type three hyphens followed by a period. Then add the title.

Atwood, Margaret. *The Tent*. Toronto: McClelland, 2006. Print.

- - -. *Lady Oracle*. Toronto: McClelland, 1976. Print.

A WORK IN AN ANTHOLOGY   When your source is a story or article in an anthology, mention the author and title of the article first.

Munro, Alice. "Boys and Girls." *Literature*. Ed. R. S. Gwynn and Wanda Campbell. Toronto: Longman, 2003. Print.

If you are using several pieces from the same anthology, include separate entries for each piece like the first entry below. Then add another entry for the anthology itself that looks like the second entry below.

Munro, Alice. "Boys and Girls." Gwynn and Campbell 313–326. Print.

Gwynn, R. S. and Wanda Campbell, eds. *Literature*. Toronto: Longman, 2003. Print.

ENCYCLOPEDIA AND DICTIONARY   When encyclopedias and dictionaries list items alphabetically, you can omit volume and page numbers. It is sufficient to list the edition and year of publication.

"Democracy." *Columbia Encyclopedia*. 6th ed. 2005. Print.

"Legitimate." *The Canadian Oxford Dictionary*. 2nd ed. 2004. Print.

Periodicals

Last name, First name. "Title of Article." *Title of the Magazine* or *Newspaper* Date: Pages. Medium of Publication.

ARTICLE IN A MAGAZINE

Geddes, Don. "Canadian Combat." *Maclean's* 20 March 2006: 21–22. Print.

ARTICLE IN A NEWSPAPER

Devlin, Keith. "Tied in Knots." *National Post* 7 Dec. 2006: A18. Print.

EDITORIAL   If the editorial is signed, begin with the editor's name. If it is unsigned, begin with the title, followed by the word *Editorial*.

"Tax Freedom Day Is Here." Editorial. *Montreal Gazette* 27 June 2006: A16. Print.

ARTICLE IN A JOURNAL

Last name, First name. "Title of Article." *Title of Journal* Volume. Issue (Date): Pages. Medium of Publication.

Seligman, Martin. "The American Way of Blame." *APA Monitor* 29.7 (1998): 97. Print.

Electronic Sources

Electronic sources include websites, information from subscription services, and reference databases. Electronic communications are frequently updated or moved, so keep track of the date you accessed a site. When using a source published on the internet, include as much of the following information as you can find. Keep in mind that some sites do not contain complete information. Also, when you write the network address, break the address only at a slash mark or period.

Last name, First name. "Title of Article." *Title of Site or Online Publication.* Date of most recent update. Medium of Publication (*Web*). Date you accessed the site. <Network Address>. (Network address is optional. Provide it if the site is difficult to find, or if your instructor requires it.)

ARTICLE ON A PERSONAL WEBSITE

Krystek, Lee. "Crop Circles from Outer Space?" *Museum of Unnatural Mystery.* Web. 16 May 2007 <http://www.unmuseum.org/cropcir.htm>.

ARTICLE IN AN ONLINE PERIODICAL   If the site mentions the volume or page reference, include it. If not, include as much information as you can find.

Grossman, Lev and Richard Lacayo. "All-Time 100 Novels." *Time.* 2005. Web. 25 Apr. 2007 <http://www.time.com/time/2005/100books/the_complete_list. html>.

GOVERNMENT SITE (OR OTHER SITES WITHOUT AUTHOR INFORMATION)
If the author is not mentioned on the site, begin with just the title and include as much information as you can find.

> "The Refugee System in Canada." 2010. *Citizenship and Immigration Canada*. Web. 28 August 2010. <http://www.cic.gc.ca/english/refugees/canada.asp#tphp idtphp>.

Other Types of Sources

INTERVIEW THAT YOU CONDUCTED

> Kumar, Nantha. Personal interview. 14 Aug. 2007.

FILM OR VIDEO   Include the name of the film, the director, the studio, the year of release, and the type of medium.

> *Casablanca*. Dir. Michael Curtiz. 1942. DVD. Warner Brothers, 2003. Film.

RADIO OR TELEVISION PROGRAM   Include the segment title, the program name, the network, the broadcast date, and the type of medium.

> "Underdogs." *The National*. CBC. 8 Jan. 2006. Television.

SOUND RECORDING   Include the name of the performer or band, the title of the song, the title of the CD, the name of the recording company, the year of release, and the type of medium.

> McLachlan, Sarah. "Shelter." *Rarities, B-Sides, & Other Stuff*. Nettwerk, 1996. CD.

 Hint   **Placement and Order of Works Cited**

The Works Cited list should be at the end of the research paper. List sources in alphabetical order of the author's last names. If there is no author, list the title (but ignore *A, An*, or *The*, which may appear at the beginning of the title).

> Bridgman, Rae. *Street Cities: Rehousing the Homeless*. Peterborough: Broadview Press, 2006. Print.
>
> - - -. *Safe Haven: The Story of a Shelter for Homeless Women*. Toronto: U of Toronto Press, 2003. Print.
>
> Fiscolanti, Michael. "The Whistle Blower." *Maclean's*. 20 February 2007. Print.
>
> *Godey's Lady's Book*. April 1850. Web. 14 July 2006. <http://www.history.rochester.edu/godeys>.
>
> Nova, Sylvia, et al. *Women on the Edge: A Decade of Change for Long-Term Homeless Women*. Ottawa: CMHC, 1999. Print.

PRACTICE 3   Imagine that you are using the following sources in a research paper. Arrange the sources for a Works Cited list using MLA style.

■ A print article by Shyman Selvaduri in *Toronto Life* magazine called "About a Boy," which was published in the March 2007 issue, and which appeared on pages 33 to 37.

■ A book by Gwynne Dyer called *With Every Mistake* that was published by Random House Canada in Toronto, in 2005.

■ A book called *Flashback: A Brief History of Film* written by Louis Giannetti and Scott Eyman. The book was published by Prentice Hall in Upper Saddle River, New Jersey, in 2006.

■ A book called *War* by Gwynne Dyer and published by Vintage Canada, Toronto, in 2004.

■ An article called "Behind the Diary" on the website *Library and Archives Canada*, which was created in 2002. You accessed the site on May 10, 2010. The web address is <http://www.collectionscanada.gc.ca/king/023011-1010-e.html>. Although you have attempted to find more source information, you cannot find the author's name on the site.

Works Cited

_____

_____

_____

_____

_____

_____

Sample Research Essay
Title Pages and Outlines

Although MLA does not insist on a title page or an outline for a research essay, your instructor may recommend or request one or both. Include the following information on your title page.

Title

Your name

Your course

Professor's name

Date

To prepare a formal outline in MLA style, use the following format.

Thesis: Goya's message regarding his feelings on religious hypocrisy and the elevation of the common Spaniard are clearly visible in *The Shootings of May 3, 1808.*

I. Context of the French occupation of Spain under Napoleon.

    A. Much bloodshed

    B. Spanish war of independence against oppression

    C. Spanish patriotism and return of the monarchy

II. Unique and revolutionary techniques in painting

    A. Limited colour palette

    B. Brutally realistic

    C. Lit central oval

III. The style has tremendous realism

    A. Peasant figure is elevated to Christ-like status

    B. Depicts the war as savage and brutal through the face-less members of the firing squad

IV. Religion is depicted without mercy

    A. Peasant is martyr

    B. Monks and monastery dark, sinister

Sample Research Essay Using MLA Style

Read the following complete student essay. Notice how the student integrates paraphrases, summaries, and quotations.

Alapi 1

Single space your name, instructor's name, course title, and date. ➤

Zachary Alapi
Mrs. Wheatcroft
ARH LFA 01
April 24, 2008

Centre the title. ➤
(Notice that the title is not underlined, boldfaced, or put in quotation marks.)

Goya's Greatest Work

Francisco José de Goya y Lucientes (1746–1828) is one of

the most renowned and famous Spanish artists whose work

has had a tremendous and lasting impact on the world of art.

Double-space the body of the essay. ➤

One of Goya's most famous paintings is titled *The Shootings of*

May 3, 1808. It is an extremely powerful and evocative work that

captures the brutality of the French occupation of Spain during the

reign of Napoleon. There is little doubt that Goya's message regard-

ing his feelings on religious hypocrisy and the elevation of the com-

mon Spaniard are clearly visible in *The Shootings of May 3, 1808.*

The Shootings of May 3, 1808 was painted in the context of

the French occupation of Spain under Napoleon. For the Spanish,

this was a war of independence against the oppression and

tyrannical rule of Napoleon, as well as an attempt to rid the

Acknowledge sources of borrowed ideas. ➤

country of the political corruption that was so rampant (Gassier

and Wilson 205). Spanish guerrilla fighters launched attacks on

French troops, which led to French firing squads killing captured

Spanish guerrilla fighters (Alexander 194). The Spaniards

killed at the hands of the firing squads became heroes and mar-
tyrs for the Spanish cause. In the work, Goya elevates the common Spaniard to a seemingly Christ-like status against the
faceless, oppressive French soldiers.

The unique and revolutionary techniques in painting used
by Goya throughout his career can be seen in *The Shootings of
May 3, 1808*. Goya used a fairly limited colour palette and his
scheme of light, shadow, line, and colour was generally subor-
dinate to the cartoon-like subject matter (Myers 20). His aim
seems to be to shock the viewer with a harsh and brutally realistic portrayal of the scene. Compositionally, "Goya seems to
have related his form in a positive way to the edge of the canvas or wall area," which essentially means that the majority of
the action in his work takes place in a lit central oval surrounded by darkness, leaving the corners of the canvas empty
(Myers 24). This focus is important in the context of the *The
Shootings of May 3, 1808* because the top half and bottom right
portion of the canvas are completely dark. "Both the night and
symmetrical composition of the subjects emphasize the drama"
("Goya"). The light, which shines specifically on the central
peasant figure, captures the attention of the viewer and places
the emphasis on what is happening to the peasant. This painting technique makes his defiance toward the firing squad even
more poignant and emphatic.

Place author's name and page number in parentheses.

For internet source, include title of site in parentheses.

Goya identified closely with the Spanish people, and through his depiction of them in *The Shootings of May 3, 1808*, he shows how he shares their sentiments (Lassaigne 96). Goya depicts "religion without mercy." While the common peasant is the martyr, the monk cowers at his feet, unable to stand up to the firing squad. Religion, which is supposed to provide stability and courage for the people, is depicted as weak and not carrying out its duties, forcing the peasant to stand up to the executioners. Furthermore, the monastery in the background is shrouded in an inauspicious darkness, which is juxtaposed by the light shining on a central peasant figure, thereby suggesting that the courage of the common man is to be celebrated, not the church, which is weak and hypocritical.

◄ *Common knowledge is not documented.*

The Shootings of May 3, 1808 is a powerful and important painting that explores the elevation of the common Spanish peasant to a seemingly divine status and criticizes the hypocrisy of the church. The realistic representation of the subject matter accentuates the emotions and messages depicted. Through his brutally honest depiction of the shootings, Goya conveys a sense of suffering, courage, and human emotions by his glorification of the common man, who is the eternal victim of war and its inhumanity.

Centre the title ➤
of the Works
Cited page.

Double-space ➤
sources.

Indent second ➤
line of each
source.

Place sources in ≺
alphabetical
order.

Works Cited

Alexander, Don. "French Replacement Methods During the

Peninsular War, 1808–1814." *Military Affairs* 44.4 (1980):

192–97. Print.

Gassier, Pierre and Juliet Wilson. *The Life and Complete Work of*

Francisco Goya. New York: Reynal, 1971. Print.

"Goya." *Spanish Arts*. Web. 22 Jan. 2007 <http://www.spanisharts.

com/prado/goya.htm>.

Lassaigne, Jacques. *Spanish Painting from Velazquez to Picasso*.

Cleveland: World Publishing, 1952. Print.

Myers, Bernard. *Goya*. London: Spring Books, 1964. Print.

Citing Sources Using APA Style

The American Psychological Association (APA) documentation style is commonly used in scientific or technical fields such as social sciences, economics, and nursing. Before you write a research essay for any course, ask your instructor which style he or she prefers.

 **APA Website**

To get some general information about some basic style questions, you can view the APA's website at **www.apastyle.org**. Use the menu on the left side of the page to direct you to specific style questions and answers.

On the same website, there is a link to information about online or "electronic" sources. Because the information about online sources is continually being updated, the site has comprehensive information about the latest citing methods. Visit **www.apastyle.org/learn/faqs/index.aspx**

APA: In-Text Citations

Here are two basic options for inserting parenthetical citations in an APA-style research essay.

1. **Enclose the author(s), the publication year, and the page number(s) in parentheses.** Include the last name(s) of the source's author(s). For two authors, separate the authors' names using & (the ampersand sign). For three to five authors, give all names in the first instance; thereafter use *et al.* after the first author's name. Follow with the publication year and then the page number or the page range where the material appears, using *p.* or *pp.* Separate the names, date, and page references with commas, and place the sentence's final period *after* the closing parenthesis.

   > Sometimes rioters lose control and "take out their anger and frustration on any individual" (Locher, 2002, p. 92).

   > A dozen men are responsible for the development of the movie camera (Giannetti & Eyman, 2006, p. 4).

2. **Introduce the source directly in the text.** When you include a short quotation within a sentence, place the publication year in parentheses immediately after you mention the author's name. Present the quotation, and then write the page number in parentheses immediately after it.

   > Sociologist David A. Locher (2002) explains, "Violent mobs often take out their anger and frustration on any individual" (p. 92).

   > As Giannettti and Eyman (2006) explained, a dozen men are responsible for the development of the movie camera (p. 4).

APA: Making a References List

Similar to the MLA Works Cited list, the APA References list gives details about each source you have used, and it appears at the end of your paper. Follow these basic guidelines to prepare References using the APA format.

1. Write "References" at the top of the page and centre it. Do not italicize it, underline it, or put quotation marks around it.
2. List each source alphabetically, using the last names of the authors.
3. Indent the second line and all subsequent lines of each reference 1.25 cm (one-half inch) from the left margin.
4. Double space the list.

 **Writing the Author, Date, Title, and Place Using APA Style**

Author
On the References page, write the complete last name and use the first and middle initials (if provided). Do not write complete first names.

Date
Put the date in parentheses immediately after the name. If you do not have the author's name, then put the date immediately after the title.

Title
Capitalize the first word in the title, the first word in the subtitle, and any proper nouns or adjectives in Reference lists. Do not add quotation marks or any other special marks around the titles of short works. Italicize titles of longer works such as books, newspapers, or magazines.

Place of Publication
Mention the name of the city and the postal abbreviation of the province or state, unless the city is a well-known publishing centre.

Complete Reference
Brainard, S. (2006). *A design manual.* Upper Saddle River, NJ: Prentice Hall.

Book

Carefully review the punctuation of the following example.

Last name, Initial(s). (date). *Title of the book.* City and Province or State of Publication: Publisher.

ONE AUTHOR   Reverse the name of the author. Put the complete last name and the first initial.

Findley, T. (1982). *Famous last words.* Toronto, ON: Penguin.

TWO OR MORE AUTHORS   Reverse the name of each author.

Ciccarelli, S. K., & Meyer, G. E. (2006). *Psychology.* Upper Saddle River, NJ: Prentice Hall.

BOOK WITH AN EDITOR INSTEAD OF AN AUTHOR Put the editor's name followed by (Ed.).

> Koppleman, S. (Ed.). (1984). *Old maids: Short stories by nineteenth-century US women writers*. Boston: Pandora Press.

TWO OR MORE BOOKS BY THE SAME AUTHOR Include the author's name in all references. Arrange the works by year of publication, putting the earliest work first.

> Atwood, M. (2006). *The tent*. New York: Doubleday.

> Atwood, M. (1976). *Lady Oracle*. New York: Doubleday.

A WORK IN AN ANTHOLOGY

> Munroe, A. (2003). Boys and Girls. In R. S. Gwynn & W. Campbell (Eds.) *Literature* (pp. 313–326). Toronto: Longman.

ENCYCLOPEDIA AND DICTIONARY

> Democracy. (2005). In *Columbia encyclopedia* (6th ed.). New York: Columbia University Press.

> Legitimate. (2004). In *The Canadian Oxford dictionary*. (2nd ed.). Toronto, ON: Oxford University Press.

Periodicals

> Last name, Initials. (Year, Month and day). Title of article. *Title of the Magazine* or *Newspaper, Volume number*, Pages.

ARTICLE IN A MAGAZINE When citing newspapers or magazines, include as much of the following information as is available.

> Shreeve, J. (2005, March). Beyond the brain. *National Geographic, 207*, 2–31.

ARTICLE IN A NEWSPAPER

> Devlin, K. (2006, December 7). Tied in knots. *National Post*, p. A18.

ARTICLE IN A JOURNAL

> Last name, Initials. (Year, Month). Title of article. *Title of Journal. Volume*(Issue), Pages.

> Seligman, M. (1998). The American way of blame. *APA Monitor, 29*(7), 97.

Electronic Sources

If the source was published on the internet, include as much of the following information as you can find. Keep in mind that some sites do not contain complete source information.

> Last name, Initials. (date of most recent update). Title of article. *Title of Site* or *Online Publication*. Retrieved date, from http://site_address.html

ARTICLE ON A PERSONAL WEBSITE

> Krystek, L. (2006). Crop circles from outer space? *Museum of unnatural mystery*. Retrieved May 16, 2007, from http://www.unmuseum.org/cropcir.htm

ARTICLE IN AN ONLINE JOURNAL   If the site mentions the volume or page reference, include it. If not, put in as much information as you can find.

> Grossman, L., & Lacayo, R. (2005). All-time 100 novels. *Time*. Retrieved May 25, 2006, from http://www.time.com/time/2005/100books/the_complete_list.html

GOVERNMENT SITE

Begin with the complete name of the government agency, followed by the date and title.

> Citizenship and Immigration Canada. (2010). The Refugee System in Canada. Retrieved August 28, 2010, from http://www.cic.gc.ca/english/refugees/canada.asp#tphp idtphp

Other Types of Sources

INTERVIEW THAT YOU CONDUCTED   In APA style, do not include a personal interview in your References list. In the actual text, just include the parenthetical notation (personal communication).

FILM OR VIDEO

> Curtiz, M. (Director). (2003). *Casablanca*. [DVD]. United States: Warner Brothers. (Original movie released 1942).

SOUND RECORDING

> McLachlan, S. (1996). Shelter. On *Rarities, B-sides, & other stuff* [CD]. Vancouver, BC: Nettwerk.

PRACTICE 4   Imagine that you are using the following sources in a research paper. Arrange the sources for a References page using APA style.

- A print article by Shyman Selvaduri in *Toronto Life* magazine called "About a Boy," which was published in the March 2007 issue, and which appeared on pages 33 to 37.
- A book by Gwynne Dyer called *With Every Mistake* that was published by Random House Canada in Toronto, in 2005.
- A book called *Flashback: A Brief History of Film* written by Louis Giannetti and Scott Eyman. The book was published by Prentice Hall in Upper Saddle River, New Jersey, in 2006.
- A book called *War* by Gwynne Dyer and published by Vintage Canada, Toronto, in 2004.
- An article called "Behind the Diary" on the website Library and Archives Canada, which was created in 2002. You accessed the site on May 10, 2010. The web address is <http://www.collectionscanada.gc.ca/king/023011-1010-e.html>. Although you have attempted to find more source information, you cannot find the author's name on the site.

References

_____

_____

_____

_____

_____

_____

_____

_____

_____

The Writer's Room **Research Essay Topics**

Writing Activity 1

Write a research paper about one of the following topics. Ask your instructor which reference style you should use. Put a Works Cited (MLA) or References (APA) page at the end of your assignment.

1. Write about a contemporary issue that is in the news.

2. Write about any issue in your career choice or field of study.

Writing Activity 2

Write a research paper about one of the following topics. First, brainstorm questions about your topic and then find a guiding research question. Then follow the process of writing a research essay.

Abortion	Holistic healing
Affirmative action	Home schooling
Assisted suicide	Immigration
Attention deficit hyperactivity disorder	Legalization of marijuana
Body image	Necessity of military intervention
Carpal tunnel syndrome	Prison reform
Censorship of the internet	Privacy and the internet
Date rape	Response to terrorism
Election reform	Same-sex marriage
Executive salaries	Sperm-donor rights
Fast food	Tobacco industry
Foreign adoptions	Consequences of war
Genetically modified food	Waste disposal
Government-sponsored gambling	Youth gangs
Health-care reform	Violence in the media

✓ CHECKLIST: RESEARCH ESSAY

When you plan a research essay, ask yourself these questions.

- [ ] Have I narrowed my topic?
- [ ] Have I created a guiding research question?
- [ ] Are my sources reliable?
- [ ] Have I organized my notes?
- [ ] Have I integrated source information using quotations, paraphrases, and summaries?
- [ ] Have I correctly documented my in-text or parenthetical citations?
- [ ] Have I correctly prepared and punctuated my Works Cited page or References list?

How Do I Get a Better Grade?

mycanadiancomplab

Go to www.mycanadiancomplab.ca for additional help with your grammar, writing, and research skills. You will have access to a variety of exercises, instruction, and video that will help you improve your basic skills and help you get a better grade.

Editing Handbook

When you speak, you have tools such as tone of voice and body language to help you express your ideas. When you write, however, you have only words and punctuation to get your message across. If your writing includes errors in style, grammar, and punctuation, you may distract readers from your message, and they may focus, instead, on your inability to communicate clearly. You increase your chances of succeeding in your academic and professional life when you write in clear, standard English.

This Editing Handbook will help you understand important grammar concepts, and the samples and practices in each chapter offer interesting information about many themes. Before you begin working with these chapters, review the contents and themes shown here.

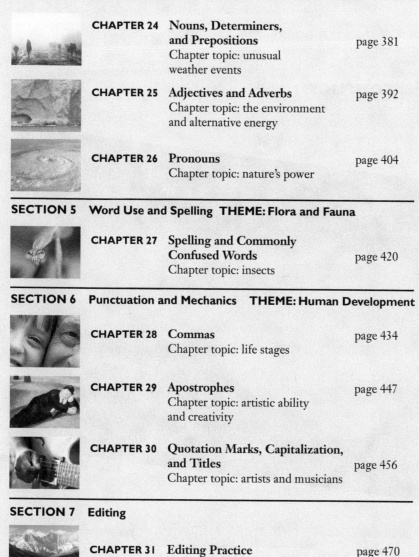

Identifying Subjects and Verbs

Section Theme **CONFLICT**

Is behaviour learned or genetic? In this chapter, you will learn about the sources of aggressive behavior.

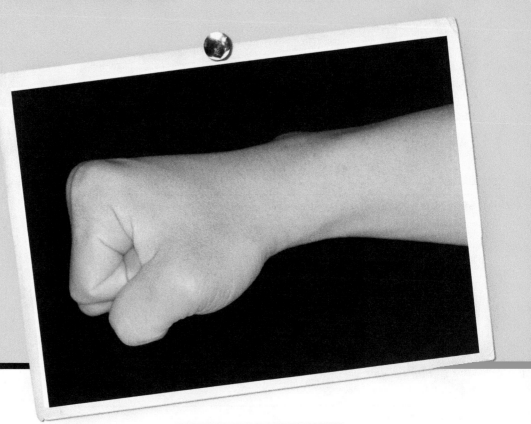

Grammar Snapsh•t

Looking at Subjects and Verbs

Psychologist Ken Low has given seminars on dealing with aggression. In the following excerpt from a seminar, he discusses the source of anger. Notice that subjects are in bold and verbs are underlined. Also observe that some sentences have no visible subjects.

Understand the source of your anger. Examine your feelings of unhappiness. In my case, the **cause** of the unhappiness was my sense of worthlessness. **Everyone** was succeeding, in my mind, and **I** was not. **I** wanted to blame my boss, my parents, or my wife. **I** was prepared to blame anybody and anything outside of myself. **Recognizing** my unhappiness gave me insight into the source of my anger. **I** held a mistaken conviction: the **world** owed me a good life.

In this chapter, you will identify subjects and verbs.

CHAPTER 16

Identifying Subjects

A **sentence** contains one or more subjects and verbs, and it expresses a complete thought. The **subject** tells you who or what the sentence is about. A **verb** expresses an action or state. If a sentence is missing a subject or a verb, it is incomplete. You will use your ability to identify subjects and verbs in the editing process.

- Subjects may be **singular** or **plural**. A subject can also be a **pronoun**. To determine the subject of a sentence, ask yourself who or what the sentence is about. It may be about a person, place, or thing.

  Detective Marcos will interview the suspects.
  Many **factors** cause people to break laws.
  It is an important case.

- A **compound subject** contains two or more subjects joined by *and*, *or*, or *nor*.

  Reporters and **photographers** were outside the prison gates.

- Sometimes a **gerund** (*-ing* form of the verb) is the subject of a sentence.

  Listening is an important skill.

 **Here and There**

Here and *There* are not subjects. In sentences that begin with *Here* or *There*, the subject follows the verb.

  There are several **ways** to find a criminal.
  Here is an interesting **brochure** about the police academy.

How to Find the Subject

To find the subject, ask yourself *who* or *what* the sentence is about. The **simple subject** is the noun or pronoun, or the name of a person or organization.

  The **Royal Canadian Mounted Police** is a large organization. **It** has branches in every province.

  When you are identifying the subject, you can ignore words that describe the noun.

  adjectives   subject
  The pompous and rude **sergeant** left the room.

PRACTICE I   Circle the subject in each sentence. Sometimes there will be more than one simple subject.

EXAMPLE: A behavioural (study) examines genetics and behaviour.

1. Research psychiatrist Carl E. Schwartz works in the Department of Psychiatry at Massachusetts General Hospital.

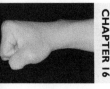

2. He conducted a study to determine hereditary factors in behaviour.

3. There were over one hundred children in his study.

4. Infants and toddlers were classed into two groups.

5. Objects, strange people, and unfamiliar settings were used to test the children.

6. Talking was not permitted.

7. The outgoing toddlers easily interacted in new surroundings.

8. The inhibited children were more likely to show signs of stress in unfamiliar surroundings.

Prepositional Phrases

A **preposition** is a word that links nouns, pronouns, and phrases to other words in a sentence. It expresses a relationship based on movement, motion, or position. A **prepositional phrase** is made up of a preposition and its object (a noun or a pronoun).

Because the object of a preposition is a noun, it may look like a subject. **However, the object in a prepositional phrase is never the subject of the sentence.**

    prepositional phrase   subject

<u>With the parents' approval</u>, the **experiment** began.

 **Using "of the"**

In most expressions containing *of the*, the subject appears before *of the*.

    subject

    Each (of the parents) agreed to participate.
    One (of the fathers) was uncomfortable with the process.

Common Prepositions

about	below	in	outside
above	beside	inside	over
across	between	into	through
after	beyond	like	to
against	by	near	toward
along	despite	of	under
among	down	off	until
around	during	on	up
at	except	onto	with
before	for	out	within
behind	from		

To help you identify the subject, put parentheses around prepositional phrases. In each of the following examples, the prepositional phrase is in parentheses. Notice that a sentence can contain more than one prepositional phrase.

(In spite of the storm), **they** drove to the hospital.

The **clinic**, (after 1971), expanded greatly.

(In the late 1990s), (during a period of cost cutting), high-tech **cameras** were placed in the room.

PRACTICE 2   Circle the subject in each sentence. Place any prepositional phrases near the subject in parentheses.

EXAMPLE: (For many years), (Schwartz) has studied genetics and behaviour.

1. In Schwartz's study, half of the babies were classified as shy. The others in the group were classified as outgoing. In unfamiliar surroundings, the shy and outgoing children reacted differently. For example, in the presence of a stranger, the shy toddlers would freeze. The outgoing toddlers would approach the stranger and interact.

2. The differences in reactions occurred in their heart rate, in the dilation of their pupils, and in the levels of the stress hormone, cortisone. Generally, the differences in the temperament of children persisted to adulthood.

3. After the first study, Carl Schwartz tracked down twenty-two of the original subjects. About one-third of the uninhibited adults showed impulsive and aggressive behaviour. Some of the shy children became extremely shy adults. However, not all outgoing infants become bold or aggressive adults. In fact, most individuals in the study did not develop behavioural problems.

Identifying Verbs

Every sentence must contain a verb. The **verb** expresses what the subject does, or it links the subject to other descriptive words.

An **action verb** describes an action that a subject performs.

Detective Rowland <u>attended</u> a seminar in Sudbury. He <u>spoke</u> to some officials.

A **linking verb** connects a subject with words that describe it, and it does not show an action. The most common linking verb is *be*, but other common linking verbs are *appear*, *become*, *look*, and *seem*.

Kim Rossmo <u>is</u> a former detective. His methods <u>seem</u> reliable.

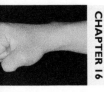

When a subject performs more than one action, the verbs are called **compound verbs**.

In 2003, Rossmo <u>wrote</u> and <u>spoke</u> about his methods.

Helping Verbs

The **helping verb** combines with the main verb to indicate tense, negative structure, or question structure. The most common helping verbs are forms of *be*, *have*, and *do*. **Modal auxiliaries** are another type of helping verb, and they indicate ability (*can*), obligation (*must*), and so on. For example, here are different forms of the verb *ask*, and the helping verbs are underlined.

<u>is</u> asking	<u>had</u> asked	<u>will</u> ask	<u>should have</u> asked
<u>was</u> asked	<u>had been</u> asking	<u>can</u> ask	<u>might be</u> asked
<u>has been</u> asking	<u>would</u> ask	<u>could be</u> asking	<u>could have been</u> asked

The **complete verb** is the helping verb and the main verb. In the following examples, the main verb is double underlined. In **question forms**, the first helping verb usually appears before the subject.

Criminal profiling techniques <u>have been</u> <u>spreading</u> across the continent.
<u>Should</u> the detective <u>have</u> <u>studied</u> the files?

Interrupting words such as *often*, *always*, *ever*, and *actually* are not part of the verb.

Rossmo <u>has</u> often <u>returned</u> to Vancouver.

 The Infinitive Is Not the Main Verb

Infinitives are verbs preceded by *to* such as *to fly*, *to speak*, and *to go*. An infinitive is never the main verb in a sentence.

infinitive
The network <u>wanted</u> **to produce** a show about geographic profiling.

PRACTICE 3   In each sentence, circle the subject and underline the complete verb. Remember to underline the helping verbs as well as the main verbs. You can place prepositional phrases in parentheses.

EXAMPLE: (According to Professor Saundra K. Ciccarelli), many (factors) <u>contribute</u> to aggressive behaviour.

1. The amygdala is located near the base of the brain. Studies have shown the amygdala's role in fear responses. In a 1939 experiment, the temporal lobe was removed from the brains of several monkeys. The lobe contains the amygdala. After the surgery, the monkeys showed absolutely no fear

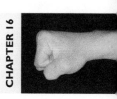

of snakes and humans. This anecdote illustrates the role of the brain in fearful or aggressive behaviour.

2. Why do people harm others? In her book *Psychology*, Ciccarelli discusses the connection between the brain and aggressive behaviour. She gives an example of a specific case. In 1966, Charles Whitman shot and killed fourteen people. Before his death in a shootout with police, Whitman wrote a note and asked doctors to examine the state of his brain. In fact, a later examination revealed the presence of a tumour next to his amygdala.

3. There are also chemical links to aggression, according to Ciccarelli. Testosterone, in high levels, has been shown to cause aggressive behaviour. Also, certain substances have an impact on the brain. Alcohol affects the amount of some brain chemicals and reduces a person's inhibitions.

FINAL REVIEW

Circle the subjects and underline the complete verbs in the following sentences. Underline *all* parts of the verb. To avoid misidentifying subjects, you can place prepositional phrases in parentheses.

EXAMPLE: (One) (of the most interesting influences on behaviour) <u>is</u> social roles.

1. Many psychologists and social scientists believe in the importance of social roles on behaviour. Thus, children can be influenced by aggressive characters on television. Young adults may be pressured or manipulated by peers. Basically, people can learn to be aggressive.

2. Most interesting of all, people of all ages can modify their behaviour due to their social roles. Psychologist Philip Zimbardo demonstrated the importance of social roles in his prison experiment at Stanford University. He recruited about seventy volunteers and gave half of them guard roles and the other half prisoner roles. Many volunteers in the guard roles exhibited violent behaviour. Other volunteers in the prisoner roles became meek. Therefore, the behaviour of the students changed due to their roles.

3. History is filled with examples of people behaving badly, often during times of conflict. Soldiers, especially, are in stressful situations and fulfill the obligations of their roles. The prison abuse scandal at Abu Ghraib in Iraq is a real-life example. Prison guards beat and humiliated prisoners. Why did the guards act so cruelly? According to psychologists, a uniform and a specific social role have powerful influences on people's behaviour.

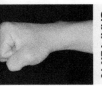

The Writer's Room **Topics for Writing**

Write about one of the following topics. After you finish writing, identify your subjects and verbs.

1. List various ways in which social roles influence people's behaviour. Support your points with specific examples.

2. Some experts suggest that personality traits are partly inherited. Are your character traits similar to a family member's traits? Compare and contrast yourself with someone else in your family.

READING LINK

Conflict

These essays contain more information about law, order, and conflict.

"The Hijab," by Naheed Mustafa (page 488)

"A Modest Proposal," by Heather Mallick (page 490)

"Seeing Red over Myths," by Drew Hayden (page 495)

✓ CHECKLIST: SUBJECTS AND VERBS

Review this chapter's main points.

☐ To identify **subjects**, look for words that tell you who or what the sentence is about.

☐ To identify **verbs**, look for words that do the following:

- **action verbs** describe the actions that the subject performs.
- **linking verbs** describe a state of being or link the subject with descriptive words.
- **helping verbs** combine with the main verb to indicate tense, negative structure, or question structure.

☐ To identify **prepositional phrases**, look for words that consist of a preposition and its object. Note: the object of a prepositional phrase cannot be the subject.

prepositional phrase   subject verb   helping verb

In spite of criticism, the police chief has released the suspect.

How Do I Get a Better Grade?

mycanadiancomplab

Go to www.mycanadiancomplab.ca for additional help with your grammar, writing, and research skills. You will have access to a variety of exercises, instruction, and video that will help you improve your basic skills and help you get a better grade.

Fragments

CONTENTS

Section Theme **URBAN DEVELOPMENT**

In this chapter, you will read about the development of suburbs and cities.

Grammar Snapshot

Looking at Sentence Fragments

In his essay "Every Day Carless," Ewan Schmidt argues for a motorized vehicle-free downtown. The sentence fragments are underlined.

    The downtown core is very quiet each Friday. There are no car horns. <u>No screeching of the brakes.</u> <u>No yelling.</u> <u>No loud motor noises.</u> <u>Because there are no cars.</u> People can walk anywhere they want without worrying about traffic. <u>Even in the middle of the street.</u>

In this chapter, you will identify sentence fragments and write complete sentences.

What Are Fragments?

A **fragment** is an incomplete sentence. It lacks either a subject or verb, or it fails to express a complete thought. You may see fragments in newspaper headlines and advertisements (*overnight weight loss*). You may also use fragments to save space when you are writing a text message. However, in college writing, it is unacceptable to write fragments.

Sentence: More and more people are moving to urban centres.

Fragment: In developing countries.

Phrase Fragments

Phrase fragments are missing a subject or a verb. In each example, the fragment is underlined.

No verb: <u>The history of cities.</u> It is quite interesting.

No subject: Ancient civilizations usually had one major city.
                   <u>Specialized in trades.</u>

How to Correct Phrase Fragments

To correct phrase fragments, add the missing subject or verb, or join the fragment to another sentence. The following examples show how to correct the previous phrase fragments.

Join sentences: The history of cities is quite interesting.

Add words: Ancient civilizations usually had one major city. **The citizens in that city** specialized in trades.

 **Incomplete Verbs**

The following example is a phrase fragment because it is missing a helping verb. To make this sentence complete, you must add the helping verb.

Fragment: Modern cities growing rapidly.

Sentence: Modern cities <u>are</u> growing rapidly.

PRACTICE I   Underline and correct ten phrase fragments.

It was founded

EXAMPLE: Damascus is one of the world's oldest cities. ~~Founded~~ in 3000 BCE.

1. The first cities began in ancient civilizations. Mesopotamia, the Indus Valley, and China. Those were large ancient civilizations. Ancient cities such as Jericho, Harappa, and Mohenjo-daro had small populations. Compared to modern cities. For example, the first cities had only around 150 000 people. Eventually, ancient empires grew. Rome reached a population of one million. Baghdad. It exceeded that number.

2. During the Middle Ages, some European cities became powerful city states. Venice and Genoa even had their own military and maritime institutions. Around that time. London became the largest city in the world. Paris as populated as Beijing and Istanbul.

3. The Industrial Revolution was an important phenomenon for the growth of cities. In the eighteenth and nineteenth centuries. Many people migrated from the countryside to the urban centres. Urbanization led to many social problems. Child labour, low wages, and unsanitary living conditions. Those were some common problems. Many reformers worked hard to improve the living conditions. Of the urban poor.

4. By the 1930s, the Great Depression raised the unemployment rate. In rural areas. Many people had to leave their farms and look for work in the cities. After World War II. Economic prosperity helped to increase the migration to the cities. Most of today's cities are growing and prospering.

CHAPTER 17

Fragments with *-ing* and *to*

A fragment may begin with a **present participle**, which is the form of the verb that ends in *-ing* (*running*, *talking*). It may also begin with an **infinitive**, which is *to* plus the base form of the verb (*to run*, *to talk*). These fragments generally appear next to another sentence that contains the subject. In the examples, the fragments are underlined.

-ing fragment:	<u>Reacting to urban sprawl.</u> City planners started a new movement in the 1980s and 1990s.
to fragment:	Urban designers believe in the new urbanism. <u>To help people live better lives.</u>

How to Correct *-ing* and *to* Fragments

To correct an *-ing* or *to* fragment, add the missing words or join the fragment to another sentence. The following examples show how to correct the two previous fragments.

Join sentences:	Reacting to urban sprawl, city planners started a new movement in the 1980s and 1990s.
Add words:	Urban designers believe in the new urbanism. **They want** to help people live better lives.

> *Hint*   **When the *-ing* Word Is the Subject**

Sometimes a gerund (*-ing* form of the verb) is the subject of a sentence. In the example, *cycling* is the subject of the sentence.

    Correct sentence: <u>Cycling</u> is a great form of exercise in urban areas.

A sentence fragment occurs when the *-ing* word is part of an incomplete verb string or when you mention the subject in a previous sentence. In the example, the fragment is underlined.

    Fragment: Many city dwellers get exercise. <u>Cycling on bike paths.</u>

PRACTICE 2   Underline and correct ten *-ing* and *to* fragments.

One principle is designing

EXAMPLE: The new urbanism movement has many principles. ~~Designing~~ walkways in neighbourhoods.

1. New urbanism is a suburban planning movement. To create people-friendly neighbourhoods. To limit the use of cars. Urban planners design self-contained neighbourhoods. Believing in the need to curtail urban sprawl. Architects pattern areas where people can walk to work and choose recreational activities close to home.

2. The new urbanism movement is a reaction against older suburban areas. After World War II, architects designed suburbs that relied heavily on the use of cars. Therefore, most people living in traditional suburbs have to commute to city centres. Creating problems such as traffic congestion and air pollution.

3. Driving to work, school, and shopping areas. Suburban dwellers waste a lot of time travelling in their cars. In addition, urban sprawl creates difficulties for people who cannot drive. Limiting their daily activities. To do errands downtown or at a mall. Non-drivers must find other means of transport.

4. To answer such concerns. Urban designers reconsidered traditional suburban models. Since 1990, the new urbanism movement has become very popular. To improve the quality of suburban life. City planners design beautiful areas for living, working, shopping, and playing. They hire innovative architects who insert skylights and green space in their designs. Presently, there are many communities in North America. Using the principles of the new urban movement.

Explanatory Fragments

An **explanatory fragment** provides an explanation about a previous sentence and is missing a subject, a complete verb, or both. These types of fragments begin with one of the following words.

also	particularly	for instance	especially	except
for example	as well as	such as	including	like

In the examples, the explanatory fragment is underlined.

Fragment: Planners in the 1960s influenced the new urbanism movement. <u>For example, Jane Jacobs.</u>

Fragment: New urbanism planners take into consideration many factors. <u>Especially reducing the use of the automobile.</u>

How to Correct Explanatory Fragments

To correct explanatory fragments, add the missing words, or join the explanation or example to another sentence. The following examples show how to correct the previous explanatory fragments.

Add words: Planners in the 1960s influenced the new urbanism movement. For example, Jane Jacobs **was an important authority on urban planning**.

Join sentences: New urbanism planners take into consideration many factors, especially reducing the use of the automobile.

PRACTICE 3   Underline and correct ten explanatory fragments. You may need to add or remove words.

EXAMPLE: Some new urbanism towns are famous. ~~Such as~~ *, such as* Celebration.

1. New urbanists plan communities with a central downtown area that is

    walking distance from all neighbourhoods. The first community built on

    the new urbanism principles is Seaside, Florida. It was started in 1981 and

    became very famous. For example, *Atlantic Monthly*. It featured Seaside

    on its cover. Robert Davis bought the land to build the community. He hired many people who followed the principles of the new urbanism philosophy. Such as architects and urban planners.

2. Seaside was relatively easy to build because the area did not have the traditional rules for developing land. For instance, no zoning regulations. The buildings in the town have uniform designs. Particularly the houses. They all have certain features, including porches that must be five metres from the sidewalk. Also, the streets. They must be made of bricks so cars cannot speed.

3. There are many other towns. Like Seaside. The most famous of these is the one Disney has built in Florida called Celebration. It also has strict rules for conformity. For example, the windows. They must be decorated with white or off-white curtains. The houses are built close together. For instance, only six metres apart. In Celebration, if neighbours complain about a barking dog, the dog can be evicted from the town.

4. Many people criticize those types of communities. Especially regarding the conformity of the design. On the other hand, people moving to those towns hope to live in an ideal community. For example, no crime or social problems. However, critics point out that all communities have some social problems.

Dependent-Clause Fragments

A **dependent clause** has a subject and verb, but it cannot stand alone. It literally depends on another clause to be a complete sentence. Dependent clauses may begin with subordinating conjunctions or relative pronouns. The following list contains some of the most common words that begin dependent clauses.

Common Subordinating Conjunctions				Relative Pronouns
after	before	though	whenever	that
although	even though	unless	where	which
as	if	until	whereas	who(m)
because	since	what	whether	whose

In each example, the fragment is underlined.

Fragment: In the city, houses are close together. <u>Whereas in the suburbs, houses have large yards</u>.

Fragment: <u>Before William Levitt built Levittown</u>. Many people lived in congested neighbourhoods.

How to Correct Dependent-Clause Fragments

To correct dependent-clause fragments, join the fragment to a complete sentence, or add the necessary words to make it a complete idea. You could also delete the subordinating conjunction. The following examples show how to correct the previous dependent-clause fragments.

Delete subordinator: In the city, houses are close together. In the suburbs, houses have large yards.

Join sentences: Before William Levitt built Levittown, many people lived in congested neighbourhoods.

PRACTICE 4   Underline and correct ten dependent-clause fragments.

EXAMPLE: William Levitt and his brother built Levittown. ~~Because~~ *because* of a shortage of affordable housing.

1. In 1948, developer William Levitt built a community in

   Pennsylvania. Which has been designated the first traditional suburb.

   Levitt wanted to give returning soldiers the opportunity to participate in

   the American dream. He called his community Levittown. This town

   consisted of similarly built single-family homes. That attracted young families. People wanted to escape the crowds of big cities like New York and Philadelphia. Homes in large cities were very expensive. Whereas Levittown contained affordable housing. The community grew to approximately 17 000 houses. Which led to the beginning of urban sprawl.

2. Some people criticized the idea of Levittown. Because all of the houses looked similar. Even though the town had four different house styles. The first residents sometimes got lost trying to find their homes. Although it began with the premise of affordable housing for everyone. Levittown initially discriminated against non-whites and did not permit them to buy houses in the community. Eventually, Levittown abandoned its "whites-only" policy. In 1957, the first African Americans to buy a house there were Bill and Daisy Meyers. Who had rocks thrown at them by the other residents.

3. Because Levittown is getting older. It has become a more attractive suburb. Many homeowners have remodelled their homes, and the saplings have grown into mature trees. Although many other suburbs have developed. Levittown remains a model of traditional suburban living.

FINAL REVIEW

The following paragraphs contain the four types of fragments: phrase, explanatory, *-ing* and *to*, and dependent clauses. Correct fifteen fragment errors.

EXAMPLE: Tourists have been coming to Tokyo. ~~Since~~ *since* World War II.

1. Tokyo, the world's largest city. It was originally called Edo. The Edo warrior family inhabited a marshy region of Japan. Where there were a few villages. Eventually, the town of Edo grew. It started to gain prominence in the 1600s. In 1603, Edo warrior Tokugawa Ieyasu

   became shogun or warlord of the region. He was so powerful that he moved the government from Kyoto to Edo. Thinking that he would have more control over politics. He acquired complete control over Japan. Quelling any opposition. His government promoted an isolationist policy. Japan had no contact with other nations. Until the nineteenth century.

2. From the seventeenth century to the nineteenth century, Japan was politically stable, allowing Edo's population to grow rapidly to about one million people. Both London and Paris had a smaller population. At that time. Edo became the economic centre of Japan. Prospering greatly due to industry. Also at that time, Japanese society developed a class system. Based on four levels of hierarchy. The samurai or warriors were at the top of the social system.

3. The Tokugawa Ieyasu family's power collapsed by the 1850s. Because of corruption within its government. At the same time, the Western powers were pressuring Japan. To open trade. England and the United States wanted Japan as a trading post. For example, in 1853, Matthew Perry. He forced Japan to open trade relations with America. Japan westernized

rapidly. After its contact with Europe and America. In 1867, Edo's name was changed to Tokyo.

4. Since the late 1800s. Tokyo has modernized like other Western capitals. In 1923, a great earthquake destroyed much of the city, and rebuilding became a priority. Many structures were built. Such as a subway system in 1927, an airport in 1931, and a port in 1941. After World War II, Tokyo greatly expanded. Today, it is a mega metropolis. Inviting visitors from all around the world.

 The Writer's Room **Topics for Writing**

Write about one of the following topics. Check that there are no sentence fragments.

1. Write about where you live. Describe your neighbourhood.

2. What are some similarities and differences between living in a city and living in a suburb?

Patricia Schwimmer (Canadian, b. 1953) "My San Francisco", 1994, Tempera, Private Collection. © Patricia Schwimmer/SuperStock.

CHECKLIST: SENTENCE FRAGMENTS

When you edit your writing, ask yourself this question.

☐ Are my sentences complete? Check for these types of fragments.

☐ ▪ phrase fragments

☐ ▪ *-ing* and *to* fragments

☐ ▪ explanatory fragments

☐ ▪ dependent-clause fragments

Los Angeles and San Francisco are moving closer

together. ~~Because~~ of the San Andreas fault. The two cities
    because

will make the largest urban area in the world. ~~If~~ the movement
    if

continues.

How Do I Get a Better Grade?

mycanadiancomplab

Go to www.mycanadiancomplab.ca for additional help with your grammar, writing, and research skills. You will have access to a variety of exercises, instruction, and video that will help you improve your basic skills and help you get a better grade.

Run-Ons

Section Theme **URBAN DEVELOPMENT**

In this chapter, you will read about architects and architecture.

Grammar Snapshot

Looking at Run-Ons

Darius Knightely is a freelance travel writer. The following excerpt about his recent trip to Barcelona contains a sentence error. The underlined error is a run-on.

> Barcelona is a city of contrasts. Visitors see medieval buildings, narrow streets, and <u>grandiose churches they also see grid-like neighbourhoods, modernist architecture, and glass and steel places of worship.</u> The modern sections of the city contrast with the older areas.

In this chapter, you will learn to correct run-on sentences.

What Are Run-Ons?

A **run-on sentence** occurs when two or more complete sentences are incorrectly joined. In other words, the sentence runs on without stopping.

There are two types of run-on sentences.

1. A **fused sentence** has no punctuation to mark the break between ideas.

   Incorrect: Skyscrapers are unusually tall buildings the Taipei 101 tower is among the tallest.

2. A **comma splice** uses a comma incorrectly to connect two complete ideas.

   Incorrect: The CN Tower is located in Toronto, it is the world's tallest communication structure.

PRACTICE 1   Read the following sentences. Write C beside correct sentences, FS beside fused sentences, and CS beside comma splices.

EXAMPLE: Gustave Eiffel was born in 1832 he designed the Eiffel
Tower and the Statue of Liberty.   _FS_

1. One of the most recognizable modern structures is the Eiffel Tower, it was built at the end of the nineteenth century.   _____

2. The French government wanted to celebrate the centennial anniversary of the French Revolution, which took place in 1789.   _____

3. The government held a competition it invited architects to submit designs to commemorate the anniversary of the revolution.   _____

4. Winners of the competition would have their designs displayed at the World's Fair of 1889.   _____

5. Many architects submitted designs, Gustave Eiffel's tower design won.   _____

6. The tower took twenty-six months to complete it was the tallest structure in the world at that time.   _____

7. It was 320 metres tall and weighed 63 500 tonnes.   _____

8. Many Parisians did not like the look of the tower, they wanted to destroy it.   _____

9. But it proved to be a very popular tourist attraction people from all over the world visit Paris and climb the tower.   _____

10. In fact, tourism experts consider the Eiffel Tower as the number one tourist attraction in the world.   _____

Correcting Run-Ons

You can correct both fused sentences and comma splices in a variety of ways. Read the following run-on sentence, and then review the four ways to correct it.

Run-On: Antoni Gaudí began his career as a secular architect he eventually became very religious.

1. Make two separate sentences by adding end punctuation, such as a period.

   Antoni Gaudí began his career as a secular architect. **He** eventually became very religious.

2. Add a semicolon (;).

   Antoni Gaudí began his career as a secular architect**;** he eventually became very religious.

3. Add a coordinating conjunction such as *for, and, nor, but, or, yet,* or *so.*

   Antoni Gaudí began his career as a secular architect, **but** he eventually became very religious.

4. Add a subordinating conjunction such as *although, because, when, before, while, since,* or *after.*

   Although Antoni Gaudí began his career as a secular architect, he eventually became very religious.

PRACTICE 2   Correct the run-ons by making two complete sentences.

EXAMPLE: Antoni Gaudí designed very interesting works, he is considered to be a genius.   *. He*

1. Antoni Gaudí was born in 1852 in Tarragona, Spain he is considered to be Catalonia's greatest architect.

2. Gaudí became a Catholic he also believed in Catalan nationalism.

3. Gaudí designed the *Sagrada Familia* he wanted to express his Catholic faith in his work.

4. Nature fascinated Gaudí, he incorporated nature's images into his creations.

5. Classical design used geometric shapes Gaudí's designs mimicked shapes from nature.

6. Gaudí's style evolved from Gothic influences, he created intricate, flowing, asymmetrical shapes.

7. Businessmen in Barcelona commissioned Gaudí to design a modern neighbourhood, he constructed many buildings like the Casa Mila.

8. His work used the *trencadis* style this style involves the use of broken tiles to decorate surfaces.

9. One of Gaudí's most famous designs is Park Guell, the park has dragon-shaped benches and tree-shaped columns.

10. Many people initially laughed at Gaudí's vision eight of his creations are now recognized as World Heritage Sites.

 Semicolons and Transitional Expressions

Another way to correct run-ons is to connect sentences with a transitional expression. Place a semicolon before the expression and a comma after it.

Example: The construction costs were too high; **therefore,** the town abandoned plans to build city hall.

The design was beautiful; **nevertheless,** it was rejected.

Some common transitional expressions are:

additionally	furthermore	however
meanwhile	moreover	nevertheless
of course	therefore	thus

PRACTICE 3   Correct the run-ons by joining the two sentences with a semicolon.

EXAMPLE: I. M. Pei has designed many famous buildings; John F. Kennedy Library is just one.

1. The Louvre Palace is one of the most recognized buildings in Paris, it was built in the Renaissance style for French monarchs.

2. The French Revolution abolished the monarchy the Louvre became a museum.

3. French officials wanted to expand the Louvre, they hired a famous architect to modify the building.

4. I. M. Pei was born in China in 1917 he immigrated to the United States to study architecture.

5. The French government commissioned Pei to enlarge the museum he designed three pyramids for the entrance.

6. The main pyramid gives light to the underground entrance, it is made of many glass squares.

7. The pyramid is about twenty-one metres high, it has two smaller pyramids on each side.

8. The pyramids were completed in 1989 many people thought the entrance was unattractive.

9. I. M. Pei is an outstanding architect his innovative designs have won many prizes.

CHAPTER 18

PRACTICE 4 Correct the run-ons by joining the two sentences with a comma and a coordinator (*for, and, nor, but, or, yet, so*).

EXAMPLE: Arthur Erickson is a Canadian architect, *and* his designs are world famous.

1. The University of British Columbia has many beautiful buildings Arthur Erickson's Museum of Anthropology is the most beautiful.

2. The museum rooms are high and spacious they can house large totems of the northwest First Nations.

Museum of Anthropology

3. The museum contains unusual artifacts, its totem pole collection is very interesting.

4. Architect Arthur Erickson considers the environment important his designs must fit into the landscape.

5. Erickson was an inexperienced architect his design won first place in a competition.

6. Many architects entered the competition Erickson's design was the most innovative.

7. The first-place winner was asked to design Simon Fraser University Erickson evaluated the surroundings.

8. The site was on top of a mountain it overlooked the ocean.

9. Erickson could follow the design trend of the time he could design according to his personal vision.

10. Simon Fraser University fits into the landscape its buildings are built into the mountainside.

PRACTICE 5   Correct the run-ons by joining the two sentences with a **subordinator.** Use one of the following subordinators: *because, before, although, when, even though,* and *although.* If the dependent clause comes at the beginning of the sentence, remember to add a comma.

EXAMPLE: European ideas have influenced African architecture, *even though* many indigenous designs reveal beauty and practicality.

1. African architecture is not that well known it is very rich and diverse.

2. African architecture was influenced by Arabs they colonized North Africa.

3. Europeans arrived in the sixteenth century Islam provided inspiration for architectural design.

4. Until the twenty-first century, there were very few famous African architects African countries were controlled by European powers.

5. Modern African buildings are beautiful they are not appreciated as World Heritage Sites.

6. The Aswan Dam, one of the most famous dams in the world, was constructed in the twentieth century the Nile River no longer flooded each year.

7. The construction of the Aswan Dam was controversial people were concerned about its impact on the environment.

8. The Eastgate Centre was built in Harare it became the world's first modern building to use natural cooling methods.

9. Modern African architecture is gaining momentum architects are considering the unique needs of Africa.

PRACTICE 6   Use a variety of methods to correct ten run-on errors. Add commas when necessary.

EXAMPLE: Many new buildings are being erected all over China, *and* modern building designs are very popular.

1. The Chinese Revolution dominated politics China's government developed policies to minimize class differences. As a result, new buildings were designed for utility, with no regard for beauty.

2. Now, China is industrializing at a great rate businesses are asking architects to design practical but beautiful buildings. The National Theatre building, for example, is controversial, it is also extremely intriguing. It was designed by French architect Paul Andreu, many people have criticized its design. It is shaped like an egg. It has three halls and a lake, it has a bridge. Another highly discussed building in Beijing is the CCTV tower it looks like the letter Z, many Chinese think it is an eyesore.

3. The cost of building these edifices is very expensive, some members of the public complain that such designs are too foreign. Others believe that

designing interesting buildings is very important. China hosted the Olympics in 2008. For example, the Olympic Stadium was a necessity, the cost was prohibitive.

4. The Beijing skyline has changed, not everybody has liked the changes. Some say that such change is the price for industrialization, average citizens are eager for Beijing to join the ranks of the most beautiful cities in the world.

FINAL REVIEW

Correct ten run-on errors.

EXAMPLE: The construction industry is the largest in the world, ∧ *and* public and private buildings consume a lot of energy.

1. When most people envision cities, they think about houses, roads, and skyscrapers built above ground they do not think about subterranean cities. However, many people use underground public and private buildings every day. In North America, there are at least five hundred public and private underground buildings for example, the Engineering Library at the University of Berkeley and the Vietnam Veterans Memorial Education Center are only two such subterranean structures. More and more underground structures are being built every day.

2. Some of the oldest underground cities are located in Cappadocia, Turkey the first underground city in that area was constructed around 2000 BCE. Archaeologists believe that at one time, up to twenty thousand

Entrance to tunnels in Cappadocia.

people lived in those underground Turkish cities the early Christians used them as a means to escape persecution.

3. Montreal contains an extremely large modern underground city. It was designed by I. M. Pei in the 1960s other architects have contributed to its expansion. It is located downtown and has around 42 kilometres of tunnels with about 120 exterior access points. More than 500 000 people use the underground city each day they want to avoid Montreal's very cold temperatures in the winter.

4. There are many reasons to build underground. First, underground buildings benefit from better climate control architects say that such buildings can be heated and cooled more efficiently than above-ground buildings. Also, building underground reduces the impact on the environment, forests and fields do not have to be cleared. Moreover, the wind, snow, and rain do not erode the walls, well-constructed underground buildings are resistant to fire and earthquakes.

5. Perhaps in the future, there will be more underground public and private buildings, they are more environmentally friendly and more energy efficient. Certainly it is time to rethink how urban planners design cities.

The Writer's Room **Topics for Writing**

Write about one of the following topics. Edit your writing and ensure that there are no run-ons.

1. Are there any buildings or areas in your neighbourhood, town, or country that you find attractive or unattractive? Describe these buildings and explain why you believe they are beautiful or unsightly.

2. Are there any changes or additions that you would make to the town or city where you live, such as adding a new park or a museum? What suggestions would you make to city planners?

 CHECKLIST: RUN-ONS

When you edit your writing, ask yourself this question.

☐ Are my sentences correctly formed and punctuated? Check for and correct any fused sentences and comma splices.

One of the most successful architects in the world is Ernest
       . He
Cormier ~~he~~ designed the Supreme Court of Canada building

in Ottawa.

How Do I Get a Better Grade?

Go to www.mycanadiancomplab.ca for additional help with your grammar, writing, and research skills. You will have access to a variety of exercises, instruction, and video that will help you improve your basic skills and help you get a better grade.

Faulty Parallel Structure

CONTENTS

- What Is Parallel Structure?
- Correcting Faulty Parallel Structure

Section Theme **URBAN DEVELOPMENT**

In this chapter, you will read about landscapes and gardens.

Grammar Snapshot

Looking at Parallel Structure

The Royal Botanic Gardens in Kew, England, supports research on conservation of the environment. The following paragraph summarizes one of the conservation schemes in Peru. Review the underlined ideas to see how they are parallel.

> The Huarango (*Prosopis pallida*) forests of the south coast of Peru are among the most highly threatened ecosystems on earth. The remaining trees are important primary producers, forming soil, preventing desertification, and providing the only refuge for biodiversity in large areas of hyperarid desert. They also furnish an extraordinary cornucopia of food, forage, and other products used by local people for thousands of years.

In this chapter, you will identify and correct faulty parallel structure.

What Is Parallel Structure?

Parallel structure occurs when pairs or groups of items in a sentence are balanced. Notice how the following sentences repeat grammatical structures but not ideas.

Parallel Nouns:	<u>Books</u>, <u>stores</u>, and <u>catalogues</u> give gardeners information.
Parallel Tenses:	Gardeners <u>dig</u> and <u>plant</u> in the soil.
Parallel Adjectives:	Kew Garden is <u>large</u>, <u>colourful</u>, and <u>breathtaking</u>.
Parallel Phrases:	You will find the public garden <u>down the road</u>, <u>over the bridge</u>, and <u>through the field</u>.
Parallel Clauses:	There are some gardens <u>that have just trees</u>, and some <u>that have only flowers and plants</u>.

Correcting Faulty Parallel Structure

Use parallel structure for a series of words or phrases, for paired clauses, for comparisons, and for two-part constructions. If you see "//" or simply "faulty parallelism" on one of your marked essays, try the following tips for correcting those errors.

Series of Words or Phrases

Use parallel structure when words or phrases are joined in a series.

Not Parallel:	The English, the Chinese, and people from Japan create luxurious gardens.
Parallel Nouns:	<u>The English</u>, <u>the Chinese</u>, and <u>the Japanese</u> create luxurious gardens.
Not Parallel:	I like to read books about gardens, to attend lectures about gardening, and buying plants for my garden.
Parallel Verbs:	I like <u>to read</u> books about gardens, <u>to attend</u> lectures about gardening, and <u>to buy</u> plants for my garden.

Paired Clauses

Use parallel structure when independent clauses are joined by *and*, *but*, or *or*.

Not Parallel:	You can find the bonsai garden on the right, and you can look left for the tea garden.

CHAPTER 19

Parallel Prepositions: You can find the bonsai garden <u>on the right</u>, and you can see the tea garden <u>on the left</u>.

Not Parallel: The tourists were dazzled, but they also had feelings of fatigue.

Parallel Adjectives: The tourists were <u>dazzled</u>, but they were also <u>fatigued</u>.

 **Use Consistent Voice**

When joining two independent clauses with a coordinating conjunction, use a consistent voice. For example, if the first part of the sentence uses the active voice, the other part should also use the active voice.

Not Parallel: The bees **flew** [active] to the flowers, and then the nectar **was tasted** [passive] by them.

Parallel Active Voice: The bees **flew** [active] to the flowers, and then they **tasted** [active] the nectar.

PRACTICE 1   Correct the faulty parallel structure in each sentence.

The Winter Palace

EXAMPLE: The Hermitage, which was the winter palace of the Russian Tsars, has a collection of valuable paintings, rare books, and
    antique furniture
<u>furniture that is antique.</u>

1. Tsar Peter the Great was cosmopolitan, educated, and

he had great determination.

2. In 1703, Peter created plans, and workers were ordered to build a new

city.

3. The Tsar commissioned a summer palace and a palace for the winter.

4. The Tsar designed parks, flower gardens, and he was also creating arboretums.

5. The summer garden contains large, exotic trees that are rare.

6. The landscaper, Domenico Trezzini, worked fastidiously, diligently, and he was creative.

7. Tourists can stroll down paths, over bridges, and walking by marble statues.

8. St. Petersburg is called the "window to the west," "the city of the white nights," and people also view it as "the northern Venice."

Comparisons

Use parallel structure in comparisons containing *than* or *as*.

Not Parallel:	Designing an interesting garden is easier than to take care of it.
Parallel -*ing* Forms:	Designing an interesting garden is easier than taking care of it.
Not Parallel:	The rock garden looks as colourful as the garden where there are roses.
Parallel Noun Phrases:	The rock garden looks as colourful as the rose garden.

Two-Part Constructions

Use parallel structure for the following paired items.

both . . . and	either . . . or	not . . . but
rather . . . than	neither . . . nor	not only . . . but also

Not Parallel:	The lecture on landscaping was both enlightening and of use.
Parallel Adjectives:	The lecture on landscaping was both enlightening and useful.

Not Parallel:	I could either see the bonsai exhibit or going to a film.
Parallel Verbs:	I could either <u>see</u> the bonsai exhibit or <u>go</u> to a film.

PRACTICE 2   Correct ten errors in parallel construction.

EXAMPLE: Cities need parks to create green areas, to prevent overcrowding,
to develop recreational facilities
and <u>people can use them for recreation.</u>

1. During the Industrial Revolution, urban life changed rapidly and
   in totality. City planners realized that more people were moving to the
   cities. Planners, politicians, and people who immigrated saw city life
   changing. Urban designers wanted to create green space rather than
   filling cities with concrete buildings.

2. One of the most important advocates of city beautification was Frederick
   Law Olmsted. He was born in 1822, in Hartford, Connecticut. He not
   only promoted urban planning, but he also was designing beautiful city
   gardens. He and collaborator Calvert Vaux designed New York's Central
   Park. Olmstead wanted the park to reflect his personal philosophy, so in it
   he created open spaces, beautiful views, and paths that wind.

3. Olmsted and Vaux designed many other projects. An important design
   was the Niagara Falls project. At that time, the falls were not completely
   visible to tourists. Olmsted wanted to create a harmonious landscape,
   to allow greater tourist accessibility, and conservation of the area

was important to him. Such a park required a great deal of planning. Goat Island separates Canada from the United States. Either the landscapers could buy Goat Island or Goat Island was continuing to be an eyesore. Olmsted and Vaux bought the island and restored it.

4. For Olmsted, contributing to the community was more important than to have fame. He designed Mount Royal Park in Montreal, and the 1893 World's Fair in Chicago was also planned by him. He was known as much for his sense of beauty as for respecting the environment. Olmsted died in 1903, but thousands of people continue to enjoy his legacy.

FINAL REVIEW

Correct fifteen errors in parallel construction. Remember: If you change a compound sentence to a simple sentence, you will have to remove a comma.

EXAMPLE: Walking through Kew Gardens is more relaxing than ~~to read~~ *reading* a book.

1. One of London's most famous sites is the Royal Botanic Gardens. Kew Gardens contains flower beds, greenhouses, and there are stone sculptures. Kew can be traced back to the mid-eighteenth century when King George III [was supporting] *supported* the garden's expansion. Since then, not only has Kew been enlarged, but it was becoming a World Heritage site. To visit Kew Gardens, travel over the Thames, along the edge of Kew village, and [you must go] past the Kew Gardens subway station.

2. Today, at Kew Gardens, botanical research is as important as attracting people who are tourists. The site is important for storing seeds, cataloguing plants, and professional gardeners go there for training. But, modernization is creating problems for Kew. Being so close to London, Kew experiences air pollution, hot weather, and the rainfall is in small amounts. Even with such problems, Kew is truly beautiful, very innovative, and it is also extremely impressive.

3. Another famous European garden is the Versailles garden near Paris, France. King Louis XIV moved his court from Paris to Versailles in 1682, and he asked the great landscaper André Le Nôtre to design the gardens. Le Nôtre worked carefully, intuitively, and with passion. Le Nôtre not only had to plan a garden, but water also had to be brought to the site by him. *he also had to bring water* The original soil was neither rich and it was not fertile. *not*

4. Le Nôtre succeeded in his design. It is perfectly laid out adhering to Renaissance principles. The gardens have walkways, fountains, statues, and there are ponds. The gardens reflect the glory of the king, the beauty of nature, and human creativity. *the creativity of human* Le Nôtre received great fame, honour, and was wealthy. Millions of visitors visit Versailles to enjoy the gardens, to understand a part of history, and seeing the splendour of the age of *to see* Louis XIV.

The Writer's Room **Topics for Writing**

Choose one of the following topics, and write a paragraph. Make sure your nouns, verbs, and sentence structures are parallel.

1. If you could be anywhere right now, where would you be? Describe that place. Include details that appeal to the senses.

2. What do you do to relax? List some steps.

 CHECKLIST: PARALLEL STRUCTURE

When you edit your writing, ask yourself this question.

☐ Are my grammatical structures balanced? Check for errors in these cases:

- when words or phrases are joined in a series
- when independent clauses are joined by *and*, *but*, or *or*
- in comparisons or contrasts

How Do I Get a Better Grade?

mycanadiancomplab

Go to www.mycanadiancomplab.ca for additional help with your grammar, writing, and research skills. You will have access to a variety of exercises, instruction, and video that will help you improve your basic skills and help you get a better grade.

Mistakes with Modifiers

CHAPTER 20

CONTENTS
- Misplaced Modifiers
- Dangling Modifiers

Section Theme **URBAN DEVELOPMENT**

In this chapter, you will read about pollution and other urban issues.

Grammar Snapshot

Looking at Mistakes with Modifiers

Myles Oka, a student in urban planning, wrote about the consequences of urban sprawl. The following excerpt contains some modifier errors.

> Because I live in a suburb, I drive many miles each day to work. <u>Last night, stuck in traffic, car horns blared constantly.</u> <u>Commuters inched their cars slowly like caterpillars wanting to get home.</u> I was stressed and anxious.

In this chapter, you will identify and correct misplaced and dangling modifiers.

Misplaced Modifiers

A **modifier** is a word, phrase, or clause that describes or modifies nouns or verbs in a sentence. To use a modifier correctly, place it next to the word(s) that you want to modify.

modifier   words that are modified
Trying to combat pollution, **city planners** have launched an anti-littering campaign.

A **misplaced modifier** is a word, phrase, or clause that is not placed next to the word that it modifies. When a modifier is too far from the word that it is describing, the meaning of the sentence can become confusing or unintentionally funny.

I saw a pamphlet about littering waiting in the mayor's office.

(How could a pamphlet wait in the mayor's office?)

Commonly Misplaced Modifiers

As you read the sample sentences for each type of modifier, notice how the meaning of the sentence changes depending on where the modifier is placed.

Prepositional Phrase Modifiers

A prepositional phrase is made of a preposition and its object.

Confusing: Helen read an article on electric cars in a café.
                 (Who was in the café: Helen or the cars?)

Clear: In a café, Helen read an article on electric cars.

Participle Modifiers

A participle modifier is a phrase that contains an *-ing* verb or an *-ed* verb.

Confusing: Jamal Reed learned about anti-littering laws touring Singapore.
                 (Can laws tour Singapore?)

Clear: While touring Singapore, Jamal Reed learned about anti-littering laws.

Relative Clause Modifiers

A modifier can be a relative clause or phrase beginning with *who, whose, which*, or *that*.

CHAPTER 20

Confusing: The woman received a $1000 fine from the officer <u>who dropped a candy wrapper</u>.
(Who dropped the candy wrapper: the woman or the officer?)

Clear: The woman who dropped a candy wrapper received a $1000 fine from the officer.

Limiting Modifiers

Limiting modifiers are words such as *almost, nearly, only, merely, just,* and *even*. In the examples, notice how the placement of *almost* changes the meaning of each sentence.

Almost all of the citizens took the steps that solved the littering problem.
(Some of the citizens did not take the steps, but most did.)

All of the citizens **almost** took the steps that solved the littering problem.
(The citizens did not take the steps.)

All of the citizens took the steps that **almost** solved the littering problem.
(The steps did not solve the littering problem.)

 **Correcting Misplaced Modifiers**

To correct misplaced modifiers, follow these steps:

1. First, identify the modifier.
   Armando saw the oil slick **standing on the pier.**

2. Then, identify the word or words being modified.
   Armando

3. Finally, move the modifier next to the word(s) being modified.
   Standing on the pier, Armando saw the oil slick.

PRACTICE I   Correct the misplaced modifier in each sentence.

who was fined $500
EXAMPLE: The man ᴧ forgot to flush the public toilet <u>who was fined $500</u>.

1. Experts recognize Singapore as the cleanest city in the world from the United Nations.

2. Singaporean police officers will immediately arrest litterbugs who patrol city streets.

3. After littering, officers give a $1000 fine to polluters.

4. For a second littering offence, a polluter must clean a public area such as a park or school yard wearing a bright yellow vest.

5. In 1992, Singapore's new law prohibited the importation, selling, or chewing of gum, which caused a large controversy.

6. Because gum was stuck on them, passengers could not close the doors to the subway trains.

7. In 2004, the law was revised to allow gum into the country that has medicinal purposes.

8. Evangeline dropped her gum on a downtown street not seeing the police officer.

9. She nearly cleaned the park for eight hours on the weekend.

10. Singaporeans with no litter are proud of their city.

Dangling Modifiers

A **dangling modifier** opens a sentence but does not modify any words in the sentence. It "dangles" or hangs loosely because it is not connected to any other part of the sentence. To avoid having a dangling modifier, make sure that the modifier and the first noun that follows it have a logical connection.

CHAPTER 20

Confusing:	While eating a candy bar, the wrapper fell on the ground.
	(Can a wrapper eat a candy bar?)
Clear:	While eating a candy bar, **Zelda** dropped the wrapper on the ground.
Confusing:	To attend the conference, a background in environmental work is necessary.
	(Can a background attend a conference?)
Clear:	To attend the conference, **participants** need a background in environmental work.

Hint   **Correcting Dangling Modifiers**

To correct dangling modifiers, follow these steps:

1. First, identify the modifier.
   When travelling, public transportation should be used.
2. Then, decide who or what the writer aims to modify.
   Who is travelling? **People**
3. Finally, add the missing subject (and in some cases, also add or remove words) so that the sentence makes sense.
   When travelling, people should use public transportation.

PRACTICE 2   Underline the dangling modifier in each sentence. Then, rewrite the sentence keeping the modifier. You may have to add or remove words to give the sentence a logical meaning.

EXAMPLE: Enjoying parks, it is difficult when there is a lot of litter.

> *It is difficult for people to enjoy parks when there is a lot of litter.*

1. Believing it is not garbage, cigarette butts are left on city streets.

   _____

   _____

2. With an unconcerned attitude, the hamburger wrapper ended up on the ground.

   _____

   _____

3. Unhappy with the garbage in the park, a major cleanup took place.

   _____

   _____

4. Playing in the sand, there were pieces of glass from broken bottles.

   _____

   _____

5. Sitting on a park bench, all sorts of plastic bags drifted by.

   _____

   _____

6. To understand the effects of littering, the cleanup costs must be examined.

   _____

   _____

7. Seeing no available trash can, the cigarette butt can be wrapped up and carried.

   _____

   _____

8. While walking barefoot on the grass, a piece of glass cut Pablo's foot.

   _____

   _____

9. The car alarm was wailing while reading my newspaper in the park.

   _____

   _____

10. By thinking about litter, parks can be kept clean.

    _____

    _____

PRACTICE 3　　Correct the dangling or misplaced modifiers in the following sentences. If the sentence is correct, write *C* next to it.

Alicia noticed that

EXAMPLE: Living in Mexico City, the air is extremely bad. _____
                              ^

1. Having the highest level of air pollution in the world, people suffer from

   asthma in Mexico City. _____

2. Coming mainly from the millions of cars on the streets, the dangers of the

   air pollution are well known. _____

3. Situated in a valley surrounded by mountains, pollution gets trapped above

   Mexico City. _____

4. Living near Ermita subway, Alicia Gutierrez suffers from pollution-related

   illnesses. _____

5. Because they are older models, the latest catalytic converters are not in

   many cars. _____

6. Mexico City planners discussed ways to combat the bad air

   in a meeting. _____

7. Several years ago, Mexico City's mayor introduced the new fuel-efficient

   buses in a state of excitement. _____

8. Because of the law requiring motorists to leave their cars home one day a

   week, Luis took a bus to work. _____

9. Trying to combat the pollution, at least five billion dollars has

   been spent. _____

10. Appreciating Mexico City's initiatives, the air quality

    is much better. _____

FINAL REVIEW

Identify fifteen dangling or misplaced modifier errors in this selection. Then, correct each error. You may need to add or remove words to ensure that the sentence makes sense.

a young boy found surprising results.

EXAMPLE: Working on his school project, ~~some surprising results were found.~~

1. Emilio discovered that there are many ways to help the environment in his school project. He sat with his parents to discuss energy-saving strategies drinking coffee. First, there are things people can do to help the environment in their kitchens. When using freezer bags or aluminium foil, washing them can reduce waste. Also, people should use cloth napkins and dishtowels instead of paper products. With airtight lids, Emilio places food in plastic containers.

2. Emilio and his parents also discussed tips for other areas of the home. Families can take measures in the bathroom who want to save energy. For example, people should take shorter showers. While Emilio is brushing his teeth, it is important to leave the faucet turned off as much as possible. People can install a toilet dam to reduce water consumption.

3. For their laundry room, Emilio's parents bought energy-efficient appliances with a smile. After washing shirts, the family hangs them out to dry instead of using a clothes dryer. They also buy phosphate-free detergent doing the shopping.

4. When Emilio's father goes to the grocery store, he makes sensible decisions about products near his house. Trying to do fewer trips and buying in bulk, the gas consumption is reduced. He buys incandescent light bulbs at the local hardware store that save energy.

5. The family's furnace needs to be upgraded, which is very old. Based on the latest technology, Emilio's parents are planning to buy an energy-efficient heater. Also, watching only one television, there is a reduction in energy consumption and the family spends more time together. Using the techniques mentioned above, Emilio's family has helped the environment and saved money.

 The Writer's Room **Topics for Writing**

Write about one of the following topics. Proofread your text to ensure that there are no modifier errors.

1. What are some steps that your neighbourhood or town could take to combat a littering or pollution problem?

2. What are some types of polluters? Write about three categories of polluters.

CHECKLIST: MODIFIERS

When you edit your writing, ask yourself these questions.

☐ Are my modifiers in the correct position? Check for errors with the following:

- prepositional-phrase modifiers
- participle modifiers
- relative clause modifiers
- limiting modifiers

  Wearing overalls, the
  ~~The~~ urban planner surveyed the garbage ~~wearing overalls~~.

☐ Do my modifiers modify something in the sentence? Check for dangling modifiers.

  the tourist got a hefty fine from the police officer
  Having thrown the plastic bag onto the street, ~~the police officer gave the tourist a hefty fine.~~

How Do I Get a Better Grade?

mycanadiancomplab

Go to www.mycanadiancomplab.ca for additional help with your grammar, writing, and research skills. You will have access to a variety of exercises, instruction, and video that will help you improve your basic skills and help you get a better grade.

READING LINK

Urban Development

These essays contain more information about urban issues.

"Friendless in North America," by Ellen Goodman (page 215)

"Yonge St., a Seedy Mystery in Plain View," by Sheila Heti (page 498)

"Living Environments," by Avi Friedman (page 503)

21 Subject–Verb Agreement

CONTENTS

Section Theme **INTERNATIONAL TRADE**

In this chapter, you will read about cultural differences in the world of international business.

Grammar Snapshot

Looking at Subject–Verb Agreement

The following excerpt, from "Canadians' Vacation Days Disappearing," is by Suzanne Beaubien. The subjects and verbs are identified. Link each verb with its subject. Do you know why some verbs end in -s?

Piers Steel, a human resources professor at the University of Calgary's Haskayne School of Business, <u>says</u> **he** <u>doesn't</u> <u>think</u> **forfeiting vacation time** necessarily <u>makes</u> businesses more productive.

"Some **people** <u>will take</u> ten hours to do five hours of work," **Steel** <u>said</u>, "but the **need** to take vacation time <u>varies</u> from job to job. Some **people** <u>love</u> their jobs and <u>do</u> not <u>want</u> to take time away."

In this chapter, you will practise making subjects and verbs agree.

Basic Subject–Verb Agreement Rules

Subject–verb agreement simply means that a subject and verb agree in number. A singular subject needs a singular verb and a plural subject needs a plural verb.

Simple Present Tense Agreement

Writers use **simple present tense** to indicate that an action is habitual or factual. Review the following rules for simple present tense agreement.

- **Third-person singular form:** When the subject is *he, she, it*, or the equivalent (*Mark, Carol, Ottawa*), add an *-s* or *-es* ending to the verb.

  Maria Orlon <u>works</u> as a marketing researcher in Regina.

- **Base form:** When the subject is *I, you, we*, or *they*, or the equivalent (*women, the Rocky Mountains*), do not add an ending to the verb.

  Many **businesses** <u>rely</u> on marketing research.

 **Be, Have, and Do**

The verbs *be, have,* and *do* have irregular third-person singular forms.

be:	I <u>am</u>	He <u>is</u>	We <u>are</u>
have:	I <u>have</u>	She <u>has</u>	They <u>have</u>
do:	I <u>do</u>	It <u>does</u>	You <u>do</u>

Agreement in Other Tenses

In the past tense, almost all verbs have one past form. The only past-tense verb requiring subject verb agreement is the verb *be*, which has two past forms: *was* and *were*.

　　I <u>was</u> tired. **Edward** <u>was</u> also tired. That day, **we** <u>were</u> very lazy.

　　In the present perfect tense, which is formed with *have* or *has* and the past participle, use *has* when the subject is third-person singular and *have* for all other forms.

　　The **travel service** <u>has raised</u> its booking fees. Other **agencies** <u>have not raised</u> their fees.

　　In the future tense and with modal forms (*can, could, would, may, might* . . .), use the same form of the verb with every subject.

　　I <u>will work</u>. **She** <u>will work</u> with me. **We** <u>can work</u> together.

GRAMMAR LINK

For more information about using the present perfect tense, see Chapter 22.

> ## Hint · Use Standard English
>
> In casual conversations and in movies, you may hear people say *He be cool*, or *She don't have the time*. In professional and academic situations, use the correct forms of *be*, *have*, and *do*.

PRACTICE 1   Underline the correct present tense form of the verbs in parentheses.

EXAMPLE: Many businesses (<u>export</u> / exports) products to other nations.

1. Although several countries (share / shares) the English language, the details in the language and culture (be / is / are) different. Business travellers (learn / learns) about these differences.

2. For example, Canadians (put / puts) gas in their cars, whereas British citizens (use / uses) petrol. In England, you (do / does) not phone people, you "ring" them. Australians also (have / has) interesting expressions. A "chalkie" (is / are) a teacher, and a "mozzie" (is / are) a mosquito.

3. In England, class-based traditions (is / are) still strong, and many people (support / supports) the monarchy. Australia, on the other hand, (have / has) a very egalitarian culture. Mr. Ian Wynn (have / has) been an Australian real estate agent for seven years, and he (does / do) not like signs of arrogance. Last spring, when some tourists (was / were) arrogant, Wynn said, "Don't be a tall poppy. The tall poppy (get / gets) its head cut off."

4. Spelling also (differ / differs) among English-speaking nations. Canada (follow / follows) British spelling much of the time. Thus, we (maintain /

maintains) the -*our* ending on words such as *flavour* or *colour*. Americans

(drop / drops) the final "u" and (write / writes) *flavor* or *color*.

More Than One Subject

There are special agreement rules when there is more than one subject in a sentence.

And

When two subjects are joined by *and*, use the plural form of the verb.

> High schools, <u>universities</u>, and <u>trade schools</u> **prepare** students for the job market.

Or / Nor

When two subjects are joined by *or* or *nor*, the verb agrees with the subject that is the closest to it.

> singular
> The layout artists or the <u>editor</u> **decides** how the cover will look.

> plural
> Neither the artist nor her <u>assistants</u> **make** changes to the design.

As Well As and Along With

The phrases *as well as* and *along with* are not the same as *and*. They do not form a compound subject. The real subject is before the interrupting expression.

<u>Japan</u>, <u>China</u>, and <u>South Korea</u> **develop** high-tech computer products.

<u>Japan</u>, as well as China and South Korea, **develops** high-tech computer products.

PRACTICE 2   Underline the correct verb in each sentence. Make sure the verb agrees with the subject.

EXAMPLE: Japan and China (<u>have</u> / has) interesting types of restaurants.

1. Tokyo and other Japanese cities (have / has) "Maid Cafés."

2. The hostess and the female servers (dress / dresses) in traditional maid

   uniforms.

3. Recently, in the Otome Road area of Tokyo, a businesswoman and her partner (have / has) opened a Butler Café.

4. Every day, Jin or another waiter (serve / serves) customers.

5. The coffee or the tea (come / comes) on a special tray.

6. The host and the waiters (treat / treats) the customers like British royalty.

7. "Mademoiselle" or "Your Highness" (is / are) said to each customer by the server in the butler uniform.

8. A crumpet as well as a large scone (appear / appears) on each table.

9. Every day, many young and old women (try / tries) to get a table at the Butler Café.

Special Subject Forms

Some subjects are not easy to identify as singular or plural. Two common types are indefinite pronouns and collective nouns.

Indefinite Pronouns

Indefinite pronouns refer to a general person, place, or thing. Carefully review the following list of indefinite pronouns.

Indefinite Pronouns

Singular	another	each	nobody	other
	anybody	everybody	no one	somebody
	anyone	everyone	nothing	someone
	anything	everything	one	something
Plural	both, few, many, others, several			

Singular Indefinite Pronouns

In the following sentences, the verbs require the third-person-singular form because the subjects are singular.

Almost <u>everyone</u> **knows** about the Free Trade Agreement.

You can put one or more singular nouns (joined by *and*) after *each* and *every*. The verb is still singular.

<u>Every</u> client **likes** the new rule. <u>Each</u> man and woman **knows** about it.

Plural Indefinite Pronouns

Both, few, many, others, and *several* are all plural subjects. The verb is always plural.

A representative from Canada and another from Mexico are sitting at a table. <u>Both</u> **want** to compromise.

Collective Nouns

Collective nouns refer to a group of people or things. Here are some common collective nouns.

army	class	crowd	group	population
association	club	family	jury	public
audience	committee	gang	mob	society
band	company	government	organization	team

Generally, each group acts as a unit, so you must use the singular form of the verb.

The <u>company</u> **is** ready to make a decision.

 **Hint**   **Police Is Plural**

Treat the word *police* as a plural noun because the word "officers" is implied but not stated.

The police **have** a protester in custody.

PRACTICE 3   Underline the correct verb in each sentence.

EXAMPLE: The Executive Planet website (have / <u>has</u>) tips for business travellers.

1. Each large and small nation (have / has) its own gift-giving rules. For

    example, Singapore (have / has) strict rules against bribery, and the

government (pride / prides) itself on being corruption-free. The police (arrest / arrests) officials who accept a bribe.

2. Specific rules (apply / applies) to gift-giving in Singapore. Certainly, everyone (love / loves) to receive a gift. Nobody (like / likes) to be left out while somebody else (open / opens) a present, so in Singapore, every businessman or businesswoman (know / knows) that gifts must be presented to a group. For example, if somebody (want / wants) to thank a receptionist, he or she (give / gives) a gift to the entire department. The group (accept / accepts) the gift graciously.

3. To be polite, most individuals (refuse / refuses) a gift initially. Some (believe / believes) that a refusal (make / makes) them appear less greedy. If the gift-giver (continue / continues) to insist, the recipient will accept the gift.

4. Singaporeans (do / does) not unwrap gifts in front of the giver. It (imply / implies) that the receiver is impatient and greedy. Everyone (thank / thanks) the gift-giver and (wait / waits) to open the gift in privacy.

5. China, as well as Japan, also (have / has) unusual gift-giving rules. In China, nobody (give / gives) a gift in white or green wrapping paper because those colours are unlucky. In Japan, the number four (sound / sounds) like the word meaning "death," so people do not give gifts that contain four items. To avoid insulting their hosts, business travellers should learn about gift-giving rules in other nations.

Verb Before the Subject

Usually the verb comes after the subject, but in some sentences, the verb is before the subject. In such cases, you must still ensure that the subject and verb agree.

There or Here

When a sentence begins with *there* or *here*, the subject always follows the verb. *There* and *here* are not subjects.

>   V   S   V   S
> Here **is** the <u>menu</u>. There **are** many different <u>sandwiches</u>.

Questions

In questions, word order is usually reversed, and the main or helping verb is placed before the subject. In the following example, the main verb is *be*.

>   V   S   V   S
> Where **is** the <u>Butler Café</u>? **Is** the <u>food</u> good?

In questions in which the main verb is not *be*, the subject agrees with the helping verb that appears before it.

>   HV   S   V   HV   S   V
> When **does** the <u>café</u> **close**? **Do** <u>students</u> **work** there?

PRACTICE 4   Correct any subject–verb agreement errors. If the sentence is correct, write C in the space.

      Have
EXAMPLE: ~~Has~~ you ever visited Turkey? _____

1. Is there etiquette rules about greetings? _____

2. Do each nation have its own rules? _____

3. There be specific rules in each country. _____

4. In Turkey, do older men or women receive preferential treatment? _____

5. If someone enters a room, he or she greet the oldest person first. _____

6. There be tremendous respect for elders. _____

7. Why is the two women holding hands? _____

8. In Turkey, handholding is a sign of respect and friendship. _____

9. In many companies, there have not been enough attention given to business etiquette. _____

10. On the other hand, there is many business professionals who learn about the customs of their foreign clients. _____

Interrupting Words and Phrases

Words that come between the subject and the verb may confuse you. In these cases, look for the subject and make sure that the verb agrees with the subject.

       S   interrupting phrase   V

Some <u>companies</u> in the transportation sector **lose** money.

       S   interrupting phrase   V

The <u>manager</u> in my office never **wears** a suit and tie.

Hint   **Identify Interrupting Phrases**

When you revise your paragraphs, place words that separate the subject and the verb in parentheses. Then you can check to see if your subjects and verbs agree.

    S   interrupting phrase   V

An <u>employee</u> **(**in my brother's company**)** **annoys** his co-workers.

When interrupting phrases contain *of the*, the subject appears before the phrase.

    S   interrupting phrase   V

<u>One</u> **(**of the most common work-related ailments**) is** carpal tunnel syndrome.

PRACTICE 5   Identify the subject and place any words that come between each subject and verb in parentheses. Then underline the correct form of the verb. (Two possible verb choices are in bold.)

EXAMPLE: (One) (of the most controversial topics in business circles) **is** / **are** stress.

1. Canadians **take** / **takes** very few vacation days. Other nations, including France, England, and Sweden, **have** / **has** many vacation days. The average employee in France **have** / **has** about thirty-nine vacation days annually. Canadians, on the other hand, only **receive** / **receives** twenty-one vacation days each year. The typical Canadian employee, for a variety of reasons, only **use** / **uses** nineteen of those days each year.

2. Why **do / does** Canadians forfeit vacation days? Some **say / says** that they

    do not schedule their vacation in advance. Others **is / are** too busy at work

    and **take / takes** cash instead of vacation days. Journalist Suzanne

    Beaubien, in a newspaper article, **suggest / suggests** that businesses

    benefit each time an employee **do / does** not take a vacation. "Over $5 billion

    in wages is handed back to employers," she **say / says**.

3. One of the problems caused by a lack of time off **is / are** stress-related illness.

    Some Canadians, according to JobCircle.com, **is / are** beginning to rebel.

    Workers increasingly **call / calls** in sick when they really **have / has** family

    responsibilities or other reasons for missing work. For example, Ted Owens, a

    Toronto-based broker, **admit / admits** to using sick days for other purposes.

    One of his co-workers **have / has** also lied to the boss on a regular basis.

Interrupting Words—Who, Which, That

If a sentence contains a clause beginning with *who, which,* or *that,* then the verb
agrees with the subject preceding *who, which,* or *that.*

> There is a <u>woman</u> in my neighbourhood *who* **works** as an executive.

Sometimes a complete dependent clause appears between the subject and verb.

> interrupting clause
> The <u>problem</u>, *which* we discussed, **needs** to be solved.

PRACTICE 6   Correct nine subject–verb agreement errors.

discusses
EXAMPLE: Jeff Geissler ~~discuss~~ maternity leave in an article for the
Associated Press.

1. Elisa Elbert, who works for an accounting firm, is expecting a child. Elisa,

    like other Australian citizens, receive up to twelve months of paid leave.

Madhuri Datta, a Canadian, is having her baby next month. Datta, who is due in November, want to share her paid leave with her husband. According to a recent poll, one of the Canadian government's best laws are the one that permits parents to divide thirty-five weeks of paid parental leave.

2. The U.S. *Family and Medical Leave Act*, which only cover workers in large companies, protect new mothers from losing their jobs. The act, according to a Harvard study, only provide for twelve weeks of paid leave.

3. Why do Canada have a parental leave program? Jeanne Brooks-Gunn, a professor at Columbia University, point out that some countries have falling birth rates and need to boost their populations. Canada, Italy, and Japan, for instance, have parental-leave policies that encourages working women to reproduce.

FINAL REVIEW

Correct fifteen errors in subject–verb agreement.

EXAMPLE: The worker ~~enjoy~~ *enjoys* his afternoon nap.

1. Is afternoon naps beneficial? In Spain, the afternoon siesta have been part of the culture for centuries. Many businesses, including shops, restaurants, and offices, close for three hours each afternoon and then opens from 5 to 7 p.m. During the long break, employees return home and has a siesta. However, the siesta culture is changing.

Mario Carreno (b. 1913/Cuban) La Siesta 1946. Oil on canvas. © Christie's Images/ SuperStock.

2. Some multinational companies that operates in Spain remain open for business in the afternoons. One of the reasons are the companies' desire to increase productivity. To give sleep-deprived Spaniards the siesta that they crave, a new type of business has opened. There is "siesta shops" throughout Spain. Each shop satisfy a need.

3. Jose Luis Buqueras, a computer programmer, work for a British multinational in Madrid, and he has a one-hour lunch break. Luckily for Buqueras, there be several siesta shops in his neighbourhood that offers short siestas. If he pays 500 pesetas, he can doze in a darkened room for twenty minutes. One of the attendants massage his neck. Then somebody cover him with a blanket. Quiet music plays in the background.

4. Although many Spanish citizens no longer enjoy three-hour breaks, they have not given up their afternoon siestas. Perhaps other nations can benefit from Spain's example. According to many medical professionals, a short afternoon nap helps reduce stress. There is also studies showing that naps reduce heart disease. David Jenkins, a government employee in Ireland, want siesta shops to open in his country.

The Writer's Room **Topics for Writing**

Write about one of the following topics. Proofread your text to ensure that your subjects and verbs agree.

1. Do you have afternoon naps? Explain why or why not. Compare yourself to someone who has, or does not have, frequent naps.

2. Describe a visit that you made to a culturally different restaurant. What happened? Use language that appeals to the senses.

CHECKLIST: SUBJECT–VERB AGREEMENT

When you edit your writing, ask yourself these questions.

☐ Do my subjects and verbs agree? Check for errors with the following:

- present tense verbs
- *was* and *were*
- interrupting phrases

The clients, whom I have never met, ~~is~~ *are* unhappy with the

new ad. It ~~be~~ *is* too dull.

☐ Do I use the correct verb form with indefinite pronouns? Check for errors with singular indefinite pronouns such as *everybody*, *nobody*, or *somebody*.

Somebody ~~have~~ *has* to modify the photograph.

☐ Do my subjects and verbs agree when the subject is after the verb? Check for errors with the following:

- sentences containing *here* and *there*
- question forms

~~Do~~ *Does* she watch commercials? There ~~is~~ *are* many funny ads on television.

Verb Tenses

CONTENTS

Section Theme INTERNATIONAL TRADE

In this chapter, you will learn about advertising and marketing.

Grammar Snapshot

Looking at Verb Tenses

The following excerpt is from Business Ethics by Richard T. De George. Look at the underlined verbs and try to determine what tense the author has used. What is the difference between *was* and *were*? Why do some verbs begin with *has*? What is the difference between *was* and *has been*? You will discover the answers to these questions in this chapter.

> The growth of giant corporations <u>has tended</u> to make competition in many areas very costly. The growth of supermarkets, which <u>began</u> in the 1940s, <u>has forced</u> most small grocers and vegetable and fruit markets out of business. The prices a supermarket <u>was</u> able to charge <u>were</u> lower than those the small operators could charge for equal-quality goods. The consequence <u>has been</u> the elimination of small grocers.

In this chapter, you will write using a variety of verb tenses.

347

What Is Verb Tense?

Verb tense indicates when an action occurred. Review the various tenses of the verb *work*. (Progressive or *-ing* forms of these verbs appear at the end of this chapter.)

Simple Forms

Present:	I <u>work</u> in a large company. My sister <u>works</u> with me.
Past:	We <u>worked</u> in Cancun last summer.
Future:	My sister <u>will work</u> in the Middle East next year.
Present Perfect:	We <u>have worked</u> together since 2001.
Past Perfect:	When Maria lost her job, she <u>had worked</u> there for six years.
Future Perfect:	By 2020, I <u>will have worked</u> here for twenty years.

CHAPTER 22

 Use Standard Verb Forms

Non-standard English is used in everyday conversation and may differ according to the region in which you live. **Standard English** is the common language generally used and expected in schools, businesses, and government institutions in Canada. In college, you should write using standard English.

Non-standard:	He don't have no money.	She be real tired.
Standard:	He <u>does not</u> have <u>any</u> money.	She <u>is</u> <u>really</u> tired.

GRAMMAR LINK

For more information about subject-verb agreement, see Chapter 21.

Present and Past Tenses

Present Tense Verbs

The simple present tense indicates that an action is a general fact or habitual activity. Remember to add *-s* or *-es* to verbs that follow third-person singular forms.

Fact:	Our fee <u>includes</u> mass mail-outs and pamphlet <u>distribution</u>.
Habitual Activity:	Carmen Cruz <u>takes</u> drawing classes every Saturday.

Saturday   Saturday   Saturday   Saturday

(past) ←————————————————————————→ (future)

She draws.   She draws.   She draws.   She draws.

Past Tense Verbs

The past tense indicates that an action occurred at a specific past time. Regular past tense verbs have a standard *-d* or *-ed* ending. Use the same form for both singular and plural past tense verbs.

Yesterday morning, we **discussed** the campaign.

Yesterday morning   **Today**

We discussed the campaign.

GRAMMAR LINK

For rules on the spelling of regular past-tense verbs, see Chapter 27, Spelling and Commonly Confused Words.

CHAPTER 22

> **PRACTICE I**   Write the present or past tense of each verb in parentheses.

EXAMPLE: In the 1960s, some American companies (attempt)
_____*attempted*_____ to enter the Japanese marketplace.

1. General Mills company (produce) _____ many food products.

   Each year, the company (sell) _____ products around

   the world. Sometimes, a product (succeed) _____ in a

   foreign marketplace, but occasionally, a product (fail) _____.

2. In 2004, Joyce Millet (publish) _____ an article called,

   "Marketing in Japan: What History Can Teach Us." To prepare

   for her article, she (research) _____ examples of product

   failures.

3. In the late 1960s, General Mills (plan) _____ to market

   Betty Crocker cake mixes in Japan. They (try) _____ to

   design a suitable product. Product developers (learn) _____

   that very few Japanese homes had ovens, so they (need) _____

   to find a new way to bake the cakes. At that time, most Japanese homes (contain) _____ a rice cooker, so designers (create)

_____ a spongy cake mix that worked in a rice cooker.

4. At first, sales of the Betty Crocker cake mix were good, but sales quickly

(tumble) _____. What was the problem? In the past, most

Japanese citizens (believe) _____ that rice was sacred, so they

(refuse) _____ to contaminate the rice with cake flavour.

Irregular Past Tense Verbs

Irregular verbs change internally. Because their spellings change from the present to the past tense, these verbs can be challenging to remember. For example, the irregular verb *go* becomes *went* when you convert it to the past tense.

> The company <u>sold</u> the patent. (*sold* = past tense of *sell*)
>
> Consumers <u>bought</u> the product. (*bought* = past tense of *buy*)

Be (Was or Were)

Most past tense verbs have one form that you can use with all subjects. However, the verb *be* has two past forms: *was* and *were*. The packing box **was** not sturdy enough. The plates <u>were</u> fragile.

PRACTICE 2   Write the correct past tense form of each verb in parentheses. Some verbs are regular, and some are irregular. If you do not know the past tense form of an irregular verb, consult the chart in Appendix 2.

EXAMPLE: Long ago, John Pemberton (have) _____*had*_____ a great idea.

1. In 1884, John Pemberton (be) _____ a pharmacist in Atlanta,

Georgia. He (know) _____ about a successful French product

called a "coca wine." Pemberton (make) _____ his own version

of the product and called it Pemberton's French Wine Coca. In 1885,

CHAPTER 22

GRAMMAR LINK

See Appendix 2 for a list of common irregular verbs.

Atlanta (pass) _____ prohibition legislation, so Pemberton

created an alcohol-free version of his drink. He (mix) _____ his

syrup with carbonated water, and he (bring) _____ some

samples to a local pharmacy. Customers (pay) _____ 5 cents a

glass for the drink.

2. Pemberton's bookkeeper (be) _____ a marketing wizard. Frank

     M. Robinson (think) _____ of a name for the drink. He also

     (feel) _____ certain that the drink required an interesting logo,

     thus Robinson (develop) _____ the handwritten Coca-Cola logo.

     In 1886, many stores (have) _____ the red logo on their awnings.

3. Pemberton never (make) _____ a lot of money from his

     invention. He (sell) _____ his company to Mr. Asa Candler for

     $2300. Candler (take) _____ the Coca-Cola company to new

     heights, and it (become) _____ a highly successful international

     company.

4. In 1889, the Coca-Cola company (do) _____ not patent the

     formula for Coca-Cola because company executives (do) _____

     not want competitors to know the secret formula of the soft drink. It

     remains one of the best-kept trade secrets in history.

> ## Hint Use the Base Form After *Did* and *To*
>
> Remember to use the base form
>
> - of verbs that follow *did* in question and negative forms.
> - of verbs that follow the word *to* (infinitive form).
>
> _invent_
> Did he ~~invented~~ a good product? Pemberton wanted to ~~promoted~~ _promote_ his
> soft drink.

PRACTICE 3   Correct twelve verb tense and spelling errors in the following essay.

like
EXAMPLE: Consumer groups didn't ~~liked~~ the marketing campaign.

1. In past centuries, breastfeeding be the most common method of feeding children. At the end of the nineteenth century, some parents fed their children cows' milk. In 1838, a German physician analyzed milk from cows and discover that larger proteins and reduced carbohydrates contributed to the increasing infant mortality rate.

2. The search for a healthy alternative to breast milk preoccupied scientists in the nineteenth century. Finally, in the 1870s, Nestlé Company produced the first infant formula. Consumers just had to mixed water with the formula.

3. In 1973, Nestlé Company wanted to sold the formula in Africa. The company putted advertisements for the product in magazines and on billboards. Nestlé also gave free samples to African women as soon as they had their babies. In hospitals, mothers seen their own breast milk dry up

after they gave formula to their babies. When the women returned home,

they did not had enough money to continue buying enough formula. They

added too much water to the formula, and the water was often

contaminated. Babies who drinked formula become malnourished. In

many villages, the level of infant malnutrition and mortality rised.

Past Participles

A **past participle** is a verb form, not a verb tense. The past tense and the past participle of regular verbs are the same. The past tense and the past participle of irregular verbs may be different.

	Base Form	**Past Tense**	**Past Participle**
Regular verb:	talk	talked	talked
Irregular verb:	begin	began	begun

GRAMMAR LINK
For a list of irregular past participles, see Appendix 2.

 **Using Past Participles**

You cannot use a past participle as the only verb in a sentence. You must use it with a helping verb such as *have, has, had, is, was* or *were*.

	helping verb	past participle	
The company	**was**	founded	in 1863.
The products	**have**	become	very popular.

PRACTICE 4   In the next selection, the past participles are underlined. Correct ten past participle errors, and write C above correct past participles.

met
EXAMPLE: The business ethics students have <u>meeted</u> many times to discuss the case.

1. Since 1973, Nestlé has <u>faced</u> a lot of criticism for its marketing techniques

   known
   in Africa. According to critics, Nestlé should have <u>knew</u> that the advertising

   made
   was dangerous and misleading. For instance, by 1980, Nestlé had <u>make</u>

hundreds of billboards showing a white woman feeding her child with a bottle. The African women were <u>teached</u> that good mothers don't breastfeed their children.   *taught*

2. The method of giving free samples to new mothers was also <u>blamed</u> for the problem. According to critics, a company spokesman has <u>admit</u> that the free samples contributed to the drying up of mothers' breast milk. In addition, the colour white was <u>weared</u> by company salespeople when they walked through hospital wards. New mothers could have <u>thinked</u> that the salespeople were nurses.

3. Nestlé's business practices have always <u>being</u> legal. In fact, Nestlé has successfully <u>used</u> the same techniques in many wealthy nations. Nonetheless, in 1977, a worldwide boycott of Nestlé products was <u>organize</u> by a group of concerned citizens.

4. Many business students have <u>studied</u> the Nestlé case. Technically, Nestlé did the same thing in Africa that it has <u>did</u> in the United States for many years. If a marketing technique has <u>work</u> successfully in wealthy countries, is a company <u>obliged</u> to revise its marketing techniques in less developed countries?

Present Perfect Tense
(*have* or *has* + past participle)

A past participle combines with *have* or *has* to form the **present perfect tense**.

> Kate **has been** a marketing manager for six years.
> Since 2001, the products **have sold** extremely well.

You can use this tense in two different circumstances.

- Use the present perfect to show that an action began in the past and continues to the present time. You will often use *since* and *for* with this tense.

PAST
(5 years ago, the
factory opened)

NOW

The factory **has flourished** for five years.

- Use the present perfect to show that one or more completed actions occurred at unspecified past times.

PAST

NOW

? ? ? ?

Mr. Jain **has visited** China four times.
(The time of the four visits is not specified.)

Choosing the Past or the Present Perfect

Look at the difference between the past and the present perfect tenses.

Simple past: In 2002, Kumar Jain **went** to Shanghai.
(This event occurred at a known past time.)

Present perfect: Since 2002, Jain **has owned** a factory in China.
(The action began in the past and continues to the present.)

He **has made** many business contacts.
(Making business contacts occurred at unknown past times.)

 **Use Time Markers**

When you try to identify which tense to use, look for time markers. **Time markers** are words such as *since, for,* or *ago* that indicate when an action occurred.

Simple past: Three weeks **ago**, Parker launched her new perfume.

Present perfect: **Since 2006**, the perfume has been successful.

PRACTICE 5   Write the past or present perfect form of the verb in parentheses.

EXAMPLE: For the last six years, my cousin Mike (be) ___*has been*___ a sales representative.

1. Since the beginning of the twentieth century, many companies (try)

   (have) ~~tried~~ to create memorable advertisements for their products.

   Before the 1920s, most ads (be) *have been was* on billboards and in

   magazines. Then, in 1922, companies (discover) *discovered* the

   potential of radio advertising. They (sponsor) *sponsored* radio

   shows. For example, the Lucky Strike Cigarette Company sponsored a

   music show. Since then, many companies (sponsor) *have sponsored*

   artistic and sporting events.

2. In the mid 1920s, radio stations (decide) *decided* to give short

   time slots to advertisers so that they could promote their products as an

   alternative to the sponsorship of shows. Ever since, commercials (be)

   have been an effective way for companies to market their products.

   Most people (see) *have seen* thousands of commercials.

 **Hint** **Past or Present Perfect?**

Use the past tense when referring to someone who is no longer living or to
something that no longer exists. Use the present perfect tense only when the
action has a relationship to someone or something that still exists.

designed
Leonardo da Vinci ~~has designed~~ many products.

△ **PRACTICE 6** Identify and correct ten verb errors.

began
EXAMPLE: The Coca-Cola Company ~~has begun~~ in 1886.

1. Since 1986, Coca-Cola ~~is~~ a familiar product throughout the world. *[has been]* For over a century, the company ~~made~~ some very successful marketing decisions. *[has made]* In 1931, Haddon Sunblom ~~has~~ illustrated a Coca-Cola advertisement with a Santa Claus figure that had a white beard, rosy cheeks, and a red suit. Since 1931, Sunblom's drawing ~~is~~ the popular image of the Christmas character. *[has been]*

2. Although the Coca-Cola company been very successful since its inception, *[has]* occasionally it has made blunders. In 1984, Coca-Cola managers ~~have~~ worried about the increasing popularity of Pepsi. That year, Coke developers modified the original formula and ~~have~~ made the product much sweeter.

3. On April 23, 1985, at a press conference, Coca-Cola's chairman ~~has~~ introduced the New Coke by calling it "smoother, rounder, and bolder." Unfortunately, when the product hit store shelves, consumers complained *[have]* about the taste.

4. On July 29, 1985, the company pulled the New Coke from the shelves and reintroduced the original product, calling it Coke Classic. Curiously, Coke Classic ~~is~~ very successful since its reintroduction. *[has been]* Since the "New Coke" fiasco, other companies learned from Coca-Cola's mistake. *[have]* If consumers love a product, do not modify it!

Past Perfect Tense
(*had* + past participle)

The **past perfect tense** indicates that one or more past actions happened before another past action. It is formed with *had* and the past participle.

PAST PERFECT   PAST   NOW

Mr. Lo **had spent** a lot on research by the time he **launched** the product.

Notice the differences between the simple past, the present perfect, and the past perfect tenses.

Simple past: Last night, Craig <u>worked</u> at Burger Town.
(The action occurred at a known past time.)

Present perfect: He <u>has owned</u> the restaurant for three years.
(The action began in the past and continues to the present.)

Past perfect: Craig <u>had had</u> two business failures before he bought Burger Town.
(All of the actions happened in the past, but the two business failures occurred before he bought the hamburger restaurant.)

PRACTICE 7   Underline the correct verb form in each sentence. You may choose the simple past or the past perfect tenses.

EXAMPLE: The Barbosas (were / <u>had been</u>) farmers for ten years when Alex Barbosa decided to sell organic beef.

1. Even though he (never studied / <u>had never studied</u>) marketing, Alex Barbosa decided to promote his organic beef.

2. He printed flyers, and then he (<u>distributed</u> / had distributed) them to private homes.

3. When most residents threw out the flyer, they (did not even read / <u>had not even read</u>) it.

4. The flyer contained a picture that Barbosa (took / <u>had taken</u>) the previous summer.

5. The image of the meat carcass (<u>was</u> / had been) unappealing.

6. After Barbosa received negative feedback about his flyer, he remembered that his daughter (warned / had warned) him about the image.

7. Also, the neighbourhood (had / had had) low-income families who could not afford the high price of the organic meat.

8. Finally, in 2005, Barbosa hired a business graduate who (learned / had learned) how to do effective marketing.

9. By December 2006, Barbosa's organic meat (found / had found) a niche in the marketplace.

Passive Voice
(be + past participle)

In sentences with the **passive voice**, the subject receives the action and does not perform the action. To form the passive voice, use the appropriate tense of the verb *be* plus the past participle. Look carefully at the following two sentences.

> **Active:** The boss **gave** documents to her assistant.
> (This is active, because the subject, *boss*, performed the action.)

> **Passive:** Several documents **were given** to the assistant.
> (This is passive because the subject, *documents*, was affected by the action and did not perform the action.)

To form the passive voice, use the appropriate past tense of the verb *be* plus the past participle.

 Avoid Overusing the Passive Voice

Generally, try to use the active voice instead of the passive voice. The active voice is more direct and friendly than the passive voice. For example, read two versions of the same message.

Passive voice: No more than two pills per day should be ingested. This medication should be taken with meals. It should not be continued if headache or nausea is experienced. Any side effects should be reported immediately.

Active voice: Do not ingest more than two pills per day. Take this medication with meals. Do not continue taking it if you experience headache or nausea. Immediately report any side effects to your doctor.

 PRACTICE 8   Complete the following sentences by changing the passive verb to the active form. Do not alter the verb tense.

EXAMPLE: Each department will be visited by the supervisor.

The supervisor will visit each department.

1. A funny commercial _was created_ by the advertising agency.

   The advertising agency created a funny commercial.

2. The ad _will be seen_ by many people.

   Many people will see the ad.

3. A well-known comedian _was hired_ by the company.

   The company hired a well-known comedian.

4. Many commercials _are created_ by Pedro Guzman.

   Pedro Guzman created many commercials.

5. Complaints about their commercials _are often ignored_ by companies.

   Companies often ignore the complaints about their commercials.

 When _Be_ Is Suggested, Not Written

In the passive voice, sometimes the verb _be_ is suggested but not written. The following sentence contains the passive voice.

   (who was)
   A man ⌃**named** Harley Cobb complained about the car company's decision.

 PRACTICE 9   Correct eight errors with past participles.

                                              found
EXAMPLE: A problem was <u>find</u> with the design.

1. When Apple Computers first developed the Macintosh, a pull-down

                                      included
   screen, or window, was <u>include</u> in the product. The computer also had a

                                                              dragged
   variety of icons for different tasks. For instance, useless files were <u>drag</u> to a

trashcan icon. A year later, Microsoft Corporation introduced its popular

~~named~~ ?

software program ~~name~~ Windows. The software, ~~create in~~ 1988, looked a

(created)

lot like Apple's software. Apple sued Microsoft for copyright infringement

and argued that Microsoft copied the "look and feel" of Apple software.

patented

2. There are strict rules about copyright. A unique product can be ~~patent.~~

However, people cannot copyright an idea. Therefore, Apple's decision to

protected

use specific icons could not be ~~protect.~~ Still, Apple argued that its original

copied

concept should not have been ~~copy.~~ The case, which lasted for four years,

won

was ~~win~~ by Microsoft.

Progressive Forms

(-ing verbs)

Most verbs have progressive tenses. The **progressive tense**, formed with *be* and the *-ing* form of the verb, indicates that an action is, was, or will be in progress. For example, the present progressive indicates that an action is happening right now or for a temporary period of time. The following timeline illustrates both the simple and progressive tenses.

Every day, he **sells** leather wallets.
(Simple present)

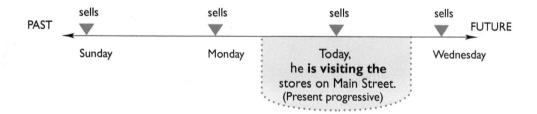

To form the progressive, use the appropriate tense of the verb *be* with the *-ing* verb.

Present progressive:	Right now, I **am** working.
Past progressive:	We **were** sleeping when you phoned us.
Future progressive:	Tomorrow, at noon, I **will be** driving.

Present perfect progressive: The receptionist **has been** <u>working</u> since 8 a.m.

Past perfect progressive: She **had been** <u>speeding</u> when the officer stopped her.

Common Errors in the Progressive Form

- Do not use the progressive form when an action happens regularly.

  complains
  Every day he ~~is complaining~~ about his job.

- In the progressive form, use the correct form of the verb *be*.

  is
  Right now, Ron ~~be~~ talking with his manager.

- In the progressive form, always include the complete helping verb.

  is   *have*
  Right now, the manager discussing the problem. They been talking

  for hours.

Non-Progressive Verbs

Some verbs do not take the progressive form because they indicate an ongoing state or a perception rather than a temporary action.

Examples of Non-Progressive Verbs

Perception Verbs	Preference Verbs	State Verbs	Possession Verbs
admire	desire	believe	have*
hear	doubt	know	own
smell*	hate	mean	possess
see	like	realize	
seem	love	recognize	
taste*	prefer	suppose	
feel*	want	think*	
	care	understand	

*Some verbs have more than one meaning and can be used in the progressive tense. Compare the following pairs of sentences.

Non-Progressive	**Progressive**
He **has** a franchise. (expresses ownership)	He **is having** a bad day.
I **think** it is unethical. (expresses an opinion)	I **am thinking** about you.

PRACTICE 10 Underline and correct one verb error in each sentence.

EXAMPLE: She $\overset{\textit{had}}{\underline{\text{been}}}$ working in the store for ten years when she was fired.

1. Ellen Peters was producing fragrances in her Toronto basement and give them away when her sister suggested that she try to market her perfume.

2. These days, Peters negotiating with a cosmetics company that hopes to market her product internationally.

3. She been looking for a product name for the last six months.

4. Last May, she be planning to call it Golden Mist when someone told her that "mist" means "manure" in German.

5. While her friends were brainstorm to help her, one of them suggested the name "Pete," which is a shortened form of Peters.

6. Unfortunately, pété is meaning "release of gassy air" in French.

7. Often, companies are having problems with bad translations.

8. For instance, the owner of the Japanese travel agency called Kinki Nippon Tours be complaining about foreign customers who wanted sex tours when a customer told him the English meaning of "kinky."

9. In another case, a Scandinavian vacuum cleaner company was making a mistake when it created the slogan "Nothing sucks like an Electrolux."

10. Ellen Peters wants her product to sell internationally, so right now she is work with a marketing firm to come up with a good name.

FINAL REVIEW

Underline and correct fifteen errors in verb form or tense.

published

EXAMPLE: The book *Business Ethics* was <u>publish</u> by Prentice Hall in 2006.

1. Since 1900, many products been defective. In his book *Business Ethics*, Richard T. De George discusses a famous product defect case. In the early 1970s, American automakers lose market share because smaller Japanese imports be flooding the market.

2. Lee Iacocca, the CEO of Ford Motor Company, was wanting the company to produce a lightweight, economical car. Engineers developed the Ford Pinto. Because Ford wanted the product on the market quickly, the car was not test for rear-end impact during the production period. Then, after the Pintos had been produce, they were put in collision tests, and they failed the tests. When the Pinto was hitted from behind, a bolt on the bumper sometimes punctured the fuel tank. It could cause an explosion.

3. Ford conducted a study and determined that a small baffle, worth about $8, could be place between the bumper and the gas tank. The company maked a cost-benefit analysis to compare the cost of adding the baffle against the estimated cost of lawsuits. The company decided that it was

less expensive to fight lawsuits than to insert the baffle. For the next seven years, the design of Ford Pintos did not changed. The company also neglected to offer the baffle to customers.

4. In 1976, Pintos had thirteen explosions from rear-end impacts, which was twice the number of explosions for cars of a comparable size. When it be too late, the Ford Motor Company realized that the lawsuits was much more expensive than the baffle installations.

5. The Pinto was recall in 1978. Since 1978, Ford has make much better business decisions. In the late 1970s, the bad publicity from the Pinto case damaged the company's reputation. Since then, Ford tried to improve its image.

The Writer's Room Topics for Writing

Write about one of the following topics. Proofread your writing and ensure that your verbs are formed correctly.

1. Write a short paragraph describing a useful product that you own. When and where did you get the product? How is it useful?

2. What are the effects of advertising on consumers? How does the deluge of commercials, spam, billboards, and other advertising affect the population?

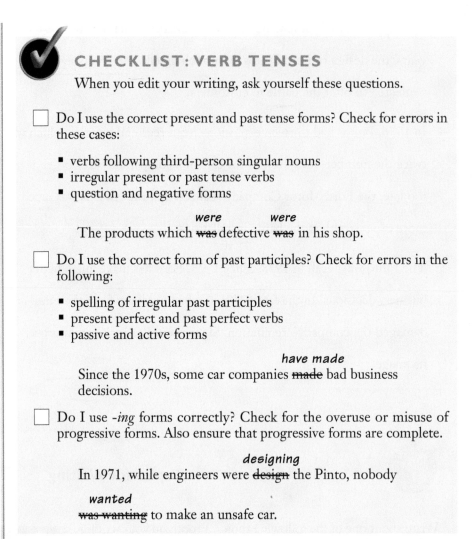

CHECKLIST: VERB TENSES

When you edit your writing, ask yourself these questions.

☐ Do I use the correct present and past tense forms? Check for errors in these cases:

- verbs following third-person singular nouns
- irregular present or past tense verbs
- question and negative forms

           were   *were*
The products which ~~was~~ defective ~~was~~ in his shop.

☐ Do I use the correct form of past participles? Check for errors in the following:

- spelling of irregular past participles
- present perfect and past perfect verbs
- passive and active forms

         have made
Since the 1970s, some car companies ~~made~~ bad business decisions.

☐ Do I use *-ing* forms correctly? Check for the overuse or misuse of progressive forms. Also ensure that progressive forms are complete.

        designing
In 1971, while engineers were ~~design~~ the Pinto, nobody

  wanted
~~was wanting~~ to make an unsafe car.

How Do I Get a Better Grade?

Problems with Verbs

CONTENTS

Section Theme **INTERNATIONAL TRADE**

In this chapter, you will read about unusual and dangerous jobs.

Grammar Snapshot

Looking at Other Verb Forms

The following excerpt is from a personal letter written by Garrett Brice, a Kelowna-based software designer who spent a summer working in a fire tower. Conditional sentences are underlined, and some modals are in bold. What types of errors do people make with the underlined or bold sentences?

> The strangest job I have ever had was working in a fire tower. Sometimes, I would spend weeks at a time completely alone. I had to alert the base camp if I saw smoke rising in the forest. I brought along a guitar because I wanted to learn how to play it. Probably I **should have tried** harder. Maybe if I had had a teacher with me, I would have learned some songs. As it was, I spent the time playing with my dog, reading, writing, and just watching the birds.

In this chapter, you will identify and write modals, conditionals, gerunds, and infinitives.

Verb Consistency

A verb tense gives your readers an idea about the time that an event occurred. A **tense shift** occurs when you shift from one tense to another for no logical reason. When you write essays, ensure that your tenses are consistent.

Tense shift: Jean Roberts travelled to Santiago, Chile, where she interviews a salon owner.

Correct: Jean Roberts travelled to Santiago, Chile, where she **interviewed** a salon owner.

 **Would and Could**

When you tell a story about a past event, use *would* instead of *will* and *could* instead of *can*.

                      couldn't

In 2001, Simon Brault wanted to be an actor. At that time, he <u>can't</u> find a good

               would

acting job. To earn extra cash, he <u>will</u> deliver telegrams wearing a costume.

PRACTICE I   Underline and correct ten tense shifts in the following paragraphs.

                       decided

EXAMPLE: In the 1990s, Gretta Zahn made a decision. She <u>decides</u> to work as a parts model.

1. Some people have very unusual jobs. In 1992, a modelling agent noticed seventeen-year-old Gretta Zahn's hands. He signed the young girl to a contract, and he said that he will make her famous as a "hand model." During Zahn's modelling years, her jobs were diverse. She soaked her fingers in dishwashing liquid, wear diamond rings, and demonstrated nail polish.

2. In the 1990s, Zahn's modelling career was lucrative. At the height of her career, she can earn up to $1500 a day. She will start her day at 5 a.m.,

and sometimes she will have to work for fourteen hours. To get a perfect shot, some photographers will take hundreds of pictures of her.

3. Zahn's agent told her that she will need to take special care of her hands. From 1992 to 2000, she cannot wear jewellery because it would leave tan lines. Also, during those years, she will not do the dishes, and she refused to pump her own gas.

4. In 2000, Zahn gave up modelling. Today, she enjoys gardening, and she likes to wear rings and bracelets. Her hands are no longer flawless, but she did not mind. "I have a life," she says. "I no longer worry about getting a cut or scrape."

Avoiding Double Negatives

A double negative occurs when a negative word such as *no* (*nothing, nobody, nowhere*) is combined with a negative adverb (*not, never, rarely, seldom,* and so on). The result is a sentence that has a double negative. Such sentences can be confusing because the negative words cancel each other.

Mr. Lee <u>doesn't</u> want <u>no</u> problems.
(According to this sentence, Mr. Lee wants problems.)

He <u>didn't</u> know <u>nothing</u> about it.
(According to this sentence, he knew something about it.)

How to Correct Double Negatives

There are two ways to correct double negatives.

- Completely remove *one* of the negative forms. Remember that you may need to adjust the verb to make it agree with the subject.

Correct:	Mr. Lee **doesn't** want ~~no~~ problems.
	Mr. Lee ~~doesn't~~ wants **no** problems.

- Change "no" to *any* (*anybody, anything, anywhere*).

Correct:	Mr. Lee doesn't want ~~no~~ problems. _(any)_

PRACTICE 2   Correct five errors with double negatives. You can correct each error in more than one way.

EXAMPLE: They don't have ~~no~~ openings. _(any)_   OR   They ~~don't have~~ no openings. _(have)_

Have you ever had a strange job? Jordan Woo has had his share of unusual occupations. In 2005, while he was living in Saskatoon, he couldn't find no summer job. Then he saw an ad for a sign holder. For three months, he stood beside a work crew and held up signs to direct traffic. Occasionally, for an hour or two, he didn't have nothing to do. The crew was working on a rural road, and sometimes there wasn't no traffic. He was bored, but he kept his job because he didn't have no better offers. Eventually, when he couldn't take it no more, he quit.

Non-Standard Forms—*Gonna, Gotta, Wanna*

Some people commonly say *I'm gonna, I gotta,* or *I wanna.* These are non-standard forms, so avoid using them in written communication.

- Write "going to" instead of *gonna.*

  (going to)
  The boss is ~~gonna~~ hire three new cashiers.

- Write "have to" instead of *gotta* or *got to.*

  (have to)
  We ~~gotta~~ stay open until midnight.

- Write "want to" instead of *wanna.*

  (want to)
  We ~~wanna~~ keep our jobs.

PRACTICE 3   Underline and correct eight non-standard verbs.

have to find
EXAMPLE: You and I <u>gotta find</u> a better job.

1. If you wanna find work, there are many job-hunting sites on the internet.
    One of the oldest and most established sites is Monster.com. The site was
    created in 1994. Jeff Taylor owned a job-recruitment agency, and he
    thought that an internet site could help his business. He decided that his
    new site was gonna match job seekers with employers. That year, he
    created Monster Board.

2. In 1995, Taylor sold his business because he didn't wanna pass up a great
    business offer. The new owners said that they were gonna change the name
    of the website. They didn't think that consumers would wanna associate
    "monster" and work. However, Taylor convinced them to keep the name.

3. In 1999, Monster Board joined with Online Career Center and became
    Monster.com. When you go on the site, you gotta find your region.
    Monster posts jobs in twenty-three countries. Then you gotta choose the
    job category that interests you. If you go on the site, you are probably
    gonna find interesting jobs in your city or area.

Problems in Conditional Forms

In **conditional sentences**, there is a condition and a result. There are three types
of conditional sentences, and each type has two parts, or clauses. The main clause
depends on the condition set in the *if* clause.

First Form: Possible Present or Future

The condition is true or very possible. Use the present tense in the *if* clause.

condition (*if* clause)   result
If you **ask** her, she **will hire** you.

Second Form: Unlikely Present

The condition is not likely, and probably will not happen.

condition (*if* clause)   result
If I **had** more money, I **would start** my own business.

Note: In formal writing, when the condition contains the verb *be*, always use "were" in the *if* clause.

If Katrina **were** younger, she **would change** careers.

Third Form: Impossible Past

The condition cannot happen because the event is over. Use the past perfect tense in the *if* clause.

condition (*if* clause)   result
If the business **had closed** in 2002, many people **would have lost** their jobs.

> *Hint*   **Be Careful with the Past Conditional**
>
> In "impossible past" sentences, the writer expresses regret about a past event or expresses the wish that a past event had worked out differently. In the "if" part of the sentence, remember to use the past perfect tense.
>
> if + past perfect tense ⟶ would have (past participle)
>
>   *had stayed*
> If the factory ~~would have stayed~~ open, many workers would have kept their jobs.

PRACTICE 4   Write the correct conditional forms of the verbs in parentheses.

EXAMPLE: If the miners (go, not) _had not gone_ on strike, their working
conditions would have remained unsafe.

1. If you do research on the internet, you (learn) _____

   that truck driving is one of the most dangerous professions. William Roach is a long-distance trucker, and he took a truck-driving course in 1992. If he

(fail) _____ the course, he would never have found his

passion.

2. Roach loves driving. "On a highway, with nothing but the road in front

of me, I feel alive and free. Even if someone offered me a better job, I

(remain) _____ a truck driver." Roach claims that the

only drawback is the time he spends away from his family. He says, "If I

(be) _____ able to, I would bring my wife and son

with me."

3. In 2003, Roach was late for a delivery. To save time, he took an unfamiliar

route. While driving, Roach fell asleep, and his truck rolled into a ditch. If

he (have) _____ a nap earlier that day, perhaps he

(not, have) _____ the accident. If he (stay)

_____ on the main highway, perhaps the accident

(involve) _____ more vehicles. According to medical

professionals, if Roach had been awake during the accident, his injuries

(be) _____ more severe. Because he was asleep, his

body was relaxed and his injuries were minor.

4. Roach claims that even if he (know) _____ about the

dangers in truck driving, he would still have chosen to be a long-distance

driver. If you could, (you, become) _____ a long-

distance driver?

Non-Standard Forms—*Would of, Could of, Should of*

Some people commonly say *would of, could of,* or *should of.* They may also say *woulda, coulda,* or *shoulda.* These are non-standard forms and you should avoid using them in written communication. When you use the past forms of *should, would,* and *could,* always include *have* with the past participle.

Dominique Brown is a nurse, but she really loves real estate. She
~~should of~~ become a real-estate agent. She ~~woulda~~ been very successful.
should have *would have*

PRACTICE 5   Underline and correct nine errors in conditional forms or in the past forms of *could* and *should.*

EXAMPLE: The workers should of stayed home.
have

1. One of the world's most successful companies began in a small village in Sweden. In 1943, seventeen-year-old Ingvar Kamprad did well in his studies, and his father gave him a gift of money. Kamprad coulda bought anything he wanted. His mother thought that he shoulda continued his studies. The young man had other ideas. He decided to create a company called IKEA, and he sold small items through a mail-order catalogue.

2. In 1947, Kamprad decided to add furniture to his catalogue. One day, an employee from IKEA removed the legs from a table so that it would fit into his car trunk. Soon, the company created flat packaging designs. If the employee woulda owned a truck, perhaps IKEA would of continued to sell completely assembled furniture. If that had been the case, the company would not of been so successful.

3. Kamprad's extreme youth helped him in his quest to take chances. Maybe

   if he woulda been older, he woulda been more conservative. If IKEA

   would not have changed, perhaps it would of remained a small company.

Recognizing Gerunds and Infinitives

Sometimes a main verb is followed by another verb. The second verb can be a gerund or an infinitive. A **gerund** is a verb with an *-ing* ending. An **infinitive** consists of *to* and the base form of the verb.

verb + gerund

Edward <u>finished</u> **installing** the carpet.

verb + infinitive

He <u>wants</u> **to take** weekends off.

Some verbs in English are always followed by a gerund. Do not confuse gerunds with progressive verb forms.

Progressive verb: Julie is working now.
(Julie is in the process of doing something.)

Gerund: Julie <u>finished</u> **working**.
(*Working* is a gerund that follows *finish*.)

Some Common Verbs Followed by Gerunds

acknowledge	deny	keep	recall
adore	detest	loathe	recollect
appreciate	discuss	mention	recommend
avoid	dislike	mind	regret
can't help	enjoy	miss	resent
complete	finish	postpone	resist
consider	involve	practise	risk
delay	justify	quit	tolerate

Some Common Verbs Followed by Infinitives

afford	decide	manage	refuse
agree	demand	mean	seem
appear	deserve	need	swear
arrange	expect	offer	threaten
ask	fail	plan	volunteer
claim	hesitate	prepare	want
compete	hope	pretend	wish
consent	learn	promise	would like

Some Common Verbs Followed by Gerunds or Infinitives

Some common verbs can be followed by gerunds or infinitives. Both forms have the same meaning.

> begin   continue   like   start

> Elaine <u>likes</u> **to read**. Elaine <u>likes</u> **reading**.
> (Both sentences have the same meaning.)

Stop, Remember, and Used to

Some verbs can be followed by either a gerund or an infinitive, but there is a difference in meaning depending on the form you use.

Term	Form	Example	Meaning
Stop	+ infinitive	He often stops <u>to buy</u> gas every Sunday.	To stop an activity (driving) to do something else.
	+ gerund	I stopped <u>smoking</u> five years ago.	To permanently stop doing something.
Remember	+ infinitive	Please remember <u>to lock</u> the door.	To remember to perform a task.
	+ gerund	I remember <u>meeting</u> him in 2004.	To have a memory about a past event.
Used to	+ infinitive	Jane used <u>to smoke</u>.	To express a past habit.
	+ gerund	Jane is used to <u>living</u> alone.	To be accustomed to something.

Prepositions Plus Gerunds

Many sentences have the structure *verb + preposition + object*. If the object is another verb, the second verb is a gerund.

> verb + preposition + gerund
> I <u>dream</u> **about** <u>travelling</u> to Greece.

Some Common Words Followed by Prepositions plus Gerunds

accuse of	be enthusiastic about	be good at	prohibit from
apologize for	feel like	insist on	succeed in
discourage him from*	be fond of	be interested in	think about
dream of	forbid him from*	look forward to	be tired of
be excited about	forgive me for*	prevent him from*	warn him about*

*Certain verbs can have a noun or pronoun before the preposition.

PRACTICE 6   Complete the sentence with the appropriate verb. Underline either the gerund or the infinitive form.

1. Do you remember (using / to use) a cellphone camera for the first time? When they first came out, I looked forward (owning / to own / to owning) one. When I first got my phone, I remember (to take / taking) pictures of myself when I accidentally hit the camera button.

2. A few weeks later, I insisted (to buy / buying / on buying) my grandfather a cellphone. I told him that he would need (using / to use) one during emergencies. My grandfather (is not used to speaking / didn't used to speak) on such tiny phones. Each time I visit him, I plan (to show / showing) him how to use it. However, my grandfather is not a technophobe. These days, he (used to work / is used to working) on a computer. He knows how to send emails, although he wishes that salespeople would stop (to send / sending) him spam. However, he just can't stand (to use / using / on using) a cellphone.

3. My grandfather is good (to think / thinking / at thinking) up solutions for problems. He wrote a letter to the cellphone manufacturer, and he

explained that some older people dislike (to try / trying / of trying) to read the tiny numbers, and they don't want (having / to have) all of the extra features such as internet links. He succeeded (to get / getting / in getting) a response. In fact, the cellphone company offered my grandfather a job as an advisor for the seniors' market. Now, some cellphone companies are excited (to promote / promoting / about promoting) a new larger-model cellphone with large numbers and no extra features.

FINAL REVIEW

Underline and correct fifteen errors with verbs.

EXAMPLE: Many jobs are ~~gonna~~ become obsolete.
going to

1. Certain jobs disappear because of advances in technology or changing habits. For instance, if you would have been born one hundred years ago, you would of worn a hat every time you went outside. However, since the 1950s, hats have not been standard attire and, as a result, hatmaking is no longer a popular profession.

2. In 1949, Joseph Wade didn't know nothing about hats, yet he decided to open a hatmaking business in Montreal. Wade created men's felt hats and sold them in his hat store. However, if he would have known what was coming, he woulda chosen another profession. By 1952, when the ducktail haircuts became popular, young men stopped wearing hats because

they did not wanna ruin their hair styles. Wade's business eventually closed. He had no idea that hatmaking was gonna become obsolete.

3. In 1964, Theo Malizia enjoyed to deliver milk in his white van. The milk was bottled in glass containers, and it was deposited on the front steps of customers. One day, he hit a pothole, a crate tipped over, and twelve bottles broke. If the bottles would have been made with a less breakable material, they would have been easier to transport. When supermarkets began carrying lighter milk containers, Malizia had to find another job. Home milk delivery wasn't popular no more.

4. In the 1990s, many people thought that any computer-related job would last for life. Carmen Morales took a nine-month course in website building in 1999. She thought that she was gonna earn a good living. Perhaps she shoulda seen what was coming. New software has become so user-friendly that many businesses simply create their own websites. Perhaps if Morales would have taken a programming course, she would have found a job more easily. Since September, Morales has been taking some business courses because she wants to be an accountant. "People always gotta do their taxes, but very few people wanna do the math," she says. Morales hopes her accounting job will never become obsolete.

The Writer's Room **Topics for Writing**

Write about one of the following topics. Ensure that your verbs are correctly formed.

1. If you had lived one hundred years ago, what job would you have done? Describe the job using details that appeal to the senses.

2. Define one of the following terms or expressions: *mindless work, balancing act, glass ceiling, success, a go-getter,* or *a "suit."*

READING LINK

International Trade

To find out more about the world of international trade, see the following essays.

"Canada Misses Its Chance to Join Major Pacific Free Trade Deal," by John Ibbitson (page 506)

"The Rich Resonance of Small Talk," by Roxanne Roberts (Page 509)

"Google's China Web," by Frida Ghitis (Page 512)

 CHECKLIST: OTHER VERB FORMS

When you edit your writing, ask yourself these questions.

☐ Are my verb tenses consistent? Check for errors with the following:

- shifts from past to present or present to past *can/could* and *will/would*

  would
  When he drove trucks, he ~~will~~ drive when he was tired.

☐ Do I use the correct conditional forms? Check for errors in the following:

- possible future forms (*If I meet . . . , I will go . . .*)
- unlikely present forms (*If I met . . . , I would go . . .*)
- impossible past forms (*If I had met . . . , I would have gone . . .*)

  had
  If he ~~would have~~ sold shoes, he would have been successful.

☐ Do I use standard verbs? Do not write *gonna, wanna, gotta, shoulda,* etc.

  want to
  If you ~~wanna~~ know the truth about the Free Trade

  have to
  Agreement, you ~~gotta~~ do some research.

How Do I Get a Better Grade?

mycanadiancomplab

Go to www.mycanadiancomplab.ca for additional help with your grammar, writing, and research skills. You will have access to a variety of exercises, instruction, and video that will help you improve your basic skills and help you get a better grade.

Nouns, Determiners, and Prepositions

CONTENTS
- Count and Non-count Nouns
- Determiners
- Prepositions

Section Theme **FORCES OF NATURE**

In this chapter, you will read about some unusual weather events.

Grammar Snapshot

Looking at Nouns, Determiners, and Prepositions

In her article "Weird Weather: Sprites, Frogs, and Maggots," Pamela D. Jacobson describes unusual weather phenomena. The nouns, determiners, and prepositions are underlined.

Sprites are barely visible to the naked eye. They sometimes look bluish closest to the clouds, but extend red, wispy flashes upward. Some occur as high as sixty miles above the storm. On images from weather satellites and space shuttles, sprites appear as marvellously complex shapes.

In this chapter, you will identify and write nouns, determiners, and prepositions.

Count and Non-count Nouns

In English, nouns are grouped into two types: count nouns and non-count nouns.

- **Count nouns** refer to people or things that you can count such as *tree, house,* or *dog.* Count nouns have both a singular and plural form.

  She wrote three <u>articles</u> about global warming.

- **Non-count nouns** refer to people or things that you cannot count because you cannot divide them, such as *sugar* and *imagination.* Non-count nouns have only the singular form.

  The <u>weather</u> is going to turn cold.

Here are some examples of common non-count nouns.

Common Non-count Nouns

Categories of Objects		Food	Nature	Substances	
clothing	machinery	bread	air	chalk	paint
equipment	mail	fish	electricity	charcoal	paper
furniture	money	honey	energy	coal	
homework	music	meat	environment	fur	
jewellery	postage	milk	radiation	hair	
luggage	software	rice	water	ink	

Abstract Nouns			
advice	effort	information	progress
attention	evidence	knowledge	proof
behaviour	health	luck	research
education	help	peace	violence

Determiners

Determiners are words that help to determine or figure out whether a noun is specific or general. Examples of determiners are articles (*a*), demonstratives (*this*), indefinite pronouns (*many*), numbers (*three*), possessive nouns (*Maria's*), and possessive adjectives (*my*).

Gabriel Daniel Fahrenheit manufactured <u>the</u> first mercury thermometer in 1714. <u>Fahrenheit's</u> product was <u>his</u> claim to fame.

Commonly Confused Determiners

Some determiners can be confusing because you can only use them in specific circumstances. Review this list of some commonly confused determiners.

a, an, the

A and *an* are general determiners and *the* is a specific determiner.

> I need to buy a new winter coat. The winter coats in that store are on sale.

- Use *a* and *an* before singular count nouns but not before plural or non-count nouns. Use *a* before nouns that begin with a consonant (*a storm*) and use *an* before nouns that begin with a vowel (*an institute*).

- Use *the* before nouns that refer to a specific person, place, or thing. Do not use *the* before languages (*He speaks Italian*), sports (*They watch tennis*), or most city and country names (*Two of the coldest capital cities in the world are Ottawa and Moscow*). Two examples of exceptions are *the United States* and *the Netherlands*.

many, few, much, little

- Use *many* and *few* with count nouns.

> Many **satellites** collect weather information, but few **forecasts** are completely accurate.

- Use *much* and *little* with non-count nouns.

> Much **attention** is focused on solar power, but North Americans use very little solar **energy**.

this, that, these, and those

This and *these* refer to things that are physically close to the speaker or in the present time. Use *this* before singular nouns and *these* before plural nouns. *That* and *those* refer to things that are physically distant from the speaker or in the past time. Use *that* before singular nouns and *those* before plural nouns.

> This **book** on my desk and those **books** on that **shelf** are about India. Did you know that in 1861, India had some very wet weather? In that **year**, Cherrapunji received 9300 millimetres of rain. In those **days**, cities had trouble coping with so much rain, but these **days**, they are better equipped.

> *Hint* **Latin Nouns**
>
> Some nouns borrowed from Latin keep the plural form of the original language.
>
> | Singular | Plural | Singular | Plural |
> |----------|--------|----------|--------|
> | alumnus | alumni | medium | media |
> | datum | data | phenomenon | phenomena |

PRACTICE I   Underline the determiner in parentheses that best agrees with the noun before it. If the noun does not require a determiner, underline *X*.

EXAMPLE: (The/A/X) driest place on earth is (the/a/X) Arica, Chile.

1. (Much/Many) people all over (the/a/X) world talk constantly about (the/a/X) weather. (A/Few/Little) phenomena are as exciting as extreme weather. For example, there are about 80 (the/X) tornadoes each year in (the/X) Canada. (A/The) tornado lasts about fifteen minutes. In 1912, the worst tornado in Canadian history hit (a/the/X) Regina. In (this/that) year, twenty-eight people died and (many/much) others were injured.

2. (Many/Much) people are fascinated with thunderstorms. (A / An/X) interesting fact about (a/the/X) CN Tower is that it is struck by lightning around seventy times per year. (The/X) golfers should be very careful during thunderstorms. They should spend as (few/little) time as possible outdoors if there is lightning. (A/The) lightning bolt can produce a few hundred megawatts of electrical power.

3. (The/X) United States launched its first weather satellite in 1961. In (these/
    those) early days, satellite pictures amazed weather researchers. Today
    (much/many) research about weather patterns is being done by meteorolo-
    gists. (These/Those) days, satellites gather (a/the/X) information about
    global weather systems that is invaluable for everybody's daily lives.

Prepositions

Prepositions are words that show concepts such as time, place, direction, and
manner. They show connections or relationships between ideas.

> <u>In</u> 1998, southern Quebec experienced nearly a week of freezing rain.
> Freezing rain fell <u>for</u> a few days.

Prepositions of Time and Place

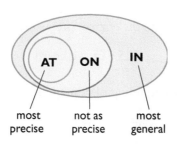

	Prepositions of Time	Prepositions of Place
in	• in a year or month (in February)	• in a city, country, or continent (in Halifax)
on	• on a day of the week (on Monday) • on a specific date (on June 16) • on a specific holiday (on Thanksgiving)	• on a specific street (on Lacombe Ave.) • on technological devices (on TV, on the radio, on the phone, on the cellphone, on the computer)
at	• at a specific time of day (at 9:15) • at night • at breakfast, lunch, dinner	• at a specific address (at 18 Oriole Crescent) • at a specific building (at the hospital)
from . . . to	• from one time to another (from 10 a.m. to 1 p.m.)	• from one place to another (from Regina to Saskatoon)
for	• for a period of time (for five hours)	• for a distance (for two kilometres)

Commonly Confused Prepositions

to versus at

Use *to* after verbs that indicate movement from one place to another. Use *at* after verbs that indicate being or remaining in one place (and not moving from one place to another). *Exception:* Do not put *to* directly before *home*.

> Each day, Suraya **runs** <u>to</u> the gym, and then she goes home and **sits** <u>at</u> the computer.

for, during, and since

Use *during* to explain when something happens, *for* to explain how long it takes to happen, and *since* to indicate the start of an activity.

> <u>During</u> the summer, the restaurant closed <u>for</u> one week because of the heat.
>
> <u>Since</u> 2006, I have been taking skiing lessons <u>during</u> the winter.

PRACTICE 2   Write the correct preposition in the blanks.

EXAMPLE: _____At_____ 5:15 a.m. we heard the news.

1. _____ the beginning of human history, people have been trying

   to predict the weather. Many writers have created almanacs to record

   weather-related events.

2. _____ 1792, _____ George Washington's second

   term as president, *The Old Farmer's Almanac* was published. Robert B.

   Thomas was its first editor. _____ 8:00 a.m. _____

   6:00 p.m., Thomas would work on his magazine. Sitting _____

   his desk, he developed a successful formula to forecast weather. He had over an 80 percent accuracy rate. Thomas died _____ 1846, but

people can go _____ Dublin, New Hampshire, and view his

secret formula _____ the *Almanac*'s office.

3. *The Farmer's Almanac* has been published each year _____ it was

first established. _____ World War II, the *Almanac* became

notoriously associated with a German spy, whom the FBI captured

_____ Long Island. The spy had the *Almanac* _____

his pocket. The U.S. government wanted to discontinue publishing the

Almanac because it contained information that was useful _____

the Germans. After discussing the issue _____ the telephone,

U.S. officials eventually allowed the *Almanac* to be published again.

Common Prepositional Expressions

Many common expressions contain prepositions. These types of expressions usually convey a particular meaning. The meaning of a verb will change if it is used with a specific preposition. Examine the difference in meaning of the following expressions.

to turn on—to start a machine or switch on the lights
to turn off—to stop a machine or switch off the lights
to turn down—to decline something
to turn over—to rotate
to turn up—to arrive

The next list contains some of the most common prepositional expressions.

accuse (somebody) of	dream of	long for	satisfied with
acquainted with	escape from	look forward to	scared of
afraid of	excited about	participate in	search for
agree with	familiar with	patient with	similar to
apologize for	fond of	pay attention to	specialize in
apply for	forget about	pay for	stop (something) from
approve of	forgive (someone) for	prevent (someone) from	succeed in
associate with	friendly with	protect (someone) from	take advantage of
aware of	grateful for	proud of	take care of
believe in	happy about	provide (someone) with	thank (someone) for
capable of	hear about	qualify for	think about / of
comply with	hope for	realistic about	tired of
confronted with	hopeful about	rely on	willing to
consist of	innocent of	rescue from	wish for
count on	insist on	responsible for	worry about
deal with	insulted by		
depend on	interested in		

PRACTICE 3   Write the correct prepositions in the next paragraphs. Use the preceding list of prepositional expressions to help you.

EXAMPLE: Many people were upset ___*about*___ the damage from the storm.

1. In southern Asia, many people look forward _____ the monsoon.

    The word monsoon comes from Arabic *mausin*, which means "the season

    of the winds." During the wet season from June to September, India

    receives an average of 300 millimetres of rain each month. During the

    monsoon, people get tired _____ dealing with the rain.

2. Throughout the year, South Asians depend _____ the monsoon.

    Farmers hope _____ adequate rainfall for their crops. Children love the monsoon because it provides them _____ the opportunity to

play in the rain and the puddles. Although South Asians are often grateful

_____ a good rainy season, they are also realistic _____ nature's

forces and think _____ possible flooding, transportation delays, and

malaria.

FINAL REVIEW

Correct fifteen errors in singular nouns, plural nouns, determiners, and prepositions.

Many   _electricity_
EXAMPLE: ~~Much~~ houses lost ~~electricities~~ during the ice storm.

1. One of the most interesting weather phenomenon is the ice storm.

   Freezing rain coats all surfaces with a heavy layer of ice. On

   January 1998, Quebec and parts of the New England

   experienced the worst ice storm of the century. About 100

   millimetres of freezing rain fell in the region since a few

   days. There were much consequences because of the ice.

2. Over 900 000 households had no electricity for about a week.

   About 100 000 people had to leave their homes and go at

   refuge centres. Many people worried of the damage to their

   homes. Some people stayed at the home, but it was difficult

   without electricity. Others relied of their neighbours. Also, the authorities

   were concerned about some people getting hypothermia.

3. The environments looked like a disaster scene from a science fiction movie. Farmers lost pigs, sheep, and other livestock. Some business lost income at that period because they had no electricity to remain open. Citizens received few information from the authorities.

4. Although this time has passed, many friends and neighbours still talk about the ice storm. Those days, it is just a distant memory.

CHAPTER 24

 The Writer's Room **Topics for Writing**

Write about one of the following topics. Proofread your text to ensure that there are no errors in singular or plural forms, determiners, and prepositions.

1. What should people do to prepare for severe weather? List some steps.
2. What are some types of severe weather phenomena? Classify severe weather into three different types.

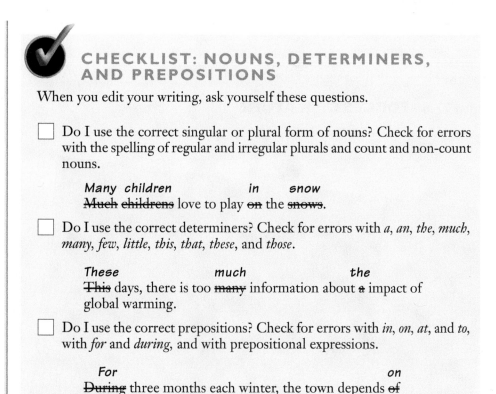

✔ **CHECKLIST: NOUNS, DETERMINERS, AND PREPOSITIONS**

When you edit your writing, ask yourself these questions.

☐ Do I use the correct singular or plural form of nouns? Check for errors with the spelling of regular and irregular plurals and count and non-count nouns.

> *Many children   in   snow*
> ~~Much~~ ~~childrens~~ love to play ~~on~~ the ~~snows~~.

☐ Do I use the correct determiners? Check for errors with *a, an, the, much, many, few, little, this, that, these,* and *those.*

> *These   much   the*
> ~~This~~ days, there is too ~~many~~ information about ~~a~~ impact of global warming.

☐ Do I use the correct prepositions? Check for errors with *in, on, at,* and *to,* with *for* and *during,* and with prepositional expressions.

> *For   on*
> ~~During~~ three months each winter, the town depends ~~of~~
>
> *at*
> tourists who stay ~~to~~ the ski resorts.

CHAPTER 24

How Do I Get a Better Grade?

mycanadiancomplab

Go to www.mycanadiancomplab.ca for additional help with your grammar, writing, and research skills. You will have access to a variety of exercises, instruction, and video that will help you improve your basic skills and help you get a better grade.

25

CHAPTER

Adjectives and Adverbs

CONTENTS

- Adjectives
- Adverbs
- Comparative and Superlative Forms

Section Theme **FORCES OF NATURE**

In this chapter, you will read about environmental issues and alternative energy sources.

Grammar Snapsh•t

Looking at Adjectives and Adverbs

In his article "Iceland's Ring Road: The Ultimate Road Trip," Mark Sundeen describes aspects of that country's landscape. The adjectives and adverbs are underlined.

Occasionally an iceberg floated beneath the highway bridge, was carried to sea, then was dashed on the beach by the windswept waves. We walked along the grey strand where the blocks of glacier rocked gently in the tide, and we gathered in our hands the cocktail-size ice cubes that had washed up on shore and flung them back to the sea.

In this chapter, you will identify and write adjectives and adverbs.

Adjectives

Adjectives describe nouns (people, places, or things) and pronouns (words that replace nouns). They add information explaining how many, what kind, or which one. They also help you appeal to the senses by describing how things look, smell, feel, taste, and sound.

> The **young** <u>students</u> convinced their **imposing** <u>principal</u> to start an **important** <u>project</u> on air quality in the schools.

 **Placement of Adjectives**

You can place adjectives either before a noun or after a linking verb such as *be, look, appear, smell,* or *become.*

Before the noun:	The **nervous** <u>environmentalist</u> gave a suitable speech.
After the linking verb:	The biologist <u>was</u> **disappointed**, and he <u>was</u> **angry**.

Problems with Adjectives

You can recognize many adjectives by their endings. Be particularly careful when you use the following adjective forms.

Adjectives Ending in *-ful* or *-less*

Some adjectives end in *-ful* or *-less*. Remember that *ful* ends in one *l* and *less* ends in double *s*.

> The Blue Oceans Club, a **peaceful** environmental organization, has promoted many **useful** projects. Protecting the environment is an **endless** activity.

Adjectives Ending in *-ed* and *-ing*

Some adjectives look like verbs because they end in *-ing* or *-ed*. When the adjective ends in *-ed*, it describes the person's or animal's expression or feeling. When the adjective ends in *-ing*, it describes the quality of the person or thing.

> The **frustrated** but **prepared** lobbyist confronted the politician, and his **challenging** and **convincing** arguments got her attention.

Keep Adjectives in the Singular Form

Always make an adjective singular, even if the noun following the adjective is plural.

>   *year*
> Lucia was a forty-five-~~years~~-old woman when she sold her five-thousand-
> *dollar*
> ~~dollars~~ car and rode a bicycle to work.

Adverbs

Adverbs add information to adjectives, verbs, or other adverbs. They give more specific information about how, when, where, and to what extent an action or event occurred. Some adverbs look exactly like adjectives, such as *early*, *late*, *soon*, *often*, and *hard*. However, most adverbs end in *-ly*.

      verb   adverb

Biologists <u>studied</u> the statistics on climate change **carefully**.

        adverb adverb

They released the results **quite** <u>quickly</u>.

   adverb adjective

The **very** <u>eloquent</u> speaker was Dr. Ying.

Forms of Adverbs

Adverbs often end in *-ly*. In fact, you can change many adjectives into adverbs by adding *-ly* endings.

If you add *-ly* to a word that ends in *l*, then your new word will have a double *l*.

               professional + ly

The journalist covered the story **professionally**.

If you add *-ly* to a word that ends in *e*, keep the *e*. Exceptions to this rule are true ➔ *truly* and *due* ➔ *duly*.

               close + ly

Scientists monitor the polar ice caps **closely**.

CHAPTER 25

 **Placement of Frequency Adverbs**

Frequency adverbs are words that indicate how often someone performs an action or when an event occurs. Common frequency adverbs are *always, ever, never, often, sometimes,* and *usually.* They can appear at the beginning of sentences, or they can appear in the following locations.

■ Place frequency adverbs before regular present and past tense verbs.

Politicians **sometimes** <u>forget</u> the importance of the environment.

■ Place frequency adverbs after all forms of the verb *be.*

She <u>is</u> **often** an advisor for environmental agencies.

■ Place frequency adverbs after helping verbs.

They <u>have</u> **never** donated to an environmental group.

PRACTICE I Correct eight errors with adjectives or adverbs.

quietly
EXAMPLE: I entered the room ~~quiet~~ because the lecture had started.

1. Many people frequent debate the issue of climate change. There are two clearly sources that cause global warming: natural and human. People forget often that natural forces have contributed to climate change throughout the history of the world. Scientists know that ice ages have developed and diminished rapid.

2. Global temperature increases naturaly for several reasons. For instance, explosions in the sun generate heat that causes the earth's temperature to rise abrupt. Another natural source for global warming is volcanic eruptions. A strong eruption gives off smoke and gases. These elements may act sometimes as a shield preventing sunlight from entering the

atmosphere. A minor change in the earth's orbit may affect also the earth's temperature. So when debating climate change, also keep in mind the natural causes of temperature fluctuations.

Problems with Adverbs

Many times, people use an adjective instead of an adverb after a verb. Ensure that you always modify your verbs using an adverb.

really quickly   *slowly*
The snowstorm developed ~~real quick~~. We had to drive very ~~slow~~.

CHAPTER 25

PRACTICE 2   Underline and correct ten errors with adjective and adverb forms.

really
EXAMPLE: Climate change is a <u>realy</u> controversial issue.

1. Human activity contributes great to global warming. With modernization, lifestyles are changing real quick. More people are driving cars, and more

   industries are consuming largely amounts of energy. When humans burn fossil fuels such as gasoline, coal, and oil, gases in the atmosphere

   that trap heat rise steady. This condition creates a dangerously greenhouse effect, which means that heat cannot escape the earth's atmosphere.

2. There is a general consensus by knowing scientists around the world that the earth is experiencing global warming. Rising temperatures could have extremely profound consequences for future generations. For instance, with melting ice caps, ocean levels could rise dramatical. Other areas in the world may experience harmfull desertification.

Using *good/well* and *bad/badly*

Good is an adjective, and *well* is an adverb. However, as an exception, you can use *well* to describe a person's health (for example, *I do not feel well*).

> **Adjective:** We will have **good** weather tomorrow.
>
> **Adverb:** She slept **well** even though the storm was noisy.

Bad is an adjective, and *badly* is an adverb.

> **Adjective:** The **bad** weather remained during the past week.
>
> **Adverb:** The meteorologist spoke **badly** during the nightly forecast.

PRACTICE 3   Underline the correct adjectives or adverbs.

EXAMPLE: Generally, public servants who listen (good / <u>well</u>) make (<u>good</u> / well) policies.

1. My biology professor explains subjects (good / well). Yesterday, he spoke about the (bad / badly) effects of greenhouse gases. The sunlight heats the earth's surface really (good / well), but not all of the heat is absorbed. The extra heat is reflected back into the earth's atmosphere, and greenhouse gases prevent this heat from escaping into the atmosphere.

2. The students in my class reacted (good / well) to a personal challenge for reducing global warming. Nobody thought (bad / badly) of the need for taking personal responsibility. They came up with (good / well) ideas to change their lifestyles, including writing a newsletter about the public's need to change (bad / badly) habits. Two (good / well) ways to reduce greenhouse gases are to reduce driving times and to recycle. Most people have (good / well) intentions and know (good / well) that humans must reduce greenhouse gases.

Comparative and Superlative Forms

Use the **comparative form** to compare two items. Use the **superlative form** to compare three or more items. You can write comparative and superlative forms by remembering a few simple guidelines.

Using -er and -est endings

Add *-er* and *-est* endings to one-syllable adjectives and adverbs. Double the last letter when the adjective ends in *one vowel + one consonant*.

short	short**er** than	the short**est**
hot	hot**ter** than	the hot**test**

When a two syllable adjective ends in *-y*, change the *-y* to *-i* and add *-er* or *-est*.

happy	happ**ier** than	the happ**iest**

Using *more* and *the most*

Add *more* and *the most* to adjectives and adverbs of two or more syllables.

beautiful	**more** beautiful than	the **most** beautiful

Using Irregular Comparative and Superlative Forms

Some adjectives and adverbs have unique comparative and superlative forms. Study this list to remember some of the most common ones.

good/well	better than	the best
bad/badly	worse than	the worst
some/much/many	more than	the most
little (a small amount)	less than	the least
far	farther/further	the farthest/the furthest

GRAMMAR LINK

Farther indicates a physical distance. *Further* means "additional." For more commonly confused words, see Chapter 27.

PRACTICE 4   Fill in the blanks with the correct comparative and superlative forms of the words in parentheses.

EXAMPLE: The problems of global warming are (serious) <u>*more serious*</u> than we previously believed.

1. The international community is trying to deal with one of the (urgent)

   _____ environmental problem the world is facing.

   Global warming is one of the (debated) _____ issues in

the scientific community. The Kyoto Protocol is an international agreement

made under the United Nations. Nations agree to reduce their greenhouse

gas emissions and prevent the greenhouse effect from becoming (bad)

_____ than in previous years.

2. Dr. Anif Mohammed is a famous climatologist. His presentation was

(short) _____ than some of the others, but it was also

the (clear) _____. In fact, he seemed to be the (little)

_____ nervous speaker at the conference.

Problems with Comparative and Superlative Forms

Using *more* and *-er*

In the comparative form, never use *more* and *-er* to modify the same word. In the superlative form, never use *most* and *-est* to modify the same word.

> The photographs of the tornado were ~~more~~ better than the ones of the rain storm, but the photos of the huge waves were the ~~most~~ best in the exhibition.

Using *fewer* and *less*

In the comparative form, use *fewer* before count nouns (*fewer people*, *fewer houses*) and use *less* before non-count nouns (*less information*, *less evidence*).

> Diplomats have **less** time than they used to. **Fewer** agreements are being made.

GRAMMAR LINK

For a complete list of non-count nouns, refer to page 382 in Chapter 24.

 Hint > **Using *the* in the Comparative Form**

Although you would usually use *the* in superlative forms, you can use it in some two-part comparatives. In these expressions, the second part is the result of the first part.

>   action   result
> The more you recycle, the better the environment will be.

PRACTICE 5 Correct the nine adjective and adverb errors in the next paragraphs.

EXAMPLE: If ~~less~~ *fewer* people drove cars, we would have ~~fewer~~ *less* air pollution.

1. The Amazon rainforest is the most largest in the world. It plays a vital role in regulating the global climate. Forests, such as the Amazon, create more better air quality for humans. Trees and plants remove carbon dioxide from the air and release oxygen into the air. The Amazon rainforest has been experiencing deforestation real rapidly.

2. There are several reasons for the deforestation of the Amazon. The most biggest causes for it are cattle ranching and road construction. Roads provide more greater access for logging and mining companies. Clearing the forest, farmers obtain more land for their cattle.

3. The depletion of the Amazon rainforest is one of the worse problems for our global climate. Less politicians than environmental activists are concerned with this issue. The more humanity waits to tackle this problem, the worst it will become. Perhaps over time, governments and the general public will try more harder to save the Amazon rainforest.

FINAL REVIEW
Correct fifteen errors in adjectives and adverbs.

EXAMPLE: We need to find ~~more~~ better sources of renewable energy.

1. Our society has depended economic on oil for the past two hundred years. Oil is a non-renewable energy source. Many politicians have reacted bad to the suggestion that we need to reduce our reliance on oil. They are concerned about economic progress, which is currently fuelled by oil. Yet worrying scientists and environmentalists believe that burning fossil fuels is causing temperatures around the world to become more warmer. Because of the threat of global warming, scientists are trying to develop alternative energy sources real quickly.

2. Wind energy is one powerfull alternative. Historically, countles efforts have been made to use wind to power millstones for grinding wheat and running pumps. Today, wind-powered turbines produce electricity 25 percent of the time because winds might not blow strong or continual. Therefore, the wind is not a dependable source of energy.

3. Less people use geothermal energy to heat homes in North America than in some other parts of the world. Nevertheless, it is also one of the most best alternative energy sources. Steam and hot water from under the earth's surface are used to turn turbines quick enough to create electricity. Around the world, there are a few areas that have steam or hot water close to the earth's surface, making geothermal energy cost-

READING LINK

Forces of Nature

These essays contain more information about weather and climate issues.

"The Rules of Survival," by Laurence Gonzales (page 515)

"The Other Side of the Mountain," by Geoff Powter (page 520)

"Monsoon Time," by Rahul Goswami (page 522)

CHAPTER 25

effective. Iceland uses geothermal energy to heat about 80 percent of its buildings.

4. The preceded energy sources are just a few of the alternative approaches that researchers are working on perfecting. These alternatives do not substitute completely for the versatility of oil. Scientists, government officials, and concerned citizens know good that our society must reduce its dependence on oil. The more money we spend on research, the best the results will be to develop and promote energy alternatives.

 The Writer's Room **Topics for Writing**

Write about one of the following topics. Proofread your text to ensure that there are no adjective and adverb mistakes.

1. Compare two types of transportation that you have owned. Explain which one you prefer.
2. Argue that our government should or should not address the issue of global warming.

 CHECKLIST: ADJECTIVES AND ADVERBS

When you edit your writing, ask yourself these questions.

☐ Do I use adjectives and adverbs correctly? Check for errors in these cases:

- the placement, order, and spelling of adjectives
- the placement of frequency adverbs, and spelling of adverbs ending in -*ly*

- the adjective and adverb form
- the use of *good/well* and *bad/badly*

>   *quietly*   *interesting*
> Magnus Forbes spoke very ~~quiet~~ about the ~~interested~~ article
>   *often*
> on El Niño at the news conference. He was asked to speak
>   ^
> ~~often~~ on environmental topics. The environmental lobbyist
>   *really well*
> hid his concern ~~real good~~.

  ☐ Do I use the correct comparative and superlative forms? Check for errors in these cases:

- *more* versus *-er* comparisons
- *the most* versus *-est* comparisons
- *fewer* versus *less* forms

> The ~~most~~ quickest tornado trackers take the first photographs.

>   *fewer*   *less*
> The organization had ~~less~~ members, but it also has ~~fewer~~ bad publicity.

How Do I Get a Better Grade?

mycanadiancomplab

Go to www.mycanadiancomplab.ca for additional help with your grammar, writing, and research skills. You will have access to a variety of exercises, instruction, and video that will help you improve your basic skills and help you get a better grade.

26 Pronouns

- Pronoun and Antecedent Agreement
- Indefinite Pronouns

- Vague Pronouns
- Pronoun Shifts

- Pronoun Case
- Relative Pronouns

Section Theme **FORCES OF NATURE**

In this chapter, you will read about nature's power.

Grammar Snapshot

Looking at Pronouns

The following quotation is from the article "The Weather: Friend and Tyrant," in which William Renaurd discusses the effects of weather on people's health. The pronouns are underlined.

"I can feel a cold weather front coming days ahead of its arrival," says Jane. "My teeth begin to hurt, and my entire lower jaw aches. I've been x-rayed, prodded by dentists, filled with pain-killing drugs, and examined by half a dozen neurologists. They can find no reason for my pain. I've decided that it's the weather and just try to bear it while waiting for the weather to change."

In this chapter, you will identify and write pronouns.

Pronoun and Antecedent Agreement

Pronouns are words that replace nouns (people, places, or things) and phrases. Use pronouns to avoid repeating nouns.

GRAMMAR LINK

For a list of common collective nouns, see page 339 in Chapter 21.

> *They*
> Hurricanes are large tropical storms. ~~Hurricanes~~ commonly form in the Caribbean.

A pronoun must agree with its **antecedent**, which is the word to which the pronoun refers. Antecedents are nouns and phrases that the pronouns have replaced, and they always come before the pronoun. Pronouns must agree in person and number with their antecedents.

> Sarah was late for **her** meeting because **she** drove slowly in the blinding rain.

> ### *Hint*   **Using Pronouns with Collective Nouns**
>
> Collective nouns refer to a group of people or things. The group acts as a unit; therefore, it is singular.
>
> The <u>organization</u> is very popular. Many people belong to **it**.
>
> The <u>company</u> was fined for polluting. **It** had to pay a large sum of money.

PRACTICE 1   Circle the pronoun and underline its antecedent.

EXAMPLE: Although hurricane <u>names</u> used to be only female, now (they) may also be male.

1. Anna Petrowski works for the <u>World Meteorological Organization</u>

   (WMO) where (she) helps to select hurricane names.

2. The <u>WMO</u> makes a list of distinctive names because (they) are easier to

   remember.

3. An <u>Atlantic hurricane</u> can have an English, a Spanish, or a French name

   because (it) mirrors the nationalities of people that may be affected.

4. In fact, when hurricanes become famous, the WMO retires their names.

5. The army usually sends its personnel to help with emergency relief during a hurricane.

Indefinite Pronouns

Use **indefinite pronouns** when you refer to people or things whose identity is not known or is unimportant. This chart shows some common singular and plural indefinite pronouns.

CHAPTER 26

Indefinite Pronouns				
Singular	another	each	nobody	other
	anybody	everybody	no one	somebody
	anyone	everyone	nothing	someone
	anything	everything	one	something
Plural	both, few, many, others, several			
Either singular or plural	all, any, half (and other fractions), some, none, more, most			

Singular

When you use a singular indefinite antecedent, also use a singular pronoun to refer to it.

Nobody remembered to bring **his** or **her** raincoat.

Plural

When you use a plural indefinite antecedent, also use a plural pronoun to refer to it.

Hurricanes and tornadoes arrive each year, and both have **their** own destructive power.

Either Singular or Plural

Some indefinite pronouns can be either singular or plural depending on the noun to which they refer.

Many meteorologists spoke at the conference. All gave important information about **their** research.

(*All* refers to meteorologists; therefore, the pronoun is plural.)

I read <u>all</u> of the newspaper and could not find **its** weather section.
(*All* refers to the newspaper; therefore, the pronoun is singular.)

 Avoid Sexist Language

Terms like *anybody, somebody, nobody,* and *each* are singular antecedents, so the pronouns that follow must be singular. At one time, it was acceptable to use *he* as a general term meaning *all people*; however, today it is more acceptable to use *he or she.*

Sexist:	<u>Everyone</u> should stay inside **his** house during a tornado.
Solution:	<u>Everyone</u> should stay inside **his or her** house during a tornado.
Better Solution:	<u>People</u> should stay inside **their** houses during a tornado.

Exception: If you know for certain that the subject is male or female, then use only *he* or only *she.*

In the men's prison, everyone has his own cell.

⚠ **PRACTICE 2** Correct nine errors in pronoun antecedent agreement by changing either the antecedent or the pronoun. If you change any antecedents, make sure that your subjects and verbs agree.

> *their*
EXAMPLE: Some of the workers had ~~his~~ own skis.

1. Everyone should know what to do if ~~they~~ *he or she* are caught in extreme weather

   conditions. For example, people should be aware of lightning storms. All

   need to avoid open spaces, and ~~he~~ *people they* should get inside a building. No one

   should remain in the open because ~~they~~ *he or she* could be struck by lightning. If

   lightning is nearby, each person who is outside should get into a crouching

   position but never lie down.

2. In the winter months, snowstorms can be dangerous. ~~Somebody~~ *People* stranded

   in a blizzard should stay with their car. Nobody should wander outside on

~~their~~ Mr&other own during a blinding snowstorm. It is very dangerous if a car gets stuck in a snowbank. One of the most common problems is carbon monoxide poisoning, which happens when snow blocks the back of the car and carbon monoxide gas backs up in ~~their~~ *the* exhaust pipe. To solve this problem, ~~everyone~~ *people* should clear the snow from their exhaust pipe.

3. Many *people* have heard ~~his or her~~ *their* weather stations reporting on tornadoes. During a tornado warning, ~~everybody~~ *everybodies* should go into a basement or windowless room in their home. Knowing what to do during extreme weather can save people's lives.

CHAPTER 26

Vague Pronouns

Avoid using pronouns that could refer to more than one antecedent.

> **Vague:** My father asked my brother where <u>his</u> umbrella was.
> (Whose umbrella? My father's or my brother's?)

> **Clearer:** My father asked my brother where **my brother's** umbrella was.

Avoid using confusing pronouns such as *it* and *they* that have no clear antecedent.

> **Vague:** <u>They</u> say that thousands of people lost their lives during the 1995 earthquake in Kobe, Japan.
> (Who are *they*?)

> **Clearer:** **Government officials** say that thousands of people lost their lives during the 1995 earthquake in Kobe, Japan.

> **Vague:** <u>It</u> stated in the newspaper that the scientific name for a thundercloud is cumulonimbus.
> (Who or what is *it*?)

> **Clearer:** **The journalist** stated that the scientific name for a thundercloud is cumulonimbus.

This, *that*, and *which* should refer to a specific antecedent.

Vague: My girlfriend said that the roads were icy. I was glad she told me <u>this</u>.
(What is *this*?)

Clearer: My girlfriend said that the roads were icy. I was glad she told me **this information.**

> ## Hint Avoid Repeating the Subject
>
> When you clearly mention a subject, do not repeat the subject in pronoun form.
>
> Thunder ~~it~~ occurs when cold air collides with hot air.

PRACTICE 3   The following paragraphs contain vague pronouns or repeated subjects. Correct the nine errors in this selection. You may need to rewrite some sentences.

The journalist reported
EXAMPLE: ~~They said on television~~ that most tornadoes occur in agricultural areas around the world.

1. Meteorologist Patricia Bowles told her friend Sheila that ~~her~~ *Sheila* photo of the tornado would appear in the newspaper. ~~They~~ *Meteorologists* say that tornadoes are the most powerful storms on earth. Tornado winds ~~they~~ can often exceed 100 miles per hour. ~~This~~ *Wind force* can cause a lot of damage to property and sometimes kill people.

2. ~~It says~~ *Meteorologists say* that tornadoes form during thunderstorms when cool air moves downward and hot air rises very quickly, creating a funnel effect. When ~~this~~ *air funnel* touches the ground, it becomes a tornado. The United States ~~it~~ has a "Tornado Alley." ~~This~~ *Tornado Alley* consists of Texas, Oklahoma, Kansas, and Nebraska. These states ~~they~~ have more tornadoes than other parts of North America because cold air from Canada meets the warm air from the Gulf of Mexico over the flat prairies.

Pronoun Shifts

If your essays contain unnecessary shifts in person or number, you may confuse your readers. They will not know exactly who or how many you are referring to. Carefully edit your writing to ensure that your pronouns are consistent.

Making Pronouns Consistent in Number

If the antecedent is singular, then the pronoun must be singular. If the antecedent is plural, then the pronoun must be plural.

> singular   his or her
> A **meteorologist** and ~~their~~ team spend years keeping meticulous records of weather patterns.

> plural   they
> When there are storm **warnings**, ~~it~~ should be taken seriously.

Making Pronouns Consistent in Person

Person is the writer's perspective. For some writing assignments, you might use the first person (*I, we*). For other assignments, especially most college essays and workplace writing, you might use the second person (*you*), or the third person (*he, she, it, they*).

Shifting the point of view for no reason confuses readers. If you begin writing from one point of view, do not shift unnecessarily to another point of view.

> They
> **Many** tourists like to travel, but **they** should be careful. ~~You~~ never
> They
> know when there will be bad weather. ~~You~~ should always be prepared for emergencies.

PRACTICE 4   Correct five pronoun shift errors.

EXAMPLE: Many people were saddened when they heard that thousands of
They
people had died in the 2001 Indian earthquake. ~~One~~ donated
money, clothes, and blankets to the victims.

In 2005, we were travelling in Pakistan. We had just finished our breakfast when you felt the ground moving. Everything in our tenth floor apartment started to shake and fall. We knew we should not panic, but one really didn't know what to do. We knew you had to get out of the high-rise and onto the ground because one could never be certain that the building would remain standing. There were no guarantees that you could make it out in time.

Pronoun Case

Pronouns are formed according to the role they play in a sentence. A pronoun can be the subject or object of the sentence, or it can show possession. This chart shows the three main pronoun cases: subjective, objective, and possessive.

Pronouns

Singular	Subjective	Objective	Possessive Adjective	Possessive Pronoun
First person	I	me	my	mine
Second person	you	you	your	yours
Third person	he, she, it, who, whoever	him, her, it, whom, whomever	his, her, its, whose	his, hers
Plural				
First person	we	us	our	ours
Second person	you	you	your	yours
Third person	they	them	their	theirs

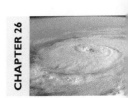

Subjective Case and Objective Case

When a pronoun is the subject of the sentence, use the subjective form of the pronoun. When a pronoun is the object in the sentence, use the objective form of the pronoun.

subject   subject   object
He left the umbrella at work, and **I** asked **him** to bring it home.

Possessive Case

A possessive pronoun shows ownership.

- **Possessive adjectives** come before the noun that they modify.

    She finished **her** research on the polar ice caps, but we did not finish **our** research.

- **Possessive pronouns** can replace the possessive adjective and the noun that follows it. In the following sentence, the possessive pronoun *ours* replaces both the possessive adjective *our* and the noun *research*.

    possessive adjective
    She finished **her** research about the polar ice caps, but we did not

    possessive pronoun
    finish **ours**.

Problems with Possessive Pronouns

GRAMMAR LINK

For more information about apostrophes, see Chapter 29.

Some possessive adjectives sound like certain contractions. When using the possessive adjectives *their*, *your*, and *its*, be careful that you do not confuse them with *they're* (they are), *you're* (you are), and *it's* (it is).

$$\overset{\textit{hers}}{} \qquad\qquad \overset{\textit{theirs}}{}$$

The book on clouds is ~~her's~~. The weather almanac is ~~their's~~.

 Hint   Choosing *His* or *Her*

To choose the correct possessive adjective, think about the possessor (not the object that is possessed).

- If something belongs to a female, use *her* + noun.

   Helena and **her** dog like to walk in the snow.

- If something belongs to a male, use *his* + noun.

   Cliff used **his** new camera to photograph storm clouds.

PRACTICE 5   Underline the correct possessive adjective or possessive pronoun in each set of parentheses.

EXAMPLE: Dr. Jane Woody wondered whether (his / <u>her</u>) theories would be accepted.

1. Scientists study volcanoes and (its / it's / their) effects on weather patterns. When a volcano erupts and throws (his / its / it's) ash particles into the surrounding air, the explosion causes a lot of lightning and thunderstorms in the region nearby.

2. I have just joined the International Society on Volcanic Studies. The members and (there / they're / their)

governments fund research into volcanic activity. A researcher and (their / his or her / its) assistants gather information about volcanic eruptions.

3. My assistant Judith, because of (her / hers) enthusiasm, painstakingly collects data from volcanic eruptions around the world. A lot of research is being done in this field. (Our / Ours) is just one small part of this study.

4. One day, we would like to present (our / ours) observations to climate scientists because we think this research will be important to (they / them). Will you be in (you're / your / yours) office next Tuesday? Let's discuss (our / ours) work and (your / yours) when we meet.

Pronouns in Comparisons with *Than* or *As*

Avoid making errors in pronoun case when the pronoun follows *than* or *as*. If the pronoun is a subject, use the subjective case, and if the pronoun is an object, use the objective case.

If you use the incorrect case, your sentence may have a meaning that you do not intend it to have. Review the following two examples. Notice that when the sentence ends with the subjective pronoun, it is advisable to add a verb after the pronoun.

objective case
I like rainy days as much as **him.**
(I like rainy days as much as I like him.)

subjective case
I like rainy days as much as **he** [does].
(I like rainy days as much as he likes rainy days.)

 **Complete the Thought**

To test which pronoun case to use, complete the thought.

He likes winter more than **I** [like winter].
(Do I want to say that he likes winter more than I like winter?)

He likes winter more than [he likes] **me**.
(Or, do I want to say he likes winter more than he likes me?)

Pronouns in Prepositional Phrases

In a prepositional phrase, the words that follow the preposition are the objects of the preposition. Therefore, always use the objective case of the pronoun after a preposition.

To **him**, global warming is not a big deal. Between **you** and **me**, I think he's misinformed.

Pronouns with *and* or *or*

Use the correct case when nouns and pronouns are joined by *and* or *or*. If the pronouns are the subject, use the subjective case. If the pronouns are the object, use the objective case.

She and I

~~Her and me~~ had to read about the causes of desertification, and then

her and me

the instructor asked ~~she and I~~ to summarize the information.

 **Finding the Correct Case**

To determine that your case is correct, try saying the sentence with either the subjective case or the objective case.

Sentence:	The professor asked her and (**I** or **me**) to research the topic.
Possible answers:	The professor asked **I** to research the topic. (This would *not* make sense.)
	The professor asked **me** to research the topic. (This would make sense.)
Correct answer:	The professor asked **her** and **me** to research the topic.

PRACTICE 6   Correct any errors with pronoun case.

EXAMPLE: Last summer, my friend and ~~me~~ *I* visited Mexico.

1. Last year, my brother and me took a vacation together.

2. He likes exotic travel more than me but convinced me to accompany him to Antarctica.

3. The tour guide told my brother and I that at its thickest point, Antarctica has an ice cap five kilometres deep. If it were to melt, it would raise the oceans' water level by many metres.

4. Between you and I, it is frightening to think about melting ice caps.

5. My brother is a photographer. Him and me took a lot of photographs.

6. I will have good memories when my brother and me look at our photo album.

Relative Pronouns

Relative pronouns can join two short sentences. They include *who, whom, whoever, whomever, which, that,* and *whose.*

Choosing *Who* or *Whom*

To determine whether to use *who* or *whom,* replace *who* or *whom* with another pronoun. If the replacement is a subjective pronoun such as *he* or *she,* use *who.* If the replacement is an objective pronoun such as *her* or *him,* use *whom.*

> I know a man **who** studies icebergs.
> (He studies icebergs.)

> The man to **whom** you gave your résumé is my boss.
> (You gave your résumé to him.)

PRACTICE 7   Underline the correct relative pronoun in the parentheses.

EXAMPLE: People (<u>who</u> / which) live in the arctic are used to harsh weather.

1. Ruth, (who / whom) I met in school, has been my best friend for twenty years.

2. Ruth, (who / whom) is a journalist, recently spent some time on Baffin Island.

3. The people on Baffin Island about (who / whom) Ruth is writing are mostly Inuit.

4. The Inuit (who / whom) are accustomed to extreme weather are active year round.

5. Ruth, (who / whom) loves the sun, sometimes feels depressed during the winter when there is very little daylight.

6. Many people (who / whom) Ruth has interviewed are worried about climate change.

FINAL REVIEW

Correct the fifteen pronoun errors in the following paragraphs.

EXAMPLE: Many people around the world have lost ~~one's~~ *their* relatives and property because of severe weather.

1. In 2004 and 2005, severe weather and natural disasters they caused havoc in the lives of people around the world. They say that the forces of nature

are uncontrollable and unpredictable. But with increasingly sophisticated technology, climatologists and there assistants should be able to improve natural disaster warnings around the world.

Katsushika Hokusai (1760–1849, Japanese) "The Wave", 19th Century, Woodcut print. © SuperStock, Inc.

2. In December 2004, my friend and me were on holiday in Thailand. At that time, the strongest earthquake in forty years occurred in the Indian Ocean. It caused a tsunami that annihilated cities, villages, and holiday resorts. My friend, whom is from Indonesia, said that all members of his uncle's family lost his homes. Many people have suffered more than me.

3. Some months after the Asian tsunami, in 2005, New Orleans experienced one of their worst hurricanes in history. Hurricane Katrina caused the levees to break and flood the city. This caused severe property damage and loss of life. Almost everybody in New Orleans had to leave their home.

4. Also in 2005, a severe earthquake in the mountainous regions of Pakistan caused death and destruction to the people of the region. They say that around 100 000 people died. I watched television reports of people living in tents and wanted to help them because you could see they had lost everything. So I collected donations from students at my college, and my brother, to who I sent the donations, passed them along to an aid organization in Pakistan.

5. The forces of nature are more powerful than us. We have no ability to control inundations, hurricanes, or earthquakes. With better warning systems and relief infrastructures, maybe one can reduce the misery caused by natural disasters.

 The Writer's Room   **Topics for Writing**

Write about one of the following topics. Proofread your text to ensure there are no pronoun errors.

1. Describe a severe weather event that you or someone you know experienced. What happened? Try to use descriptive imagery.

2. Argue that bicycles should be the only type of vehicle allowed in city centres. Support your argument with specific examples.

 CHECKLIST: PRONOUNS

When you edit your writing, ask yourself these questions.

☐ Do I use the correct pronoun case? Check for errors with the following:

- subjective, objective, and possessive cases
- comparisons with *than* or *as*
- prepositional phrases
- pronouns following *and* or *or*

                    me

Between you and I, my sister watches the weather reports

     I (do)

more than <u>me</u>.

☐ Do I use the correct relative pronouns? Check for errors with *who* or *whom*.

           whom

My husband, <u>who</u> you have met, is a meteorologist.

☐ Do my pronouns and antecedents agree in number and person? Check for errors with indefinite pronouns and collective nouns.

> *its*
> The bad weather and <u>their</u> aftermath were reported on the news.

☐ Are my pronoun references clear? Check for vague pronouns and inconsistent points of view.

> *Scientists*
> <u>They</u> say the weather will change rapidly. I read the report
> *I*
> and <u>you</u> could not believe what it said.

How Do I Get a Better Grade?

mycanadiancomplab

Go to www.mycanadiancomplab.ca for additional help with your grammar, writing, and research skills. You will have access to a variety of exercises, instruction, and video that will help you improve your basic skills and help you get a better grade.

CHAPTER 27

Spelling and Commonly Confused Words

CONTENTS
- Spelling Rules
- 120 Commonly Misspelled Words
- Look-Alike and Sound-Alike Words

Section Theme **FLORA AND FAUNA**

In this chapter, you will read about insects.

Grammar Snapshot

Looking at Spelling

In this excerpt from the article, "Songs of Insects," writer Sy Montgomery discusses how insects communicate. Writers often misspell the underlined words.

If you share this poet's <u>sensibilities</u>, now is the time to <u>fulfill</u> your longing. Though <u>widely</u> loved for <u>its</u> changing <u>leaves</u> and migrating birds, early fall is, in some circles anyway, yet more <u>renowned</u> for the sweetness of <u>its</u> insect voices.

In this chapter, you will identify and correct misspelled words.

Spelling Rules

It is important to spell correctly because spelling mistakes can detract from important ideas in your work. Here are some strategies for improving your spelling skills.

How to Become a Better Speller

- **Look up words** using the most current dictionary because it will contain new or updated words. For tips on dictionary usage, see page 485.
- **Keep a record of words that you commonly misspell.** For example, write the words and definitions in a spelling log, which could be in a journal or binder. See Appendix 5 for more information about your spelling log.
- **Use memory cards or flash cards** to help you memorize the spelling of difficult words. With a friend or a classmate, take turns asking each other to spell difficult words.
- **Write out the spelling of difficult words at least ten times** to help you remember how to spell them. After you have written these words, try writing them in a complete sentence.

Six Common Spelling Rules

Memorize the following common rules of spelling. If you follow these rules, your spelling will become more accurate. Also try to remember the exceptions to these rules.

1. **Writing *ie* or *ei*** Write *i* before *e*, except after *c* or when *ei* is pronounced as *ay*, as in *neighbour* and *weigh*.

i before *e*:	chief	field	grief
ei after *c*:	receipt	deceit	receive
ei pronounced as *ay*:	weigh	beige	vein

   Here are some exceptions:

ancient	either	neither	foreigner	leisure	height
science	species	society	seize	their	weird

2. **Adding *-s* or *-es*** Add *-s* to form plural nouns and to create present-tense verbs that are third-person singular. However, add *-es* to words in the following situations.

   - When words end in *s*, *sh*, *ss*, *ch*, or *x*, add *-es*.

     Noun: box → boxes
     Verb: miss → misses

   - When words end in consonant *y*, change the *y* to *i* and add *-es*.

     Noun: baby → babies
     Verb: marry → marries

- When words end in *o*, you usually add -*es*. Exceptions are *pianos*, *radios*, *logos*, *stereos*, *autos*, *typos*, and *casinos*.

  Noun: tomato ➔ tomatoes
  Verb: go ➔ goes

- When words end in *f*, or *fe*, change the *f* to a *v* and add -*es*. Exceptions are *beliefs* and *roofs*.

  life ➔ lives
  wolf ➔ wolves

3. **Adding Prefixes and Suffixes** A **prefix** is added to the beginning of a word, and it changes the word's meaning. For example, *con-*, *dis-*, *pre-*, *un-*, and *il-* are prefixes. When you add a prefix to a word, keep the last letter of the prefix and the first letter of the main word.

   i**m** + **m**ature = im**m**ature
   mi**s** + **s**pell = mi**ss**pell

   A **suffix** is added to the ending of a word, and it changes the word's tense or meaning. For example, -*ly*, -*ment*, -*ed*, and -*ing* are suffixes. When you add the suffix -*ly* to words that end in *l*, keep the *l* of the root word. The new word will have two *l*s.

   casua**l** + **l**y = casua**ll**y
   factua**l** + **l**y = factua**ll**y

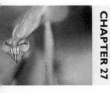

4. **Adding Suffixes to Words Ending in *e*** If the suffix begins with a vowel, drop the *e* on the main word. Some common suffixes beginning with vowels are -*ed*, -*er*, -*est*, -*ing*, -*able*, -*ent*, and -*ist*.

   bak**e** ➔ baking
   creat**e** ➔ created

   Some exceptions are words that end in *ge*, which keep the *e* and add the suffix.

   outrag**e** ➔ outrageous
   manag**e** ➔ manageable

   If the suffix begins with a consonant, keep the *e*. Some common suffixes beginning with consonants are -*ly*, -*ment*, -*less*, and -*ful*. Some exceptions are *acknowledgment*, *argument*, and *truly*.

   sur**e** ➔ surely
   awar**e** ➔ awareness

5. **Adding Suffixes to Words Ending in *y*** If the word has a consonant before the final *y*, change the *y* to an *i* before adding the suffix. Some exceptions are *ladybug*, *dryness*, and *shyness*.

   prett**y** ➔ prettiest
   happ**y** ➔ happiness

If the word has a vowel before the final *y*, if it is a proper name, or if the suffix is *-ing*, do not change the *y* to an *i*. Some exceptions are *daily*, *laid*, and *said*.

employ ➔ employed
apply ➔ applying
Levinsky ➔ Levinskys

6. **Doubling the Final Consonant** Double the final consonant of one-syllable words ending in a consonant-vowel-consonant pattern.

ship ➔ shi**pp**ing
swim ➔ swi**mm**er
hop ➔ ho**pp**ed

Double the final consonant of words ending in a stressed consonant-vowel-consonant pattern.

re<u>fer</u> ➔ preferred
oc<u>cur</u> ➔ occurred

Do not double the final consonant in two syllable words ending in consonant-vowel-consonant pattern if the stress falls on the first syllable.

enter ➔ entering
open ➔ opening

Exceptions: travel ➔ travelling
label ➔ labelling

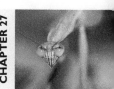

120 Commonly Misspelled Words

This list contains some of the most commonly misspelled words in English.

absence	believable	definitely	government
absorption	business	desperate	grammar
accommodate	calendar	developed	harassment
acquaintance	campaign	dilemma	height
address	careful	disappoint	immediately
aggressive	ceiling	embarrass	independent
already	cemetery	encouragement	jewellery
aluminum	clientele	environment	judgment
analyze	committee	especially	laboratory
appointment	comparison	exaggerate	ledge
approximate	competent	exercise	leisure
argument	conscience	extraordinarily	licence (n.)
athlete	conscientious	familiar	license (v.)
bargain	convenient	February	loneliness
beginning	curriculum	finally	maintenance
behaviour	definite	foreign	mathematics

medicine	personality	rhythm	truly
millennium	physically	schedule	Tuesday
minuscule	possess	scientific	until
mischievous	precious	separate	usually
mortgage	prejudice	sincerely	vacuum
necessary	privilege	spaghetti	Wednesday
ninety	probably	strength	weird
noticeable	professor	success	woman
occasion	psychology	surprise	women
occurrence	questionnaire	technique	wreckage
opposite	receive	thorough	writer
outrageous	recommend	tomato	writing
parallel	reference	tomatoes	written
performance	responsible	tomorrow	zealous
perseverance			

PRACTICE I   Edit the following paragraphs for twenty misspelled words.

strength
EXAMPLE: Some insects have an incredible amount of ~~strenght~~.

1. Throughout history, humans have either been fascinated or repulsed by insects. In fact, humans have developped a close connection to insects and recognize the power and importance of insects for sustaining life. For example, insects pollinate plants and aerate soil. Without such help, the enviroment would suffer. Thus, human cultures have acknowleged insects through art, literature, and religion.

2. First, the ancient Egyptians honoured different insects. The dung beetle or scarab was definatly an important religious symbol. The Egyptians called it Khepera, the god of virility and rebirth. They beleived that he was responsable for pushing the sun along the horizon. To honour Khepera, the Egyptians wore scarab amulets as precious jewlry and buried them in pots and boxs with the dead. The ancients thought that the scarabs helped

CHAPTER 27

the dead who were enterring the afterlife. Furthermore, ancient Egyptian kings took the name of Khepera when they became rulers. For example, Tutankhamen's royal name was Neb Kheperu Ra.

3. Another insect, the cricket, was valued in Chinese culture. The Chinese kept both singing and fighting varieties. Singing crickets were expecialy crucial to farmers. They knew it was time to plough when crickets and other insects began to wake and sing. Wealthy ladyes and palace concubines kept crickets as pets in cages. People surmised that the crickets represented the women themselfs who had very little status in the community. Fighting crickets were also very popular, and many people lost much of their savings beting on cricket fights.

4. Western artists are also fascinated with insects. There are many fables that feature different speceis as the main characters. In modern literature, insects play a noticable role. For example, in Franz Kafka's *Metamorphosis*, the main character turns into a giant cockroach. Insects are common symbols in modern film. Jiminy Cricket is Pinocchio's consceince. In the movie *The Fly*, a scientist is unaturaly transformed into a six-foot human fly. Flys and other insects can also symbolize human fear and repugnance.

5. Humans and insects have had a truely unique relationship for many millennia. Different cultures have integrated insects into the fields of art, music, religion, and history. Indeed, some people say that the teeny creepy crawlers are survivors and will surly outlive humans.

CHAPTER 27

Look-Alike and Sound-Alike Words

Sometimes two English words can sound the same but have different spellings and meanings. These words are called **homonyms**. Here are a few commonly confused words and basic meanings. (For more specific definitions for these and other words, consult a dictionary.)

CHAPTER 27

accept	to receive; to admit	We must accept the vital role that insects play in our culture.
except	excluding; other than	I like all insects except ants.
allowed	permitted	We were not allowed to view the exhibit.
aloud	spoken audibly	We could not speak aloud, so we whispered.
affect	to influence	Pesticides affect the environment.
effect	the result of something	Scientists are examining the effects of pesticides on our health.
been	past participle of the verb *to be*	He has been to the Imax film about caterpillars.
being	present progressive form (the *-ing* form) of the verb *to be*	She was being kind when she donated to the butterfly museum.
by	preposition meaning *next to*, *on*, or *before*	A bee flew by the flowers. By evening, the crickets were making a lot of noise.
buy	to purchase	Will you buy me that scarab necklace?
complement	to add to; to complete	The film about the monarch butterfly was a nice complement to the exhibit.
compliment	to say something nice about someone	The film was informative and the director received many compliments.
conscience	a personal sense of right or wrong	After spraying pesticides, the gardener had a guilty conscience.
conscious	to be aware; to be awake	He made us conscious of the important role insects play in our society.

PRACTICE 2 Underline the correct word in parentheses.

EXAMPLE: Many people (by / <u>buy</u>) clothes made out of silk.

1. Silk has (been / being) produced (by / buy) the Chinese for at least four thousand years. The silkworm is actually a caterpillar that eats nothing (accept / except) mulberry leaves, grows quickly, and then encircles itself

into a cocoon of raw silk. The cocoon contains a single thread about 300 to 900 metres in length, so it's not surprising that it takes about 2000 cocoons to make one pound of silk. (Been / Being) very (conscious / conscience) of the long and intense silk-making process, most people (accept / except) the high cost of the material.

2. The Chinese valued silk and guarded the secret of its making carefully. In ancient China, only the emperor and his family were (allowed / aloud) to wear silk garments. Sometimes, members of royalty wore the fabric as a (complement / compliment) to their regular clothes. Of course, less fortunate people admired the emperor's beautiful clothes and always (complimented / complemented) him on them.

3. By the fifth century, the secret of silk making had been revealed to Korea, Japan, and India. How did the secret get out? Legend says that a princess with no (conscious / conscience) smuggled out silkworm larvae to Korea by hiding them in her hair. The emperor was outraged (by / buy) the actions of the princess, and there was great debate about her treachery.

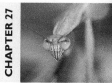

everyday	ordinary or common	Swatting mosquitoes is an <u>everyday</u> ritual of camping.
every day	each day	<u>Every day</u>, I check my roses for aphids.
imminent	soon to happen	The journalist reported that the arrival of locusts in parts of Africa was <u>imminent</u>.
eminent	distinguished; superior	Professor Maurice Kanyogo is an <u>eminent</u> entomologist.
imply	to suggest	The entomologist <u>implied</u> that he received a large grant.
infer	to conclude	His students <u>inferred</u> that they would have summer jobs because of the grant.
its	possessive case of the pronoun *it*	The worker bee went into <u>its</u> hive.
it's	contraction for *it is*	<u>It's</u> well-known that the queen bee is the largest in the colony.

knew	past tense of *to know*	I <u>knew</u> that I should study for my test on worms.
new	recent or unused	But my <u>new</u> book on honey making was more interesting.
know	to have knowledge of	The beekeepers <u>know</u> that there has been a decline of bees in recent years.
no	a negative	There were <u>no</u> books on beekeeping in the library.
lose	to misplace or forfeit something	Do not <u>lose</u> the mosquito repellent.
loose	too baggy; not fixed	You should wear <u>loose</u> clothes when camping.
loss	a decrease in an amount; a serious blow	Farmers would experience a <u>loss</u> if there were no bees to pollinate crops.
peace	calmness or an end to violence	The <u>peace</u> in the woods was wonderful.
piece	a part of something else; one item in a group of items	The two <u>pieces</u> of amber had insects in them.
principal	director of a school; main	The <u>principal</u> of our school is an expert on beetles. They are his <u>principal</u> hobby.
principle	rules or standards	Julius Corrant wrote a book about environmental <u>principles</u>.
quiet	silent	The crickets remained <u>quiet</u> this evening.
quite	very	They usually make <u>quite</u> a noise.
quit	stop	I would like them to <u>quit</u> making so much noise.

CHAPTER 27

PRACTICE 3   Identify and correct ten word choice errors.

peace
EXAMPLE: I need some ~~piece~~ and quiet.

1. I am reading a book on pollination by Professor Zoe Truger, an imminent entomologist who specializes in butterfly behaviour. Its very interesting. On it's cover, there is a beautiful photograph of a butterfly. Everyday, during the summer, thousands of monarch butterflies are found in southern Canada, their summer home. As autumn arrives, these butterflies know that migration to warmer climates is eminent.

2. The principle of Jake's school took the students on a nature walk to look for earthworms. The students were very quit when the guide told them there are 2700 species of earthworms.

3. Did you no that beekeeping is one of the world's oldest professions? Some beekeepers may loose their businesses because bees are dying due to pesticide overuse. Citizens need to quite spraying their fields, parks, and gardens with pesticides.

taught	past tense of *to teach*	I taught a class on pollination.
thought	past tense of *to think*	I thought the students enjoyed it.
than	word used to compare items	There are more mosquitoes at the lake than in the city.
then	at a particular time or after a specific time	He found the termite nest. Then he called the exterminators.
that	word used to introduce a clause	They told him that they would come immediately.
their	possessive form of *they*	They wore scarab amulets to show their respect for the god Khepera.
there	a place	The ant colony is over there.
they're	contraction of *they are*	The ants work hard. They're very industrious.
to	part of an infinitive; indicates direction or movement	I want to hunt for bugs. I will go to the hiking path and look under some rocks.
too	also; very	My friend is too scared of bugs. My brother is too.
two	the number after *one*	There were two types of butterflies in the garden today.
where	question word indicating location	Where did you buy the book on ladybugs?
were	past tense of *be*	There were hundreds of ladybugs on the bush.
we're	contraction of *we are*	We're wondering why we have this infestation.

who's	contraction of *who is*	Ishbelle, <u>who's</u> a horticulturist, also keeps a butterfly garden.
whose	pronoun showing ownership	<u>Whose</u> garden is that?
write	to draw symbols that represent words	I will <u>write</u> an essay about the common earthworm.
right	correct; the opposite of the direction left	In the <u>right</u> corner of the garden, there is the compost bin with many worms in it.
		You are <u>right</u> when you say that earthworms are necessary for composting.

PRACTICE 4   Identify and correct sixteen word choice errors.

There
EXAMPLE: ~~Their~~ are many different types of hobbies.

1. Their are both professional and amateur beekeepers. Beekeepers wear special clothes, but even with protective gear, there usually stung at least once while practising there profession. Some beekeepers have a greater resistance to stings then others have. All of them know than there is a small danger of death from anaphylactic shock because of a bee sting. A person whose interested in beekeeping should know the risks. Than he or she can make the write choices about hobbies.

2. We recently read to books on ladybugs. We went to the library were an expert thought us about ladybugs. The expert, who's bug collection was on display, said each ladybug controls pests because it eats around 5000 aphids in its lifetime. Ladybugs eat other pests to. We where extremely surprised when we heard that fact. Were going to do more research on ladybugs. I will right an email to the expert asking for more information.

FINAL REVIEW

Correct the twenty spelling errors and mistakes with commonly confused words in the following essay.

carries
EXAMPLE: The bee ~~carrys~~ pollen grains from one plant to another.

1. Around the world, unatural causes such as climate change, pollution, and human activities are threatening the enviroment. Forests are expecialy vulnerable to these pressures because of loging, increasing pests, and global warming. Conserving biodiversity is important for protecting forests.

2. Biodiversity, a contraction of the words *biological diversity*, means that a variety of plants, animals, and micro-organisms co-exist in an ecosystem. Today, imminent scientists concerned with species' extinction refer to the necesity of maintaining biodiversity on our planet. Scientists are conscience of the value of each species. Argueing for conserving biodiversity, scientists believe that if species become extinct, than the ecosystem will become unstable.

3. Insects are crucial to sustain the biodiversity of an ecosystem and are the most diverse life form on earth. Currently, there are approximately 800 000 identified species of insects, all of which are usefull in balancing the ecosystem. For example, they pollinate plants, and they eat other insects and plants. Their also important to the global economy. For instance, insects are used for honey production, silk making, and agricultural pest

control. If an insect species becomes extinct, they're will be a variety of consequences on the remaining species in the ecosystem, such as an increase in predatory insects or a lost of another species higher on the food chain. Such a change in the ecosystem would have an eminent effect on all life forms.

4. Most people think that insects are troublesome and should be eradicated. Of course, insects such as mosquitos carry diseases, including malaria and West Nile Virus, which are harmfull to human health. But its important to keep in mind that most insects provide important services for the natural world, to. Were there are insects, there is a thriving ecosystem. Extinction of an insect species will have a serious affect on nature, so the next time you are tempted to swat a fly or step on an ant, you might think twice.

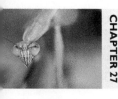

CHAPTER 27

READING LINK
Flora and Fauna
These readings contain more information on plant and animal life.
"Living Among the Bees," by Lucie L. Snodgrass (page 116)
"Make a Difference," by David Suzuki and David R. Boyd (page 525)

The Writer's Room **Topics for Writing**

Write about one of the following topics. Proofread your text to ensure there are no spelling and commonly confused word errors.

1. Discuss types of insects that are particularly annoying, repulsive, or frightening.
2. Are laws banning the use of pesticides on lawns a good idea? Explain your views.

CHECKLIST: SPELLING RULES

When you edit your writing, ask yourself these questions.

☐ Do I have any spelling errors? Check for errors in words that contain these elements:

- any *ie* or *ei* combinations
- prefixes and suffixes

> *Dragonflies*   *lovely*   *Their*
> ~~Dragonflys~~ are ~~lovly~~. ~~There~~ wings are transparent, but
>
> *their*
> ~~they're~~ bodies are a variety of colours. They eat other
>
>   *mosquitoes*
> insects such as ~~mosquitos~~.

☐ Do I repeat spelling errors that I have made in previous assignments? I should check my previous assignments for errors or consult my spelling log.

CHAPTER 27

How Do I Get a Better Grade?

mycanadiancomplab

Go to www.mycanadiancomplab.ca for additional help with your grammar, writing, and research skills. You will have access to a variety of exercises, instruction, and video that will help you improve your basic skills and help you get a better grade.

CHAPTER 28

Commas

CONTENTS

- What Is a Comma?
- Commas in a Series
- Commas After Introductory Words or Phrases
- Commas Around Interrupting Words or Phrases
- Commas in Compound Sentences
- Commas in Complex Sentences

Section Theme
HUMAN DEVELOPMENT

In this chapter, you will read about life stages.

Grammar Snapshot

Looking at Commas

On an episode of the ABC news program *Primetime*, Connie Chung interviewed citizens from Yuzuri Hara, Japan, a small mountainous village two hours outside of Tokyo. In the excerpt that follows, the commas are highlighted.

> Mr. Takahashi attributes his smooth skin, even after working fifty years in the sun, to sticking to the local traditional diet. The skin on his arms felt like a baby's, and the skin on his legs barely had a wrinkle. Some of what Mr. Takahashi eats is on the menu every day at a hotel in Yuzuri Hara. The innkeeper, Mrs. Ishi, is eighty and looks pretty good herself.

In this chapter, you will learn to use commas correctly.

What Is a Comma?

A **comma** (,) is a punctuation mark that helps identify distinct ideas. There are many ways to use a comma. In this chapter, you will learn some helpful rules about comma usage.

Notice how comma placement changes the meanings of the following sentences.

The baby hits, her mother cries, and then they hug each other.

The baby hits her mother, cries, and then they hug each other.

Commas in a Series

Use a comma to separate items in a series of three or more items. Remember to put a comma before the final "and."

| Unit 1 | , | unit 2 | , | and/or | unit 3. |

Canada, the United States, and Mexico have psychology conferences.

The experiment required patience, perseverance, and energy.

Some teens may do part-time work, volunteer in the community, and maintain high grades at school.

 **Comma Before *and***

There is a trend in the media to omit the comma before the final *and* in a series. However, in academic writing, it is preferable to include the comma because it clarifies your meaning and makes the items more distinct.

PRACTICE I Underline series of items. Then add fifteen missing commas.

EXAMPLE: Some psychological studies are <u>simple</u>, <u>obvious</u>, and <u>extremely important</u>.

1. Mary Ainsworth was born in Ohio attended the University of Toronto and worked in Uganda. She became an expert in the childhood development field. Ainsworth's most significant research examined the attachment of infants to their caretakers.

2. Ainsworth designed an experiment called *The Strange Situation*. She measured how infants reacted when the primary caretaker left the room a stranger entered and the primary caretaker returned. She determined that children have four attachment styles. They may be secure avoidant ambivalent or disoriented.

3. Secure children may leave their mother's lap explore happily and return to the mother. Avoidant babies are not upset when the mother leaves do not look at the stranger and show little reaction when the mother returns. Ambivalent babies are clinging unwilling to explore and upset by strangers. Disoriented infants react oddly to their mother's return. They look fearful avoid eye contact and slowly approach the returning mother.

Commas After Introductory Words or Phrases

Place a comma after an **introductory word** or **phrase**. Introductory words include interjections (*well*), adverbs (*usually*), or transitional words (*therefore*). Introductory phrases could be transitional expressions (*of course*), prepositional phrases (*in the winter*), or modifiers (*born in Egypt*).

Introductory word(s)	,	sentence.

Introductory word:	<u>Yes</u>, the last stage of life is very important.

Introductory phrase:	<u>After the experiment</u>, the children returned home.
	<u>Feeling bored</u>, he volunteered at a nearby clinic.

PRACTICE 2   Underline each introductory word or phrase. Then add twelve missing commas.

EXAMPLE: <u>Before leaving home,</u> adolescents assert their independence.
_∧

1. In *Childhood and Society* Erik Erikson explained his views about the stages of life. According to Erikson there are eight life stages. In his opinion each stage is characterized by a developmental crisis.

2. In the infancy stage babies must learn to trust others. Wanting others to fulfill their needs babies expect life to be pleasant. Neglected babies may end up mistrusting the world.

3. During adolescence a young man or woman may have an identity crisis. Confronted with physical and emotional changes teenagers must develop a sense of self. According to Erikson some adolescents are unable to solve their identity crisis. Lacking self-awareness they cannot commit to certain goals and values.

4. In Erikson's view each crisis must be solved before a person develops in the next life stage. For example a person may become an adult chronologically. However that person is not an adult emotionally.

Commas Around Interrupting Words or Phrases

Interrupting words or phrases appear in the middle of sentences, and while they interrupt the sentence's flow, they do not affect its overall meaning. Some interrupters are *as a matter of fact*, *as you know*, and *for example*. Prepositional phrases can also interrupt sentences.

Sentence,	interrupter,	sentence continued.

The doctor, <u>for example</u>, has never studied child psychology.

Adolescence, <u>as you know</u>, is a difficult life stage.

The child, <u>with no prompting</u>, started to laugh.

> ### Hint · Using Commas with Appositives
>
> An appositive gives further information about a noun or pronoun. The appositive can appear at the beginning, in the middle, or at the end of the sentence. Set off appositives with commas.
>
> beginning
> A large hospital, the Hospital for Sick Children has some of the world's best researchers.
>
> middle
> Gail Sheehy, a journalist, has written about life passages.
>
> end
> The doctor's office is next to Sims Wholesale, a local grocery store.

PRACTICE 3   The following sentences contain introductory words and phrases, interrupters, and series of items. Add the missing commas. If the sentence is correct, write C in the space provided.

EXAMPLE: Erik Erikson, a child development expert, wrote about his identity crisis._____

1. Erik Erikson during his youth, had an identity crisis. _____

2. At the age of sixteen he learned more about his past. _____

3. His mother admitted that Erik was the result of an extramarital affair. _____

4. He felt surprised, confused and angry. _____

5. At that time, he did not know his birth father. _____

6. Erikson's mother a Danish woman had moved to Germany. _____

7. His adopted father a pediatrician named Theodore Homburger was Jewish. _____

8. Erikson felt confused about his nationality his religion, and his genealogy. _____

9. In the early 1920s, Erikson went to Vienna. _____

10. Erikson, at a conference met Anna Freud. _____

11. Anna Freud Sigmund Freud's daughter, analyzed Erikson. _____

12. Using psychoanalysis she helped him resolve his identity crisis. _____

Commas in Compound Sentences

In compound sentences, place a comma before the coordinating conjunction (*for*, *and*, *nor*, *but*, *or*, *yet*, *so*).

Sentence	**, and**	**sentence.**

Adulthood has three stages, **and** each stage has its particular challenge.

Carolina lives with her mother, **but** she is very independent.

She goes to school, **yet** she also works forty hours a week.

Hint **Commas and Coordinators**

To ensure that a sentence is compound, cover the conjunction with your finger and read the two parts of the sentence. If one part of the sentence is incomplete, then no comma is necessary. If each part of the sentence contains a complete idea, then you need to add a comma.

> **No comma:** Ben still lives with his parents **but** is very self-sufficient.
>
> **Comma:** Ben still lives with his parents, **but** he is very self-sufficient.

PRACTICE 4   Edit the following paragraphs and add ten missing commas.

EXAMPLE: She is not an adult, yet she is not a child.

1. Adulthood is another stage in life but the exact age of adulthood is unclear.

    Some cultures celebrate adulthood with high school graduation

    ceremonies and others celebrate with marriage. Some people define

    adulthood as the moment a person has full-time work and is self-sufficient

    yet many people become independent only in their thirties.

2. Cultures treat early adulthood differently. Irene Berridge, who was born and raised in Medicine Hat, Alberta, has a culturally mixed background. Her mother is German and her father is British. She was encouraged to leave home and get an apartment at age nineteen. Today, twenty-one-year-old Irene washes her clothing at a laundromat and she does her own cooking. She has a part-time job and she splits the bills with her roommate.

3. Alexis Khoury's parents are recent immigrants from Greece and they want their daughter to stay home until she marries. Alexis is a thirty-one-year-old Montrealer and she sometimes feels embarrassed to be living at home. She does not feel like an adult and her parents encourage her dependence. However, Alexis will respect her parents' wishes and she will not leave home until she has found a life partner.

Commas in Complex Sentences

A **complex sentence** contains one or more dependent clauses (or incomplete ideas). When you add a **subordinating conjunction**—a word such as *because*, *although*, or *unless*—to a clause, you make the clause dependent.

        dependent clause   independent clause

After <u>Jason graduated from college</u>, he moved out of the family home.

Use a Comma After a Dependent Clause

If a sentence begins with a dependent clause, place a comma after the clause. Remember that a dependent clause has a subject and a verb, but it cannot stand alone. When the subordinating conjunction comes in the middle of the sentence, it is not necessary to use a comma.

> **Dependent clause,**   main clause.

Comma: <u>When I find a better job,</u> I will move into an apartment.

> Main clause   **dependent clause.**

No comma: I will move into an apartment <u>when I find a better job</u>.

PRACTICE 5   Edit the following sentences by adding or deleting commas.

EXAMPLE: Although twenty-eight-year-old Samuel Chong lives at home, he
is not ashamed.
        ^

1. When he examined the 2001 census Mark Noble noticed a clear trend.

2. Although most people in their twenties lived on their own about forty
   percent of young adults still lived with their parents.

3. In 1981, the results were different, because only twenty-five percent of
   young adults lived at home.

4. After examining the statistics Noble determined several causes for the shift.

5. Because the marriage rate is declining fewer people buy their own homes.

6. When the cost of education increases people cannot afford to study and
   pay rent.

7. Other young adults stay with their parents, because the rents are so high.

8. Because these conditions are not changing many young adults will likely
   continue to stay with their parents.

CHAPTER 28

Use Commas to Set Off Non-restrictive Clauses

Clauses beginning with *who*, *that*, and *which* can be restrictive or non-restrictive. A **restrictive clause** contains essential information about the subject. Do not place commas around restrictive clauses. In the following example, the underlined clause is essential to understand the meaning of the sentence.

No commas: The only local company <u>that creates computer graphics</u> has no job openings.

A **non-restrictive clause** gives non-essential or additional information about the noun but does not restrict or define the noun. Place commas around non-restrictive clauses. In the following sentence, the underlined clause contains extra information, but if you removed that clause, the sentence would still have a clear meaning.

Commas: Her book, <u>which is in bookstores</u>, is about successful entrepreneurs.

 Hint   **Which, That, and Who**

Which   Use commas to set off clauses that begin with *which*.
   The brain, **which** is a complex organ, develops rapidly.
That   Do not use commas to set off clauses that begin with *that*.
   The house **that** I grew up in was demolished last year.
Who   If the *who* clause contains non-essential information, put commas around it. If the *who* clause is essential to the meaning of the sentence, then it does not require commas.

   Essential: Many people **who** have brain injuries undergo subtle personality changes.

   Not essential: Dr. Jay Giedd, **who** lives in Maryland, made an important discovery.

PRACTICE 6   Edit the following sentences by adding twelve missing commas.

EXAMPLE: The neurologist, whom I have never met, made an exciting discovery.

1. Twenty years ago, scientists thought that the brain stopped changing at an early age. They believed that after children reached twelve years of age their brains would stop growing. In 1997, a team of doctors who specialized in brain research made an exciting discovery. Neuroscientist Dr. Jay Giedd who works at the National Institute of Mental Health realized that brain cells have a growth spurt just before puberty. Scientists discovered that myelin which connects brain cells increases during adolescence. However, not all parts of the brain receive myelin at once, and the last region to receive it is the frontal lobe.

2. The frontal lobe, which is responsible for rational decision making stops an individual from making impulsive choices. For example imagine that you are driving your car. When another car cuts you off the primitive part of your brain wants to hurt the other driver. The frontal lobe helps you to think about alternatives. Thus, you may simply accept that all drivers make mistakes.

3. According to specialists the delay in receiving myelin to the frontal lobe affects many teens, and they may have trouble curbing their impulses. They may react quickly violently or irrationally, and are more likely than people in other age groups to engage in risky behaviour. When the frontal lobe has fully developed people generally become less impulsive.

FINAL REVIEW

Edit this essay by adding seventeen missing commas and removing three unnecessary commas.

EXAMPLE: If people want to have longer lives they can exercise, eat well, and avoid risky behaviour.

1. In 350 BCE, Aristotle wrote an essay about life spans. Everybody has a maximum life span and nothing can be done to prolong that span. Until recently scientists agreed with Aristotle. They would argue that today's life expectancies are about as high as they can possibly get. However a group of researchers believes that human life expectancy will increase significantly in the future.

2. Dr. James Vaupel a researcher at Duke University, believes that our lifespan can be extended significantly. He gives a concrete example. In 1840, Swedish women had the world's longest life expectancy and the average Swedish woman lived to age forty-five. Today, Japanese women,

who live to an average age of eighty-five have the world's longest life expectancy. This huge increase in life expectancy was partly due to the decrease in infant mortality. In 1800, about 25 percent of babies died in the first year of life. Surgery vaccines and antibiotics have helped to lower the childhood death rates. Also, because they have access to new medical interventions people over age sixty-five are living longer. Still, only about 2 percent of the population lives to one hundred years of age.

3. According to Dr. Vaupel, today's babies will have much longer life expectancies than their parents had and half of all newborns could live to one hundred years of age. Dr. Aubrey De Grey, a professor at Cambridge University believes that human life expectancy will increase to five hundred years or more. Certainly, there are very promising discoveries on the horizon. Cures for cancer, and heart disease will help increase life expectancy. Also, because so many women delay childbirth the period of human fertility may lengthen which could have an eventual impact on life expectancy.

4. Some experts disagree with Vaupel and De Grey. Leonard Hayflick, discovered that human cells divide and reproduce about fifty times before slowing down and stopping. The longest average lifespan humans can attain in Hayflick's view is 120 years of age. However, some research labs are experimenting with ways of increasing the lifespan of cells. For example scientists have isolated a part of the chromosome that shrinks with age. If scientists find a way to slow down cell aging the results could significantly increase life expectancies of all humans.

5. A very long life expectancy, would force humans to rethink life stages. When would childhood end? Would you want to live to 150 years of age or more?

The Writer's Room **Topics for Writing**

Write about one of the following topics. After you finish writing, make sure that you have used commas correctly.

1. What problems could occur if human life expectancy were to become a lot longer? Think about the effects of an increased lifespan.

2. Which life stage is the most interesting? Give anecdotes to back up your views.

 CHECKLIST: COMMAS

When you edit your writing, ask yourself these questions.

☐ Do I use commas correctly? Remember to use commas in these situations:

- between words in a series of items
- after an introductory word or phrase
- around an interrupting word or phrase

   The conference will be in Halifax, Edmonton, or Vancouver.

   Beyond a doubt, many psychologists will attend.

   The key speaker, in my opinion, is extremely interesting.

☐ Do I use commas correctly in compound and complex sentences? Remember to use commas in these situations:

- before the coordinator in a compound sentence
- after a dependent clause in a complex sentence

   She will discuss brain development, and she will present case studies.

   When her presentation ends, participants can ask questions.

CHAPTER 28

How Do I Get a Better Grade?

mycanadiancomplab

Go to www.mycanadiancomplab.ca for additional help with your grammar, writing, and research skills. You will have access to a variety of exercises, instruction, and video that will help you improve your basic skills and help you get a better grade.

Apostrophes

CHAPTER 29

CONTENTS

- What Is an Apostrophe?
- Apostrophes in Contractions
- Apostrophes to Show Ownership
- Apostrophes in Expressions of Time

Section Theme **HUMAN DEVELOPMENT**

In this chapter, you will read about artistic ability and creativity.

Man Reclining, 1978, Fernando Botero, Private Collection.

Grammar Snapshot

Looking at Apostrophes

In an interview with Diane Sawyer for *ABC News*, musician Paul McCartney discusses his art show and his initial feelings about painting. Review the highlighted words. Discuss what the long form of each contraction is.

The way I was brought up, in the working class, only people who went to art school painted. It wasn't for us to paint. We didn't ride horses. They did. You know, we'd ride bikes if we were lucky. I would've felt like I was a bit uppity to paint, you know. "Oh, you're painting now, are you?"

In this chapter, you will learn to use apostrophes correctly.

What Is an Apostrophe?

An **apostrophe** is a punctuation mark showing a contraction or ownership.

Emma **Chong's** art gallery is very successful, and **it's** still growing.

Apostrophes in Contractions

To form a **contraction**, join two words into one and add an apostrophe to replace the omitted letter(s). The following are examples of common contractions.

- **Join a verb with *not*.** The apostrophe replaces the letter *o* in not.

is + not = isn't	has + not = hasn't
are + not = aren't	have + not = haven't
could + not = couldn't	should + not = shouldn't
do + not = don't	would + not = wouldn't
does + not = doesn't	

  Exceptions: will + not = <u>won't</u>   can + not = can't

- **Join a subject and a verb.** Sometimes you must remove several letters to form the contraction.

I + will = I'll	she + will = she'll
I + would = I'd	Tina + is = Tina's
he + is = he's	they + are = they're
he + will = he'll	we + will = we'll
Joe + is = Joe's	who + is = who's
she + has = she's	who + would = who'd

  Exception: Do not contract a subject with the past tense of *be*. For example, do not contract *he + was* or *they + were*.

Hint **Common Apostrophe Errors**

- Do not use apostrophes before the final *-s* of a verb or a plural noun.

  Mr. Gaudet ~~want's~~ to open several ~~gallery's~~.

- In contractions with *not*, remember that the apostrophe usually replaces the missing *o*.

  doesn't
  He ~~does'nt~~ understand the problem.

PRACTICE 1 Edit the following sentences for fifteen apostrophe errors. Each word counts as one error.

EXAMPLE: Making a great work of art ~~isnt~~ *isn't* a simple process.

1. Whos a great artist? Why do some people have amazing artistic abilities whereas others do'nt? Researchers in biology, sociology, and psychology haven't unlocked the keys to human creativity. However, expert's in each field have proposed theories about creativity.

2. Sigmund Freud proposed that creativity is an occurrence of the subconscious. If someones in pain, he or she may create an artwork to relieve the suffering. Near the end of his life, Freud changed his mind. He said that he didnt believe that suffering was a prerequisite to creativity.

3. Neurologists look inside the brain to answer questions about creativity. Theyve said that the left portion of the brains responsible for logical processing and verbal skills. The right sides responsible for artistic, abstract thinking. In the past, neurologists did'nt believe that the left side of the brain had an impact on creative impulses, but recent brain scan's have shown that both sides of the brain are used in creative thinking.

4. Whats the source of creativity? Maybe its never going to be understood. What everybody know's for certain is that artistic talent isnt evenly distributed. Some people are'nt as talented as others.

> ## Hint > Contractions with Two Meanings
>
> Sometimes one contraction can have two different meanings.
>
> **I'd** = I had *or* I would   **He's** = he is *or* he has
>
> When you read, you should be able to figure out the meaning of the contraction by looking at the words in context.
>
> **Joe's** working on a painting. **Joe's** been working on it for a month.
> (Joe is)   (Joe has)

PRACTICE 2   Look at each underlined contraction, and then write out the complete words.

EXAMPLE: They <u>weren't</u> ready to start a business.   ___*were not*___

1. Rachel <u>Wood's</u> very happy with her sculpture.   _____

2. <u>She's</u> been a professional artist since 2002.   _____

3. <u>She's</u> an extremely creative woman.   _____

4. I wish <u>I'd</u> gone to art school.   _____

5. <u>I'd</u> like to be an artist, too.   _____

Apostrophes to Show Ownership

You can also use apostrophes to show ownership. Review the following rules.

Possessive Form of Singular Nouns

Add -'s to the end of a singular noun to indicate ownership. If the singular noun ends in *s*, you add -'s if you would pronounce it (boss's). If you would not pronounce the additional *s*, then just add an apostrophe (Moses').

Lautrec's artwork was very revolutionary.

Morris's wife is a professional dancer.

Possessive Form of Plural Nouns

When a plural noun ends in *-s*, just add an apostrophe to indicate ownership.
Add *-'s* to irregular plural nouns.

> Many **galleries'** websites contain images of some of the artworks.
>
> The **men's** and **women's** paintings are in separate rooms.

Possessive Form of Compound Nouns

When two people have joint ownership, add the apostrophe to the second name.
When two people have separate ownership, add apostrophes to both names.

Joint ownership: Marian and **Jake's** gallery is successful.

Separate ownership: **Marian's** and **Jake's** studios are in different buildings.

PRACTICE 3   Write the possessive forms of the following phrases.

EXAMPLE: the sister of the doctor   *the doctor's sister* _____

1. the brush of the artist   _____

2. the brushes of the artists   _____

3. the lights in the studio   _____

4. the room of the child   _____

5. the rooms of the children   _____

6. the entrances of the galleries   _____

7. the photo of Ross and Anna   _____

8. the photo of Ross and the
   photo of Anna   _____

> ### Hint > Possessive Pronouns Do Not Have Apostrophes
>
> Some contractions sound like possesive pronouns. For example, *you're* sounds like *your* and *it's* sounds like *its*. Remember that possesive pronouns never have apostrophes.
>
>   *its*
> The conference is on ~~it's~~ last day.
>
>   *yours*   *hers*
> The document is ~~your's~~ and not ~~her's~~.

PRACTICE 4   Correct nine errors. You may need to add, move, or remove apostrophes.

1. Many artist's paintings are unique. Have you ever heard of Fernando Botero? The Colombian painters work has been exhibited in a Quebec City museum. Several of his painting's have also appeared in Vancouver galleries.

2. Botero's paintings usually contain images of people. What makes his work unique is it's humour. He makes generals, religious figures, and dictators look like children. Theyre small and bloated, and the images are filled with colour.

3. Another great artist is Georgia O'Keeffe. Its not difficult to recognize an artwork that is her's. Shes known for her paintings of white bones, bull skulls, and flowers. In many art collections, youll find her artwork.

Apostrophes in Expressions of Time

If an expression of time (*year, week, month, day*) appears to possess something, you can add -'s.

> Alice Ray gave two **weeks**' notice before she left the dance company.

When you write out a year in numerals, an apostrophe can replace the missing numbers.

> The graduates of the class of '**99** hoped to find good jobs.

However, if you are writing the numeral of a decade or century, do not put an apostrophe before the final -s.

> In the **1900s**, many innovations in art occurred.

PRACTICE 5 Correct ten errors. You may need to add, move, or remove apostrophes.

                   doesn't
EXAMPLE: Octavio Cruz ~~doesnt~~ have a studio.

1. In the summer of 2000, Winnipeg construction worker Octavio Cruz did a

   years worth of painting. He felt incredibly inspired. In the early 1990's,

   hed sold some artworks, but his paintings were uninspired, and he had

   trouble becoming motivated. Then, in 1999, he was in a car accident. He

   spent three week's in a hospital. Since then, hes been extremely creative.

   His wife's astonishment is evident: "Hes a different man," she says. "His

   paintings are so much more vivid and colourful."

2. Cruz has been studied by a neurologist, Dr. Wade. The doctors theory is

   that Cruzs injury "disinhibited" his right brain, thus allowing him to

   become more creative. Many other peoples stories are similar to Cruz's. In

   fact, since the 1970's, scientists have recognized that certain brain injuries

   can stimulate creativity.

FINAL REVIEW

Edit the following paragraphs and correct fifteen apostrophe errors. You may need to add, remove, or move apostrophes.

Donald Martin, after Van der Weyden (20th Century American), "Portrait", Airbrush on wood. © Donald C. Martin/SuperStock.

EXAMPLE: What is an ~~artists~~ *artist's* motivation to create?

1. In 1982, Dr. Teresa Amabile made an interesting study in creativity. For Amabiles study, she divided schoolgirl's into two groups. Both groups rooms were filled with collage material, including coloured paper, paste, and construction paper. The doctor chose collage-making because it doesnt require drawing skills.

2. Each group was invited to an "art party" in a separate room. The first groups goal was to create art to win a prize, such as a toy. The doctor offered toys to the best three artists. Thus, the childrens motivation to create was to win the exciting prize. The girls in the second group didnt have to compete for a prize. They were simply told that three name's would be randomly drawn for prizes.

3. The doctors hypothesis was that a persons creativity would lessen if he or she were motivated by a reward. Amabile asked local artists and art critics to judge the collages when the children werent in the room. The judges scores for the first group were consistently lower than those for the second group. Thus, the doctors hypothesis was correct. A reward, such as money or a prize, isnt helpful to the creative process. When people create art for arts sake, they tend to be more imaginative.

The Writer's Room Topics for Writing

Write about one of the following topics. After you finish writing, make sure that you have used apostrophes correctly.

1. Describe the work of a painter, illustrator, photographer, or sculptor that you like. Explain what is most interesting about that artist's work.

2. Define one of these terms: *creativity, graffiti, art, vandalism,* or *beauty.*

CHECKLIST: APOSTROPHES

When you edit your writing, ask yourself these questions.

☐ Do I use apostrophes correctly? Check for errors in these cases:

- contractions of verbs + *not* or subjects and verbs
- possessives of singular and plural nouns (*the student's* versus *the students'*)
- possessives of irregular plural nouns (*the women's*)
- possessives of compound nouns (*Joe's and Mike's cars*)

> *shouldn't*   *Wong's*
> You ~~should'nt~~ be surprised that Chris ~~Wong'~~ going to exhibit his paintings.
>
> *Chris's*
> ~~Chris'~~ artwork will be on display next week.

☐ Do I place apostrophes where they do not belong? Check for errors in possessive pronouns and present tense verbs.

> *looks*   *its*
> It ~~look's~~ as if the gallery is moving ~~it's~~ collection to Houston.

How Do I Get a Better Grade?

mycanadiancomplab

Go to www.mycanadiancomplab.ca for additional help with your grammar, writing, and research skills. You will have access to a variety of exercises, instruction, and video that will help you improve your basic skills and help you get a better grade.

30 CHAPTER

Quotation Marks, Capitalization, and Titles

Section Theme **HUMAN DEVELOPMENT**

In this chapter, you will read about artists and musicians.

Grammar Snapsh•t

Looking at Quotation Marks

This excerpt is translated from Paul Gauguin's book, *Avant et Après*. It recounts when Vincent Van Gogh cut off part of his own ear. Notice that the quotation marks and some capital letters are highlighted.

> The man in the bowler hat harshly questioned me:"Well, sir, what have you done to your friend?"
>
> "I don't know," I replied.
>
> "But you know that he is dead," he said.
>
> I would not wish such a moment on anyone, and it took me a while before I could think. My heart pounded, and I was choking with anger and pain. I felt everyone's eyes staring at me. I stammered, "Sir, let's go upstairs and discuss it there."

In this chapter, you will learn how to use direct quotations correctly. You will also learn about capitalization and title punctuation.

Quotation Marks (" ")

Use **quotation marks** to set off the exact words of a speaker or writer. When you include the exact words of more than one person in a text, then you must make a new paragraph each time the speaker changes. If the quotation is a complete sentence, punctuate it in the following ways.

- Capitalize the first word of the quotation.
- Place quotation marks around the complete quotation.
- Place the end punctuation inside the closing quotation marks.

> Oscar Wilde declared, "All art is useless."

Generally, attach the name of the speaker or writer to the quotation in some way. Review the following rules.

1. **Introductory phrase**   When the quotation is introduced by a phrase, place a comma after the introductory phrase.

    > Pablo Picasso said, "Art is a lie that makes us realize the truth."

2. **Interrupting phrase**   When the quotation is interrupted, place a comma before and after the interrupting phrase.

    > "In the end," says dancer Martha Graham, "it all comes down to breathing."

3. **End phrase**   When you place a phrase at the end of a quotation, end the quotation with a comma instead of a period.

    > "Great art picks up where nature ends," said Marc Chagall.

    If your quotation ends with other punctuation, put it inside the quotation mark.

    > "Who is the greatest painter?" the student asked.

    > "That question cannot be answered!" the curator replied.

4. **Introductory sentence**   When you introduce a quotation with a complete sentence, place a colon (:) after the introductory sentence.

    > Choreographer George Balanchine explains his philosophy about dance: "Dance is music made visible."

5. **Inside quotations**   If one quotation is inside another quotation, then use single quotation marks (' ') around the inside quotation.

    > To her mother, Veronica Corelli explained, "I am not sure if I will succeed, but you've always said, 'Your work should be your passion.'"

>  **Integrated Quotations**
>
> If the quotation is not a complete sentence, and you simply integrate it into your sentence, do not capitalize the first word of the quotation.
>
> Composer Ludwig van Beethoven called music "the mediator between the spiritual and the sensual life."

PRACTICE 1   In each sentence, the quotation is set off in bold. Add quotation marks and periods, commas, or colons. Also, capitalize the first word of the quotation, if necessary.

Susan Valadon (1867–1938 French) "Portrait of Madam Coquiot", 1915. Oil on canvas. Musée du Palais Carnoles, Menton, France. © Artists Rights Society (ARS), New York.

EXAMPLE: Professor Wayne Johnson asks ~~where are~~ , "W where are the great female artists?"

1. Art student Alex Beale says **the lack of great female artists throughout history is puzzling**

2. Professor Aline Melnor states **one must consider the conditions for producing art**

3. **Art schools did not accept women** she points out.

4. **Until a hundred years ago, the only alternative to family life for women was the convent** proclaimed writer and feminist Germaine Greer.

5. **Suzanne Valadon** says historian Maria Sage **went from being an artist's model to being an artist**

6. Historian Andre Villeneuve writes that sculptor Camille Claudel was **the mistress of Auguste Rodin**

7. Germaine Greer shows the connection between female and male artists **the painter Rosa Bonheur learned about art from her father, who was also an artist**

CHAPTER 30

8. **In the twer**   **bers of female artists exploded**

   declared gall

9. Angel Trang to   **t I shouldn't have drawn on the walls, but you**   **rself**

10. Louise Otto-Pete   bout women in the arts **women will be forgotten**   **bout themselves**

PRACTICE 2   rors in the following dialogue.

EXAMPLE: She told me   nds ⁑.

Jamilla was concerned   understand why you are leaving college".

Omar looked at her and r   nake it as a musician."

"How will you make a livir

He replied, "I do not need t   e happy."

"You're being very naïve." Ja

Shocked, Omar said, "I'm simp   ou always say, "Find work that you love." "

"Perhaps you have to take some   nded, "and learn from your own mistakes."

Omar stated firmly, "my decision

Using Quotations in   says

Use quotations to reveal the opinions of   leas that are particularly memorable and important. W   ber to limit how many you use in a single paper and t   using both direct and indirect quotations.

CHAPTER 30

(Handwritten note overlay): Quiz #1 Name: Jing Total: 22.5/36

Direct and Indirect Quotations

A **direct quotation** contains the exact words of an author, and the quotation is set off with quotation marks.

> A shopping tip from *Consumer 4 Kids Reports* states, "The name brands are always displayed up front, when you first walk into the department."

An **indirect quotation** keeps the author's meaning but is not set off by quotation marks.

> A shopping tip by the *Consumer 4 Kids Reports* states that name brand clothes are always put on view at the front of the clothing department.

Integrating Quotations

Short Quotations

Introduce short quotations with a phrase or sentence. (Short quotations should not stand alone.) Read the following original selection, and then view how the quotation has been introduced using three common methods. The selection, written by Mary Lou Stribling, appeared on page 6 of her book *Art from Found Materials*.

CHAPTER 30

> **Original Selection**
> Picasso is generally acknowledged as being the first major artist to use found objects in his paintings. About the same time, however, a number of other artists who were active in the Cubist movement began to make similar experiments. The collages of Braque and Gris, which were made of printed letters, newspapers, wallpaper scraps, bottle labels, corrugated cardboard, and other bits of trivia, are especially notable.

1. **Phrase introduction**
   In *Art from Found Materials*, Mary Lou Stribling writes, "Picasso is generally acknowledged as being the first major artist to use found objects in his paintings" (6).

2. **Sentence introduction**
   In her book, *Art from Found Materials*, Mary Lou Stribling suggests that Picasso was not the only artist to use found objects in his work: "About the same time, however, a number of other artists who were active in the Cubist movement began to make similar experiments" (6).

3. **Integrated quotation**
   In *Art from Found Materials*, Mary Lou Stribling reveals that artists incorporated everyday objects into their paintings, including "wallpaper scraps, bottle labels, corrugated cardboard, and other bits of trivia" (6).

CHAPTER 30

> **Hint** **Words That Introduce Quotations**
>
> Here are some common words that can introduce quotations.
>
> | | | | |
> |---|---|---|---|
> | admits | concludes | mentions | speculates |
> | claims | explains | observes | suggests |
> | comments | maintains | reports | warns |
>
> The doctor **states**, "_____."
>
> "_____," **observes** Dr. Hannah.
>
> Dr. Hannah **speculates** that _____.

Long Quotations

If you use a quotation in MLA style that has four or more lines or in APA style that has more than forty words, insert the quotation in your research paper in the following way.

- Introduce the quotation with a sentence ending with a colon.
- Indent the entire quotation about ten spaces from the left margin of your document.
- Use double spacing.
- Do not use quotation marks.
- Cite the author and page number in parentheses after the punctuation mark in the last sentence of the quotation.

Review the next example from a student essay about art history. The quotation is from page 132 of Germaine Greer's *The Obstacle Race*. The explanatory paragraph introduces the quotation and is part of an essay.

> Much great art has been lost due to a variety of factors:
>> Panels decay as wood decays. Canvas rots, tears, and sags. The stretchers spring and warp. As color dries out it loses its flexibility and begins to separate from its unstable ground; dry color flakes off shrinking or swelling wood and drooping canvas. (Greer 132)

> **Hint** **Using Long Quotations**
>
> If your research paper is short (two or three pages), avoid using many long quotations. Long quotations will only overwhelm your own ideas. Instead, try summarizing a long passage or using shorter quotations.

Using Ellipses (. . .)

If you want to quote key ideas from an author, but do not want to quote the entire paragraph, you can use **ellipses**. These three periods show that you have omitted unnecessary information from a quotation. Leave a space before and after each period, and if the omitted section includes complete sentences, add a period before the ellipses.

> The original selection, written by Jeremy Yudkin, appeared in his book *Understanding Music* on page 446. Notice how the quotation changes when the essay writer uses ellipses.

Original Selection
In his early years, Elvis Presley symbolized something very important for American youth. He was the symbol of freedom and rebellion. His unconventional clothes, the messages of his music, and especially his raw sexuality appealed to the new and numerous groups of American teenagers. The spirit of rebellion was in the air.

Quotation with Omissions
In his book *Understanding Music*, Jeremy Yudkin describes the impact of Elvis: "In his early years, Elvis Presley symbolized something very important for American youth. . . . The spirit of rebellion was in the air" (446).

CHAPTER 30

PRACTICE 3   Read the following selection and then use information from it to write direct and indirect quotations. The selection, written by David G. Martin, appeared on page 567 of his book *Psychology*.

Until fairly recently, up to the early or mid-nineteenth century, events that could not be explained were often attributed to supernatural causes. Human behaviour that was bizarre was thought to be the work of demons. Demonology is the study of the ancient belief that mental disorders are caused by possession by demons. Autonomous evil beings were thought to enter a person and control his or her mind and body.

1. Make a direct quotation.

_____

_____

_____

2. Make an indirect quotation.

_____

_____

_____

Capitalization

Remember to capitalize the following:

■ the pronoun **I**

■ the first word of every sentence

> **My** brothers and **I** share an apartment.

There are many other instances in which you must use capital letters. Always capitalize in the following cases.

■ **Days of the week, months, and holidays**

> Thursday   June 22   Labour Day

Do not capitalize the seasons: summer, fall, winter, spring

■ **Titles of specific institutions, departments, companies, and schools**

> Bombardier   Department of Finance   Elmwood Collegiate

Do not capitalize general references.

> the company   the department   the school

■ **Names of specific places such as buildings, streets, parks, cities, provinces, and bodies of water**

> Eiffel Tower   Yonge Street
> Times Square   Saskatchewan
> Edmonton, Alberta   Lake Erie

Do not capitalize general references.

> the street   the province   the lake

■ **Specific languages, nationalities, tribes, races, and religions**

> Greek   Mohawk   Buddhist   a French restaurant

■ **Titles of specific individuals**

> General Dallaire   Professor Sayf
> the President   Prime Minister Blair
> Doctor Blain   Ms. Robinson

CHAPTER 30

If you are referring to the profession in general, or if the title follows the name, do not use capital letters.

my doctor	the professors	Elise Roy, a doctor

- **Specific course and program titles**

Physics 201	Marketing 101	Advanced German

If you refer to a course, but do not mention the course title, then it is not necessary to use capitals.

He is in his math class.	I study engineering.

- **Major words in titles of literary or artistic works**

the *Calgary Herald*	*Corner Gas*	*The Lord of the Rings*

- **Historical events, eras, and movements**

World War II	Post-Impressionism	Baby Boomers

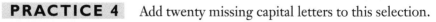

PRACTICE 4   Add twenty missing capital letters to this selection.

EXAMPLE: Mozart was born in ~~s~~alzburg, Austria.
S

1. Erich Schenk describes the life of Wolfgang Amadeus Mozart in his book *Mozart and his times*. Mozart, born on january 27, 1756, was a gifted musician who composed his first pieces at age five. By the age of thirteen, he had written a german and an italian opera. In Salzburg, his employer was prince-archbishop Colloredo. Then, in Vienna, he wrote compositions for emperor joseph II. At that time, Austria was a part of the holy roman empire.

2. Mozart's best-known works include *the marriage of figaro* and *the magic flute*. Mozart, a catholic, died mysteriously at the age of thirty-five, and his body was put into a communal grave, which was the common practice for paupers in Vienna at that time. His final resting place is near a river called the danube.

Titles

Place the title of a short work in quotation marks. Italicize (or underline, if you are not using a computer) the title of a longer document.

Short Works		Long Works	
Short story:	"The Hockey Sweater"	**Novel:**	*The Blind Assassin*
Web article:	"Music Artists Lose Out"	**Website:**	*CNET News.com*
Chapter:	"Early Accomplishments"	**Book:**	*The Art of Emily Carr*
Newspaper article:	"The City's Hottest Ticket"	**Newspaper:**	*Globe and Mail*
Magazine article:	"New Artists"	**Magazine:**	*Rolling Stone*
Essay:	"Hip-Hop Nation"	**Textbook:**	*Common Culture*
TV episode:	"The Search Party"	**TV series:**	*Lost*
Song:	"Mouths to Feed"	**CD:**	*Release Therapy*
Poem:	"Howl"	**Anthology:**	*Collected Poems of Beat Writers*
		Movie:	*Mission Impossible*
		Artwork:	*The Mona Lisa*

Capitalizing Titles

When you write a title, capitalize the first letter of the first and last words and all the major words.

To Kill a Mockingbird
"Stairway to Heaven"
Eight Men Out

Do not capitalize the word ".com" in a web address. Also, do not capitalize the following words, unless they are the first or last word in the title.

Articles:	a, an, the
Coordinators:	but, and, or, nor, for, so, yet
Prepositions:	of, to, in, off, out, up, by . . .

> **Your Own Essay Titles**
>
> In essays that you write for your courses, do not underline your title or put quotation marks around it. Simply capitalize the first word and the main words.
>
> Why Music Is Important

PRACTICE 5 Add twelve capital letters to the following selection. Also, add quotation marks or underlining to five titles.

>   B   W
> **EXAMPLE:** The magazine ~~business week~~ featured successful female entrepreneurs.

1. The singer known as Pink was born Alecia Moore on september 8, 1979. During her teen years, she regularly performed at Club fever near girard street in Philadelphia. One saturday night, after her five-minute slot, a representative from MCA records spotted her and asked her to audition for the band, Basic instinct.

2. After some time playing in bands, Pink decided to become a solo artist. Her first album, called Can't take me home, was released in 2000. It was a double platinum hit, and spun off three singles. Pink then went on to record Patti LaBelle's hit song Lady Marmalade with three other artists. In the april 2006 issue of Rolling Stone, Barry Walter reviewed Pink's fourth album I'm Not Dead. He had particular praise for her song Stupid girls.

FINAL REVIEW

Identify and correct twenty-five errors. Look for capitalization errors. Also ensure that titles and quotations have the necessary capital letters, quotation marks, punctuation, and underlining.

EXAMPLE: The marketing manager said, "Each generation is distinct."
                                              ^

1. People who belong to a generation may have wildly different life experiences. Nonetheless, as Ted Rall points out in his book Marketing Madness, "you are more likely to share certain formative experiences and attitudes about life with your age cohorts".

2. In the last century, each generation was anointed with a title. F. Scott Fitzgerald named his cohorts when he wrote the book, The Jazz Age, which described 1920s flappers who frequented jazz clubs. Tom Brokaw, in his book <u>The greatest generation</u>, discussed people who came of age in the 1930s. Born between 1911 and 1924, they grew up during the Great depression. However, perhaps the best-known spokesperson for a generation is Douglas Coupland.

CHAPTER 30

3. Douglas Coupland was born in 1961 and raised in Vancouver, british Columbia. Even as a young student at Sentinel secondary school, Coupland knew that he would be an artist. When he got older, he took Sculpture classes at Vancouver's Emily Carr institute of Art and design. He also studied at the European Design Institute in italy. As a sculptor,

Coupland had some success and, in november 1987, he had a solo show called "The floating world" at an art gallery in Vancouver.

4. Most know Coupland from his second career. While writing a comic strip for the magazine Vista, Coupland was approached by St. Martin's press and asked to write a guidebook about his generation. Instead, he wrote a complete novel called <u>generation X.</u>

5. Coupland's novel, which describes the generation that came of age in the 1970s and 1980s, is filled with original terminology. For instance, Coupland writes: "Clique maintenance is the need of one generation to see the generation following it as deficient so as to bolster its own collective ego". One chapter in his book is called "Our Parents had more." On page 27, a character has a mid-twenties breakdown that occurs because of "An inability to function outside of school or structured environments coupled with a realization of one's essential aloneness in the world."

6. Every current generation has unique characteristics. Music, clothing, and slang words help define a generation. What name will define the youths who are growing up today?

The Writer's Room **Topics for Writing**

Write about one of the following topics. Include some direct quotations. Proofread to ensure that your punctuation and capitalization is correct.

1. List some characteristics of your generation. What political events, social issues, music, and fashion bind your generation?

2. List three categories of art. Describe some details about each category.

3. Examine the photograph. What do you think the people are saying to each other? Write a brief dialogue from their conversation.

READING LINK

Human Development

These readings contain more information about human development.

"Twixters," by Betsy Hart (page 529)

"Religious Faith versus Spirituality," by Neil Bissoondath (page 531)

"Medicating Ourselves," by Robyn Sarah (page 534)

 CHECKLIST: QUOTATION MARKS

When you edit your writing, ask yourself these questions.

☐ Are there any direct quotations in my writing? Check for errors with these elements:
- punctuation before or after quotations
- capital letters
- placement of quotation marks

  "Art is making something out of nothing and selling it," said musician Frank Zappa.

☐ Do my sentences have all the necessary capital letters?

  War
  Carr's greatest works were painted after World ~~war~~ I.

☐ Are the titles of small and large artistic works properly punctuated?

  Above the Trees.
  Emily Carr's painting was called ~~Above the Trees~~.

How Do I Get a Better Grade?

Editing Practice

To conquer Mount Everest, climbers meet the physical and mental challenges through practice and training. To write good essays, students perfect their skills by revising and editing.

Why Bother Editing?

After you finish writing the first draft of an essay, always make time to edit it. Editing for errors in grammar, punctuation, sentence structure, and capitalization can make the difference between a failing paper and a passing one or a good essay and a great one. Editing is not always easy; it takes time and attention to detail. But it gets easier the more you do it. Also, the more you edit your essays (and your peers' essays, too), the better your writing will be, and the less time you will need to spend editing!

PRACTICE I   EDIT AN ESSAY

Correct fifteen errors in this student essay. An editing symbol appears above each error. To understand the meaning of each symbol, refer to the revising and editing symbols on the inside back cover of this book.

Climbing Everest

1   The Nepalese and Indians name it Sagarmatha, and people from Tibet call

it Qomolangma. The rest of the world knows it as *cap* mount Everest. In 1852, a

geological survey of the Himalayan mountain range identified the highest peak as

"Peak XV." By 1865, the British named the peak "Everest" after a surveyor named

Sir George Everest. For mountain climbers, Everest became a challenge as soon

shift
as it is named the highest peak in the world.

2   By 1921, Tibet opened *sp* it's borders to the outside and gave climbers easy access

to Everest. The first Europeans to attempt to climb Everest were George Mallory

ro
and Andrew Irvine in 1924, unfortunately, they both perished in the attempt.

Many other unsuccessful endeavours were made to reach the Everest summit.

Then in 1953, Edmund Hillary, a New Zealander, and Tenzing Norgay, a Nepalese

Sherpa, became the first climbers to reach the top of the world at 8848 metres

above sea level. Both men became world-famous *sp* heros. In addition, in 1978, two

Austrian climbers, Reinhold Messner and Peter Habeler, reached the Everest summit without the aid of supplemental oxygen. Two years later, Messner again

frag

attained the summit without extra oxygen. A solo climb.

vt

3   Since 1921, around 2200 mountaineers reached the summit; others have paid

sp

a great price. About 185 climbers have died in the attemt. There is a graveyard on the ascent to the summit. Mountaineers see the remains of corpses, tents, and

//

bottles that were filled with oxygen. The dead remain on Everest. Even if climbers

shift

wanted to carry the corpses down, you could not because of altitude.

ad

4   The popularity of climbing the world's most highest peak has become so great that critics call Everest just another tourist trap. Many climbers set up businesses

pl

as guides. A Nepalese businessmen is planning to develop a cyber café at the base

agr

camp, and some snowboarders want to surf down from the summit. There are also a lot of trash on the summit trail. Nonetheless, Everest still catches the

pl

imagination of persons all over the world.

PRACTICE 2 EDIT AN ESSAY

Correct fourteen errors in this student essay. An editing symbol appears above each error. To understand the meaning of each symbol, refer to the revising and editing symbols on the inside back cover of this book.

The Man Who Discovered King Tutankhamen

1   Howard Carter's persistence helped him make a great contribution to the history of human civilization. Carter was born in 1874 near London, England. He became interested in Egyptology at the age of 17, when he was working in Egypt on an archaeological sight. His job was to trace drawings and inscriptions. Howard Carter discovered one of the greatest archaeological finds in history: the tomb of King Tutankhamen.

2   At the age of twenty-five Carter became the first inspector general for monuments in Upper Egypt. He was responsible for supervising digs around the area of the Valley of the Kings. Which had a great number of tombs. He became very fascinating by the story of the young pharaoh, King Tutankhamen, and he was absolutly certain that the king's tomb was located in the general area of the Valley of the Kings.

3   For excavations, Carter received funding from Lord Carnarvon, a wealthy

patron of many digs. From 1914 to 1922, Carnarvon funded Carters search for the

legendary tomb of King Tut. By 1922, Lord Carnarvon became frustrated at the

lack of success and decided that he would support the search for only one more

year. Carter got real lucky when, one morning, one of his workers tripped over a

flat rock, when Carter went to see what it was, he realized that it was the top of a

staircase.

4   Carter was elated by the discovery but his workers had a completely different

reaction. They were convinced that the tomb had a curse on it. Whoever broke

the door seal was doomed for death. Carter ignored the superstition. And went

inside the tomb. Inside he found everything intact and spent the next ten years

cataloguing his find. Some people continued to believe at the curse and blamed

it for the death of six workers. An urban legend eventually formed called the

Mummy's Curse, which exagerated the power of the curse. Carter never believed

in no curse, and he dies of natural causes at the age of sixty-six.

PRACTICE 3   EDIT A FORMAL LETTER

Correct twelve errors in this formal business letter.

George Bates

5672 Manet street west

St.-Jérôme, QC J7Z 4V2

August 15, 2008

Customer Service

The Furniture store

1395 Division Street

Montreal, QC H3T 1L9

Subject: Desk

Attention: Sales manager

I bought a desk from your store on august 13 2008, and the store delivered it thursday morning. After the delivery people had left, I discovered a large scratch on the surface of the desk. Its also lopsided. Since I have always found your products to be of excellent quality I would like to have replacement desk delivered to my home and the damaged desk taken away. If you do not have replacement desk of the same model, then I would like to have a full reimbursement.

Thank you very much for your co-operation in this matter I look forward to receiving my new desk.

Yours sincerly,

George Bates

George Bates

PRACTICE 4   EDIT AN ESSAY

Correct twenty errors in the following essay.

Discovering Venice

1   My brother and me are spending this summer in one of the most beautiful city in the world. Venice, Italy. It is unique because it is composed of a number of small islands in the Adriatic sea. It has over one hundred canals and over four hundred bridges. One of Italy's must-see places, Venice has an intriguing history.

2   Venice was founded in the fifth century by Romans escaping the ferocious Gothic tribes. According to legend. In the tenth century, Venice became a city of wealthy merchants who profited from the Crusades. By the twelfth century, after its successful war against Genoa, Venice had become a powerful city-state, trading with the Byzantines, the Arabs, and many others.

3   One of it's most famous citizens was the explorer Marco Polo (1254–1324), a businessman who was one of the first europeans to reach China. Him and his father spent about twenty-four years in China and was reputedly friends and confidants of Kublai Khan, the emperor of China. Polo may have brought back noodles from China. Which have become the basis for italian pasta.

4   When the Polos returned from China, they recounted the adventures they had had. The citizens of Venice did not believe them. Even today, scholars differ about weather Marco Polo actually reached China. Some say it was highly unlikly because he did not mention things such as chopsticks tea, or Chinese script. Others think that Polo reached China because he talked about paper money and the Chinese postal system.

5   Venice been written about in many works of fiction. For example, Shakespeare's *Merchant of Venice* is set in this city. Shakespeare also set the first part of his tragedy *Othello* in Venice. In fact, the first scenes of the Shakespearean tragedy takes place in the Duke's palace. Another famous book, Thomas Mann's Death in Venice, takes place on a Venetian island that is popular among tourists.

6   My brother has travelled more than me, and he says that of all the cities he's seen, Venice is his absolute favourite. If I would have known how fascinating the city is, I would have visited it a long time ago.

PRACTICE 5   EDIT A WORKPLACE MEMO

Correct ten errors in the following excerpt from a memo.

To: Career development faculty members

From: Maddison Healy

Re: Internships

I'm gonna take this opportunity to remind you that their are financial resources to hiring two new interns for the Career development Program. If anyone wishes to participate in this collaboration, please let Danielle or I know. The current deadline for applying to the internship program is the beginning of april. The internship program, provides valuable mentoring to college students. Treating an intern with respect, it is very important. If you hire an intern, you are responsible for training them. Also, you must provide constructive feedback to the intern and to the college administrator. For those who are interested, please let me know as quick as possible.

PRACTICE 6   EDIT A SHORT ARTICLE

Correct fifteen errors in the following selection.

Forget What Your Grade Five Teacher Taught You

1   The solar system no longer has nine planets, on August 24, 2006, the International Astronomical union, which has a voting membership of about 2500 scientists, met in Prague. It decided to demote Pluto from a planet to a dwarf planet. The astronomers said that Pluto does not exhibit the same characteristics as the other major planets. According to scientists, a planet must orbit the sun, it must be having a spherical shape, and it must have a clear orbit. Unfortunatly, Pluto's orbit overlaps Neptune's orbit, so it does not meet the third criterion for a planet.

2   At the begining of the twentieth century, much astronomers suspected the possibility of another planet in the solar system. In 1930, while working for the Lowell Conservatory in Flagstaff, Arizona, astronomer Clyde Tombaugh took photographs of a sphere that was composed mainly of ices and rocks. It also had a satellite, Charon, orbiting it. Eventualy, this sphere became the nineth planet in the solar system.

3   Scientists were very exciting about the discovery. People from all over the world suggested names for the new planet. The scientists from the observatory received so many suggestions that they had difficulty choosing one. An eleven-years-old girl from Oxford, England, suggested the name Pluto. Venetia Burney was interested in Greek and Roman mythology, and Pluto is the Roman name

for Hades, the Greek god of the Dead. She was giving her suggestion to her grand-father, who then wired it to the Lowell Observatory.

4   The scientific community and the public have had a mixed reaction to the declassification of Pluto. As a planet. Some refuse to accept it. But I wonder why are they resistant. Perhaps teachers don't wanna change astronomy textbooks. Maybe humans feel particularly wary when the scientific community "revises" what it once asked them to accept as fact.

How Do I Get a Better Grade?

mycanadiancomplab

Go to www.mycanadiancomplab.ca for additional help with your grammar, writing, and research skills. You will have access to a variety of exercises, instruction, and video that will help you improve your basic skills and help you get a better grade.

Reading Strategies and Selections

PART V

In this chapter, the essays are organized according to the same themes used in the grammar chapters. The predominant writing pattern of each essay is shown in parentheses.

From Reading to Writing

Aspiring actors study ordinary people, psychological profiles, and the work of other actors to fully develop the characters they play. In the same way, by observing how different writers create their work, you can learn how to use those techniques in your own writing.

Reading Strategies

The reading strategies discussed in this chapter can help you develop your writing skills. They can also help you become a more active reader. You will learn about previewing, finding the main and supporting ideas, understanding difficult words, and recognizing irony. When you read, you expand your vocabulary and learn how other writers develop topics. You also learn to recognize and use different writing patterns. Finally, reading helps you find ideas for your own essays.

"You don't have to burn books to destroy a culture. Just get people to stop reading them."

RAY BRADBURY, AUTHOR

Previewing

Previewing is like glancing through a magazine in a bookstore; it gives you a chance to see what the writer is offering. When you preview, look quickly for the following visual clues so that you can determine the selection's key ideas:

- Titles or subheadings (if any)
- The first and last sentence of the introduction
- The first sentence of each paragraph
- The concluding sentences
- Any photos, graphs, or charts

Finding the Main Idea

After you finish previewing, read the selection carefully. Search for the **main idea**, which is the central point that the writer is trying to make. In an essay, the main idea usually appears somewhere in the first few paragraphs in the form of a thesis statement. However, some professional writers build up to the main idea and state it only in the middle or at the end of the essay. Additionally, some professional writers do not state the main idea directly.

 **Hint** **Making a Statement of the Main Idea**

If the reading does not contain a clear thesis statement, you can determine the main idea by asking yourself *who, what, when, where, why,* and *how* questions. Then, using the answers to those questions, make a statement that sums up the main point of the reading.

Making Inferences

If a professional writer does not state the main idea directly, you must look for clues that will help you to **infer** or figure out what the writer means to say. For example, the next paragraph does not have a topic sentence. However, you can infer the main idea. Underline key words that can lead you to a better understanding of the passage.

> Algie Crivens III was 18 and fresh out of high school in 1991 when he was sentenced to twenty years in prison for a murder he did not commit. He spent the next eight-and-a-half years consumed with educating himself while his appeals crawled through the courts. Crivens is nothing if not energetic; he tends to speak in paragraphs, not sentences. While in prison, he channeled this energy into earning an associate's degree in social science and a bachelor's in sociology. He also took courses in paralegal studies and culinary arts. His fellow prisoners used to ask how he could spend so much time reading. But, to him, reading was a way to escape the boredom of prison life.

—From "Righting a Wrong" by Liliana Ibara

PRACTICE I   Ask yourself the following questions.

1. What is the subject of this text?

   _____

2. What points can you infer that the writer is making? _____

   _____

   _____

Finding the Supporting Ideas

Different writers use different types of supporting ideas. They may give steps for a process, use examples to illustrate a point, give reasons for an argument, and so on. Try to identify the author's supporting ideas.

Highlighting and Making Annotations

After you read a long text, you may forget some of the author's ideas. To help you remember and quickly find the important points, you can highlight key ideas and make annotations. An **annotation** is a comment, question, or reaction that you write in the margins of a passage.

Each time you read a passage, follow these steps:

- Look in the introductory and concluding paragraphs. Underline sentences that sum up the main idea. Using your own words, rewrite the main idea in the margin.
- Underline or highlight supporting ideas. You might even want to number the arguments or ideas. This will allow you to understand the essay's development.
- Circle words that you do not understand.
- Write questions in the margin if you do not understand the author's meaning.
- Write notes beside passages that are interesting or that relate to your own experiences.
- Jot down any ideas that might make interesting writing topics.

Here is an example of a highlighted and annotated passage from an essay titled "Sprawl Fallout" by Patricia L. Kirk.

1   For suburbanites who spend hours in traffic each day commuting to city jobs, the concept of urban sprawl is more than a (euphemism) batted around by city planners. Many commuters know the psychological tolls of their long, slow journeys—irritation, anxiety, less time at home—but the negative impacts might be broader than most realize.

◄ What is a euphemism?

◄ General background for the introduction

◄ Main point suggests urban sprawl is not good.

2   Urban sprawl—a phenomenon that results in people living far from their workplaces—has been linked to asthma, obesity, and just plain foul

◄ Definition of sprawl

Shows the effects of sprawl

Traffic jams drive me crazy.

➤ moods. In one study, people with long commutes reported more headaches, stomach problems, and fatigue than people with shorter drives. Irritability from long commutes was also shown to transfer to job performance, ➤ resulting in lower productivity.

Understanding Difficult Words

When you come across an unfamiliar word in a passage, do not stop reading to look up its definition in the dictionary. First, try using context clues to figure out the term's meaning on your own. If you still do not understand the word, circle it to remind you to look up its meaning in the dictionary when you have finished reading through the passage. You can keep a list of new vocabulary in the "Vocabulary Log" at the end of this book in Appendix 5.

Using Context Clues

Context clues are hints in the selection that help to define a word. To find a word's meaning, try the following:

- **Look at the word.** Is it a noun, a verb, or an adjective? Knowing how the word functions in the sentence can help you guess its meaning.
- **Look at surrounding words.** Look at the entire sentence and try to find a relation between the difficult word and those that surround it. There may be a **synonym** (a word that means the same thing) or an **antonym** (a word that means the opposite), or other terms in the sentence that help define the word.
- **Look at surrounding sentences.** Sometimes you can guess the meaning of a difficult word by looking at the sentences, paragraphs, and punctuation marks surrounding it. When you use your logic, the meaning becomes clear.

In most cases, you can guess the meaning of a new word by combining your own knowledge of the topic with the information conveyed in the words and phrases surrounding the difficult word.

PRACTICE 2 Can you define the words *strewn, emanate,* or *haven*? Perhaps you are not quite sure. Looking at the words in context makes it much easier to guess the definitions of the words.

When I arrived in my hometown, I was baffled by the changes in my old neighbourhood. Garbage was **strewn** across front lawns, paint peeled on the greying wooden homes, and roofs sagged. The auto body shop on the corner **emanated** horrible fumes of turpentine and paint, forcing me to cover my nose when I passed it. I wondered what had happened to my former safe **haven**.

Now write your own definition of the words as they are used in the context.

strewn _____   emanated _____   haven _____

 **Cognates**

Cognates (also known as word twins) are English words that may look and sound like words in another language. For example, the English word *responsible* is similar to the Spanish word *responsable*, although the words are spelled differently.

If English is not your first language, and you read an English word that looks similar to a word in your language, check how the word is being used in context. It may or may not mean the same thing in English as it means in your language. For example, in English, *sensible* means "to show good sense," but in Spanish, *sensible* means "emotional." In German, *bekommen* sounds like "become" but it really means "to get," and the German word *gift* means "poison" in English. If you are not sure of a word's meaning, you can always consult a dictionary.

Using a Dictionary

If you cannot understand the meaning of an unfamiliar word even after using context clues, then look up the word in a dictionary. A dictionary is useful if you use it correctly. Review the following tips for proper dictionary usage:

- **Look at the dictionary's front matter.** The preface contains explanations about the various symbols and abbreviations. Find out what your dictionary has to offer.
- **Read all of the definitions listed for the word.** Look for the meaning that best fits the context of your sentence.
- **Look up root words, if necessary.** For example, if you do not understand the word *unambiguous*, remove the prefix and look up *ambiguous*.

Here is an example of how dictionaries set up their definitions:

Word-Break Divisions	**Stress Symbol (') and Pronunciation**	**Parts of Speech**
Your dictionary may indicate places for dividing words with heavy black dots.	Some dictionaries provide the phonetic pronunciation of words. The stress symbol lets you know which syllable has the highest or loudest sound.	The *n* means that *formation* is a noun. If you do not understand the "parts of speech" symbol, look in the front or the back of your dictionary for a list of symbols and their meanings.

for•ma′•tion / fȯr′māshən/ *n* 1, the process of shaping. 2, that which is shaped. 3, formal structure or arrangement, esp. of troops.

From *The New American Webster Handy College*, A Signet Book, 2000.

Determining Connotation and Denotation

A **denotation** is the literal meaning for a word that may be found in the dictionary. For example, the dictionary definition of *mother* is "a female parent."

A **connotation** is the implied or associated meaning. It can be a cultural value judgment. For instance, the word *mother* may trigger feelings of comfort, security, anger, or resentment in a listener, depending on that person's experience with mothers.

Authors can influence readers by carefully choosing words that have specific denotations. For example, review the next two descriptions. Which one has a more negative connotation?

Terry left his family.   Andrew abandoned his family.

PRACTICE 3   Read the next passages and underline any words or phrases that have strong connotations. Discuss how the words support a personal bias.

1. There is no question about whom Ms. Politkovskaya held responsible in years of unflinching reporting from Chechnya: the Russian Army and Mr. Putin himself. When he finally got around to acknowledging her death yesterday, it was in a cold-blooded statement that the authorities "will take every step to investigate objectively the tragic death of the journalist Politkovskaya."

    from "Another Killing in Moscow" (*The New York Times* editorial)

2. Rohe could have chosen to give a substantive speech detailing why she believes "pre-emptive war is dangerous and wrong"— or as she so categorically put it, how she "knows" that it is. Instead she took the easy way out by insulting the speaker and throwing out some leftist chestnuts about the still missing Osama bin Laden and weapons of mass destruction. But the former would have required her to grapple with ideas; she chose to take potshots.

    from "The Real Meaning of Courage" by Linda Chavez

Recognizing Irony

Irony is a technique that some writers use to make a point. When an author is being ironic, he or she says one thing but really means the opposite. When the author uses an ironic tone, he or she does not intend the reader to interpret the words literally. Sarcasm is a type of verbal irony.

EXAMPLE: The charred burger lay in a grease-soaked bun. "That looks wonderful," he muttered.

PRACTICE 4   Read the following selection from an essay called "The Greatest Player" by Gary Lautens. Then answer the questions.

Occasionally, I run into sports figures at cocktail parties, on the street, or on their way to the bank. "Nice game the other night," I said to an old hockey-player pal.

"Think so?" he replied.

"You've come a long way since I knew you as a junior."

"How's that?"

"Well, you high-stick better for one thing—and I think the way you clutch sweaters is really superb. You may be the best in the league." He blushed modestly. "For a time," I confessed, "I never thought you'd get the hang of it."

"It wasn't easy," he confided. "It took practice and encouragement. You know something like spearing doesn't come naturally. It has to be developed."

"I'm not inclined to flattery but, in my book, you've got it made. You're a dirty player," I continued. . . . "There isn't a player in the league who knows as many obscene gestures."

How is the selection ironic? What does the author really mean?

_____

_____

From Reading to Writing

After you finish reading a selection, you could try these strategies to make sure that you have understood it.

Summarize the reading. When you summarize, you use your own words to write a condensed version of the reading. You leave out all information except for the main points. You can find a detailed explanation about summaries in Chapter 14.

Outline the reading. An outline is a visual plan of the reading that looks like an essay plan. First, you write the main idea of the essay, and then write down the most important idea from each paragraph. You could make further indentations, and under each idea, include a detail or example.

Analyze the reading. When you read, look critically at the writer's arguments and evaluate them, point by point. Also analyze how the writer builds the argument and ask yourself questions such as *Do I agree? Are the author's arguments convincing?* Then, when you write your analysis, you can break down the author's explanations and either refute or agree with them, using your own experiences and examples to support your view.

Write a response. Your instructor may ask you to write about your reaction to a reading. These are some questions you might ask yourself before you respond in writing.

- What is the writer's main point?
- What is the writer's purpose? Is the writer trying to entertain, persuade, or inform?
- Who is the audience? Is the writer directing his or her message at someone like me?
- Do I agree or disagree with the writer's main point?
- Are there any aspects of the topic to which I can relate? What are they?

After you answer the questions, you will have more ideas to use in your written response.

Reading Selections

Theme: **Conflict**

READING I

The Hijab

Naheed Mustafa

> Naheed Mustafa, a North-America-born Muslim woman, has taken to wearing the traditional hijab scarf. She wrote this article while studying in a Canadian university.

1   I often wonder whether people see me as a radical, fundamentalist Muslim terrorist packing an AK-47 assault rifle inside my jean jacket. Or maybe they see me as the poster girl for oppressed womanhood everywhere. I'm not sure which it is. I get the whole gamut of strange looks, stares, and covert glances. You see, I wear the hijab, a scarf that covers my head, neck, and throat. I do this because I am a Muslim woman who believes her body is her own private concern.

2   Young Muslim women are reclaiming the hijab, reinterpreting it in light of its original purpose—to give back to women ultimate control of their own bodies. The Qur'an teaches us that men and women are equal, and that individuals should not be judged according to gender, beauty, wealth, or privilege. The only thing that makes one person better than another is her or his character.

3   Nonetheless, people have a difficult time relating to me. After all, I'm young, Canadian born and raised, and university-educated. Why would I do this to myself, they ask. Strangers speak to me in loud, slow English and often appear to be playing charades. They politely inquire how I like

living in Canada and whether or not the cold bothers me. If I'm in the right mood, it can be very amusing. But, why would I, a woman with all the advantages of a North American upbringing, suddenly, at 21, want to cover myself so that only my face and hands show?

4   Women are taught from early childhood that their worth is proportional to their attractiveness. Women feel compelled to pursue abstract notions of beauty, half realizing that such a pursuit is futile. When women reject this form of oppression, they face ridicule and contempt. Whether it is women who refuse to wear makeup or to shave their legs or to expose their bodies, others have trouble dealing with them.

5   In the Western world, the hijab has come to symbolize either forced silence or radical, unconscionable militancy. Actually, it's neither. It is simply a woman's assertion that judgment of her physical person is to play no role whatsoever in social interaction. Wearing the hijab has given me freedom from constant attention to my physical self. Because my appearance is not subjected to public scrutiny, my beauty, or perhaps lack of it, has been removed from the realm of what can legitimately be discussed. No one knows whether my hair looks as if I just stepped out of a salon, whether or not I can pinch an inch, or even if I have unsightly stretch marks. And because no one knows, no one cares.

6   Feeling that one has to meet the impossible male standards of beauty is tiring and often humiliating. I should know; I spent my entire teenage years trying to do it. I was a borderline bulimic and spent a lot of money I didn't have on potions and lotions in hopes of becoming the next Cindy Crawford. The definition of beauty is ever-changing; waifish is good, waifish is bad, athletic is good—sorry, athletic is bad. Narrow hips? Great. Narrow hips? Too bad.

7   Women are not going to achieve equality with the right to bear their breasts in public, as some people would like to have you believe. That would only make us party to our own objectification. True equality will be had only when women don't need to display themselves to get attention and won't need to defend their decision to keep their bodies to themselves.

COMPREHENSION AND CRITICAL THINKING

1. In paragraph 1, find a synonym for "the whole range or scope."

    _____

2. Find a word in paragraph 4 that means pressured.

    _____

3. Describe the author's background.

    _____

4.   Why does Mustafa choose to wear the hijab?

_____

_____

5.   How does Mustafa define the hijab? Give both the literal and symbolic meanings.

_____

_____

6.   According to Mustafa, what does the hijab symbolize to non-Muslim North Americans?

_____

7.   Using inferences, what assumptions is the author making about men?

_____

_____

_____

8.   In paragraph 6, the author argues that women have to meet "impossible standards of beauty." Respond to her opinion.

_____

9.   Who is the intended audience for this essay?

_____

WRITING TOPICS

Write about one of the following topics. Remember to explore, develop, and revise and edit your work.

1.   What causes women to think they are being judged on their beauty?
2.   The author describes being judged because of the hijab. Write about how people are judged based on the clothing they wear.

READING 2

A Modest Proposal
Heather Mallick

Heather Mallick is a Toronto-based columnist for the *Toronto Star*. Her latest book is *Cake or Death*. The following argument essay takes a stance on the wearing of the niqab.

1   Women in niqabs look like scary black crows as they flutter along a Canadian sidewalk. So what? Black crows are common enough birds. But

they might as well be big red fire trucks when you consider the reactions of other Canadians, we who generally dress like drab sparrows: sensibly, comfortably and in shades of brown.

2   What is to be done?

3   In the latest standoff an immigrant from Egypt has refused to adjust her full-body niqab to uncover her mouth in the French-language class that the government hopes will help new Canadians fit into Quebec society. Told that it would be difficult to learn any language under those conditions, she spoke only when facing away from her male classmates and spoke to her female instructor one-on-one. Then she was reported to have asked the male students to move farther away from her.

4   The CEGEP de Saint-Laurent in Montreal was not happy. Neither was the Quebec government, which backed its immigration minister in saying that the woman, Naima Ahmed, could not remain in the class.

5   "This is the first time I felt racism [in Canada]," Ahmed told a newspaper in an interview after her story hit the headlines.

6   And I, a lifelong feminist—a stance that earns me almost daily hate mail—am pondering who I will most annoy with today's column.

7   What Ahmed calls racism is what I call feminism. Is Ahmed, as she says, protecting her modesty? If so, from what? Canadian men aren't easily inflamed by a mouth. Or a nose. Even the most crass men will remain reasonably polite when confronted by a female classmate with face, hair, ankles, the whole package.

Threat of Exposure

8   But Ahmed, 29, is new to this country. She has seen ill-treatment. She comes from a nation ranked by the World Economic Forum at the bottom of 58 countries in every aspect of women's rights: economic participation and opportunity, political power, education and health. Women in Cairo cannot walk on the street without enduring male assaults, as this shocking BBC report reveals.

9   Ahmed's problem is that she thinks she'll endure the same problems in Montreal, not realizing that the niqab can seem threatening even to other women on a Canadian street.

10   This is how the great travel writer Jonathan Raban once described the sight of Arab women visiting London while retaining their modesty, and I wouldn't call his description inaccurate: "It was the masks I noticed first. They made the women look like hooded falcons, and they struck me not as symbols of Islamic female modesty so much as objects of downright menace. Round every corner, one came upon these masks, and the black silk sheaths that encased the women as if they were corpses risen in their shrouds."

11   In Canada your face is your fortune. Along with clothing and speech, it is a way of quickly assessing another human being and figuring out a means of being social. Ahmed does not realize that if she doesn't adapt to this, she will never fit in Canadian society and will likely not work in her chosen field as a pharmacist, a job that requires clarity and obvious empathy.

12   On the other hand, immigrants' unwillingness to adapt to Canadian mores has also improved our lives immeasurably. I recall the shrimp cocktail, the iceberg lettuce salad, turkey served with marshmallows, boiled cabbage served on the plate like the earth humps on top of fresh graves. All classic Canadian cuisine.

13   At this immigrants did the equivalent of turning away from the class and gave us pizza, hummus, dim sum, tapas, boudin noir, Époisses, pero-gies, pickled herring, dal, pasteis de nata, vinho verde, burritos, polenta, baklava, etc. This has enhanced my life, given it an enchantment my Scottish mother and East Indian father, hardly foodies, never explored.

14   When Muslims offered us Shariah law, Muslim-Canadian feminists braved some very dire elderly imams and told us to turn our backs on it. So far we have and it has helped us all.

15   Canadians aim to welcome immigrants with courtesy and patience. Immigrants come here because they like us. They bend; we bend; neither of us breaks.

Stigmatizing Assumptions

16   I have two daughters, which makes me a practical species of feminist with a meticulous interest in the daily lives of women. I want to hustle over to women in niqabs and whisper, "You don't have to wear that here." Politeness always triumphs and I have never done this. But I see myself from the black-cloaked woman's eyes—my tight clothing and exposed legs, long hair, lipstick, a real boldness with the men who are my equals—and I assume, perhaps unfairly, that she regards me as sluttish.

17   So women are at odds with each other over the niqab. It gets worse. A niqab inevitably insults all the men and women who encounter it, just by implication. I can take a niqab-wearer's incorrect assumptions about me personally, but I dislike her stigmatizing men, whose co-operation this feminist needs to build a society that will be fair to our daughters.

18   Ahmed is comfortable only in the company of females. She assumes that men are only at ease in the company of men (a reference to a brilliant Neil LaBute movie you may not wish to see).

19   But I believe all single-sex institutions are bad news. Book groups, single-sex schools, male top-heavy workplaces, police forces, armed forces, girl gangs, anywhere where one gender predominates or rules is

headed for trouble. Am I alone in noticing that sexual segregation ends in tears and sometimes blood? Just read Margaret Atwood's novel *Cat's Eye* and study the mechanism.

20   Ahmed hopes that no man will ever see her face, and that men will never truly interact or compete with her. We had that era in Canada, before the Persons Case (and long after), when women were fired from their jobs when they married, when women, Jews and other undesirables couldn't get into good universities, when men ruled on sexual and reproductive matters, when society was compartmentalized to the extreme.

21   Ahmed wants Canada to give way and revert to an era of cruelty, nay perversion. Canada asks that she concede. Inevitably, both sides will adjust. But someone has to decide where it stops, and I believe niqabs are it.

Open and Shut Case

22   Here's a Canadian snapshot. Last night, I asked my male bus driver to let me off at my front door instead of the regular stop. It's a practice the Toronto transit system began years ago, when Paul Bernardo was capturing women as they got off the bus in order to rape and torture them. The rule was left in place after he was imprisoned.

23   The bus driver, a nice man, was happy to help. I was effusive in my thanks. In Cairo, a smart Ahmed wouldn't ride a bus at night. In fact, it was only in 2008 that Egyptian women were allowed even to apply for jobs driving buses.

24   In Egypt, the niqab might be practical. In Canada, it is nothing more than female self-harming. When anguished young women cut their arms and legs with knives to let out emotional pain, our health-care system sends them to doctors and counsellors.

25   I see no difference between hurting yourself in private with scissors and hurting yourself in public by rendering yourself both scary and invisible. The second course hurts the rest of us too.

26   I say we dispense with it, and with all the kindness and warmth I can offer, I welcome Naima Ahmed to this country.

COMPREHENSION AND CRITICAL THINKING

1.   What does Mallick mean by "your face is your fortune" in paragraph 11?

_____

2.   What is the meaning of *enchantment* in paragraph 13?
      a. charm   b. delight   c. bewitch

3.   Mallick uses a direct example of a woman from Cairo. Why does she mention this?

_____

4.   Briefly explain the meaning of author's "Canadian snapshot" in paragraphs 22 to 23.

_____

5.   Using your own words, explain what the author's thesis is.

_____

_____

6.   Mallick uses an argument structure in her essay. What is the opposing point of view?

_____

7.   Does Mallick feel that wearing the niqab is ever permissible?

_____

8.   Although this is mainly an argument essay, it also touches on comparison and contrast. Briefly sum up the main similarities and differences discussed.

_____

_____

_____

_____

_____

9.   The author begins this essay with a shocking description. Why is this scene crucial to the main focus of the essay?

_____

10.   Who is the audience for this essay? Look closely at the tone and vocabulary.

_____

_____

WRITING TOPICS

Write about one of the following topics. Remember to explore, develop, and revise and edit your work.

1.   Write about your name. You could write about the following: the meaning of your name, the story of how your parents named you, the evolution of your feelings about your name, and so on.
2.   Write about your reaction to this essay. Do you think Mallick's description is inappropriate?

READING 3

Seeing Red Over Myths
Drew Hayden Taylor

> Drew Hayden Taylor is an Ojibway playwright and novelist, and he is a regular contributor to *Now* magazine. He discusses common misconceptions about Canadian Natives in the following essay.

1   A year and a half ago, my Mohawk girlfriend and I (a fellow of proud Ojibway heritage) found ourselves in the history-rich halls of Europe, lecturing on Native issues, the propaganda and the reality, at a university deep in the heart of northeastern Germany. Then one young lady, a student at this former communist university, put up her hand and asked an oddly naïve question, something like, "Do Indian women shave their legs and armpits like other North American women?" This was not the strangest question I've had put to me. I keep a list, which includes, "I'm phoning from Edinburgh, Scotland, and am doing research on natives in the 1930s. Can you send information?" or "Where can I get my hands on some Inuit throat singers?"

2   But unbeknownst to me, the shaving of extremities in Europe is a largely unexplored area of female hygiene; evidently this topic warranted investigation as to its possible Aboriginal origin. But the question presented a rather obvious example of the issue that permeates North America: the myth of pan-Indianism. The young lady had begun her question with "Do Indian women . . . ?" Sometimes the questioner substitutes First Nations/Native/Aboriginal/Indigenous for Indian. However it's worded, it reveals a persistent belief that we are all one people.

3   Within the borders of what is now referred to as Canada, there are more than fifty distinct and separate languages and dialects. And each distinct and separate language and dialect has emerged from a distinct and separate culture. I tried to tell this woman that her question couldn't be answered because, technically, there is no "Indian/First Nations/Aboriginal." To us, there is only the Cree, the Ojibway, the Salish, the Innu, the Shuswap, and so on.

4   I find myself explaining this point with annoying frequency, not just in Europe, but here in Canada, at the Second Cup, Chapters, or the bus station. The power of that single myth is incredible. When people ask me, "What do First Nations people want?" how do I answer? Some of the Mi'kmaq want to catch lobster, some of the Cree want to stop the flooding and logging of their territory in northern Manitoba, Alberta and Quebec, the Mohawk want the right to promote their own language, and I know bingo is in there somewhere.

5   That's why every time I see a TV news report talking about the plight of the Aboriginal people, I find myself screaming "Which people? Be specific!" That's why I never watch television in public.

6   Such is the power of myths. By their very definition, they're inaccurate or incomplete. Now you know why we as Native people (see, I do it myself) prefer not to use the term "myth" when referring to the stories of our ancestors, as in "The Myths and Legends of Our People." There is something inherently wrong about starting a traditional story with "This is one of the myths that was passed down from our grandfathers. . . ." Literally translated, it means, "This is a lie that was handed down by our grandfathers. . . ."

7   The preferred term these days is *teachings*—as in, "Our teachings say. . . ." It's certainly more accurate because it recognizes the fact that most teachings exist for a purpose—that there's some nugget of metaphor or message within the subtext. And in the Native (there I go again!) way, we like to accentuate the positive. (Important note: The word *legend* can also be used instead of *teachings*, provided you have oral permission from a recognized elder, or written permission from an Aboriginal academic—any Nation will do.)

8   The myth of pan-Indianism is not the only one rooted in the Canadian psyche. A good percentage of Canadians believe that there's a strong Aboriginal tradition of alcoholism. In Kenora, a decade or so ago, someone told me that in one month alone there had been almost three hundred arrests of Aboriginals for alcohol-related offences. And Kenora's not that big a town. The statistic frightened me—until it was explained that rather than confirming the mind-boggling image of three hundred drunken Indians running through the Kenora streets, it signified the same dozen people who just got arrested over and over and over again. It's all in how you read the statistic. And nobody told me how many white people had been arrested over and over again. It's all in how you read that statistic.

9   While acknowledging that certain communities do, indeed, suffer from substance-abuse problems (like many non-Native communities, I might add), I can safely say that not myself, my girlfriend, my mother, my best friend, and most of the other people of Aboriginal descent I consider friends and acquaintances are alcoholics. I wonder why this myth is so persuasive.

10   It's also believed by a good percentage of Canadians that all Native people are poor. Unfortunately, many communities do suffer from mind-numbing poverty, as do many non-Native communities. But contrary to popular belief, capitalism was not a foreign concept to Canada's earliest inhabitants. There were levels of wealth and status back then; today, instead of counting their horses, the rich might count their horsepower.

11   Several weeks ago, a Toronto newspaper attacked a rumour about a coalition of Aboriginal people who had expressed interest in buying the Ottawa Senators [hockey team]. The columnist thought the idea preposterous: "These are the same people who can't afford to pay tax on a pack of smokes; the same people who are so poor they claim government policy is

forcing them to live in neighbourhoods where a rusted car with more than one flat tire is considered a lawn ornament." Well, the ratio of rusted-car-on-lawn to no-rusted-car-on-lawn is so disproportionate it's hardly worth mentioning.

12   Yes, there are some wealthy Native people out there (I wish I knew more of them personally). But their existence is a hard idea to accept when the media only feature First Nations stories on the desperate and the tragic.

13   So where does this leave us? I was asked to write an essay on the "myths of a common Indian identity," which, as I translate it, means that I was asked to comment on lies about something that doesn't exist. That sounds more like politics to me. But if you're still curious about whether Indian women shave their legs and armpits, you'll have to ask one. I'm not telling.

COMPREHENSION AND CRITICAL THINKING

1. In paragraph 2, what is the meaning of *permeates*? _____

2. Find a word in paragraph 11 that means "ridiculous." _____

3. What are some alternative terms for *Native*?

    _____

4. With what does the author introduce his essay?

    a. historical information

    b. a contrasting position

    c. an anecdote

5. Using your own words, write a thesis statement for this essay.

    _____

    _____

6. According to Taylor, what are some incorrect beliefs that people have about Natives?

    _____

    _____

7. What is the difference between a *teaching* and a *myth*?

    _____

    _____

8. Paragraph 11 is missing a topic sentence. Which sentence best expresses the main idea of that paragraph?

    a. Aboriginal people wanted to buy the Ottawa Senators.

    b. Many people have the mistaken notion that all Aboriginals are poor.

    c. Aboriginals do not have rusted cars on their lawns.

    d. People make broad generalizations about Aboriginals.

9. Taylor refutes common misconceptions with factual, anecdotal, and statistical support. Give an example of each one.

    Fact: _____

    Anecdote: _____

    Statistic: _____

    _____

WRITING TOPICS

Write about one of the following topics. Remember to explore, develop, and revise and edit your work.

1. Define a term that relates to your race, religion, or nationality.
2. How do people from other nations view Canadians? How do Canadians view themselves? Compare the stereotypes about Canadians with the reality.

Theme: Urban Development

READING 4

Yonge St., a Seedy Mystery in Plain View
Sheila Heti

Sheila Heti is a Toronto-based writer whose most recent books include *The Middle Stories, Ticknor,* and *How Should a Person Be?* The following narrative essay comes from the online *Toronto Star*.

1   The luckiest person in the world is the person who has never been talked about. No one has talked about them to others, no one has told them what they're like to their face, and they have never spoken to themselves about who they are, muttering, for instance, walking down the street, under their breath, "You're a liar, you're a s---, you've never done an honest day's work in your life."

2   Riding my bicycle up and down Yonge Street all day Wednesday, from its base at Captain John's floating restaurant to as far north as I

wanted to go (Sheppard) I was reminded of my two favourite TV shows about Toronto ever made. They were like twins, and they aired on Global in the 1980s from 3 to 5 in the morning. The shows were called *Night Walk* and *Night Ride* and the premise was simple: The cameraman would carry a camera over his shoulder and walk slowly through a deserted Toronto at night—down a street in Chinatown (a cabbie stands outside his car and makes a note in a book; the camera moves past, sizing him up), through an empty mall, all the shops closed for the night. Or else the camera was held out the window of a car as it drove slowly through the mostly empty Toronto streets.

3   Every streetlight, every light from a car or illuminated sign over a store left a comet trail of light. There was no voice or opinion, just soft jazz playing over top. It was Toronto without commentary—just the eyes. The time slot and its mysterious minimalism, and the fact that it was seemingly made on the cheap, to substitute as a slightly more interesting version of the colour bar that would otherwise appear when programming had ceased, gave it an aura of mystery, banality, and a bit of low-rent seediness. It was both comforting and slightly sinister. It made you feel good and alone.

4   Being on my bike felt like being that camera's POV. Moving up and down Yonge, I had so many associations—from every stage in my life, since I have lived in this city all my life. There was not one block that did not hold a significant memory—more because I have no idea about anyone else's associations with Yonge Street. Other cities with famous streets—people know how prominent locals feel and think about them. Art has been made about them, or people have talked. But I don't know what any prominent locals have thought of Yonge Street, or what their associations might be.

5   I don't know what Glenn Gould made of Yonge Street. I don't know what Karen Kain thought of Yonge Street. I don't know how Wayne Gretzky felt on Yonge Street. I don't know what David Cronenberg likes about Yonge Street.

6   It is as though everyone who's ever had a thought or feeling about Yonge Street has held it close. They refrained from trying to universalize it. No one has said anything about Yonge Street that has claimed it or remade it. It reeks of no one's experience or imagination except—when you're the one travelling on it—your own. That's maybe what made the *Night Walk* and *Night Ride* shows so good, and so typically Toronto: They were silent about themselves.

7   Tourists go to Yonge Street, but what is there to say about Yonge? It is no longer accepted as the longest street in the world. It is Toronto's first street, yes. There is every sort of store on it: purse stores; currency exchanges; wig shops. Near St. Clair there is a cemetery. Canada's first subway runs along it.

8   Sonya, who for 28 years has run a fortune-telling business out of a second-floor walk-up on the north-west corner of Yonge and Wellesley,

says that Yonge Street has changed. I met her because there was a sign that was very old that I had never noticed before. It advertised tea. I went inside but there was no tea, just fortunes.

9   "It grows more unsafe," she said. She wouldn't walk it at night. Earl, the 72-year-old man who works for her, said he's not afraid to walk it at even 2 in the morning. Sonya, hearing this, shakes her head and remarks, in a dark way: "I don't know what business you have on Yonge Street at 2 in the morning."

10   People say people change. People also say people never change. When people say people change, it is because a woman who feels bad for always being reticent about giving herself fully in a relationship, but gets into relationships all the same, after a conversation with her uncle realizes that she doesn't have to want what she doesn't want, and begins behaving in a way that is new—same as when she talked to him at the age of 14 and he said if she didn't want to have sex with her boyfriend she should not. When we say people don't change, it's because at 40 as at 14, she still goes to her uncle for advice. And he still gives his advice over a meal he pays for on Yonge Street.

11   My father believes people don't change, so naturally he said of Yonge: "Yonge Street hasn't changed in the past 40 years." I felt dubious. At its beginnings, Yonge Street was a portage route. Yet on my bike the other day, I saw a car on Queens Quay West, waiting to make a right turn on to Yonge to drive north. Tied to the top of the car was a canoe. Ah! A portage route still!

12   If the characteristics of a person can be identified within days of their birth—if there is something in the baby that is expressed in the grown-up—this might be true of Yonge Street as well. Seeing the canoe tied to that car was like imagining a yawning baby who will yawn with the same muscles as a man.

13   The fortune teller said of the changes on Yonge: "People move in, people move out, stores close. It's good and bad. A lot of things happening and a lot of things not happening." Same as with any street in the city, she made a point of saying, and same as with any city in the world.

14   "Save your money," she advised. "In three years it will be depression."

15   On the website of the City of Toronto Archives there are photographs of Toronto during the Depression. Streetcars and carriages run up and down it—on wooden planks, on mud. Men stroll with packages under their arms and women carrying purses jaywalk with their daughters. In some pictures the streets look wet and rainy—wet like any street in Toronto might be wet, or like any street in the world.

16   Yonge and Dundas, after its latest renovation, looked like ugly prosperity. But its growth stopped or stalled and it doesn't look like prosperity today, just more buildings, not too tall.

17   The fortune teller says stores are closing around her and soon we'll see more newspaper-covered windows. The Coach House Tavern, which is the diner below her, is closed for vacation for the first time ever. And her business is faltering, too. She used to employ six people—other card-readers, people to keep the tea room clean—and regulars jammed the stairwell. Now business is slow. Her customers are being called out west to where the money and jobs are—to Calgary.

18   "So what's more important?" she asks. "Bread in their mouth or fortune telling?"

19   Yonge Street was the beginning of industrial Toronto. It separates east from west. For one reason or another, no one holds up lucky Toronto and looks at the long line down the centre of it and says what it means or who it is or what it portends. Toronto is a folded palm.

COMPREHENSION AND CRITICAL THINKING

1.   What is the meaning of *banality* in paragraph 3?
      a.   trivial   b.   boring   c.   commonplace

2.   Find a word in paragraph 6 that means *make accessible to all*. _____

3.   Underline the thesis statement. Remember that it may not be in the first paragraph.

4.   Look in paragraph 3, and underline examples of imagery that appeal to hearing, taste, and/or sight.

      _____

      _____

      _____

      _____

      _____

      _____

      _____

      _____

      _____

5.   Why does Heti refer to the television shows described in paragraph 2?

      _____

6. Although this is mainly a narrative essay, it also touches on comparison and contrast. Briefly sum up the main similarities and differences discussed.

    _____

    _____

    _____

    _____

    _____

7. Explain why Heti refers to Glenn Gould, Karen Kain, Wayne Gretzky, and David Cronenberg in paragraph 5.

    _____

    _____

8. At what point in the essay is the fortune-teller mentioned? Why is this reference important to the essence of the article?

    _____

    _____

9. What does the metaphor *folded palm* mean in the last paragraph?

    _____

    _____

10. Think about the title. Why does Heti call this essay "Yonge St., a Seedy Mystery in Plain View"?

    _____

    _____

    _____

WRITING TOPICS

Write about one of the following topics. Remember to explore, develop, and revise and edit your work.

1. Write about you're a part of your city or town.
2. Write about your reaction to this essay. Do you think Heti's description is vivid?

READING 5

Living Environments
Avi Friedman

Avi Friedman is professor at the McGill School of Architecture. In the following article, which appeared in the *Montreal Gazette*, Friedman reflects on designing an appropriate house for the individual needs of families.

1   When invited to design a home, I first like to know what kind of dwellers my clients are. In our first meeting, I ask them to take me on a guided tour of their current residence and describe how each room is used—when and by whom. Walking through hallways, scanning the interior of rooms, peeping into closets, looking at kitchen cupboards, and pausing at family photos have helped me devise several common categories of occupants.

2   The "neat" household regards the house as a gallery. The home is spotless. The placement of every item, be it hanging artwork, a memento on a shelf, or furniture, is highly choreographed. The color scheme is coordinated and the lighting superb. It feels as if one has walked into an *Architectural Digest* magazine spread. Recent trends, professional touches, and carefully selected pieces are the marks of the place.

3   The "utilitarian" family is very pragmatic. They are minimalists, believing that they get only what they need. Environmental concerns play an important role in buying goods. The place, often painted in light tones, is sparsely decorated with very few well-selected items. Souvenirs from a recent trip are displayed and some photos or paintings are on the wall. They will resist excess consumption and will squeeze as much use as they can from each piece.

4   The home of the "collector" family is stuffed to the brim. It is hard to find additional space for furniture or a wall area to hang a painting. Books, magazines, and weekend papers are everywhere. Newspaper cutouts and personal notes are crammed under magnets on the fridge door. The collector family seems to pay less attention to how things appear and more to comfort. Stress reduction is a motto. Being an excessively clean "show house" is not a concern. Placing dirty breakfast dishes in the sink and the morning paper in the rack before leaving home is not a priority as long as things are moving along.

5   Of course, these are only a few household types, but at the end of a house tour, I have a pretty good idea about my clients. More than the notes that I take during a meeting, these real-life images tell me all about my client's home life and desired domestic environment. When I began practicing, I quickly realized house design is about people more than

architecture. As hard as I might try, I will never be able to tailor a new personality to someone by placing them in a trendy style, one that does not reflect who they really are. I can attempt to illustrate options other than their current life habits and decorating choices. But in the end, when they move into their new place, they will bring along their old habits.

6   My experience has taught me some homeowners have been trying hard to emulate lifestyles and décors that are really not theirs. The endless decorating shows on television and the many magazines that crowd supermarket racks provide a tempting opportunity to become someone else. Some homeowners are under constant pressure, it feels, to undergo extreme makeovers and borrow rather than mature into their natural selves. They search for a readymade packaged interior style rather than discovering their own.

7   I am often at a loss when clients ask me what style I subscribe to, or solicit advice on the style they are to adopt. I reply that styles are trendy and comfort is permanent, and that they should see beyond the first day of occupancy into everyday living. Sipping a freshly brewed coffee on the back porch on a summer Sunday and letting the morning paper litter the floor while watching a squirrel on the tree across the yard is a treasured moment. It will never be able to fit into a well-defined architectural style. Home design needs to create the backdrop for such opportunities. It is these types of moments that make us enjoy life.

8   If someone wants to read, why not have a wall of books? Does someone love listening to music? Then a music room or corner should be created, even if it is not trendy. Does someone want to interact with the children? He or she might add a hobby space, even if it is outdated and cannot be found in most magazines.

9   Referring to technological advances, the renowned French architect Le Corbusier once described the home as a "machine for living." It is partially true. Home is the site where mundane and utilitarian activities take place. It is also where special moments, uniquely ours, are created and treasured.

COMPREHENSION AND CRITICAL THINKING

1.   Find a four-word expression in paragraph 4 that means "completely filled."

     _____

2.   Find a word in paragraph 6 that means "to copy."

     _____

3.   Underline the thesis statement.
4.   Underline the topic sentences in paragraphs 2–7.

5. Paragraph 8 is missing a topic sentence. Which sentence best expresses the main idea of that paragraph?
   a. People can create a music room in their homes.
   b. Everybody should think about his or her likes and dislikes.
   c. People should create spaces in their homes to accommodate their personal interests.
   d. Hobby rooms and bookshelves can help make a home feel very unique.

6. How does Friedman assess the needs of families when designing a house?

   _____

   _____

   _____

7. What are the three categories of households that Friedman describes in this article?

   _____

8. In your own words, describe the characteristics for each type of household.

   _____

   _____

   _____

   _____

9. a. What influences families when they choose a design for their homes?

   _____

   b. Does Friedman think that such influences are positive or negative? Explain your answer.

   _____

   _____

10. According to Friedman, what is the most important factor that home design should take into consideration?

   _____

   _____

WRITING TOPICS

Write about one of the following topics. Remember to explore, develop, and revise and edit your work.

1. Use a different classification method to describe types of living environments.
2. Friedman writes, "Home is the site where mundane and utilitarian activities take place. It is also where special moments, uniquely ours, are created and treasured." Write about different categories of special or memorable moments.

Theme: **International Trade**

READING 6

Canada Misses Its Chance to Join Major Pacific Free Trade Deal

John Ibbitson

> John Ibbitson is a columnist and bureau chief. His most recent work is *Open and Shut: Why America Has Barack Obama and Canada Has Stephen Harper.* The following is a cause and effect essay on the Trans-Pacific Partnership (TPP) negotiations.

1   Canada has been shut out of a potentially historic Pacific free trade agreement involving the United States and seven other countries.

2   When asked in 2006 to join the Trans-Pacific Partnership negotiations that only recently got under way in Australia, the Harper government refused, largely to protect the Quebec and Ontario dairy industry from foreign competition. When Canada changed its mind earlier this year and asked to join, we were told it was too late, according to several sources.

3   As a result, this country could miss out on being part of a new free trade zone that would encompass 470 million people with a combined GDP of more than $16-trillion.

4   "It is foolish to hamstring our participation in these negotiations" just to protect the dairy industry, said Jayson Myers, president of the Canadian Manufacturers and Exporters association.

5   "There are much bigger economic interests at stake here," he maintained.

6   New Zealand Prime Minister John Key will meet with Prime Minister Stephen Harper Wednesday in Ottawa. High on the agenda: Canada's participation in the Trans-Pacific Partnership.

7   Until recently, TPP, as it's known, was an obscure trade agreement that went into effect in 2006 involving New Zealand, Singapore, Chile and Brunei.

8   But the TPP suddenly began attracting a whole lot of attention, when President Barack Obama last year committed the United States to join with Australia, Peru and Vietnam in a second round of negotiations aimed at expanding the pact.

9   Mr. Obama, who dubs himself the "first Pacific President" wants to expand American trade in the Pacific region. Joining the TPP would counter increasing Chinese domination of Asian-Pacific trade.

10   When TPP members approached Canada to be a part of an expanded pact, Canada refused, mostly because any new agreement would threaten this country's dairy industry.

11   Dairy and poultry farmers belong to marketing boards, which assign production quotas and exclude foreign competition. New Zealand is a dairy juggernaut, and would insist that supply management, as it's known, be dismantled as part of any trade deal. So the Conservative government decided to leave the talks alone.

12   But with the United States in the game, Ottawa suddenly wanted to join, too. That won't happen anytime soon, however, because the United States has vetoed Canadian admission.

13   "You don't want countries joining every other round, because we have a very complex process for launching negotiations," an unnamed source stated in the April, 2010, issue of *Inside U.S. Trade*.

14   The *Globe and Mail* was able to independently confirm that Canada will not be asked to join the negotiations at this time.

15   However, that is not the understanding of Peter Van Loan, the Minister for International Trade.

16   "I don't believe that we're at a point where we have been told there's no place for us, or where we've made a formal ask that we be included either," he said. "It probably would be more fair to say that we've expressed an interest in being kept in the picture."

17   The dairy lobby in both the United States and Canada will fight any agreement that opens the dairy sector to foreign competition.

18   "If you were to fully liberalize dairy between Canada and New Zealand, it would devastate the whole Canadian dairy industry," said Yves Leduc, director of international trade for Dairy Farmers of Canada.

19   There are about 57,500 jobs on dairy farms, but most of the jobs are located in rural Quebec and Eastern Ontario ridings, giving the dairy lobby a political clout far beyond its size.

20   The dairy industry wasn't the only factor that kept Canada out of TPP four years ago. David Emerson, who was international trade minister at the time, said his department was focusing on trade negotiations with Singapore and South Korea at the time.

21   But those negotiations ultimately failed, leaving Canada without any free trade agreement with any Asian nation.

22   This worries Mr. Emerson greatly. "Not having strong Asian trade and investment linkages over the next few decades is a recipe for economic marginalization in the global economy," he said in an e-mail.

23   The TPP talks could fail. The Americans will also demand dairy exemptions. And many Americans will be reluctant to join a trade zone that includes Vietnam.

24   But if the talks do succeed, and if Canada is ultimately asked to join, the question will come down to this: Are we a trading nation that reaches out to new and expanding markets overseas, or do we turn away from those opportunities to protect dairy farmers?

COMPREHENSION AND CRITICAL THINKING

1. Find a word in paragraph 1 that means "capable of coming into being or action." _____

2. In paragraph 7, what is the meaning of *obscure*?
    a. obvious   b. unclear   c. rare

3. What is the cause–effect relationship that occurs in this essay?

    _____

    _____

    _____

4. In your own words, explain Ibbitson's thesis.

    _____

    _____

5. What was the main reason why the Harper government refused to join the Trans-Pacific Partnership (TPP) negotiations?

    _____

    _____

6. Which source confirmed that Canada would not be asked to join the negotiations?

    _____

7. Why was Canada shut out of the trade negotiations?

    _____

8. Who does Ibbitson rely on as credible sources to support his thesis?

    _____

9. Does the author present an unbiased view of his topic? ____

10. With what does the author conclude his essay?
    a. a suggestion   b. a quotation   c. a prediction

WRITING TOPICS

Write about one of the following topics. Remember to explore, develop, and revise and edit your work.

1. Locate a more recent article on the Trans-Pacific Partnership (TPP) negotiations, and write a cause and effect essay about the current developments.

2. Write an essay related to the TPP negotiations, but from the dairy farmers' perspective.

READING 7

The Rich Resonance of Small Talk

Roxanne Roberts

> Roxanne Roberts is a staff writer for the *Washington Post*. In the following article, she muses about the importance of small talk.

1   I talk too much. The good news is that I can enter a room full of strangers, walk up to anyone, and start yammering away. The bad news is . . . well, you can guess that I bore people. All things considered, this has worked out pretty well. In my sixteen years as a social reporter for a newspaper, I've marched up to presidents, movie stars, and kings and felt unafraid to make small talk, otherwise known as the mother's milk of party coverage. I have an advantage, of course, in that I have a press pass and a notebook.

2   But small talk is a big deal for everyone; it is one of those essential social skills that separate the men from the boys. The ability to connect in short, casual conversations can make or break careers, friendships, and romances—it's how we gather information, and hopefully, make a favorable impression. There are only three golden rules for small talk: First, shut up and listen; second, when in doubt, repeat Rule 1; third, get others to talk about themselves.

3   First, Rule 1 and Rule 2 take a lifetime for the average extrovert or egomaniac to master. To listen that intently, to focus with every muscle, takes not only great skill but also great discipline, which is why mere mortals fall short. It is so easy to respond to a casual comment by unwittingly turning the spotlight back on yourself: "You're going to Italy? We stayed at this great little place outside of Florence." It seems so natural—your small talk might be helpful, witty, and even relevant, but you're nonetheless talking instead of listening—and you can never learn anything while talking, except that you talk too much.

4   In the meantime, there are a few other tricks for small talk with strangers and acquaintances. For example, introduce yourself by name, even if you think they know it. "I don't think we've met. I'm Queen Elizabeth II." It's gracious, it's efficient, and it's smart. It's very awkward when someone starts a conversation with "Remember me?" and you don't. Second, ask simple questions. "What do you think of the [party, conference, cheese puffs]?" Then listen. When you run into a casual acquaintance, ask what he or she has been doing lately. Then listen. Ask follow-up questions based on the answers. If you are genuinely interested, most people will be surprised and flattered. Resist the temptation to display your own special brand of brilliance, and when you catch yourself doing so, shift the focus back. Later on, when the relationship has evolved beyond small talk, you can strut your fabulousness.

5   Furthermore, mastering the art of small talk is important for drawing shy people into a conversation. If this is done right, they walk away thinking *you're* great. "A great small talker is someone who has three to four open-ended questions that make the person open up," says Ann Stock, former White House social secretary for the Clintons and currently the vice president of the Kennedy Center. "It ignites something in them that makes them start talking. After that, you ask leading questions."

6   Use your body language. There's nothing worse than chatting with people who simultaneously scan the room for someone more important. Give someone your full and real attention during your conversation. Face him or her directly, and look in his eyes. Never underestimate small talk—even though many people dread it or think it's silly, boring, or superficial.

7   Once in a rare while, someone comes along who innately gets it and turns a brief, casual moment into a truly memorable encounter. Former president Bill Clinton is a genius at it. In the course of two minutes, he can lock eyes with a person, ask a seemingly simple question, and make a person feel like the center of the universe. Clinton's remarkable memory for names and faces means he can meet someone and—months or years later—ask about his or her family or golf game. People are shocked and delighted.

8   Another legendary master at the art of small talk was the late Pamela Harriman, Democratic fundraiser, ambassador to France, and the woman once called the "greatest courtesan of the century"—a nod to her many high-profile lovers. What set her apart was her laser-like ability to make anyone feel like the most important person in the room. She wanted to know everything about the people she met. She hung on every word and seldom talked about herself. She made people feel like brilliant, under-appreciated jewels. "She had the power to make people want to talk with her," William Pfaff wrote in the *International Herald Tribune* shortly after her death in 1997. "She was—or certainly made herself seem to be—interested in everyone with whom she spoke, and in what they had to say. She, in turn, had something intelligent to say to them." She was not, he wrote, an intellectual or particularly sophisticated in matters of international relations. She knew enough to ask the right questions. But mostly she let others do the talking: "The willingness to listen is seduction itself—certainly to vain men, and in the world in which she functioned, all men are vain."

9   Finally, consider the famous story about British Prime Minister Benjamin Disraeli and his great political rival, William Gladstone. Legend has it that a lady was taken to dinner one evening by Gladstone and the next by Disraeli. When asked her impression of the two men, she replied, "When I left the dining room after sitting next to Mr. Gladstone, I thought he was the cleverest man in England. But after sitting next to Mr. Disraeli, I thought I was the cleverest woman in England."

COMPREHENSION AND CRITICAL THINKING

1. What is the meaning of *nod to* in paragraph 8?
   a. acknowledgment of
   b. an indication of agreement
   c. falling asleep
2. Underline the thesis statement.
3. Why does the author begin with the first-person pronoun/in the introductory paragraph, but use third-person pronouns for the rest of the essay?

   _____

4. Why does the author think that learning the art of small talk is important?

   _____

   _____

5. Using your own words, list at least five pieces of advice the author gives to master the art of small talk.

   _____

   _____

   _____

6. According to the author, why is it difficult for people to follow the first rule of small talk?

   _____

   _____

7. Why does the author use Bill Clinton and Pamela Harriman as examples to support her thesis?

   _____

8. How are Clinton's and Harriman's strategies for making small talk similar?

   _____

9. How are Clinton's and Harriman's strategies for making small talk different?

   _____

   _____

   _____

10.   How is the anecdote in the concluding paragraph a good support for mastering the art of small talk?

_____

_____

_____

_____

WRITING TOPICS

Write about one of the following topics. Remember to explore, develop, and revise and edit your work.

1.   Explain steps that people can take to have better relationships with their life partners.
2.   Describe a process people can go through to make their guests feel more comfortable. You can discuss houseguests, dinner guests, or party guests.

READING 8

Google's China Web
Frida Ghitis

> Frida Ghitis is a journalist, businesswoman, and writer who authored *The End of Revolution: A Changing World in the Age of Live Television.* In the following essay, Ghitis examines the role that Google and other internet providers play in supporting China's severe censorship laws.

1   A few years ago, I walked into an Internet room in Tibet's capital, Lhasa. There were no Chinese soldiers in the room and no visible government censors nearby. A sign on the wall, however, reminded Web users that even after entering the stateless world of the Web, China's all-seeing eye had not disappeared. "Do not use Internet," the warning instructed crassly, "for any political or other unintelligent purposes."

2   Since then, China's ruling regime has perfected the science of controlling what the Chinese can read or write on the Internet to such a degree that it has become the envy of tyrants and dictators the world over. We might have expected that from a regime that has proven it will do whatever it takes to stay in power. What we never expected was to see Google, the company whose guiding motto reads "Don't be evil," helping in the effort. Google's decision to help China censor searches on the company's Chinese website is not only a violation of its own righteous-sounding principles, and it's not just an affront to those working to bring international standards of human rights for the Chinese people.

No, Google's sellout to Beijing is also a threat to every person who has ever used Google anywhere in the world.

3   Google saves every search, every e-mail, every fingerprint we leave on the Web when we move through its Google search engine, or its Gmail service, or its fast-growing collection of Internet offerings. Google knows more about us than the **FBI** or the **CIA** or the **NSA** or any spy agency of any government, and nobody regulates it. When a company that holds digital dossiers on millions of people decides profits are more important than principles, we are all at risk. Google will now participate actively in a censorship program whose implications, according to Harvard's Berkman Center for Internet and Society, "are profound and disturbing." The Chinese government blocks thousands of search terms—including censorship.

4   To be fair, Google is hardly alone in its decision to capitulate to Beijing's rulers in order to gain a Web share of China's 1.3 billion inhabitants. The country's tantalizing market has tested the ethics of many Western corporations—and almost all have failed the test. That is particularly true in the Internet business. Just last year, Yahoo helped Beijing's Web goons track down the identity of a Chinese journalist who wrote an e-mail about the anniversary of the 1994 Tiananmen Square massacre—a massacre of thousands of Chinese democracy advocates perpetrated by the same regime whose efforts Google now abets. The journalist, Shi Tao, was sentenced to ten years in prison. Reporters Without Borders labeled Yahoo an "informant" that has "collaborated enthusiastically" with the Chinese regime. Microsoft, too, plays by the dictatorship's rules. Bloggers on MSN's service cannot type words such as "democracy" or "freedom." Internet users cannot read or write about anything that even hints of opposition to the ruling Communist Party. Even pro-Western commentary can trigger a block. And forget anything about Tibet or the Dalai Lama. Chinese bloggers, incidentally, must all register and identify themselves to authorities.

5   Neither Yahoo nor Microsoft claims to have higher ethical standards than the competition. The often-stated desire to "do good" and make the world a better place was one of the traits that endeared Google to the public. It was one of the reasons we trusted them to guard the precious and valuable contents of their thousands of servers. Now Google has become a company like all others, one with an eye on the bottom line before anything else. The company has decided to help China's censors even as it fights a request for records from the US Justice Department's investigation of online child pornography. Skeptics had claimed Google was resisting the request to protect its technology, rather than to protect users' privacy. That explanation now sounds more plausible than ever.

FBI:
U.S. Federal Bureau of Investigation

CIA:
U.S. Central Intelligence Agency

NSA:
U.S. National Security Agency

6   We've long known about China's disdain for individual freedoms. But Google, we hardly knew you. It's definitely time to rethink that Gmail account and demand some safeguards from a potentially dangerous company. Perhaps here, too, we will need to heed the Tibetan cybercafé warning, "Do not use Internet for any political or unintelligent purposes."

COMPREHENSION AND CRITICAL THINKING

1. Find a word in paragraph 4 that means "to give in to."

    _____

2. The verb *abet* in paragraph 4 means
    a. hurt   b. encourage   c. help or assist

3. Underline the thesis statement.

4. In your own words, explain the author's main point.

    _____

    _____

5. With what does the author introduce the text?
    a. general background
    b. historical background
    c. an anecdote
    d. a contrasting position

6. Why is the author so upset about Google's actions in China? Give at least two reasons.

    _____

    _____

    _____

7. According to the author, how are Google's policies in China hypocritical?

    _____

    _____

    _____

8. Examine paragraph 4. Is the author acknowledging the opposing position? Explain your answer.

    _____

    _____

    _____

    _____

    _____

9. Why do western businesses agree to participate in the violation of personal freedoms in China?

_____

_____

10. In which paragraphs does the author use an anecdote to support her point of view? _____

11. Name two informed sources that the author quotes.

_____

_____

12. What is the author's predominant tone?

contemplative	outraged	lighthearted	sarcastic
humorous	friendly	casual	supportive

WRITING TOPICS

Write about one of the following topics. Remember to explore, develop, and revise and edit your work.

1. Take the opposite position to the author, and argue that Google has every right to act as it does in China.
2. Argue that the censorship rules should (or should not) be more severe. Consider censorship of the internet, music, film, or television.

Theme: Forces of Nature

READING 9

The Rules of Survival

Laurence Gonzales

Laurence Gonzales won the National Magazine Award in 2001 and 2002. His work has appeared in such publications as *Harper's*, *National Geographic Adventure*, and *Smithsonian Air and Space*, just to name a few. The following excerpt is from his best-seller, *Deep Survival*.

1 As a journalist, I've been writing about accidents for more than thirty years. In the last fifteen or so years, I've concentrated on accidents in outdoor recreation, in an effort to understand who lives, who dies, and why. To my surprise, I found an eerie uniformity in the way people survive seemingly impossible circumstances. Decades and sometimes centuries apart, separated by culture, geography, race, language, and tradition,

the most successful survivors—those who practice what I call "deep survival"—go through the same patterns of thought and behavior, the same transformation and spiritual discovery, in the course of keeping themselves alive. It doesn't seem to matter whether they are surviving being lost in the wilderness or battling cancer; the strategies remain the same.

2   Survival should be thought of as a journey, a vision quest of the sort that Native Americans have had as a rite of passage for thousands of years. Once people pass the precipitating event—for instance, they are cast away at sea or told they have cancer—they are enrolled in one of the oldest schools in history. Here are a few things I've learned about survival.

Stay Calm

3   In the initial crisis, survivors are not ruled by fear; instead, they make use of it. Their fear often feels like (and turns into) anger, which motivates them and makes them feel sharper. Aron Ralston, the hiker who had to cut off his hand to free himself from a stone that had trapped him in a slot canyon in Utah, initially panicked and began slamming himself over and over against the boulder that had caught his hand. But very quickly he stopped himself, did some deep breathing, and began thinking about his options. He eventually spent five days progressing through the stages necessary to convince him of what decisive action he had to take to save his own life.

Think, Analyze, and Plan

4   Survivors quickly organize, set up routines, and institute discipline. When Lance Armstrong was diagnosed with cancer, he organized his fight against it the way he would organize his training for a race. He read everything he could about it, put himself on a training schedule, and put together a team from among friends, family, and doctors to support his efforts. Such conscious, organized effort in the face of grave danger requires a split between reason and emotion in which reason gives direction and emotion provides the power source. Survivors often report experiencing reason as an audible "voice."

5   Steve Callahan, a sailor and boat designer, was rammed by a whale, and his boat sunk while he was on a solo voyage in 1982. Adrift in the Atlantic for seventy-six days on a five-and-a-half-foot raft, he experienced his survival voyage as taking place under the command of a "captain" who gave him his orders and kept him on his water ration, even as his own mutinous (emotional) spirit complained. His captain routinely lectured "the crew." Thus under strict control, he was able to push away thoughts that his situation was hopeless and take the necessary first steps of the survival journey: to think clearly, analyze his situation, and formulate a plan.

Celebrate Every Victory

6   Survivors take great joy from even their smallest successes. This attitude helps keep motivation high and prevents a lethal plunge into hopelessness. It also provides relief from the unspeakable strain of a life-threatening situation.

7   Lauren Elder was the only survivor of a light plane crash in the High Sierra. Stranded on a 12,000 foot peak, one arm broken, she could see the San Joaquin Valley in California below, but a vast wilderness and sheer and icy cliffs separated her from safety. Wearing a wrap-around skirt and blouse but no underwear, with two-inch heeled boots, she crawled "on all fours, doing a kind of sideways spiderwalk," as she put it later, "balancing myself on the ice crust, punching through it with my hands and feet." She had thirty-six hours of climbing ahead of her—a seemingly impossible task. But Elder allowed herself to think only as far as the next big rock. Once she had completed her descent of the first pitch, Elder said that she looked up at the impossibly steep slope and thought, "Look what I've done! Exhilarated, I gave a whoop that echoed down the silent pass." Even with a broken arm, joy was Elder's constant companion. A good survivor always tells herself, "Count your blessings—you're alive."

Enjoy the Survival Journey

8   It may seem counterintuitive, but even in the worst circumstances, survivors find something to enjoy, some way to play and laugh. Survival can be tedious, and waiting itself is an art. Elder found herself laughing out loud when she started to worry that someone might see up her skirt as she climbed. Even as Callahan's boat was sinking, he stopped to laugh at himself as he clutched a knife in his teeth like a pirate while trying to get into his life raft. And Viktor Frankl ordered some of his companions in **Auschwitz** who were threatening to give up hope to force themselves to think of one funny thing each day. Singing, playing mind games, reciting poetry, and doing mathematical problems can make waiting tolerable, while heightening perception and quieting fear.

Auschwitz: a Nazi concentration camp

Never Give Up

9   Yes, you might die. In fact, you will die—we all do. But perhaps it doesn't have to be today. Don't let it worry you. Forget about rescue. Everything you need is inside you already. Dougal Robertson, a sailor who was cast away at sea for thirty-eight days after his boat sank, advised thinking of survival this way: "Rescue will come as a welcome interruption of . . . the survival voyage." One survival psychologist calls that "resignation without giving up. It is survival by surrender."

10   Survivors are not easily discouraged by setbacks. They accept that the environment is constantly changing and know that they must adapt. When they fall, they pick themselves up and start the entire process over again, breaking it down into manageable bits. When *Apollo 13*'s oxygen tank exploded, apparently dooming the crew, Commander Jim Lovell chose to keep on transmitting whatever data he could back to mission control, even as they burned up on re-entry. Elder and Callahan were equally determined and knew this final truth: If you're still alive, there is always one more thing that you can do.

Copyright © 2010 by Laurence Gonzales

COMPREHENSION AND CRITICAL THINKING

1. What is the meaning of *precipitating* in paragraph 2?
   a. ending   b. unexpected   c. initiating or beginning
2. In paragraph 7, what is the meaning of *pitch*?
   a. throw   b. slope   c. tone
3. With what does the author introduce the text?
   a. general background
   b. historical background
   c. an anecdote
   d. a contrasting position
4. In this process essay, the author describes the experiences of several survivors. Briefly explain what challenge the following people faced.

   Aron Ralston: _____

   _____

   Lance Armstrong: _____

   _____

   Lauren Elder: _____

   _____

   Viktor Frankl: _____

   _____

   Dougal Robertson: _____

   _____

5. a. What do most of these stories of survival have in common? What kinds of threats were they surviving?

   _____

   _____

   _____

    b. How is Frankl's journey different from those of the others mentioned in the essay?

_____

_____

6. This process essay also uses elements of narration and cause and effect. What are some of the effects of positive thinking while in a dangerous situation?

_____

_____

_____

7. What is the author's specific purpose?

_____

_____

8. Who was likely the targeted audience for this essay?
    a. an academic or intellectual audience
    b. children
    c. a general audience
    Give some reasons for your choice.

_____

_____

9. What lessons does this essay have for the reader?

_____

_____

_____

10. Using your own words, explain why it is important to enjoy the survival journey.

_____

WRITING TOPICS

Write about one of the following topics. Remember to explore, develop, and revise and edit your work.

1. Describe a difficult physical ordeal that you or someone you know went through. What happened? What steps were taken to get through the ordeal?
2. Explain the steps people should take when they have an emotional crisis. For example, how can they survive a breakup, a public humiliation, or the loss of a friend?

READING 10

The Other Side of the Mountain
Geoff Powter

> Geoff Powter is the author of *Strange and Dangerous Dreams: The Fine Line between Adventure and Madness.* The following is an article from *Canadian Geographic.*

1   I was in trouble. My day on southeastern British Columbia's 3,176-metre Bugaboo Spire had begun well enough: a fast walk up a glacial bowl on perfect sun-braised snow, a crescent moon snagged on a rim of alpenglowing peaks, the silence of an ascent without another soul in sight and then joyous movement, weaving my way up a dragon's-back ridge of immaculate granite to a million-mile view. But barely a few hundred metres from the summit, the descent down the other side of the mountain quickly turned into something dramatically, and stupidly, different.

2   At dawn, the climb had made perfect sense. After 10 days of rain, I was so thrilled to see a cloudless sky out the window of the empty alpine hut that I'd bounded out with barely a thought about a partner or a rope. I happily convinced myself that breaking these basic rules didn't matter. I was feeling strong, the route up the mountain was supposed to follow an obvious and moderate line, and the descent had been climbed in *1916*, for God's sake.

3   But now, with my feet slipping on dirty ledges still wet from the rain and 1,000 metres of air yawning below me, I slowed to a crawl, my heart in my throat. The ridge was a mess of options, and for nearly an hour, I battled with problems of will and skill, going up and down, back and forth, terrified of the exposure, baffled about the proper line, cursing my choice to come up without a partner or a rope. I desperately needed help.

4   The Hopi of the American Southwest, I once read, believe that one of the surest ways to summon a spirit is to walk backwards through a place where the spirit has lived. It strikes me now, when I look back to that moment high on the ridge years ago, that I may have been doing my own conjuring when I started down the mountain, walking backwards over terrain first covered by the great Austrian mountain guide Conrad Kain.

5   The hubris of youth had kept me from learning much about Kain before I found myself stuck on Bugaboo Spire—in my mind he was just another of the old men who'd climbed easy mountains in a long-gone era—but I had a very different appreciation of the man by the time I reached the bottom. In my high-tech rock shoes, the climb was still frighteningly uncertain; Kain had climbed it in hobnailed boots. I had a hut and the possibility of rescue just a couple of kilometres away; in Kain's day, the nearest road was a 40-kilometre bushwhack away. I knew the climb was possible; he certainly didn't.

6   But Kain's legacy was redefining the possible. Everywhere he climbed—in the Alps, where the young goatherd quickly became one of the most respected guides; in New Zealand, where Kain spent three winters; and especially here in Canada, which became his home in 1909— his routes became the benchmarks. If I struggled to get myself down Bugaboo Spire, it was little wonder. Kain may have climbed it in 1916, but as mountain historian Chic Scott points out, Kain's climb of the peak was "one of the great moments in Canadian mountaineering" and one of the hardest things ever climbed anywhere in the world by that date. Since then, Kain's spirit has guided just about every climber who has come to Canada's western mountains.

7   My long-ago summer turned out to be a whole season of conjuring Kain. I traced his footsteps back down all three of his great Canadian climbs—Bugaboo, Mount Louis near Banff and Mount Robson—and finally understood just how often we climb on the invisible shoulders of others. I also, thankfully, began to absorb some of Kain's way of looking at the mountains around me. I began that year seeing mountains as physical challenges and ended it understanding they could be spiritual temples. As Kain's biographer J. Monroe Thorington wrote, Kain "saw a peak first as something beautiful—the technical problem was always secondary—and nothing counted beside that vision."

8   No other mountain lesson could have been as important.

COMPREHENSION AND CRITICAL THINKING

1. In paragraph 4, *conjuring* means
    a. magical tricks   b. configuring   c. climbing
2. What type of narrator is telling this story?
    a. first-person narrator   b. third-person narrator
3. What can you infer about his personality?

    _____

4. In your own words, sum up the story in a couple of sentences. Remember to answer who, what, when, where, why, and how questions.

    _____

    _____

5. Describe the author's physical and mental state at the beginning of the essay.

    _____

6. Why does the author refer to the Hopi of the American Southwest?

    _____

7. What does *the hubris of youth* mean in paragraph 5?

    _____

8. Who was Conrad Kain? Why does Powter make reference to him?

_____

9. What were some of the obstacles that the narrator faced during his climb to Bugaboo Spire?

_____

10. This essay contains examples of imagery (description using the senses). Give examples of imagery that appeal to touch, sight, and hearing.

_____

WRITING TOPICS

Write about one of the following topics. Remember to explore, develop, and revise and edit your work.

1. Specifically describe a memorable outdoor adventure that you or someone you know has had.
2. Argue for or against engaging in dangerous extreme sports.

READING 11

Monsoon Time
Rahul Goswami

Rahul Goswami is a journalist for *Orientation: Middle East*. In the following essay, he reminisces about the weather in his homeland. Pay closs attention to the descriptive details.

1   My father used to tell me about the monsoon in Bangladesh. He was born in Handiyal, a village in the north-central district of the country. Behind his parents' house was a river, the Padma, a part of the immense water system that crisscrosses Bangladesh. Big even during the sweltering dry months, the Padma would become an inland ocean at the height of the monsoon. My father would talk about the river swelling day after day as the rain drove down. He loved the monsoon, despite the inevitable annual floods, the misery, and the hardship.

2   Years later, I moved to Dubai, where I lived until just recently. It is a modern metropolis—built on the edge of the great Arabian sand sea— glittering with glazed glass and proud of its impeccably maintained highways. It scarcely ever rains here. On perhaps five days a year, a few millimeters of rain will reluctantly descend. More frequent are the sandstorms, which clog drains that are tested no more than annually. This past year was my first full one in Dubai and the first time in my life I have missed an entire monsoon.

squalls: sudden violent gusts of wind

3   By June in India, when the first wet **squalls** explode over Bombay [Mumbai], one has been anticipating the rain for a month and more. Then

in July, the massive, heavy cloud systems have settled immovably over the subcontinent, and they let fall torrents of rain, day after day. Indoors a patina of moisture coats everything, clothes will not dry, and head colds make one miserable. Outside, the city struggles with its everyday routines. Suburban trains do not run, their tracks submerged under feet of muddy water. City drains, routinely untended and choked with tons of garbage, refuse to do their work. Housing colonies turn into **archipelagos**. Mosquitoes assume fearsome proportions.

archipelagos: groups of small islands

4   By August, the monsoon has dulled the world. Trees appear a uniform drab green, the sea stays gray and forbidding, and the city stinks. When, in September, the rains have at last weakened into ineffectual evening drizzles, one is relieved.

5   The monsoon season has, I discovered, a rhythm that the mind and body grow accustomed to. In Dubai last June, when the temperature reached 48° Celsius, I would catch myself glancing at the sky, wondering idly if there was a hint of interesting cloud. My rational self knew there could not be a monsoon here, but the subconscious would not be denied. Some mornings I would awake in my darkened, air-conditioned room and imagine rain drumming on the window. It was an illusion that persisted several seconds into wakefulness, and even after I rose I would resist drawing the curtain aside, preferring instead to retreat to the even darker bathroom. Then I'd tell myself there is no rain, and I'd lace my shoes and step outside into the pitiless heat of Arabia.

6   Late in July, I noticed that the illusions persisted at work, too. With the window blinds down and the central air-conditioning humming along at a cool 22° Celsius, I occasionally caught myself wondering whether I'd find a cab that would be willing to drive me home in the rain. After all, it must be raining outside by now. At these times it took some courage to walk into the passageway between the office suites, face the window, stare at the Dubai skyline carelessly shimmering in the late evening sun, and remind myself that the monsoon lay on the other side of the Indian Ocean.

7   The sounds of rain would still visit, sometimes surprising, always comforting, while outside Dubai still blazed with heat and light. August slipped into September and as the body readjusted itself, the mind played along. As the Gulf's fall months began, the harsh absence of monsoon faded. I no longer looked for that high and lonely cloud in the sky. The time for rain had passed, and I wondered whether next year my longing would be the same.

COMPREHENSION AND CRITICAL THINKING

1.   Define *monsoon*.

_____

2. Circle a word in paragraph 3 that means "violent flow or downpour."

3. In paragraph 3, the author uses the word *patina*. What does it mean?

   _____

4. What are some effects of the author's decision to move to Dubai?

   _____

5. Using your own words, sum up the main idea of the essay.

   _____

   _____

6. What impression does the writer give of Dubai? Using your own words, describe that place.

   _____

   _____

7. What impression does the writer give of Mumbai during the monsoon season? Using your own words, describe what the city is like.

   _____

   _____

8. What is the dominant impression in Goswami's essay? Circle the letter of the best answer.

   a. joy   b. tension   c. homesickness   d. anger   e. despair

9. The writer appeals to more than one sense. Give an example for each type of imagery.

   sight:_____

   _____

   hearing:_____

   _____

   smell:_____

   _____

10. Monsoons disrupt everyday life with intense and unending rainfall. Moreover, the extreme humidity is unpleasant. Why would the author prefer the chaos and rain of his homeland over the dryness and order of Dubai? To answer this question, you will have to make inferences.

   _____

   _____

   _____

   _____

WRITING TOPICS

Write about one of the following topics. Remember to explore, develop, and revise and edit your work.

1. Which season do you like the most? Describe that season using vivid imagery.
2. Describe an extreme weather phenomenon that you lived through. What happened? Include descriptive details that appeal to the senses.

Theme: **Flora and Fauna**

READING 12

Make a Difference
David Suzuki and David R. Boyd

> David Suzuki is an environmental activist and writer. David R. Boyd is an environmental lawyer and author. The following is excerpted from their book, *David Suzuki's Green Guide*.

1   There's an ancient story about an old man who used to love walking near the ocean. He'd walk along the beach every morning. One day he saw a person moving like a dancer, bending, then wading into the waves with arms extended. It pleased him that someone would dance to the beauty of the day and the rhythm of the waves. As he got closer, he saw that it was a young girl. The girl wasn't dancing, but was reaching down to the sand, picking something up, and carrying it carefully out into the ocean.

He called out, "Good morning! What are you doing?"

The girl replied, "I'm returning starfish to the ocean."

"Why?"

"The sun is up and the tide is going out. If I don't rescue them, they'll be stranded on the beach and die."

"But there are miles upon miles of beach and starfish all along the way. What difference can you possibly make?"

2   The girl didn't answer right away. She bent down, picked up another starfish, and gently placed it in the sea. She watched a wave lift it high, and then, as it sank into the life-giving water, she turned to the man, smiled, and said, "I made a difference for that one."

3   He nodded and reflected for a moment. Then he bent down, picked up a starfish, and returned it to the sea.

4   The mutually beneficial relationship between personal and planetary well-being comes as no surprise to those who recognize that humans are part of nature, but runs contrary to the common misconception that reducing your footprint will somehow diminish your standard of living.

5   Your personal actions may seem like drops in the ocean, but everything you do has a ripple effect that multiplies your impact. When you turn off a light, you save up to three times as much energy as the light would have consumed. When you reduce your material consumption by a kilogram, you save up to 200 kilograms of natural resources and prevent up to 200 kilograms of waste and pollution. When you walk to work, ride a bicycle to the store, or enjoy a vacation closer to home, you prevent pollution, save natural resources, save money, improve your health, decrease wear and tear on roads, and boost your happiness. When you eat a meal of local organic food, you support the regional economy, decrease greenhouse gas emissions, protect wildlife habitat and soil quality, and feel healthy and happy. When you increase your home's energy efficiency you save money, take a bit of pressure off the planet, increase your level of comfort, and improve air quality. When you choose environmentally friendly products you send a signal to the market, and the market responds. When you vote for candidates based on their environmental platform, you start to change how governments operate. The ripple effect expands as you share your stories and experiences with family, friends, colleagues, and acquaintances. And remember that in a world of more than 6 billion people, each of us is a drop in the bucket, but with enough drops we can fill any bucket.

6   When we make changes at the individual level we are not alone. More and more people are discovering that environmentally responsible behavior is enriching, not impoverishing. Millions of people belong to international and national environmental groups, local green groups, and community sustainability groups. Thousands more join each day. As this wild and organic movement grows, it approaches what is known as a tipping point. Small changes that appear to have little or no effect on a system keep occurring until a critical mass is reached. Then one further small change "tips" the system and a large effect is observed. Exactly where a tipping point lies is unknown. Every person who joins the movement for a sustainable future brings us a little bit closer. Every builder working on zero energy or energy-plus homes brings us a little bit closer. Every farmer producing food sustainably brings us closer. Every business that shifts its practices and products towards cradle-to-cradle design brings us closer. Every government policy that rewards pro-environmental behavior and prohibits or penalizes ecologically

destructive actions moves us towards the tipping point of the sustainability revolution.

7   Unfortunately, the natural world may also be teetering towards unknown tipping points, where climate change could accelerate or the rate of extinction could snowball. In this sense, we are in a race against time, making it imperative that we act now to put the brakes on our unsustainable levels of consumption, waste, and pollution.

8   If we can harness our knowledge, the deep reservoirs of human wisdom accumulated over millennia, and our unique gift of foresight, then we can achieve sustainability within one or two generations. Saving ourselves and countless other species from the brink of ecological disaster would be the greatest comeback of all time, outshining Team Canada's hockey victory in the 1972 Summit Series against the Soviet Union, won after early losses suggested there was no hope, Lance Armstrong's seven Tour de France championships, won after the cyclist battled testicular cancer, or the 1951 New York Giants baseball victory, won after the team overcame a thirteen-game deficit against archrival Brooklyn Dodgers. Today, Stanford ecologist Paul Ehrlich says there are a thousand ecological Pearl Harbors happening at once and we must mount an immediate and comprehensive response.

9   This book outlines, on the basis of the best scientific evidence, the most important steps you can take to reduce your ecological footprint. There's no expectation that you'll wake up tomorrow and change all the habits developed over your lifetime that contribute to environmental degradation. Striving for a sustainable lifestyle is like training for a marathon in that it requires dedication to develop healthy new habits. Every marathon begins with a first step. It's best to start slowly and gradually build on your successes. In the end you'll be a healthier, happier person. Be more mindful of the choices you make and their environmental implications. Think about where you choose to live, what you eat, how you travel, what you do for a living, what kind of stuff you buy, and how you exercise your democratic rights. Reflect on what makes you genuinely happy. Sign up for David Suzuki's Nature Challenge. Get out there and enjoy the natural world. Make your ecological footprint as small as possible.

10   Ultimately, you make the choices. As Dr. Seuss wrote in his 1971 classic *The Lorax*, "unless someone like you cares a whole awful lot, nothing is going to get better. It's not."

COMPREHENSION AND CRITICAL THINKING

1. Why do Suzuki and Boyd begin this excerpt with an anecdote about starfish?

   _____

   _____

2. Explain the term *reducing your footprint* (paragraph 9).

   _____

3. Underline the thesis statement.
4. What misconception do the authors refer to in paragraph 9?

   _____

5. Provide at least five ways in which individual actions can impact the environment. _____

6. What do the authors mean by a *ripple effect* in paragraph 5?

   _____

7. Why are people not alone when they make environmental changes?

   _____

8. What do the authors mean by *the tipping point* in paragraph 6?

   _____

   _____

   _____

   _____

9. According to the authors, what is the answer to achieving sustainability?

   _____

   _____

10. What is the significance of the Dr. Seuss quotation at the end of the excerpt? _____

WRITING TOPICS

Write about one of the following topics. Remember to explore, develop, and revise and edit your work.

1. Consider one environmental disaster. What are the causes of the disaster, or how have governments and the public responded to it?
2. What steps are you taking to reduce your environmental footprint? You may want to research David Suzuki's Nature Challenge as the authors suggest in paragraph 9.

Theme: **Human Development**

READING 13

Twixters

Betsy Hart

> Betsy Hart is a journalist for the Scripps Howard News Service. In the following essay, she examines adults who do not want to grow up.

1   Meet the Twixters: "Michelle, Ellen, Nathan, Corinne, Marcus, and Jennie are friends. All of them live in Chicago. They go out together three nights a week, sometimes more. Each of them has had several jobs since college; Ellen is on her seventeenth." They are all ages twenty-four to twenty-eight. They don't own homes, they are not married, and they don't have kids. Most telling: They don't want to own homes, be married, or have kids. As one Twixter, charming twenty-seven-year-old Matt—who took six and a half years to graduate from college—put it, "I do not ever want a lawn . . . I do not want to be a parent. I mean, hell, why would I? There's so much fun to be had while you're young." Ah, out of the mouths of babes. Why would he want such things, indeed? He's still a child, just in a man's body. It used to be that our culture presented adulthood as something valuable, so there was prestige in attaining it. Now we teach our children to fear adulthood—and so they stay children.

2   All of this comes from the current *Time* magazine cover story, "They Just Won't Grow Up." Well put. *Time* reports, "Everybody knows a few of them—full-grown men and women who still live with their parents, who dress and talk and party as they did in their teens, hopping from job to job and date to date, having fun but seemingly going nowhere." Ten years ago, they might have been called, well, losers. But not anymore. There are just too many of them. As *Time* puts it, "This is a much larger phenomenon, of a different kind and a different order." Now, the age from eighteen to twenty-five—and often much later—is seen as a distinct phase in life.

3   Some sociologists who observe this trend say growing up is just harder than it used to be. They are wrong. The problem is, growing up is easier and cushier than ever. And so, the 20 percent of all twenty-six-year-olds who live with their parents—you read right, one-fifth, typically rent-free or heavily subsidized—don't want to go. (How does one put a price on someone doing or helping you with the laundry, anyway?) No one is making them leave the family nest. It's incredibly cushy there, and why in the world would they go through the hard work of building their own nest when they have access to a much fancier one ready-made?

4   The idea that this is all about finances is silly. We're living in a great economy. And the Twixters are such big spenders, on eating out, new cars, and flat-screen TVs, that advertisers are now targeting these adult adolescents, seeing them as something of a gold mine. The Twixters have money. They just want to spend it on the fun toys and leisure activities.

5   Fewer young adults want to take a job they are not crazy about, one that isn't "meaningful enough," or perhaps live in an efficiency apartment and do their laundry down the street, while saving and working for something better. It is more fun to live better now, often at someone else's expense: mom and dad's.

6   Look, I'm not suggesting there should not be a place in the family nest for young adults during a trauma. Sure, parents should help those who are truly getting on their feet—meaning they are working, paying rent, helping around the house—and making plans to move on. I do know some young adults who move in with their parents to help take care of them. It might even be that some generations enjoy living together as equals. I'm just lamenting the adults who want to stay kids, whether they are living with mom and dad or not—and the parents who not only encourage it but subsidize it.

7   Growing up, becoming an adult, and taking on adult responsibilities brings joy and satisfaction and disappointment and heartache and even fun. As a culture, the less we encourage that transition, the more we encourage young adults to stay in their "it's all about me" cocoon. The real problem? If we as a culture make it easy for these young adults to have no real responsibilities either for themselves or to others, we rob them of a tangible way to be plugged into and connected to their community and their world—and something bigger than just themselves.

COMPREHENSION AND CRITICAL THINKING

1.   Find a verb in paragraph 6 that means "mourning or grieving."

_____

2.   Find a word in paragraph 7 that means the opposite of "elusive and vague."

_____

3.   What are the main characteristics of a Twixter?

_____

_____

4.   Underline the thesis statement.
5.   The author is defining a Twixter, but she is also making an argument. What is her point of view?

_____

_____

_____

6. What is the author implying in paragraph 3?
   a. It is society's fault that some people never grow up.
   b. Parents contribute to the problem of Twixters by making home too comfortable.
   c. Young adults can't easily move out because it is too expensive these days.
7. What is the author's main point in paragraph 4?
   a. Twixters have a lot of money.
   b. Twixters spend a lot of money on games and toys.
   c. Our economy is doing extremely well.
   d. Twixters would rather spend money on themselves than move out of their parents' home.
8. According to the author, how does delayed adulthood hurt the Twixters?

   _____

   _____

   _____

WRITING TOPICS

Write about one of the following topics. Remember to explore, develop, and revise and edit your work.

1. Choose a term that refers to a particular type of adolescent or young adult and write a definition essay about that term. For example, you might write about *rappers*, *punks*, *skaters*, or *jocks*, or you can define a new term that people in your area use.
2. Define adulthood. What are the main characteristics of an adult?

READING 14

Religious Faith versus Spirituality
Neil Bissoondath

> Neil Bissoondath, a journalist and writer, immigrated to Canada from Trinidad when he was eighteen years old. He has written novels, essay collections, and short story collections. His works include *A Casual Brutality* and *Digging Up the Mountains*. In the following essay, he contrasts religion and spirituality. As you read this comparison and contrast essay, also look for elements of argument writing.

1   *Wait till someone you love dies. You'll see. You'll know God exists. You'll want Him to.*

2   The prediction, repeated with minimal variation through the years by believers challenged by my non-belief, was never offered as a promise but as a vague threat, and always with a sense of satisfied superiority, as if the speakers relished the thought that one day I would get my comeuppance.

3   They were, without exception, enthusiastic practitioners of their respective faiths—Roman Catholics, Presbyterians, Hindus, Muslims, God-fearing people all. Which was, to me, precisely the problem: Why all this fear?

4   And then one day, without warning, my mother died. Hers was the first death to touch me to the quick. Her cremation was done in the traditional Hindu manner. Under the direction of a **pundit**, my brother and I performed the ceremony, preparing the body with our bare hands, a contact more intimate than we'd ever had when she was alive.

pundit:
Hindu priest

5   As I walked away from her flaming **pyre**, I felt myself soaring with a lightness I'd never known before. I was suddenly freed from days of physical and emotional **lassitude**, and felt my first inkling of the healing power of ritual, the solace that ceremony can bring.

pyre:
a pile of burning wood used to cremate a dead body

lassitude:
weariness, fatigue

6   Still, despite the pain and the unspeakable sense of loss, the oft-predicted discovery of faith eluded me. I remained, as I do today, a non-believer, but I have no doubt that I underwent a deeply spiritual experience. This was when I began to understand that religious faith and spirituality do not necessarily have anything to do with each other—not that they are incompatible but that they are often mutually exclusive.

7   Western civilization has spent two thousand years blurring the distinction between the two, and as we enter the third millennium we are hardly more at peace with ourselves than people were a thousand years ago. Appreciating the distinction could help soothe our anxieties about the days to come.

8   Spirituality is the individual's ability to wonder at, and delight in, the indecipherable, like a baby marveling at the wiggling of its own toes. It is to be at ease with speculation, asking the unanswerable question and accepting that any answer would necessarily be incomplete, even false. It is recognizing that if scientific inquiry has inevitable limits, so too do religious explanations, which base themselves on unquestioning acceptance of the unprovable: neither can ever fully satisfy.

9   A sense of the spiritual comes from staring deep into the formation of a rose or a hibiscus and being astonished at the intricate delicacy of its symmetry without needing to see behind its perfection of form the fashioning hand of deity.

10   It comes from watching your child being born and gazing for the first time into those newly-opened eyes, from holding that child against your chest and feeling his or her heartbeat melding with yours.

11   It comes from gazing up into the sparkling solitude of a clear midnight sky, secure in the knowledge that, no matter how alone you may feel at moments, the message of the stars appears to be that you most indisputably are not.

12   At such moments, you need no **dogma** to tell you that the world seen or unseen, near or distant, is a wonderful and mysterious place.

dogma: principle, tenet

13   Spirituality, then, requires neither science nor religion, both of which hunger after answers and reassurance—while the essence of spirituality lies in the opening up of the individual to dazzlement. Spirituality entails no worship.

14   At the very moment of my mother's cremation, her brother, trapped thousands of miles away in England by airline schedules, got out his photographs of her and spread them on his coffee table. He reread her old letters and spent some time meditating on the life that had been lived—his way, at the very moment flames consumed her body, of celebrating the life and saying farewell, his way of engaging with the spiritual.

COMPREHENSION AND CRITICAL THINKING

1. In paragraph 2, *comeuppance* means:
    a. rising up
    b. punishment
    c. reward

2. Write a synonym for the word *solace* in paragraph 5. _____

3. Underline the thesis statement. Be careful because it may not necessarily be in the first paragraph.

4. How does Bissoondath define spirituality? Give examples from the essay.

    _____

    _____

5. Why does the author object to believers who try to challenge his non-belief?

    _____

6. How does the death of the author's mother change him?

    _____

    _____

7. Why does the author give a lesser value to science and religion than to spirituality?

    _____

    _____

    _____

8. To support his belief in spirituality, why does Bissoondath give the example of his uncle in paragraph 14?

_____

_____

_____

9. Bissoondath "soared with lightness" during the traditional Hindu ceremony and mentions the "healing power of ritual." How do such words contradict his strong opinions about religion? Explain your answer.

_____

_____

WRITING TOPICS

Write about one of the following topics. Remember to explore, develop, and revise and edit your work.

1. Bissoondath went to a traditional Hindu ceremony. All human cultures have special ceremonies, festivals, and holidays. For example, Canadians may celebrate Valentine's Day, Victoria Day, Thanksgiving Day, birthdays, anniversaries, and marriages. Compare and contrast two special events that people celebrate.

2. Present an opposing point of view to the one presented in this essay. Defend the belief in religion. You can use yourself or others as examples.

READING 15

Medicating Ourselves

Robyn Sarah

> Robyn Sarah is a poet and a writer. Her work has appeared in the *Threepenny Review*, *New England Review*, and *The Hudson Review*, and she is a frequent contributor to the *Montreal Gazette*. In the following essay, Sarah reflects on society's overreliance on medication.

1   It is hard to pick up a magazine these days without finding an article attacking or defending some pharmaceutical remedy for syndromes of mood or behaviour. These drugs are in vogue because they have shown themselves spectacularly effective for a range of conditions, though their exact workings are not well understood and their long-term effects are not known. Yet for all the noise we continue to hear about, say, Ritalin, for children with attention deficit disorders and related learning or behaviour problems—or Prozac and the new family of anti-depressants prescribed to the stressed and distressed of all ages—the real debate on pharmaceuticals has yet to begin.

2   The enormous strides science has made in understanding brain chemistry have precipitated a revolution no less significant than the "cyber-revolution" now transforming our lives. The biochemical model has brought relief to many suffering individuals and families, removing devastating symptoms and lifting blame from parents whose contorted responses to a child's **anomalous** behaviour were once mistaken for its cause. But the very effectiveness of corrective pharmacology engenders an insidious imperative: we can, therefore we must. The realization that we can chemically fine-tune personalities—that we may be able to "fix" what were once believed innate flaws of character—has staggering implications for our understanding of morality, our standards for acceptable behaviour, our mental pain threshold, and our expectations of self and others.

anomalous: unusual

3   The medication debate should not be a matter of "whether or not," but of where to stop. Mental illness is real and can be life-threatening. But when is something truly a disorder, and when are we **pathologizing** human difference, natural human cycles and processes? How do we decide what needs fixing, and who should decide? These are not simple matters.

pathologizing: making a disease of

4   During my own school years, the boy who today would be prescribed Ritalin used to spend a lot of time standing in the hall outside the classroom. His "bad boy" reputation dogged him year to year and became part of his self-image. He learned to wheel-and-deal his way out of trouble by a combination of charm and **subterfuge**; he learned to affect a rakish persona to mask what anger he might feel about his **pariah** status. But in spite of his often superior intelligence, anything else he learned in school was hit-and-miss. Such "bad boys" rarely lasted beyond the second year of high school.

subterfuge: evasion

pariah: outcast

5   Defenders of Ritalin point out that in making it possible for such a child to focus and sustain attention, to complete tasks and take satisfaction from them, the stimulant breaks a cycle of disruptive behaviour, punishment, anger, and acting out. Begun early, Ritalin can prevent the battering of self-esteem such children undergo in school; introduced later, it allows a child to rebuild self-esteem. These are powerful arguments for a drug that, when it works, can effect what seems a miraculous transformation in a "problem child," giving him a new lease on life in a system that used to chew him up and spit him out.

6   But Ritalin is not a benign drug, and many are alarmed at the frequency and casualness with which it is prescribed (often at the school's prompting) for a disorder that has no conclusive medical diagnosis. Some argue that children who may simply be high-spirited, less compliant, or more physically energetic than the norm are being "drugged" for the convenience of teachers and smooth classroom functioning. Others wonder if the frequency of **ADD** and **ADHD** diagnoses says more about the state of schools than it does about the state of children. Do our schools

ADD: attention-deficit disorder

ADHD: attention-deficit hyperactivity disorder

give children enough physical exercise, enough structure and discipline, or enough real challenge? A proliferation of troublemakers can be an indication of something wrong in the classroom—witness any class with an inexperienced substitute teacher. Pills to modify the behaviour of "disturbers" may restore order—at the cost of masking the true problem.

7   Something similar may be going on as diagnoses of depression and other disorders proliferate, especially among groups in the throes of life change (adolescent, mid-life, or geriatric). Just as physical pain is our body's way of alerting us to a problem, psychic pain can be a response to our changed position in the world. Psychic pain might indicate that we should reorient ourselves by reassessing and rebuilding our primary relationships. If I swallow a pill to conceal my existential problems—an "equanimity" pill—I may be easier to live with, but I may also be masking the need for some fundamental work to be done, some exercise of the spirit. Giving a boost to my brain chemistry might help me do this work, but it is just as likely to take away the urgency to do it.

8   I am myself no stranger to depression, but in eschewing the chemical solution, I have begun to sense I am swimming against the tide. For a while, I felt all the worse because so many of my peers, with lives no less complicated than mine, seemed to be handling mid-life pressures better than I was. Slowly it emerged that several had taken antidepressants at some point "to get over a rough spot." Some are still taking them.

9   The arguments are seductive. Why make things harder for ourselves, and why inflict our angst on others, when there is an alternative? One father I know, the stay-at-home parent of small children, told me he put himself back on Prozac (originally prescribed for migraines) because under stress he tended to be irritable, and things were more stressful with a new baby in the house. His irritability was not something he wanted to inflict on his children. Who could fault him for such a decision?

10   If we can really smooth our rough edges by popping a pill, why not make life pleasanter for our loved ones and associates by popping a pill? If a pill can make saints of us all, where is the virtue in resisting this pill? But the effect may be to mask how many people would otherwise be doing "badly," which not only induces the unmedicated to bash themselves for their human frailties, but blinds us all to societal ills that may explain why so many of us get depressed.

11   The new pharmaceutical culture could stigmatize the unmedicated. It could make us all less tolerant of our frailties and those of others. It could keep us reconciled to the values that have put us in the pressure cooker to begin with: the worship of youth and success, the pursuit of comfort and expediency, and a model of wellness based on uninterrupted productivity.

12   Shall we lose the sense of what it is to be unique, struggling, evolving souls in the world, and instead use designer drugs to make ourselves smooth-functioning cogs of an unexamined societal machine? Aldous Huxley predicted it in 1932, in his Utopian novel *Brave New World.* Remember the drug *soma*? It has "the advantages of Christianity and alcohol; none of their defects [. . .]. Anyone can be virtuous now. You can carry half your morality around in a bottle." Huxley's book, on the high school reading list a generation ago, enjoys that same place today. But I am beginning to think the satire may have been lost on us. Perhaps it was too late for the message even when he wrote it. With our complicity, his vision gets closer every day.

COMPREHENSION AND CRITICAL THINKING

1. In paragraph 7, what does *proliferate* mean? _____
2. Define the word *stigmatize* in paragraph 11. _____
3. In your own words, restate the thesis statement.

   _____

   _____

4. In which paragraph(s) does the author acknowledge an opposing viewpoint?

   _____

5. Which strategies does the author use to support her argument? There is more than one answer.
   a. fact
   b. anecdote
   c. quotations from informed sources
   d. statistics
   e. logical consequences
   For each type of support that you have identified, underline a sentence from the text.
6. Using your own words, list at least four of the author's main arguments.

   _____

   _____

   _____

   _____

   _____

   _____

   _____

7. The author suggests some causes of overmedicating in our culture. What are they?

_____

_____

8. What are some of the effects of using medication to modify behaviour problems?

_____

_____

9. How does the author conclude her essay?
   a. suggestion   b. prediction   c. call to action
10. Why does the author quote Aldous Huxley in her concluding paragraph?

_____

_____

WRITING TOPICS

Write about one of the following topics. Remember to explore, develop, and revise and edit your work.

1. Argue for the use of mood-altering drugs.
2. Argue that vaccinations should or should not be mandatory. You will have to do some research and support your points with the opinions of experts. See Chapter 15 for information about writing a research essay.

Appendix 1
Grammar Glossary

Parts of Speech	Definition	Some Examples
Noun	Names a person, place, or thing.	singular: woman, horse, person plural: women, horses, people
Verb	Expresses an action or state of being.	action: look, make, touch, smile linking: is, was, are, become
Adjective	Adds information about the noun.	small, pretty, red, soft
Adverb	Adds information about the verb, adjective, or other adverb; expresses time, place, and frequency.	quickly, sweetly, sometimes, far, usually, never
Pronoun	Replaces one or more nouns.	he, she, it, us, ours, themselves
Preposition	Shows a relationship between words (source, direction, location, etc.).	at, to, for, from, behind, above
Determiner	Identifies or determines if a noun is specific or general.	a, an, the, this, that, these, those, any, all, each, every, many, some
Conjunction	Coordinating conjunction: Connects two ideas of equal importance. Subordinating conjunction: Connects two ideas when one idea is subordinate (or inferior) to the other idea.	but, or, yet, so, for, and, nor although, because, even though, unless, until, when
Conjunctive adverb	Shows a relationship between two ideas. It may appear at the beginning of a sentence, or it may join two sentences.	also, consequently, finally, however, furthermore, moreover, therefore, thus
Interjection	Is added to a sentence to convey emotion.	hey, yikes, ouch, wow

How Do I Get a Better Grade?

mycanadiancomplab

Go to www.mycanadiancomplab.ca for additional help with your grammar, writing, and research skills. You will have access to a variety of exercises, instruction, and video that will help you improve your basic skills and help you get a better grade.

Appendix 2
Irregular Verbs

Base Form	Simple Past	Past Participle	Base Form	Simple Past	Past Participle
arise	arose	arisen	eat	ate	eaten
be	was, were	been	fall	fell	fallen
bear	bore	borne / born	feed	fed	fed
beat	beat	beat / beaten	feel	felt	felt
become	became	become	fight	fought	fought
begin	began	begun	find	found	found
bend	bent	bent	flee	fled	fled
bet	bet	bet	fly	flew	flown
bind	bound	bound	forbid	forbade	forbidden
bite	bit	bitten	forget	forgot	forgotten
bleed	bled	bled	forgive	forgave	forgiven
blow	blew	blown	forsake	forsook	forsaken
break	broke	broken	freeze	froze	frozen
breed	bred	bred	get	got	got, gotten
bring	brought	brought	give	gave	given
build	built	built	go	went	gone
burst	burst	burst	grind	ground	ground
buy	bought	bought	grow	grew	grown
catch	caught	caught	hang[1]	hung	hung
choose	chose	chosen	have	had	had
cling	clung	clung	hear	heard	heard
come	came	come	hide	hid	hidden
cost	cost	cost	hit	hit	hit
creep	crept	crept	hold	held	held
cut	cut	cut	hurt	hurt	hurt
deal	dealt	dealt	keep	kept	kept
dig	dug	dug	kneel	knelt	knelt
do	did	done	know	knew	known
draw	drew	drawn	lay	laid	laid
drink	drank	drunk	lead	led	led
drive	drove	driven	leave	left	left

[1]When hang means "to kill or die by hanging," then it is a regular verb: hang, hanged, hanged.

Base Form	Simple Past	Past Participle	Base Form	Simple Past	Past Participle
lend	lent	lent	slit	slit	slit
let	let	let	speak	spoke	spoken
lie²	lay	lain	speed	sped	sped
light	lit	lit	spend	spent	spent
lose	lost	lost	spin	spun	spun
make	made	made	split	split	split
mean	meant	meant	spread	spread	spread
meet	met	met	spring	sprang	sprung
mistake	mistook	mistaken	stand	stood	stood
pay	paid	paid	steal	stole	stolen
put	put	put	stick	stuck	stuck
prove	proved	proved / proven	sting	stung	stung
quit	quit	quit	stink	stank	stunk
read	read	read	strike	struck	struck
rid	rid	rid	swear	swore	sworn
ride	rode	ridden	sweep	swept	swept
ring	rang	rung	swell	swelled	swollen
rise	rose	risen	swim	swam	swum
run	ran	run	swing	swung	swung
say	said	said	take	took	taken
see	saw	seen	teach	taught	taught
sell	sold	sold	tear	tore	torn
send	sent	sent	tell	told	told
set	set	set	think	thought	thought
shake	shook	shaken	throw	threw	thrown
shine	shone	shone	thrust	thrust	thrust
shoot	shot	shot	understand	understood	understood
show	showed	shown	upset	upset	upset
shrink	shrank	shrunk	wake	woke	woken
shut	shut	shut	wear	wore	worn
sing	sang	sung	weep	wept	wept
sink	sank	sunk	win	won	won
sit	sat	sat	wind	wound	wound
sleep	slept	slept	withdraw	withdrew	withdrawn
slide	slid	slid	write	wrote	written

²*Lie* can mean "to rest in a flat position." When *lie* means "tell a false statement," then it is a regular verb: *lie, lied, lied.*

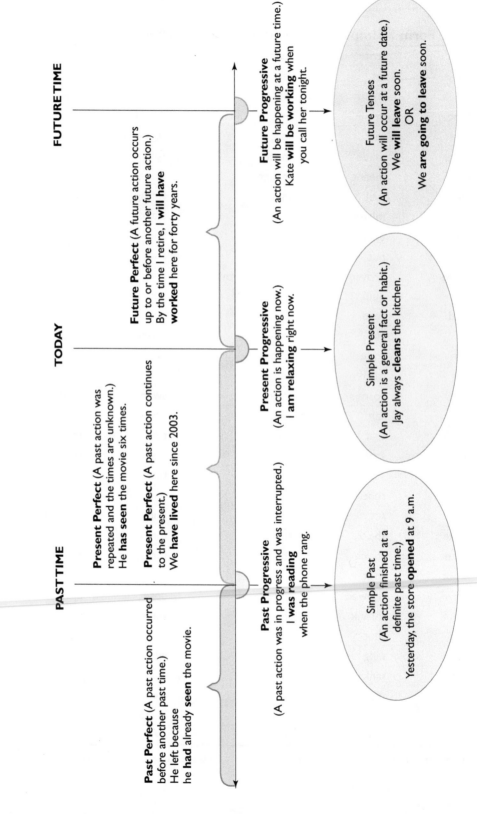

Appendix 3
Verb Tenses

542

PAST TIME

TODAY

FUTURE TIME

Past Perfect (A past action occurred before another past time.)
He left because he **had** already **seen** the movie.

Present Perfect (A past action was repeated and the times are unknown.)
He **has seen** the movie six times.

Present Perfect (A past action continues to the present.)
We **have lived** here since 2003.

Future Perfect (A future action occurs up to or before another future action.)
By the time I retire, I **will have worked** here for forty years.

Past Progressive
(A past action was in progress and was interrupted.)
I **was reading** when the phone rang.

Present Progressive
(An action is happening now.)
I **am relaxing** right now.

Future Progressive
(An action will be happening at a future time.)
Kate **will be working** when you call her tonight.

Simple Past
(An action finished at a definite past time.)
Yesterday, the store **opened** at 9 a.m.

Simple Present
(An action is a general fact or habit.)
Jay always **cleans** the kitchen.

Future Tenses
(An action will occur at a future date.)
We **will leave** soon.
OR
We **are going to leave** soon.

Making Compound Sentences

A.

Complete idea

, coordinator
, for
, and
, nor
, but
, or
, yet
, so

complete idea.

B.

Complete idea

;

complete idea.

C.

Complete idea

; transitional expression,
; however,
; in fact,
; moreover,
; therefore,
; furthermore,

complete idea.

Making Complex Sentences

D.

Complete idea

subordinator
although
because
before
even though
unless
when

incomplete idea.

E.

Subordinator
Although
Because
Before
Even though
Unless
When

incomplete idea

,

complete idea.

Appendix 5
Spelling, Grammar, and Vocabulary Logs

In the first few pages of your writing portfolio or copybook, try keeping three "logs" to help you avoid repeating errors and improve your writing.

Spelling Log

The goal of keeping a spelling log is to stop repeating errors. Every time you misspell a word, record both the mistake and the correction in your spelling log. Then, before you hand in a writing assignment, consult the list of misspelled words.

> **EXAMPLE:**
>
> | *Incorrect* | *Correct* |
> |---|---|
> | *finaly* | *finally* |
> | *responsable* | *responsible* |

Grammar Log

The goal of keeping a grammar log is to stop repeating errors in sentence structure, mechanics, and punctuation. Each time a writing assignment is returned to you, identify one or two repeated errors and add them to your grammar log. Next, consult the grammar log before you hand in new writing assignments in order to avoid making the same errors. For each type of grammar error, you could do the following:

1. Identify the assignment and write down the type of error.
2. In your own words, write a rule about the error.
3. Include an example from your writing assignment.

> **EXAMPLE:** *Cause and Effect Essay* (Mar. 10)   Fragment
>
> *Sentences must have a subject and verb and express a complete thought.*
>
> *Also, an overbearing parent. ~~That~~ can cause a child to become controlling.*

Vocabulary Log

The vocabulary log can provide you with interesting new terms to incorporate in your writing. As you use this book, you will learn new vocabulary. Keep a record of the most interesting and useful words and expressions. Write a synonym or definition next to each new word.

> **EXAMPLE:** *ubiquitous means widespread*

Spelling Log

Spelling Log

Grammar Log

Grammar Log

Vocabulary Log

_____

_____

_____

_____

_____

_____

_____

_____

_____

_____

_____

_____

_____

_____

_____

_____

_____

_____

_____

_____

_____

_____

_____

_____

_____

_____

Vocabulary Log

_____
_____
_____
_____
_____
_____
_____
_____
_____
_____
_____
_____
_____
_____
_____
_____
_____
_____
_____
_____
_____
_____
_____

Credits

TEXT:

T. Morehead. A Signet Book, Penguin © 2000; **p. 487:** Reprinted by permission of Jackie Lautens; **pp. 488–489:** Reprinted by permission of Naheed Mustafa; **pp. 490–493:** Reprinted by permission of Heather Mallick; **pp. 495–497:** © 2001 Drew Hayden Taylor; **pp. 498–501:** Reprinted by permission of Sheila Heti; **pp. 503–504:** Reprinted with permission of Dr. Avi Frideman; **pp. 506–507:** John Ibbitson, 2010. © CTVglobemedia Publishing Inc. All Rights Reserved; **pp. 509–510:** From *The Washington Post*, © 2004 The Washington Post. All rights reserved. Used by permission and protected by the Copyright Laws of the United States. The printing, copying, redistribution, or retransmission of the Material without express written permission is prohibited; **pp. 512–514:** Reprinted by permission of Frida Ghitis; **pp. 515–518:** Copyright © 2010 Laurence Gonzales; **pp. 520–521:** Reprinted by permission of Geoff Powter; **pp. 522–523:** Reprinted with the permission of The Atlantic Online; **pp. 525–527:** Excerpt from David Suzuki's Green Guide by David Suzuki & David R. Boyd, published 2008 by Greystone Books: an imprint of D&M Publishers Inc. Reprinted with permission from the publisher; **pp. 529–530:** Reprinted with permission of the Scripps Howard News Service; **pp. 531–533:** Reprinted by permission of Neil Bissoondath; **pp. 534–537:** Reprinted with permission of Robyn Sarah.

PHOTOS:

Page 3: Photos.com; **p. 15:** Courtesy of www.istockphoto.com; **p. 17:** Courtesy of www.istock.photo.com; **p. 32:** Courtesy of www.istockphoto.com; **p. 44:** Courtesy of www.istockphoto.com; **p. 61:** Courtesy of www.istockphoto.com; **p. 62:** Courtesy of www.istockphoto.com; **p. 63:** Courtesy of www.istockphoto.com; **p. 65, top:** Courtesy of www.istockphoto.com; **p. 65, mid:** Pixtal/Superstock Royalty Free; **p. 68:** Courtesy of www.istockphoto.com; **p. 81:** Milos Jokic/Shutterstock; **p. 100:** Courtesy of www.istockphoto.com; **p. 102:** Courtesy of www.istockphoto.com; **p. 120:** Courtesy of www.istockphoto.com; **p. 122:** Courtesy of Daniel Gilbey Photography/Shutterstock; **p. 137:** Courtesy of www.istockphoto.com; **p. 139:** Courtesy of www.istockphoto.com; **p. 157:** Photos.com; **p. 159:** Photos.com; **p. 180:** Purestock/Superstock Royalty Free; **p. 182:** Courtesy of www.istockphoto.com; **p. 199:** Photos.com; **p. 201:** Courtesy of www.istockphoto.com; **p. 218:** Courtesy of www.istockphoto.com; **p. 220:** Photos.com; **p. 240:** Courtesy of www.istockphoto.com; **p. 243:** Photos.com; **p. 244:** Photos.com; **p. 253:** Photos.com; **p. 273:** Execution of the Defenders of Madrid, 3rd May, 1808, 1814 (oil on canvas), Goya y Lucientes, Francisco Jose de (1746–1828)/Prado, Madrid, Spain/The Bridgeman Art Library International; **p. 286:** Photos.com; **p. 293:** Photos.com; **p. 297:** Courtesy of www.istockphoto.com; **p. 302:** Steve Vidler/SuperStock, Inc.; **p. 303:** Patricia Schwimmer (Canadian, b. 1953) "My San Francisco", 1994, Tempera, Private Collection. © Patricia Schwimmer/SuperStock; **p. 305:** Courtesy of www.istockphoto.com; **p. 310:** Richard Cummins/SuperStock, Inc.; **p. 313:** Michele Burgess/SuperStock, Inc.; **p. 315:** Richard Cummins/SuperStock, Inc.; **p. 316:** Courtesy of www.istockphoto.com; **p. 318:** Yoshio Tomii/SuperStock, Inc.; **p. 321:** Hidekazu Nishibata/SuperStock, Inc.; **p. 324:** Photos.com; **p. 332:** Courtesy of www.istockphoto.com; **p. 334:** Courtesy of www.istockphoto.com; **p. 344:** Mario Carreno (b. 1913/Cuban) *La Siesta* 1946. Oil on canvas. © Christie's Images/SuperStock; **p. 346:** Photos.com; **p. 347:** Photos.com; **p. 365:** Ritu Manoj Jethani/Shutterstock; **p. 367:** Courtesy of www.istockphoto.com; **p. 369:** Robert Llewellyn/SuperStock, Inc.; **p. 378:** SuperStock, Inc.; **p. 380:** Courtesy of www.istockphoto.com; **p. 381:** Courtesy of www.istockphoto.com; **p. 389:** Photos.com; **p. 390:** Superstock Royalty Free; **p. 392:** Courtesy of www.istockphoto.com; **p. 396:** Pixtal/Superstock Royalty Free; **p. 400:** Tony Linck/SuperStock, Inc.; **p. 404:** Photos.com; **p. 412:** Donna and Steve O'Meara/Superstock Royalty Free; **p. 417:** Katsushika Hokusai (1760–1849, Japanese) "The Wave", 19th Century, Woodcut print. © SuperStock, Inc.; **p. 420:** Courtesy of www.istockphoto.com; **p. 424:** SuperStock, Inc.; **p. 430:** Charles Marden Fitch/SuperStock, Inc.; **p. 434:** Courtesy of www.istockphoto.com; **p. 444:** Photos.com; **p. 447:** The Bridgeman Art Library International; **p. 454:** Donald Martin, after Van der Weyden (20th Century American), "Portrait", Airbursh on wood. © Donald C. Martin/SuperStock; **p. 455:** Photos.com; **p. 456:** Courtesy of www.istockphoto.com; **p. 458:** © 2007 Artists Rights Society (ARS), New York; **p. 469:** Photos.com; **p. 470:** Photos.com; **p. 481:** Courtesy of www.istockphoto.com.

Index